SAYONARA, FOOTBALL

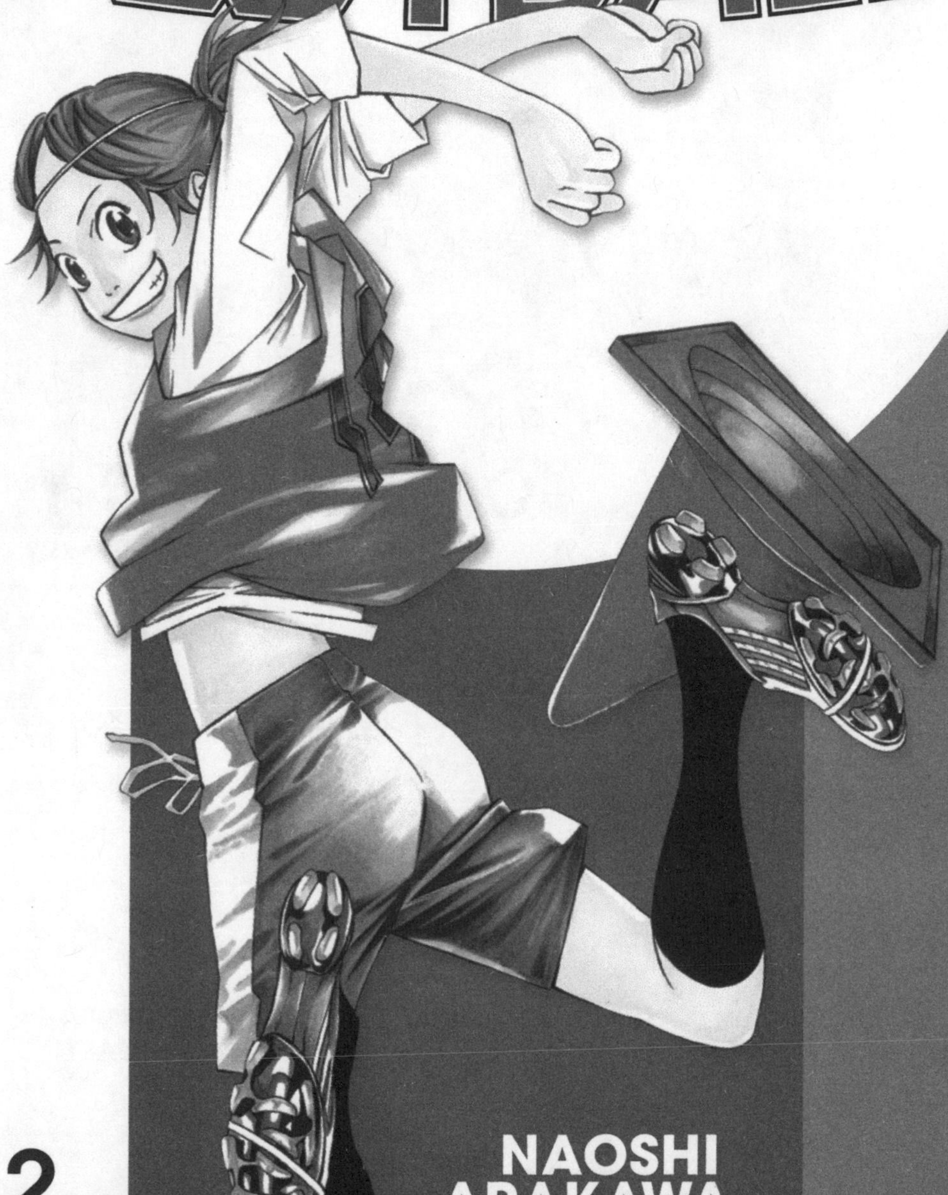

2

NAOSHI ARAKAWA

2

SAYONARA FOOTBALL CONTENTS

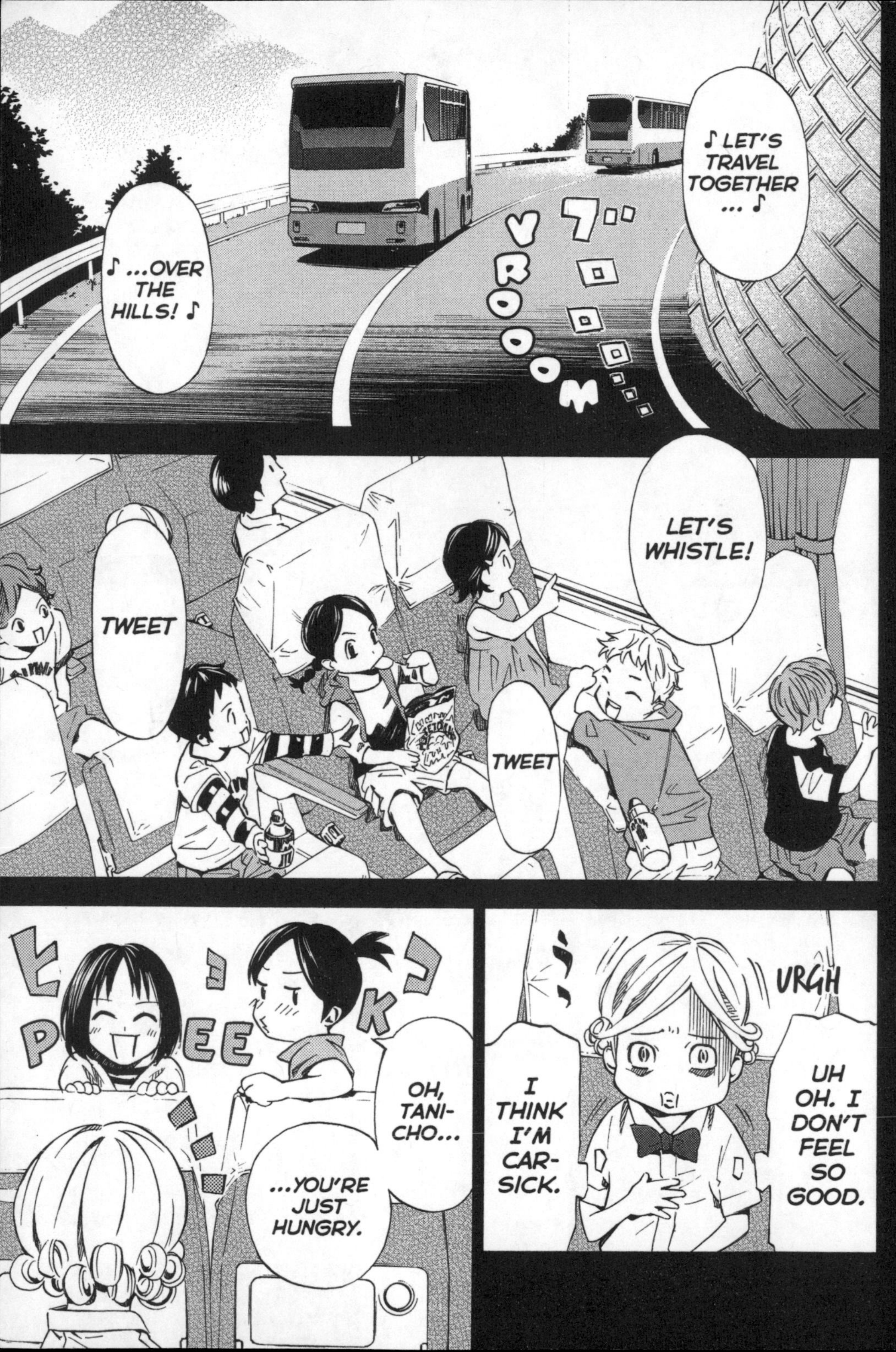

♪ LET'S TRAVEL TOGETHER ... ♪
VROOOOM
♪ ...OVER THE HILLS! ♪
LET'S WHISTLE!
TWEET
TWEET
URGH
UH OH. I DON'T FEEL SO GOOD.
I THINK I'M CAR-SICK.
PEEK
OH, TANI-CHO...
...YOU'RE JUST HUNGRY.

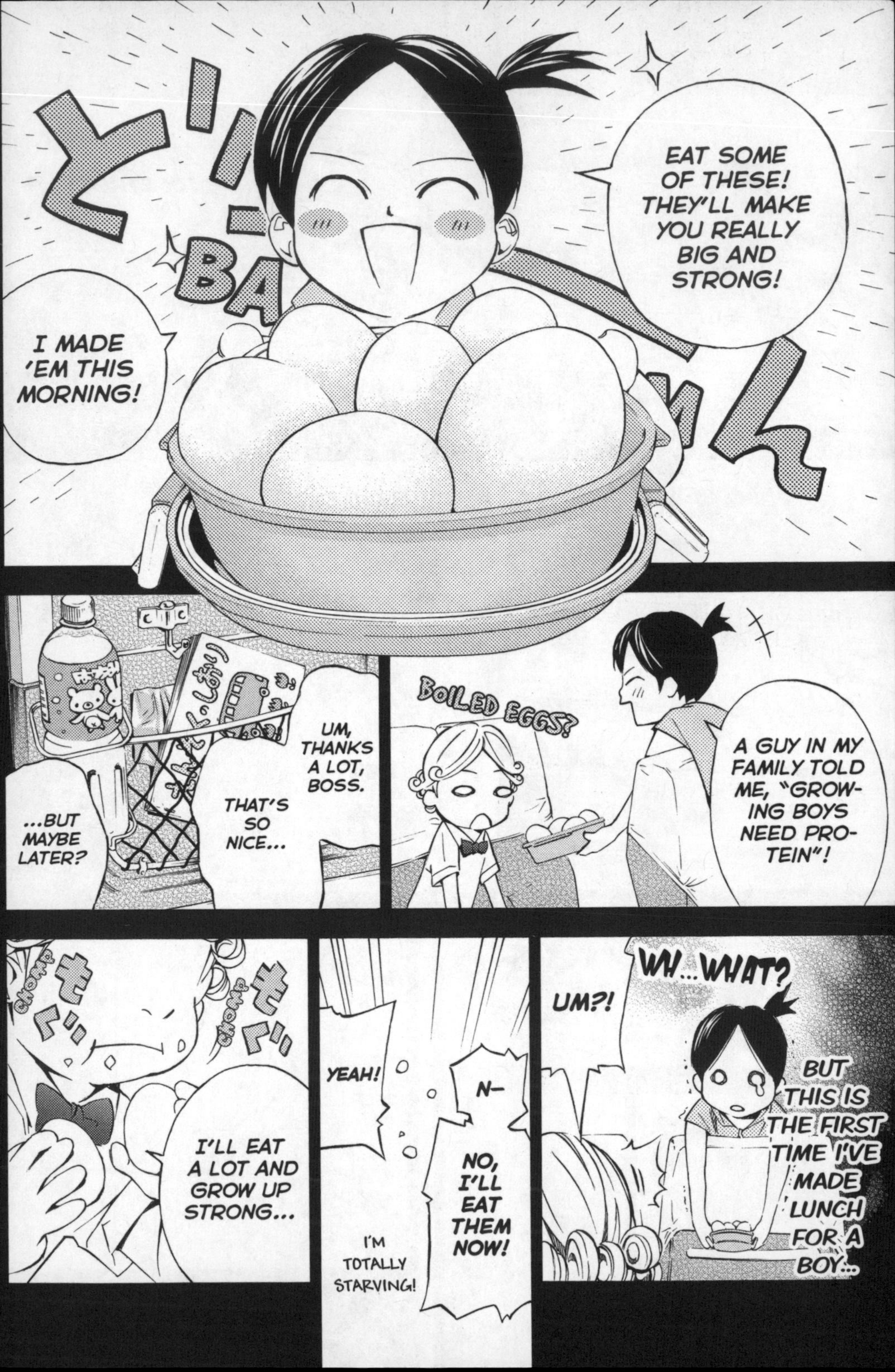

BA
M
EAT SOME OF THESE! THEY'LL MAKE YOU REALLY BIG AND STRONG!
I MADE 'EM THIS MORNING!
A GUY IN MY FAMILY TOLD ME, "GROWING BOYS NEED PROTEIN"!
BOILED EGGS?
UM, THANKS A LOT, BOSS.
THAT'S SO NICE...
...BUT MAYBE LATER?
WH... WHAT?
UM?!
BUT THIS IS THE FIRST TIME I'VE MADE LUNCH FOR A BOY...
N—
NO, I'LL EAT THEM NOW!
YEAH!
I'M TOTALLY STARVING!
CHOMP
CHOMP
I'LL EAT A LOT AND GROW UP STRONG...

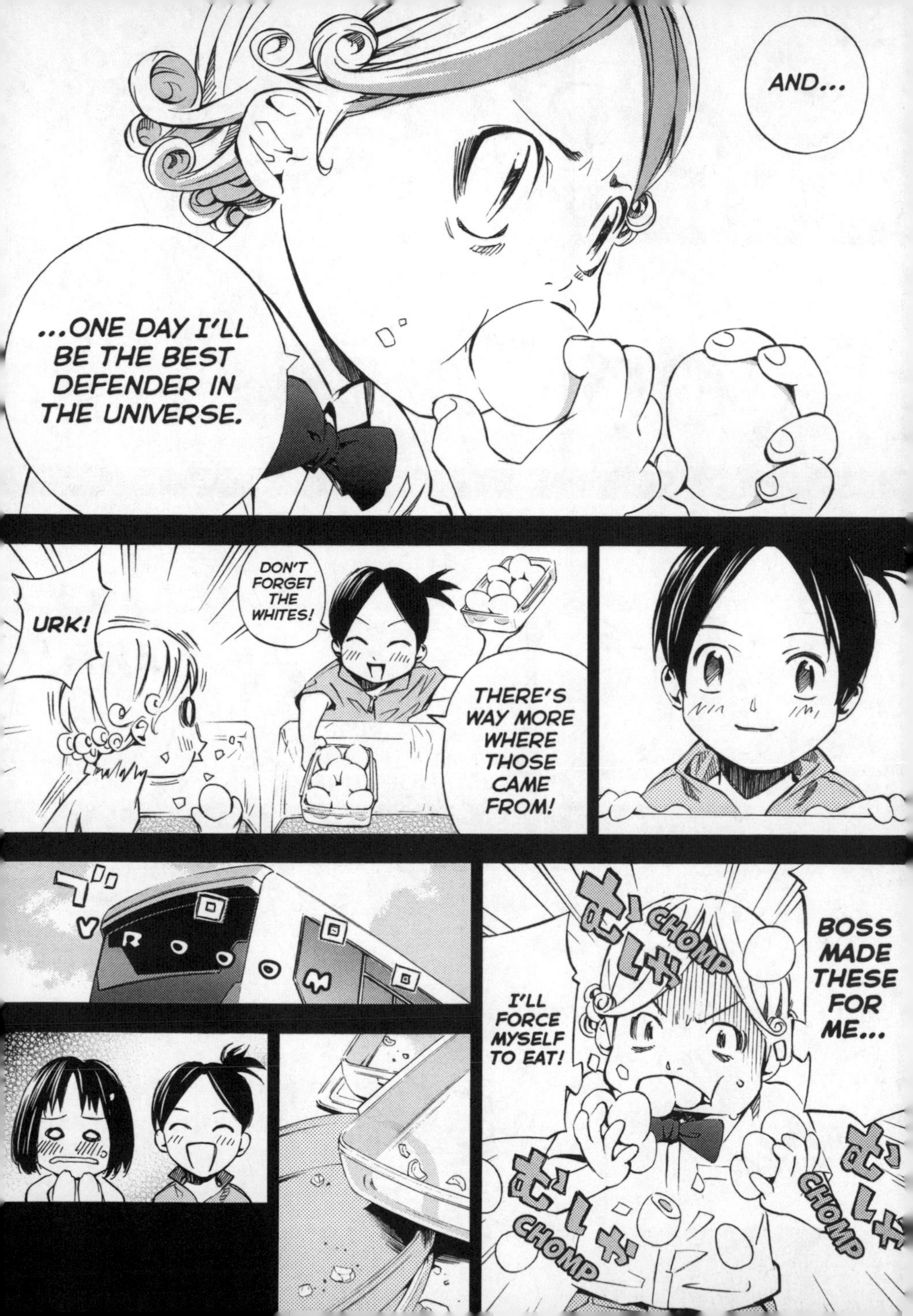
AND...
...ONE DAY I'LL BE THE BEST DEFENDER IN THE UNIVERSE.
DON'T FORGET THE WHITES!
THERE'S WAY MORE WHERE THOSE CAME FROM!
URK!
BOSS MADE THESE FOR ME...
CHOMP
I'LL FORCE MYSELF TO EAT!
CHOMP
CHOMP
VROOOM

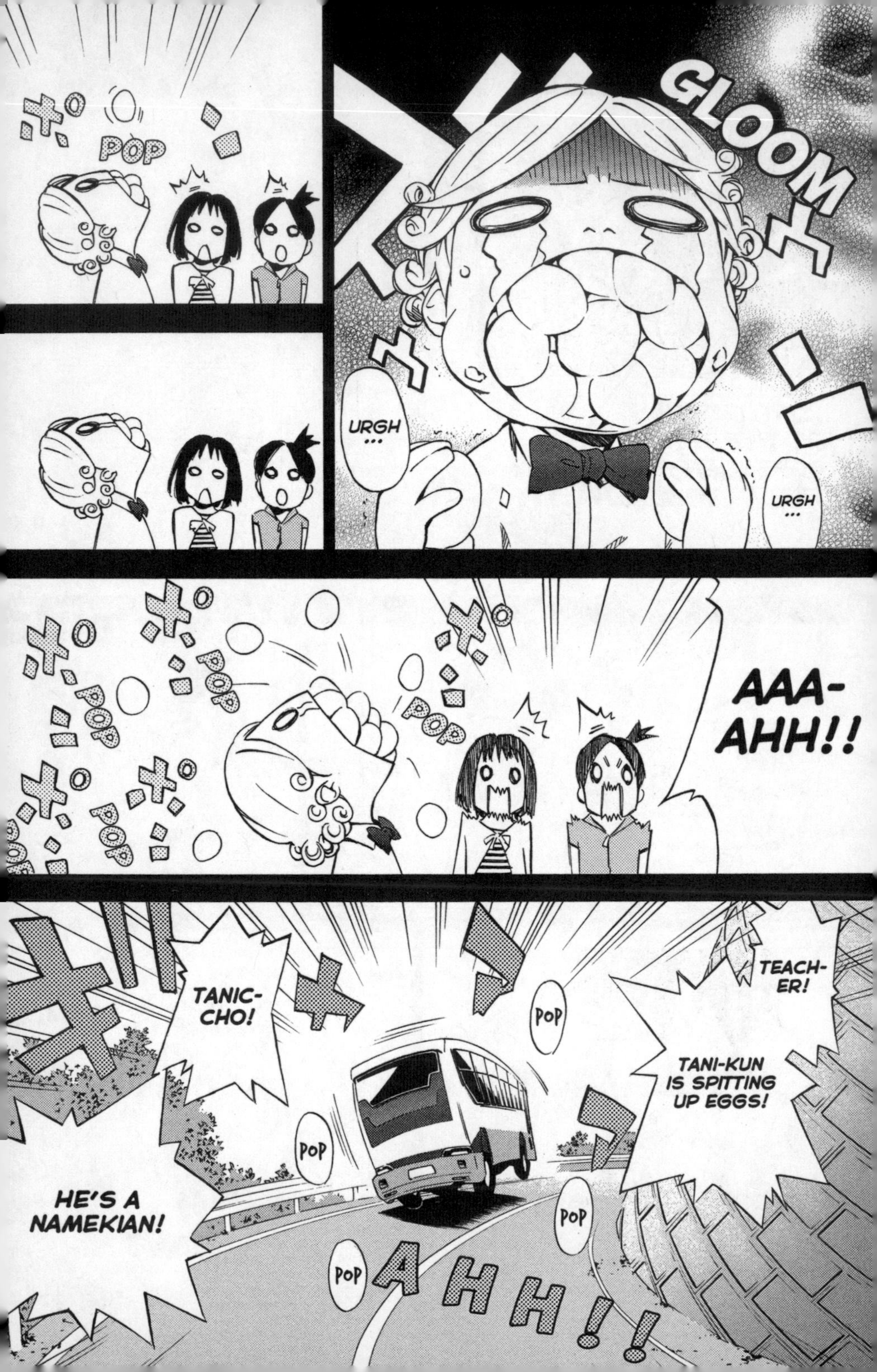
GLOOM
URGH...
URGH...
POP
AAA-AHH!!
POP
POP
POP
POP
POP
TEACHER!
TANI-KUN IS SPITTING UP EGGS!
POP
TANIC-CHO!
POP
POP
HE'S A NAMEKIAN!
POP
AHH!!

ESTROOMS

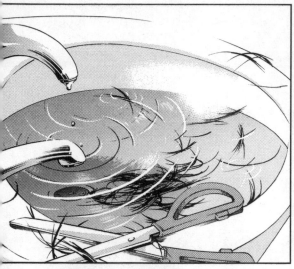

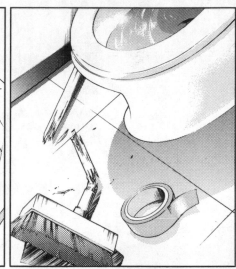

...IS...

...BETTER?!

WHICH OF US...

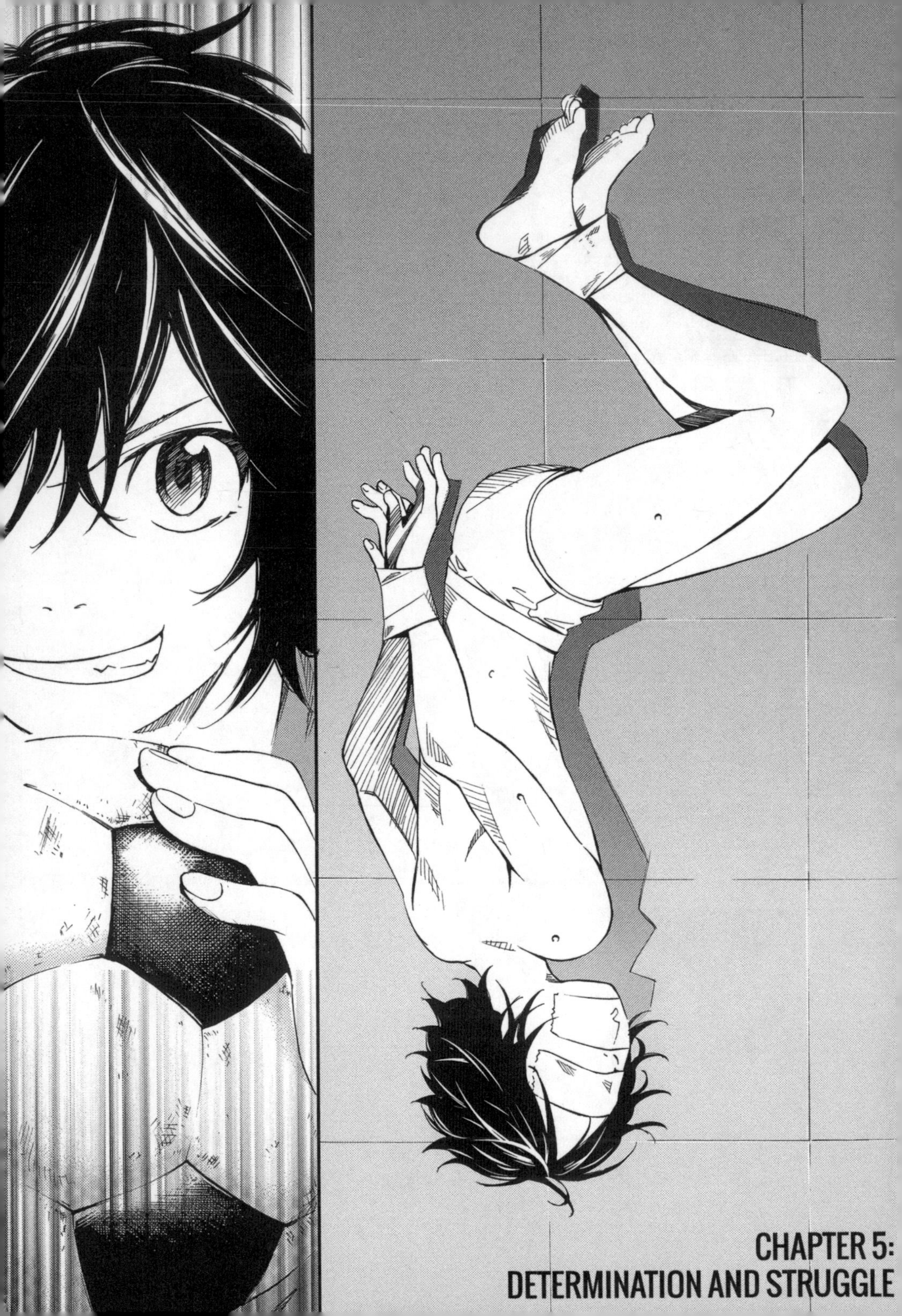
CHAPTER 5:
DETERMINATION AND STRUGGLE

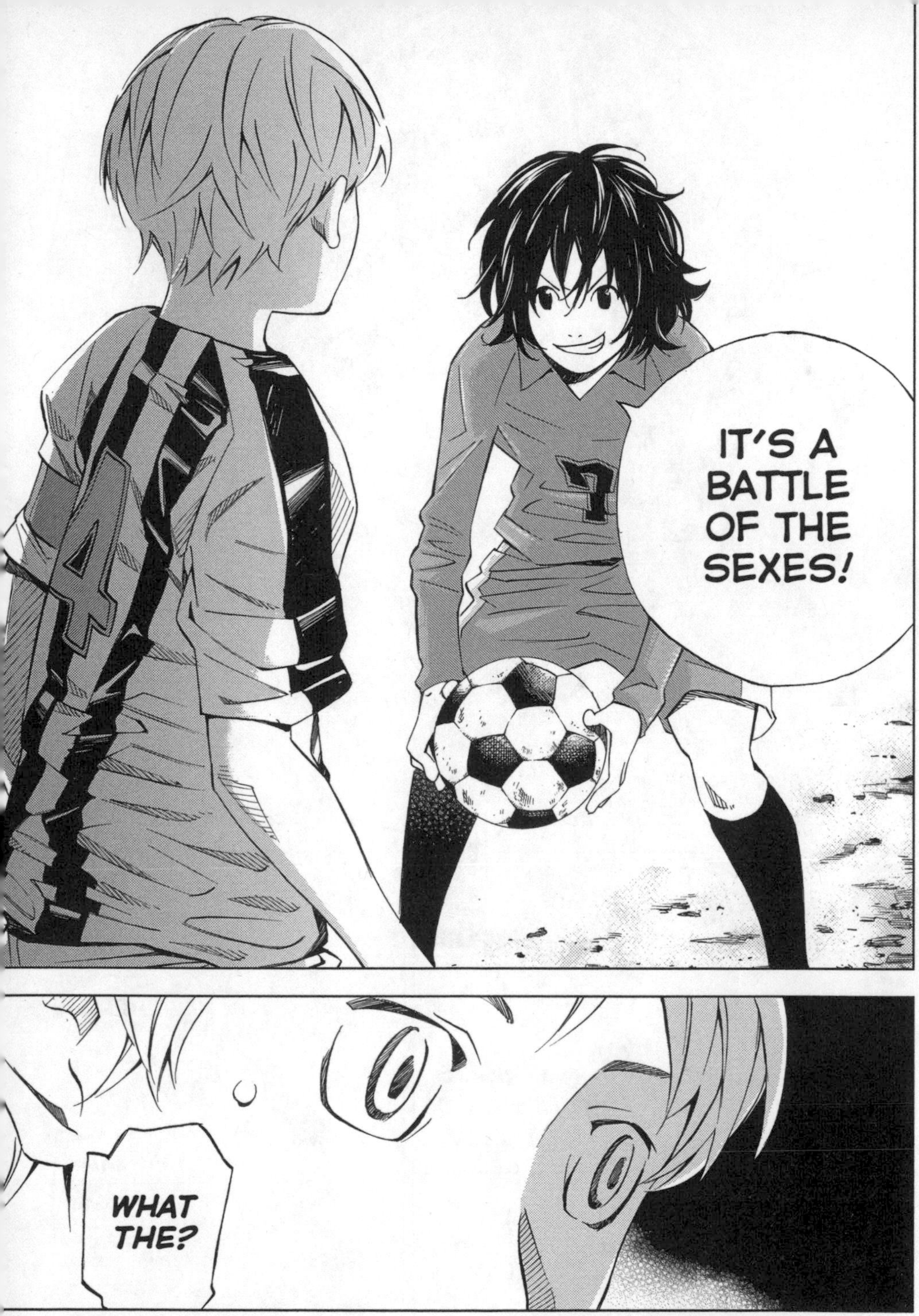
IT'S A BATTLE OF THE SEXES!
WHAT THE?

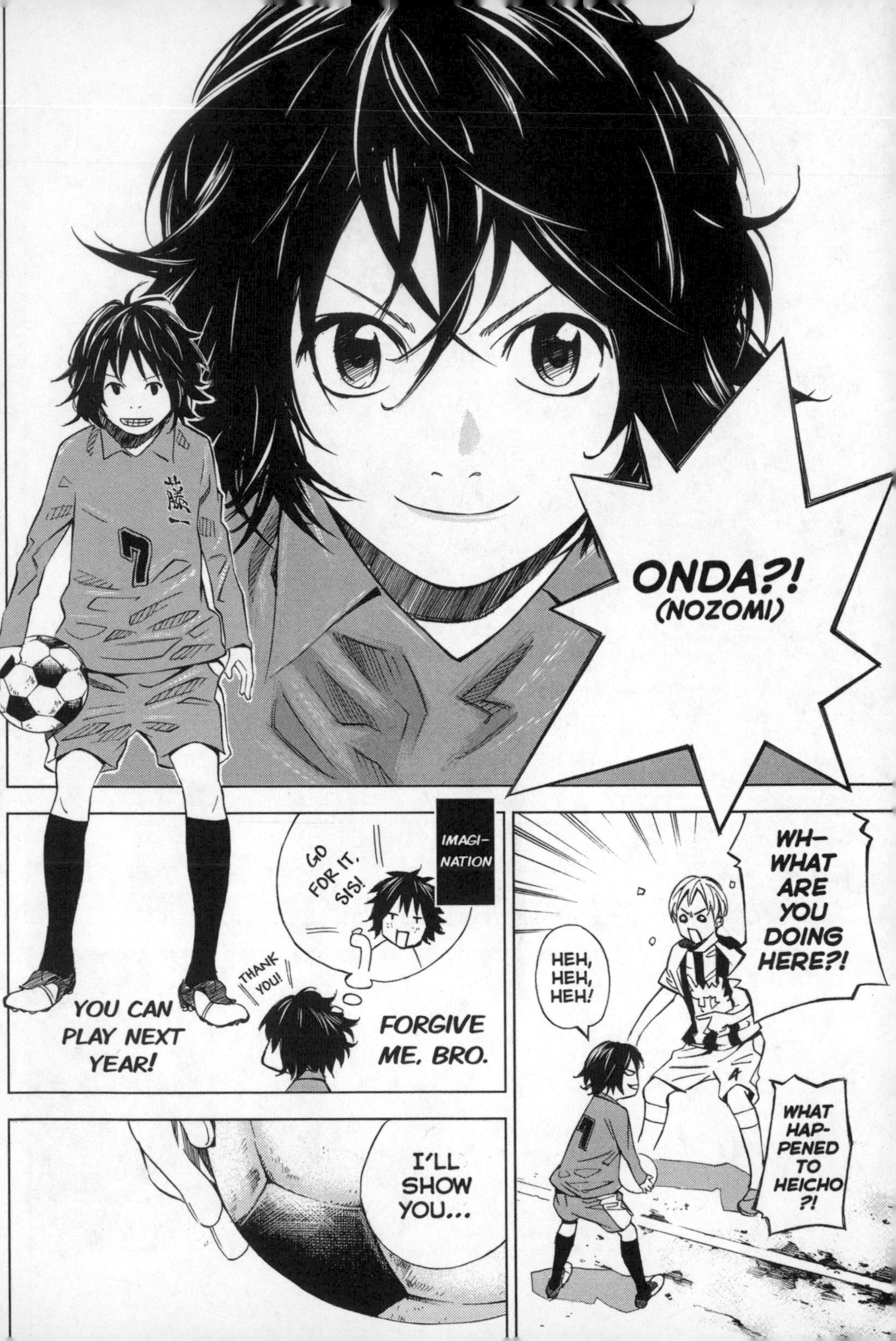
ONDA?!
(NOZOMI)
WH-WHAT ARE YOU DOING HERE?!
HEH, HEH, HEH!
WHAT HAP-PENED TO HEICHO?!
IMAGI-NATION
GO FOR IT, SIS!
THANK YOU!
FORGIVE ME, BRO.
YOU CAN PLAY NEXT YEAR!
I'LL SHOW YOU...

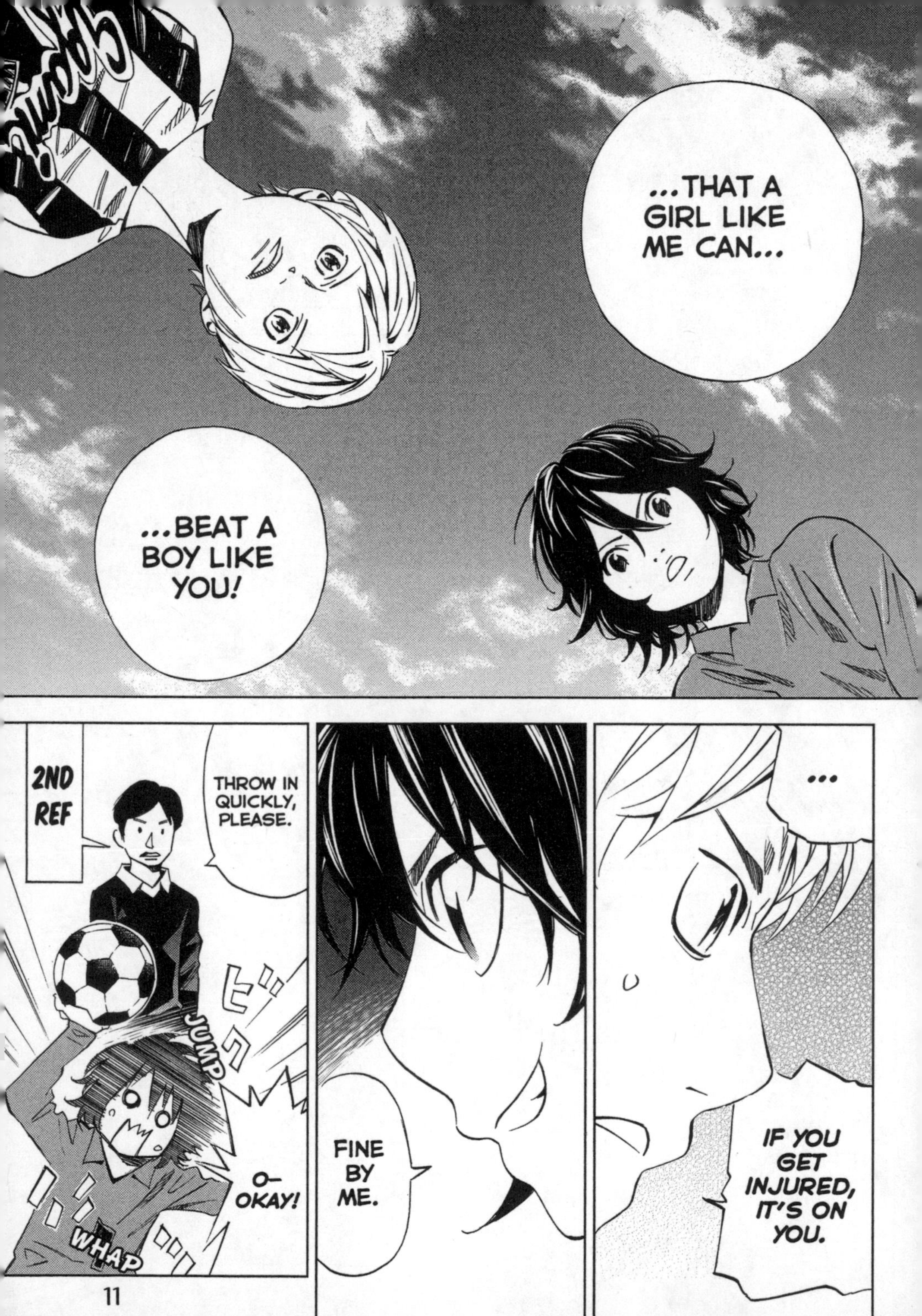
...THAT A GIRL LIKE ME CAN...
...BEAT A BOY LIKE YOU!
...
IF YOU GET INJURED, IT'S ON YOU.
FINE BY ME.
2ND REF
THROW IN QUICKLY, PLEASE.
ビク
JUMP
O-OKAY!
WHAP

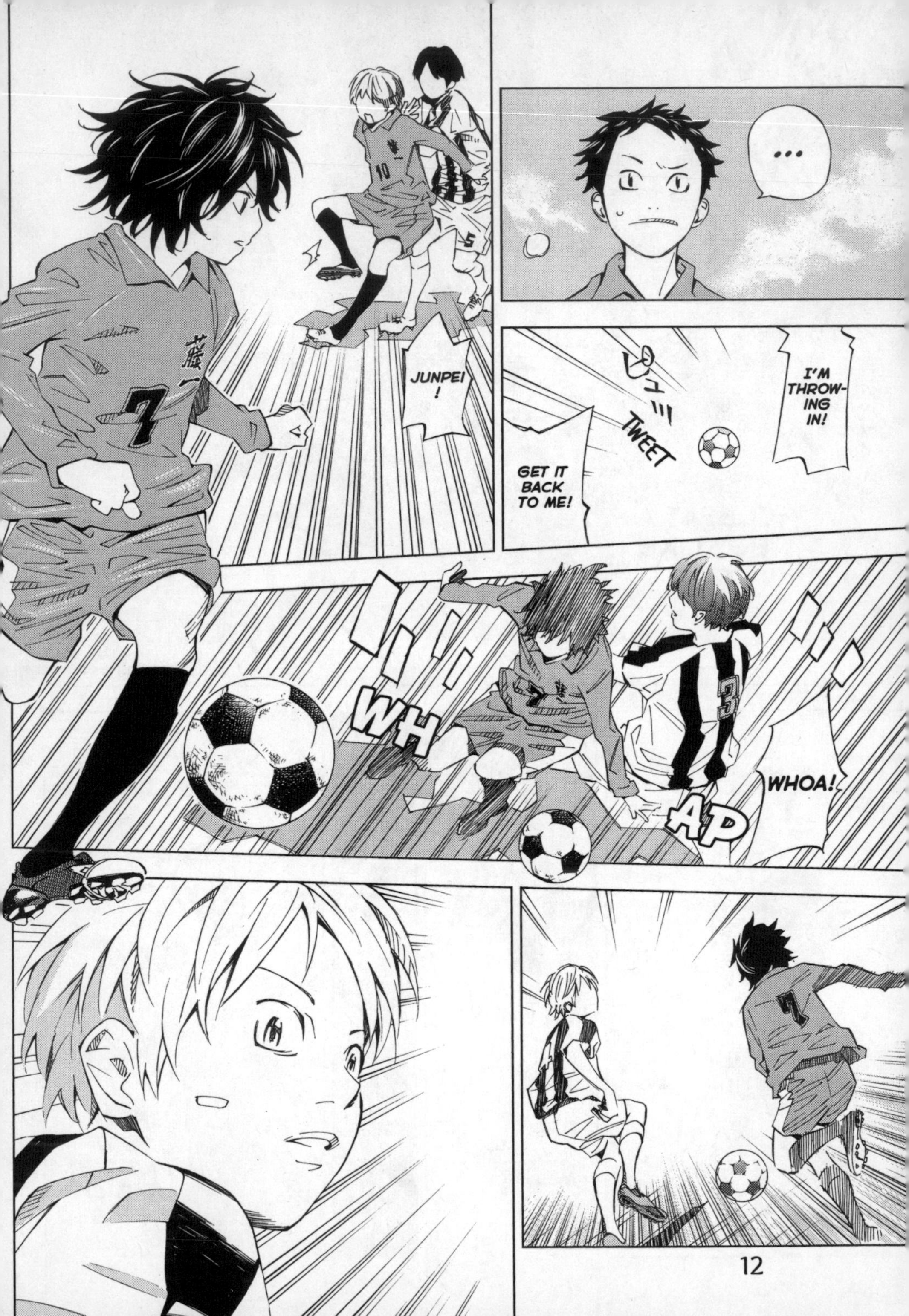
...
I'M THROWING IN!
ピュ
TWEET
GET IT BACK TO ME!
WHOA!
WH
AP
JUNPEI!

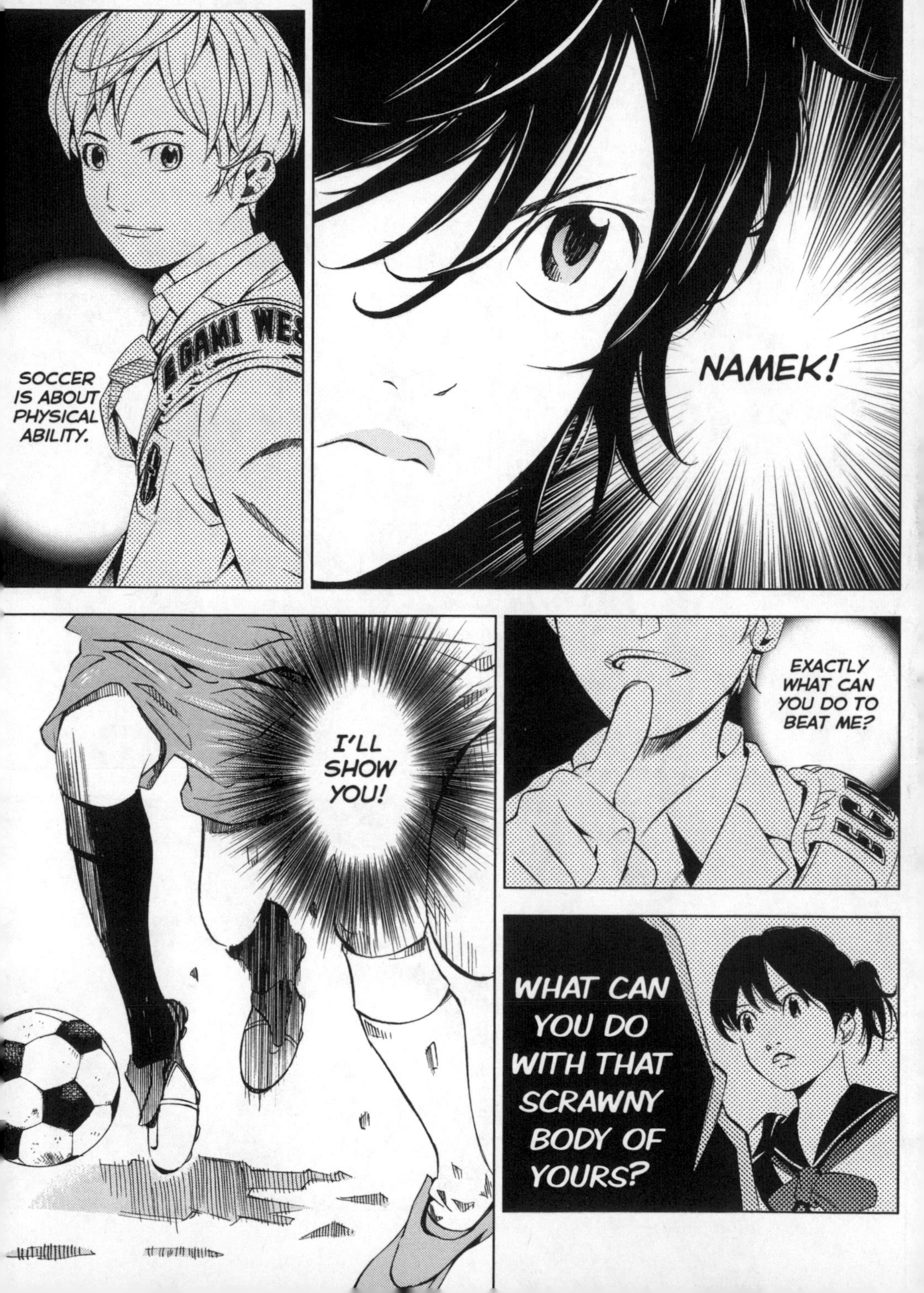
NAMEK!
SOCCER IS ABOUT PHYSICAL ABILITY.
EXACTLY WHAT CAN YOU DO TO BEAT ME?
WHAT CAN YOU DO WITH THAT SCRAWNY BODY OF YOURS?
I'LL SHOW YOU!

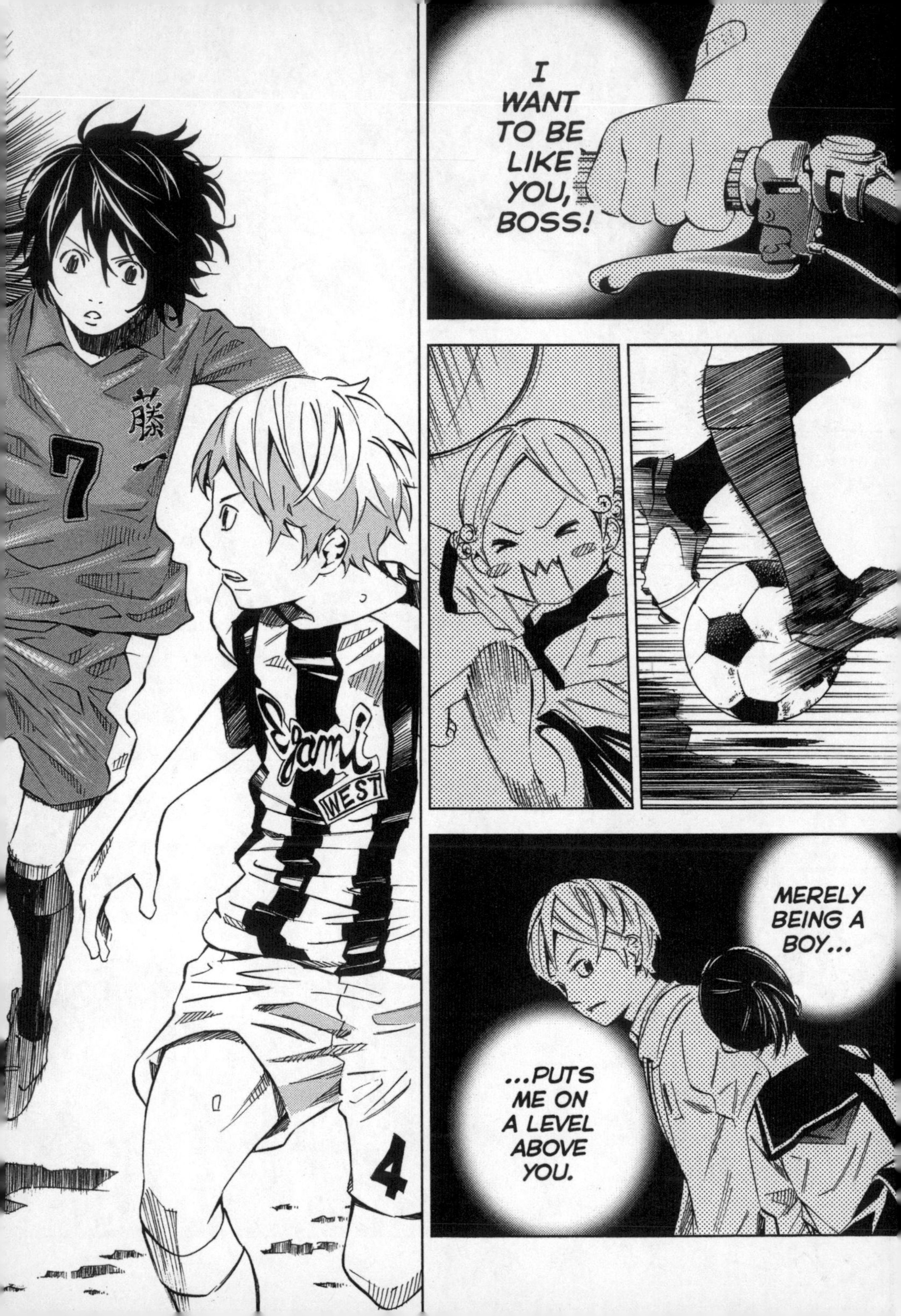
I WANT TO BE LIKE YOU, BOSS!
MERELY BEING A BOY...
...PUTS ME ON A LEVEL ABOVE YOU.
WEST

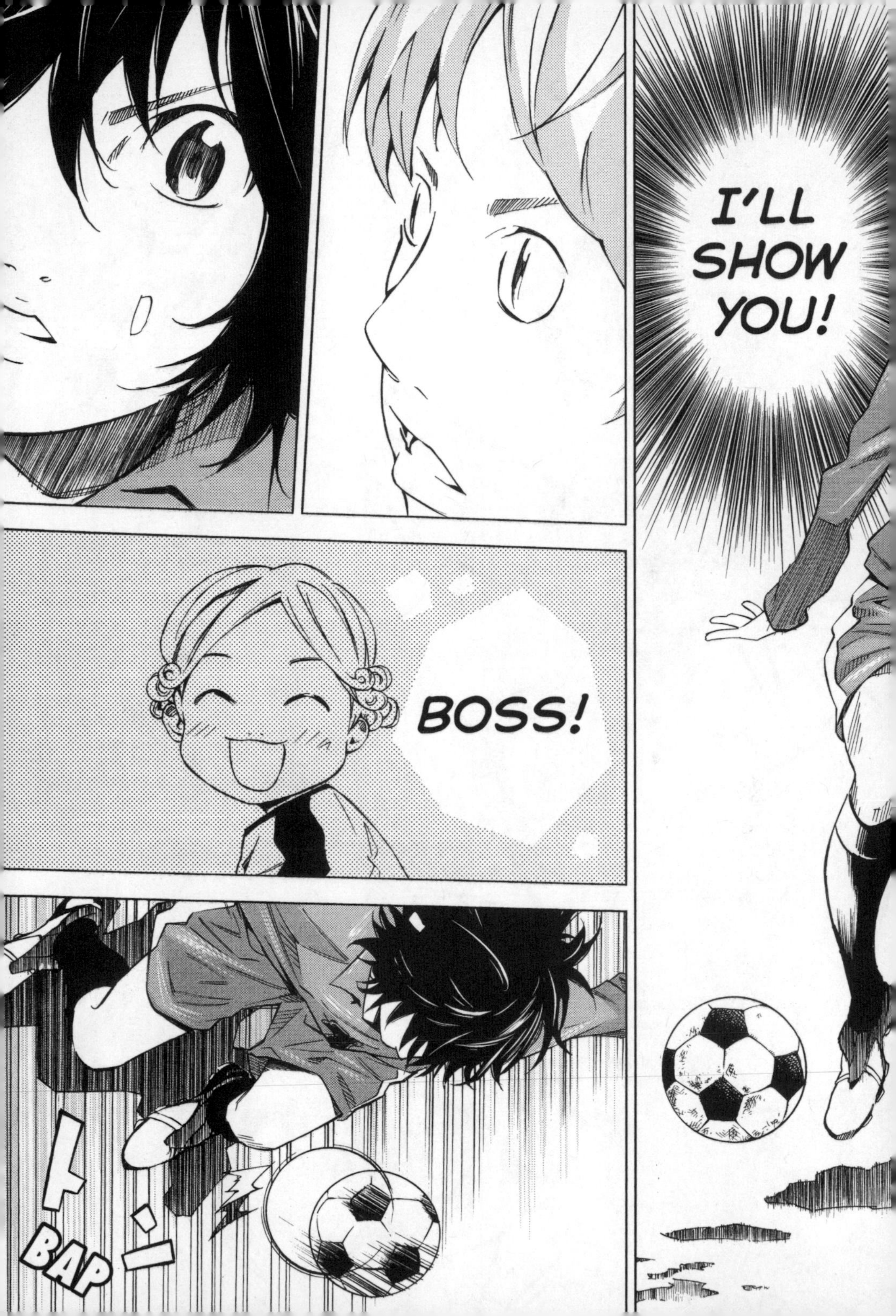
I'LL SHOW YOU!
BOSS!
BAP

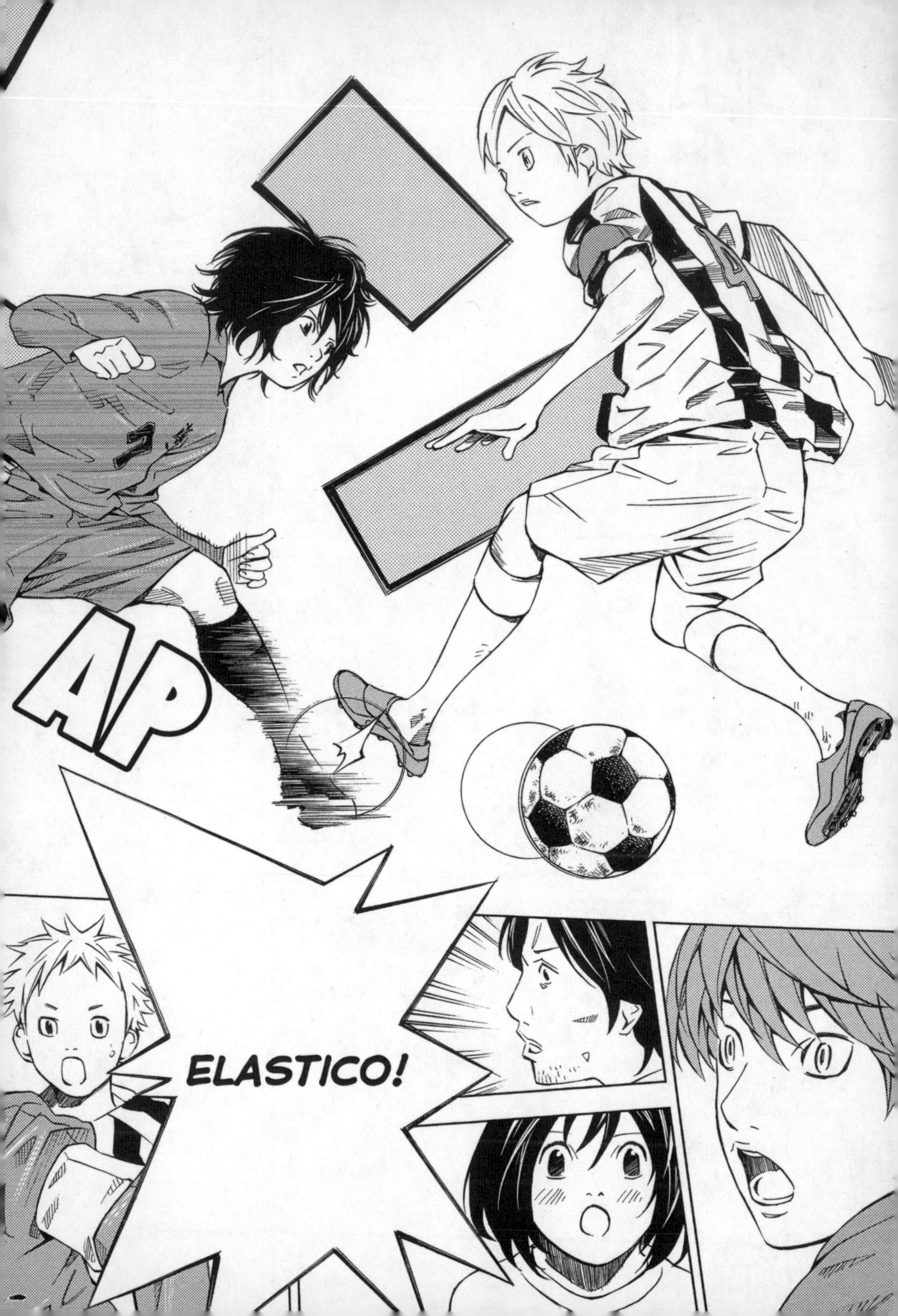
AP
ELASTICO!

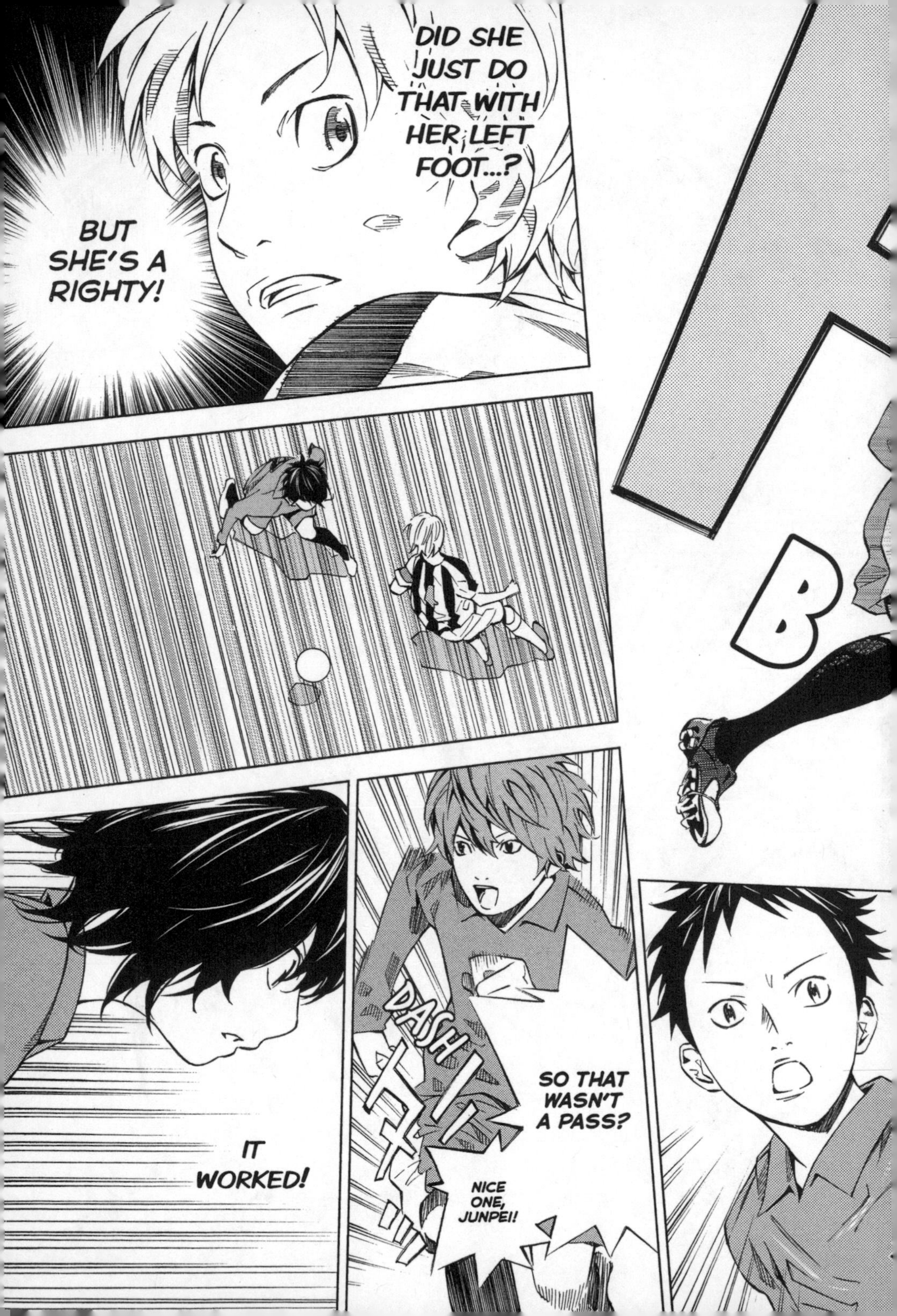
B
DID SHE JUST DO THAT WITH HER LEFT FOOT...?
BUT SHE'S A RIGHTY!
SO THAT WASN'T A PASS?
DASH
NICE ONE, JUNPEI!
IT WORKED!

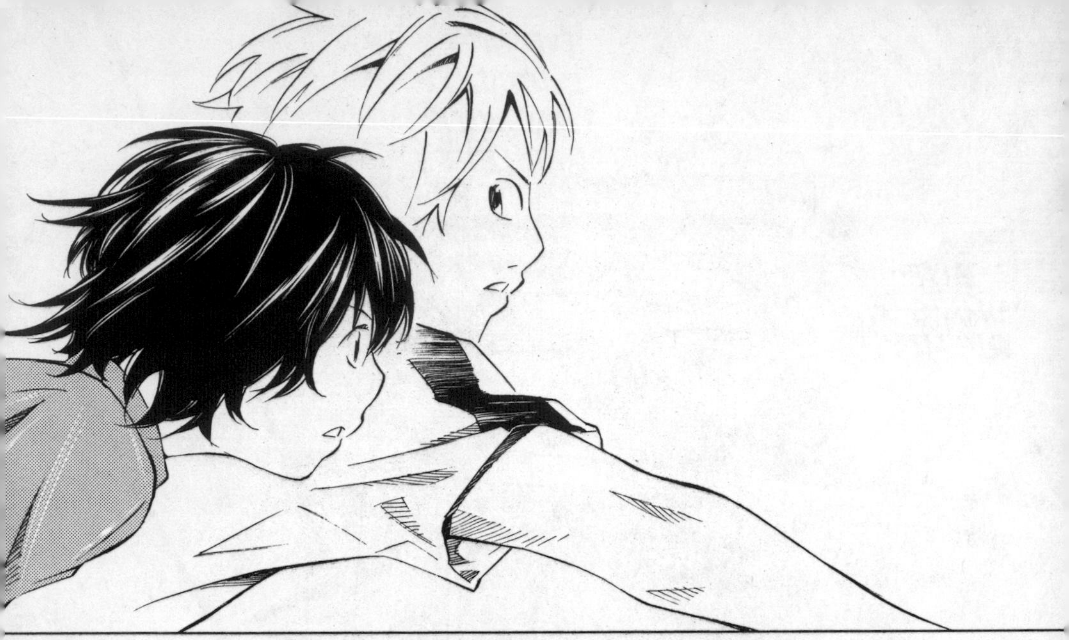
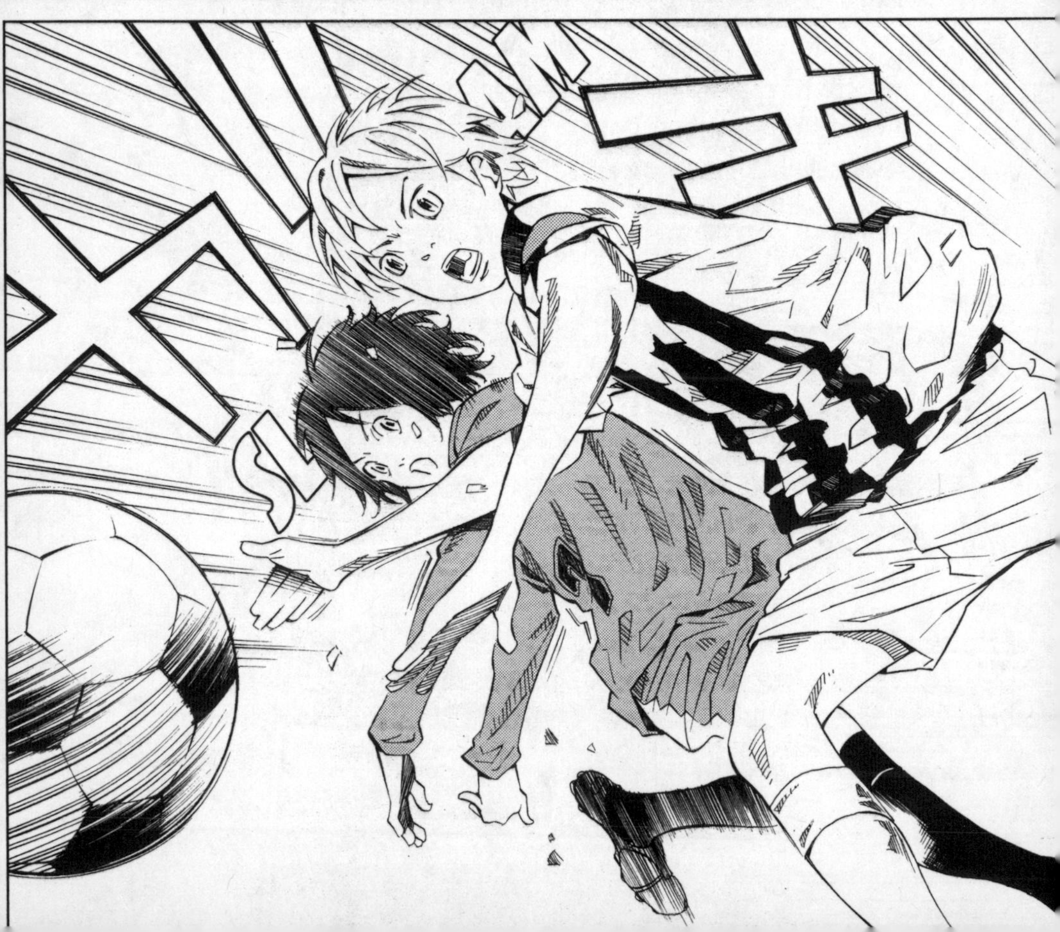

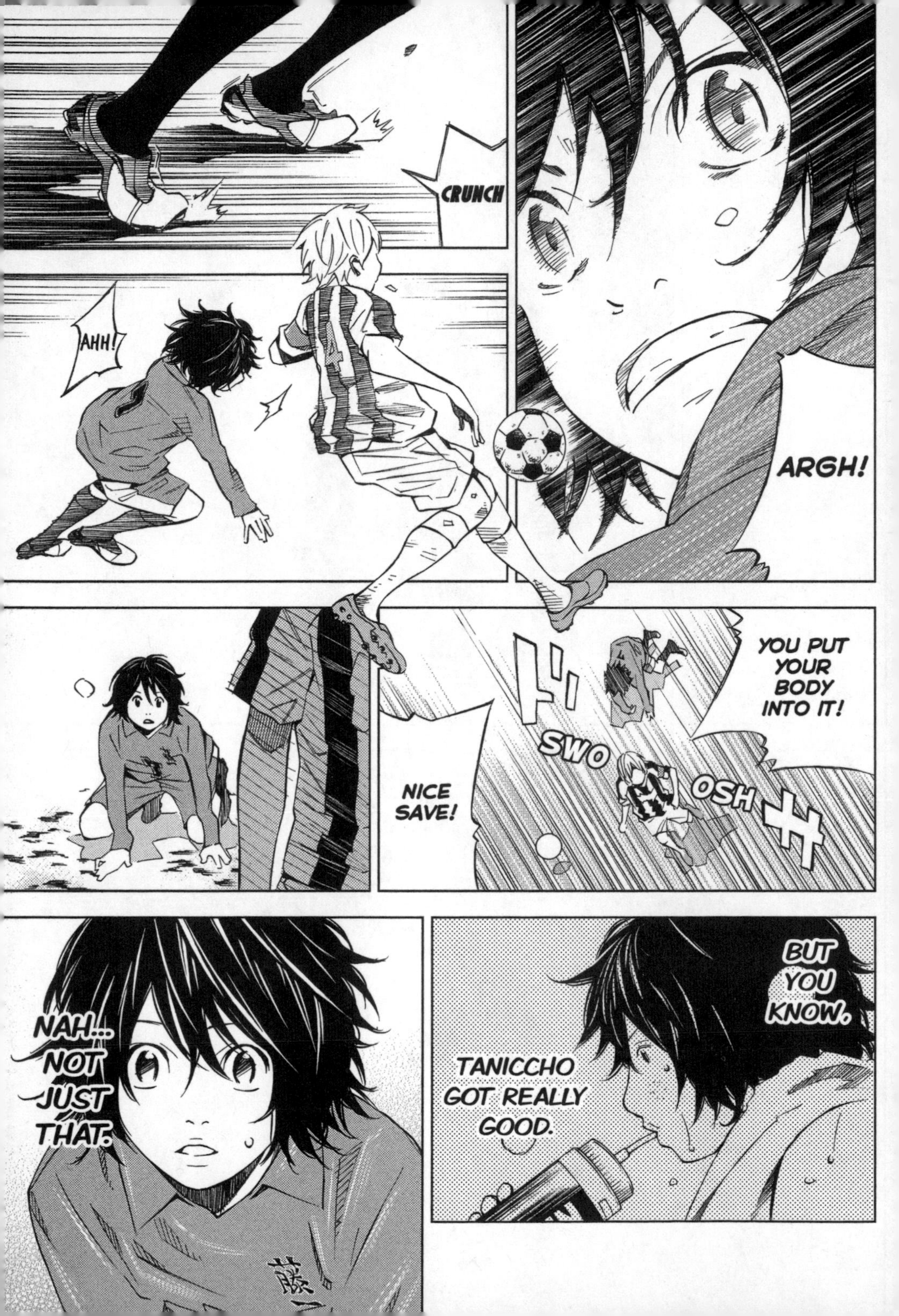
ARGH!
CRUNCH
AHH!
YOU PUT YOUR BODY INTO IT!
SWO OSH
NICE SAVE!
BUT YOU KNOW.
TANICCHO GOT REALLY GOOD.
NAH... NOT JUST THAT.
藤

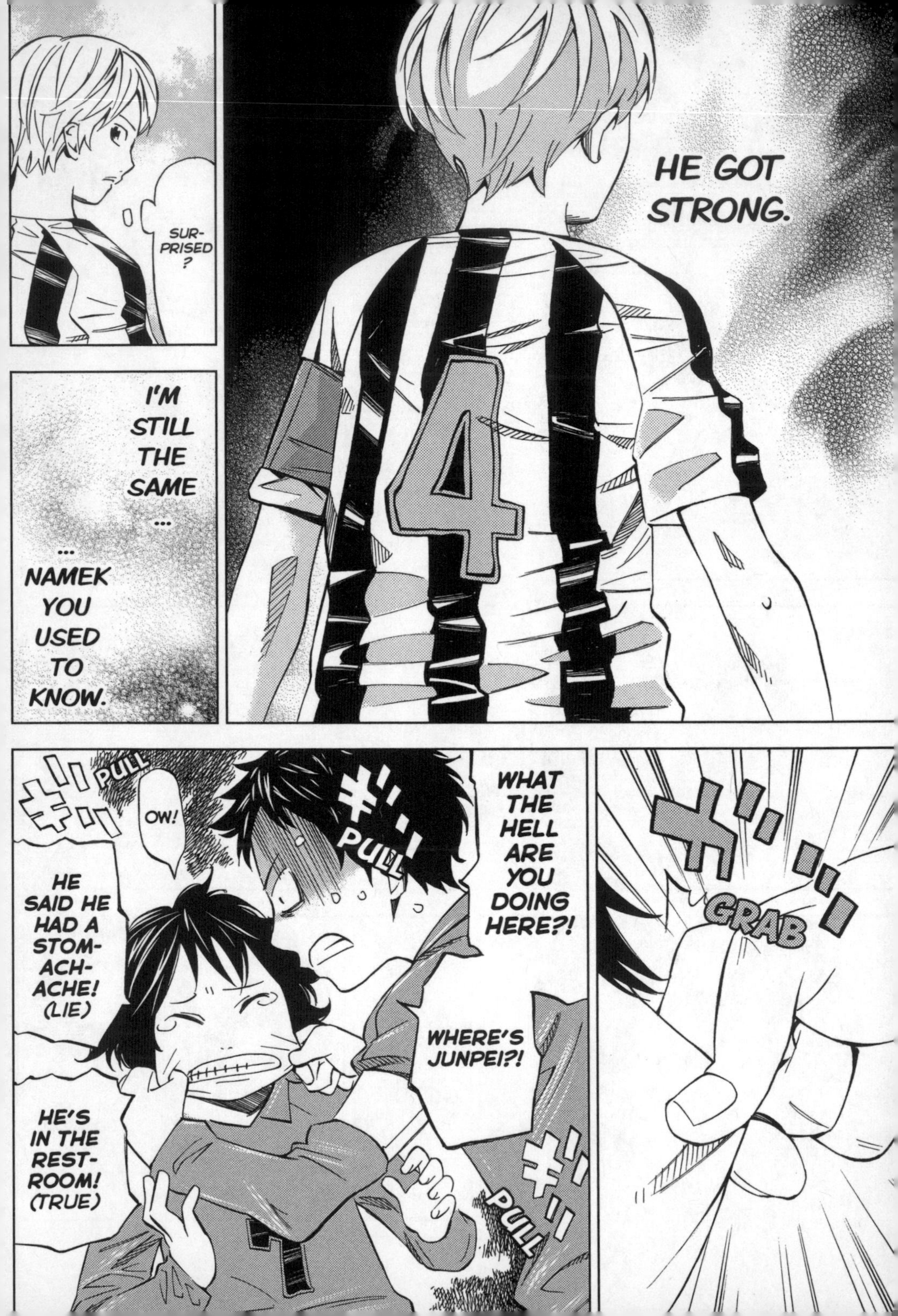
HE GOT STRONG.
SUR-PRISED?
I'M STILL THE SAME...
...NAMEK YOU USED TO KNOW.
GRAB
WHAT THE HELL ARE YOU DOING HERE?!
PULL
PULL
OW!
HE SAID HE HAD A STOMACH-ACHE! (LIE)
WHERE'S JUNPEI?!
HE'S IN THE REST-ROOM! (TRUE)
PULL

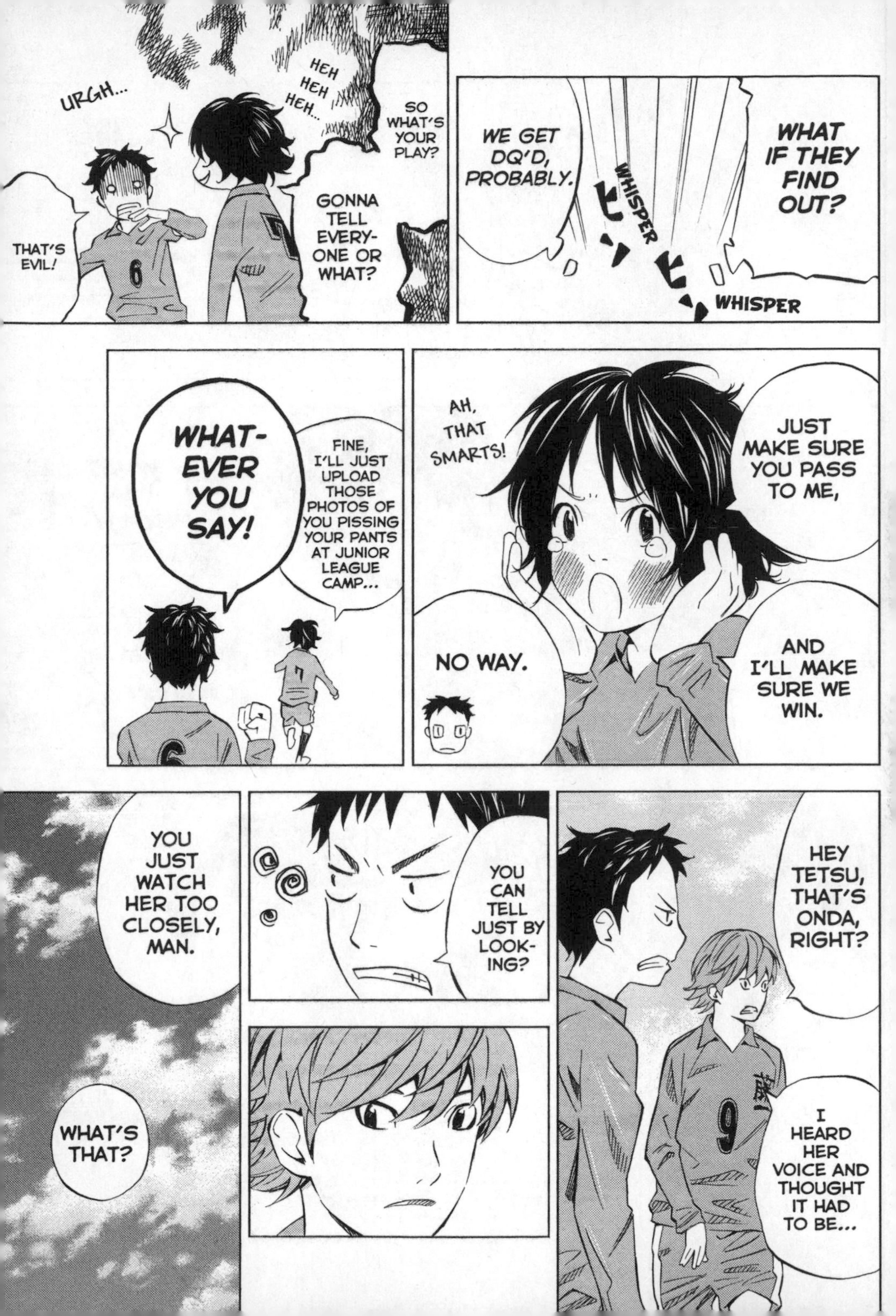
WHAT IF THEY FIND OUT?
WHISPER
WHISPER
WE GET DQ'D, PROBABLY.
SO WHAT'S YOUR PLAY?
GONNA TELL EVERY-ONE OR WHAT?
HEH HEH HEH...
URGH...
THAT'S EVIL!
JUST MAKE SURE YOU PASS TO ME,
AH, THAT SMARTS!
AND I'LL MAKE SURE WE WIN.
NO WAY.
FINE, I'LL JUST UPLOAD THOSE PHOTOS OF YOU PISSING YOUR PANTS AT JUNIOR LEAGUE CAMP...
WHAT-EVER YOU SAY!
HEY TETSU, THAT'S ONDA, RIGHT?
I HEARD HER VOICE AND THOUGHT IT HAD TO BE...
YOU CAN TELL JUST BY LOOK-ING?
YOU JUST WATCH HER TOO CLOSELY, MAN.
WHAT'S THAT?

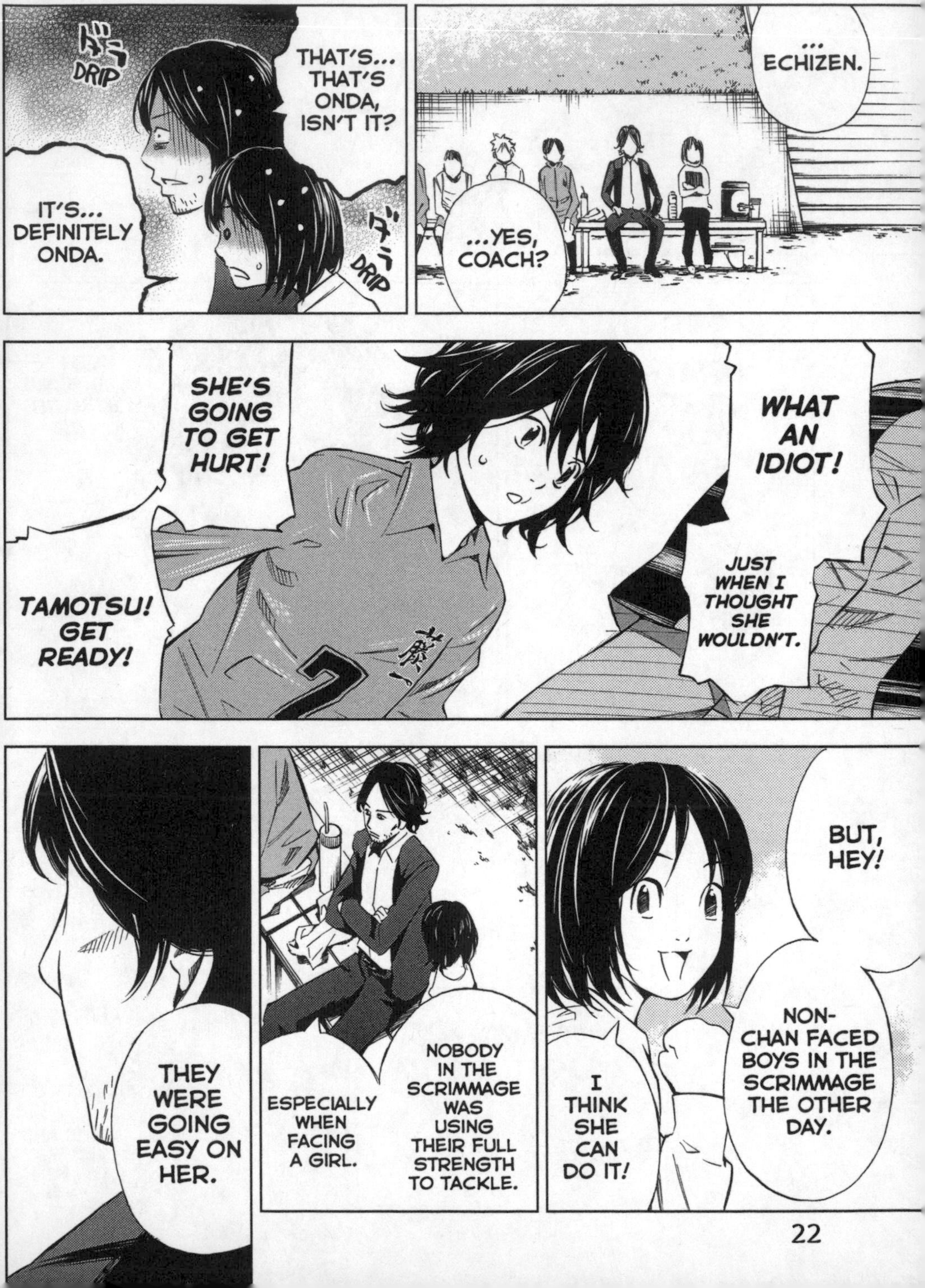
...
ECHIZEN.
...YES, COACH?
THAT'S... THAT'S ONDA, ISN'T IT?
ダラ DRIP
IT'S... DEFINITELY ONDA.
ダラ DRIP
WHAT AN IDIOT!
JUST WHEN I THOUGHT SHE WOULDN'T.
SHE'S GOING TO GET HURT!
TAMOTSU! GET READY!
BUT, HEY!
NON-CHAN FACED BOYS IN THE SCRIMMAGE THE OTHER DAY.
I THINK SHE CAN DO IT!
NOBODY IN THE SCRIMMAGE WAS USING THEIR FULL STRENGTH TO TACKLE.
ESPECIALLY WHEN FACING A GIRL.
THEY WERE GOING EASY ON HER.

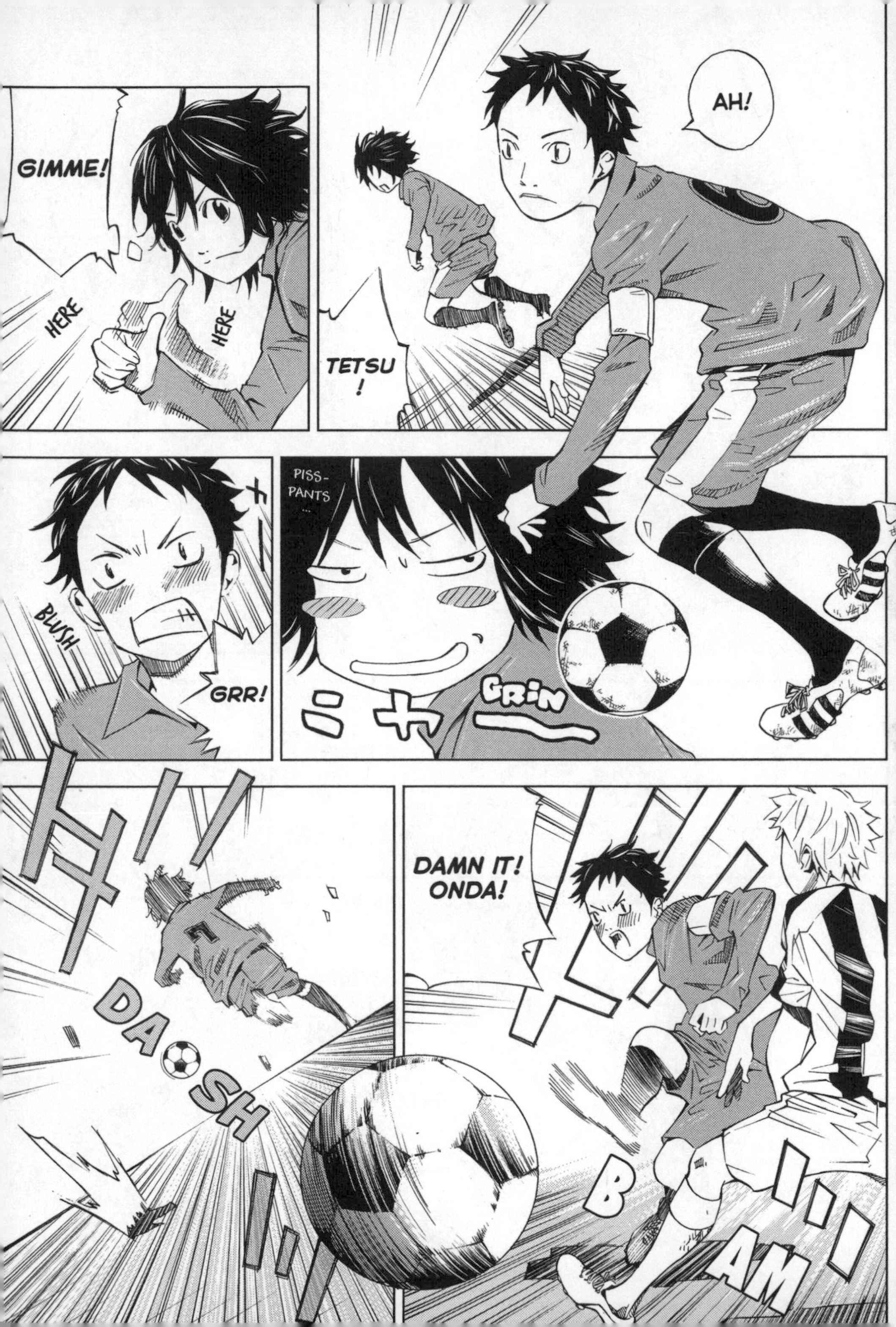
AH!
TETSU!
GIMME!
HERE
HERE
PISS-PANTS ...
GRIN
BLUSH
GRR!
DAMN IT! ONDA!
BAM
DASH

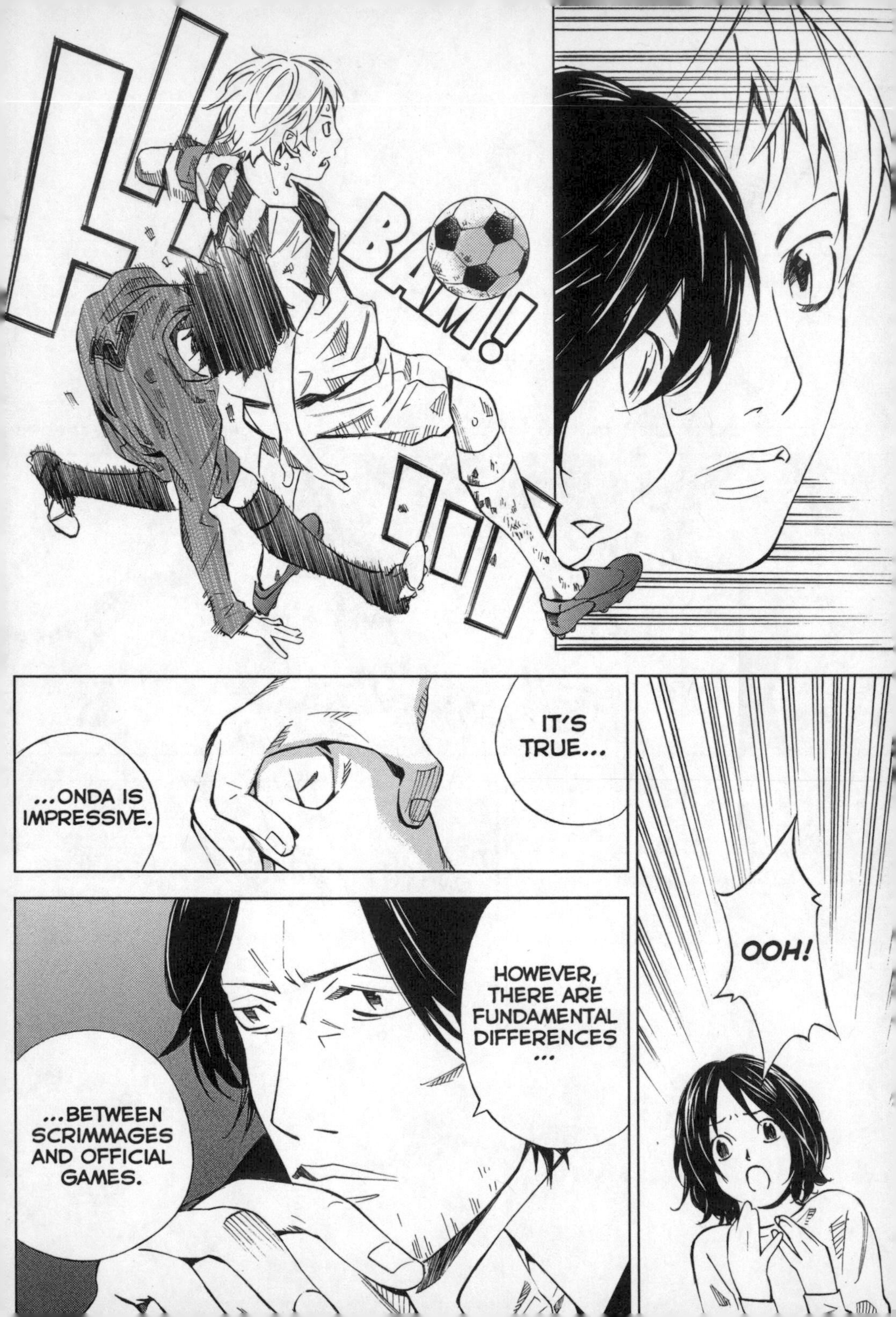
BAM!
OOH!
IT'S TRUE...
...ONDA IS IMPRESSIVE.
HOWEVER, THERE ARE FUNDAMENTAL DIFFERENCES...
...BETWEEN SCRIMMAGES AND OFFICIAL GAMES.

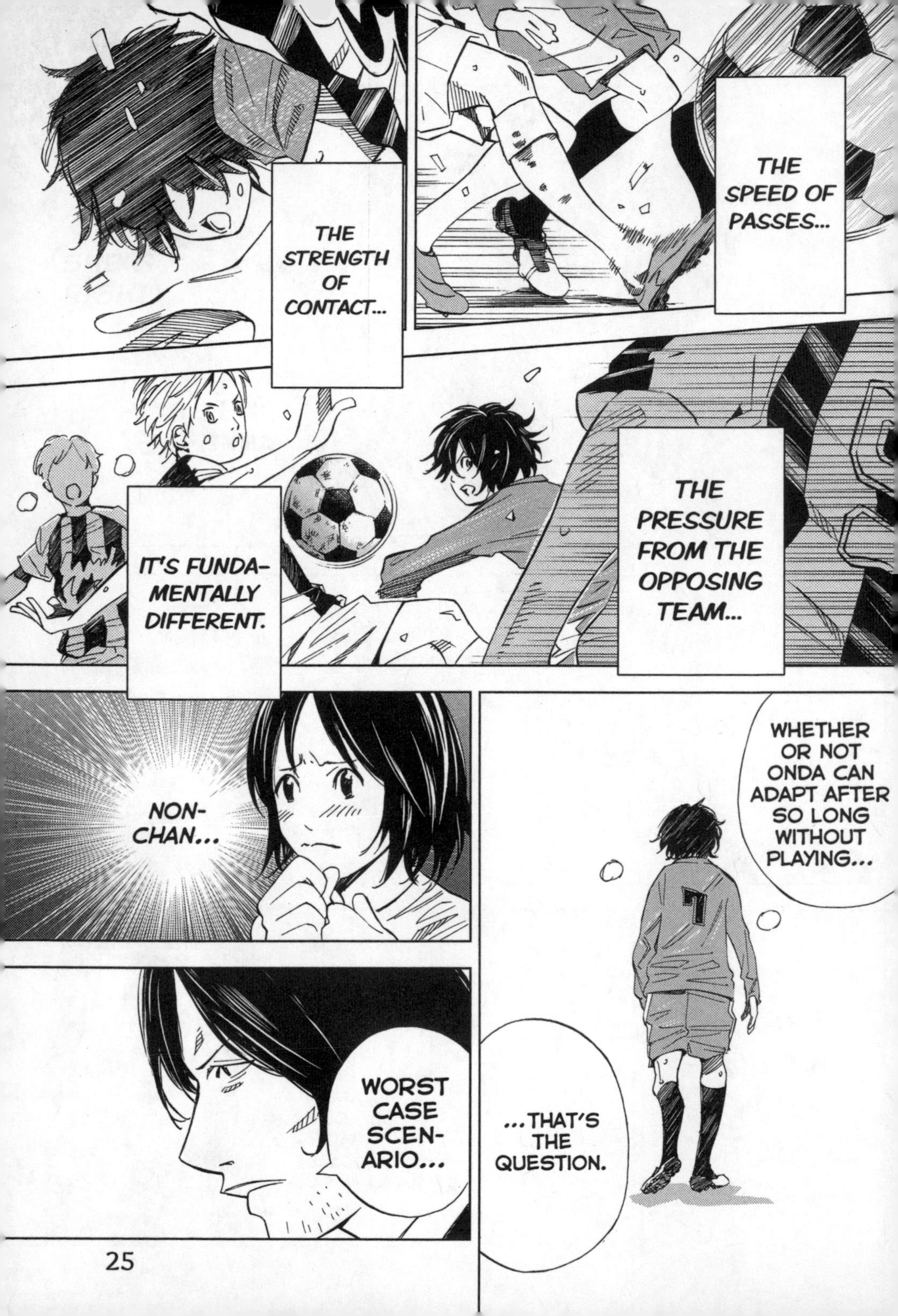
THE SPEED OF PASSES...
THE STRENGTH OF CONTACT...
THE PRESSURE FROM THE OPPOSING TEAM...
IT'S FUNDAMENTALLY DIFFERENT.
WHETHER OR NOT ONDA CAN ADAPT AFTER SO LONG WITHOUT PLAYING...
...THAT'S THE QUESTION.
NON-CHAN...
WORST CASE SCENARIO...

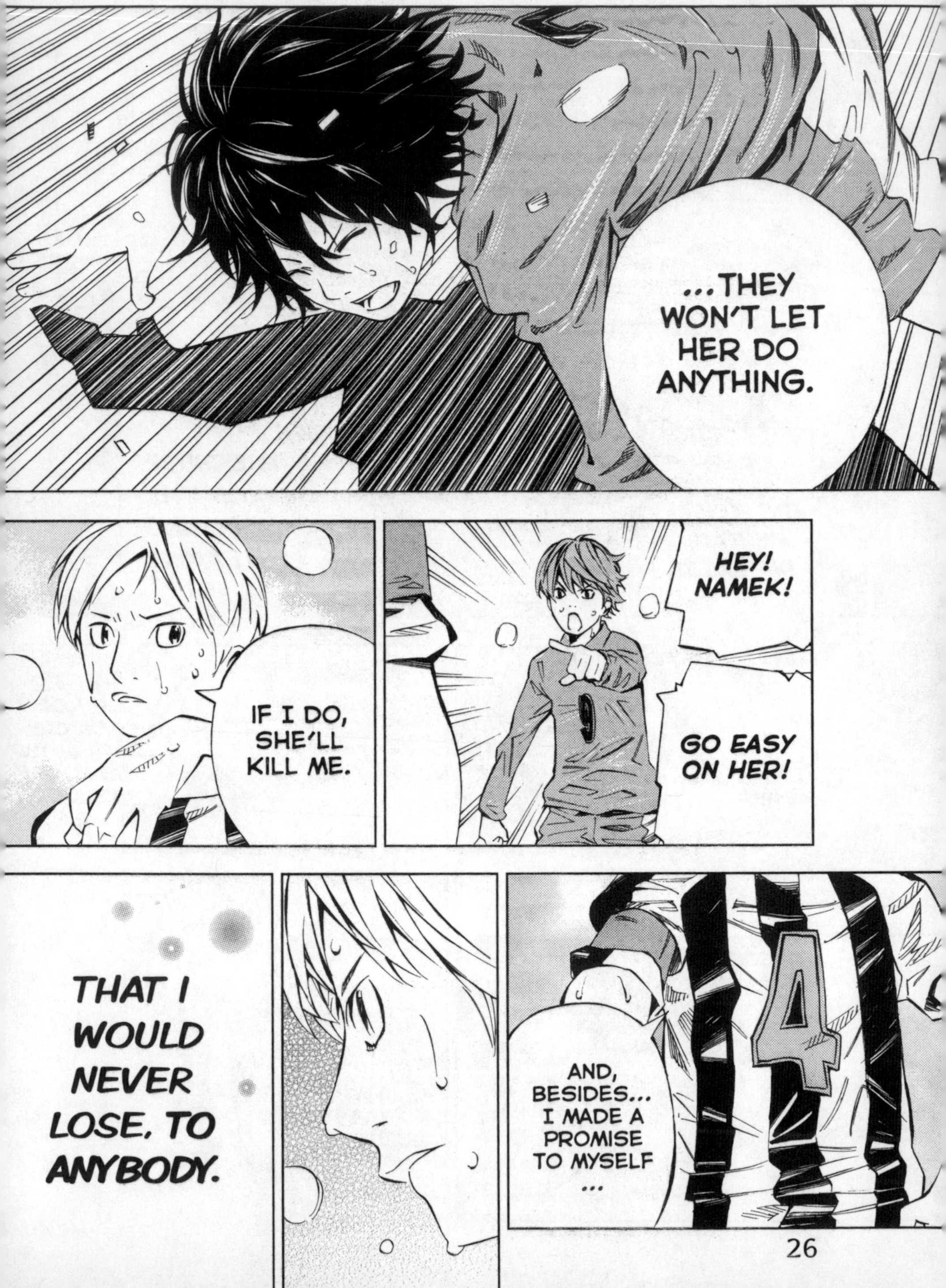
...THEY WON'T LET HER DO ANYTHING.
HEY! NAMEK!
GO EASY ON HER!
IF I DO, SHE'LL KILL ME.
AND, BESIDES... I MADE A PROMISE TO MYSELF ...
THAT I WOULD NEVER LOSE, TO ANYBODY.

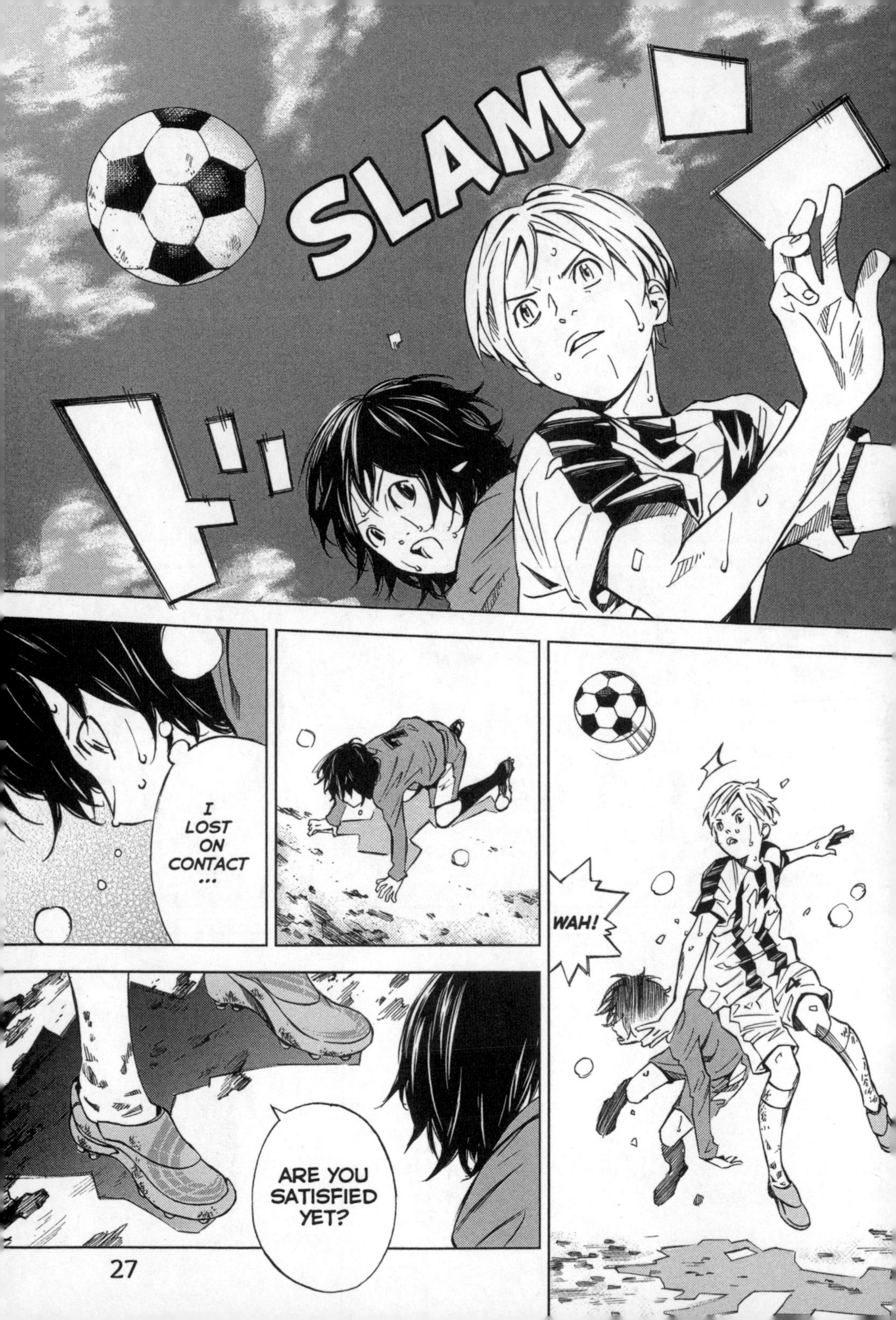
SLAM
WAH!
I LOST ON CONTACT...
ARE YOU SATISFIED YET?

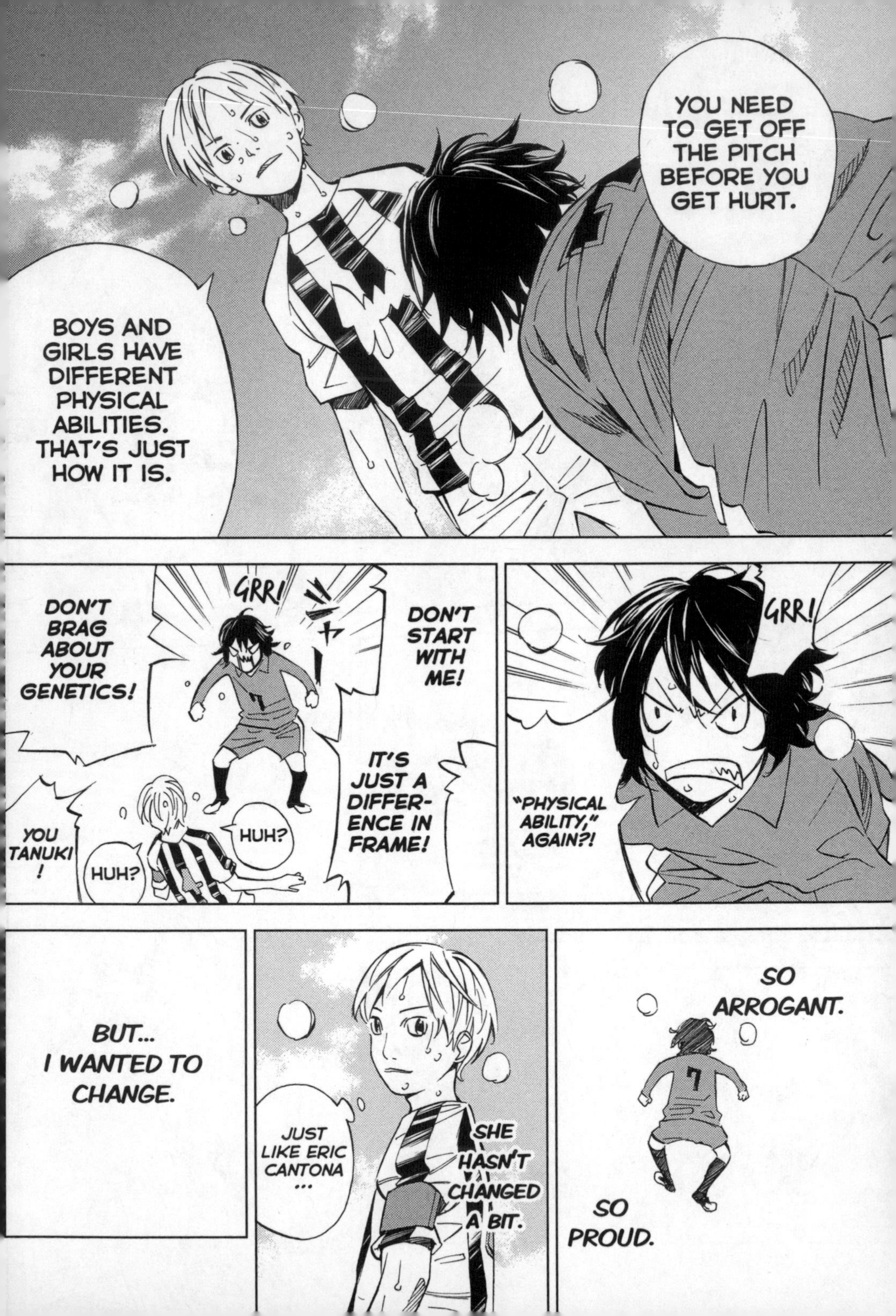
YOU NEED TO GET OFF THE PITCH BEFORE YOU GET HURT.
BOYS AND GIRLS HAVE DIFFERENT PHYSICAL ABILITIES. THAT'S JUST HOW IT IS.
GRR!
"PHYSICAL ABILITY," AGAIN?!
DON'T START WITH ME!
GRR!
DON'T BRAG ABOUT YOUR GENETICS!
IT'S JUST A DIFFERENCE IN FRAME!
HUH?
HUH?
YOU TANUKI!
SO ARROGANT.
SO PROUD.
SHE HASN'T CHANGED A BIT.
JUST LIKE ERIC CANTONA...
BUT... I WANTED TO CHANGE.

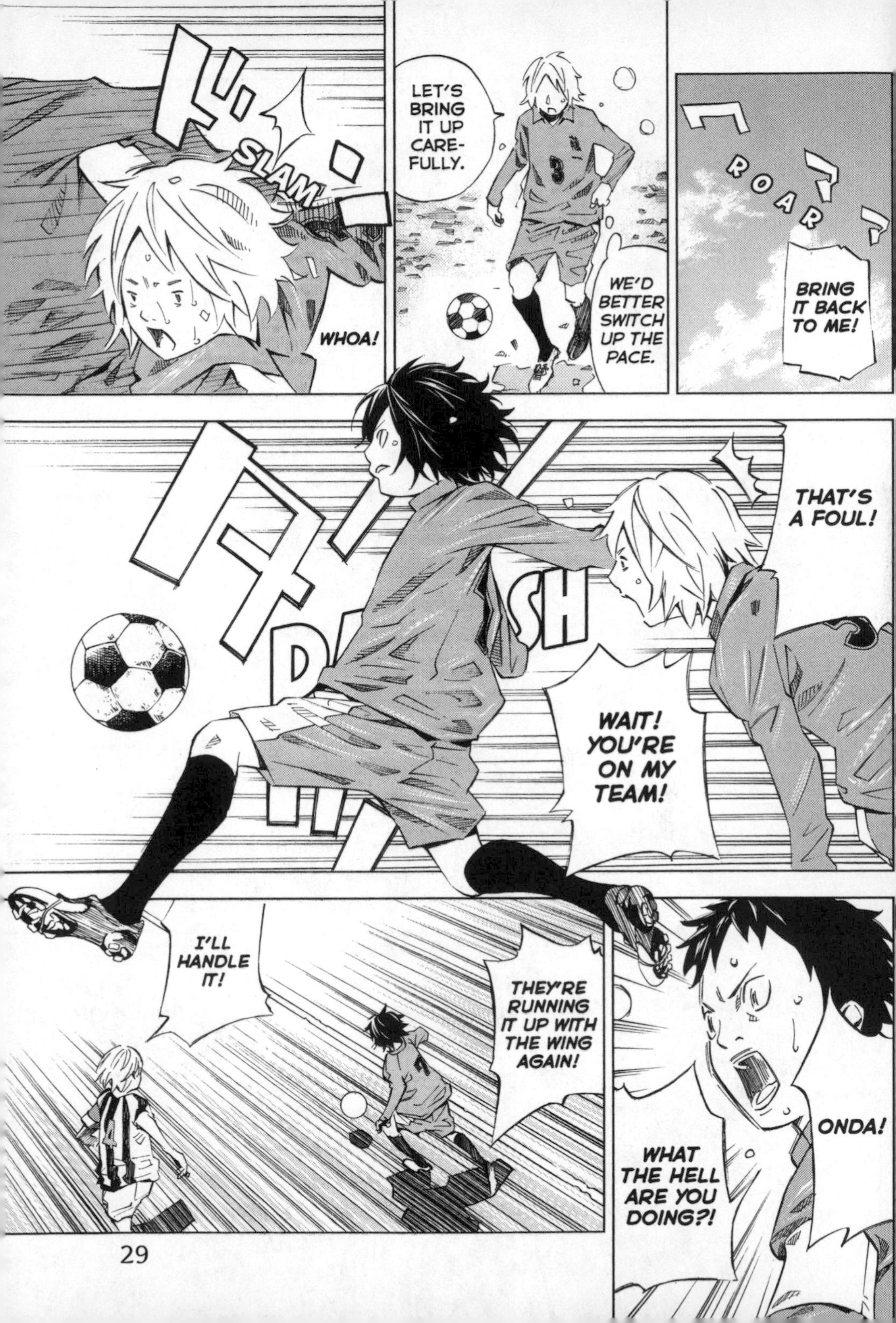
ROAR
BRING IT BACK TO ME!
LET'S BRING IT UP CAREFULLY.
WE'D BETTER SWITCH UP THE PACE.
SLAM
WHOA!
THAT'S A FOUL!
WAIT! YOU'RE ON MY TEAM!
DASH
ONDA!
WHAT THE HELL ARE YOU DOING?!
THEY'RE RUNNING IT UP WITH THE WING AGAIN!
I'LL HANDLE IT!

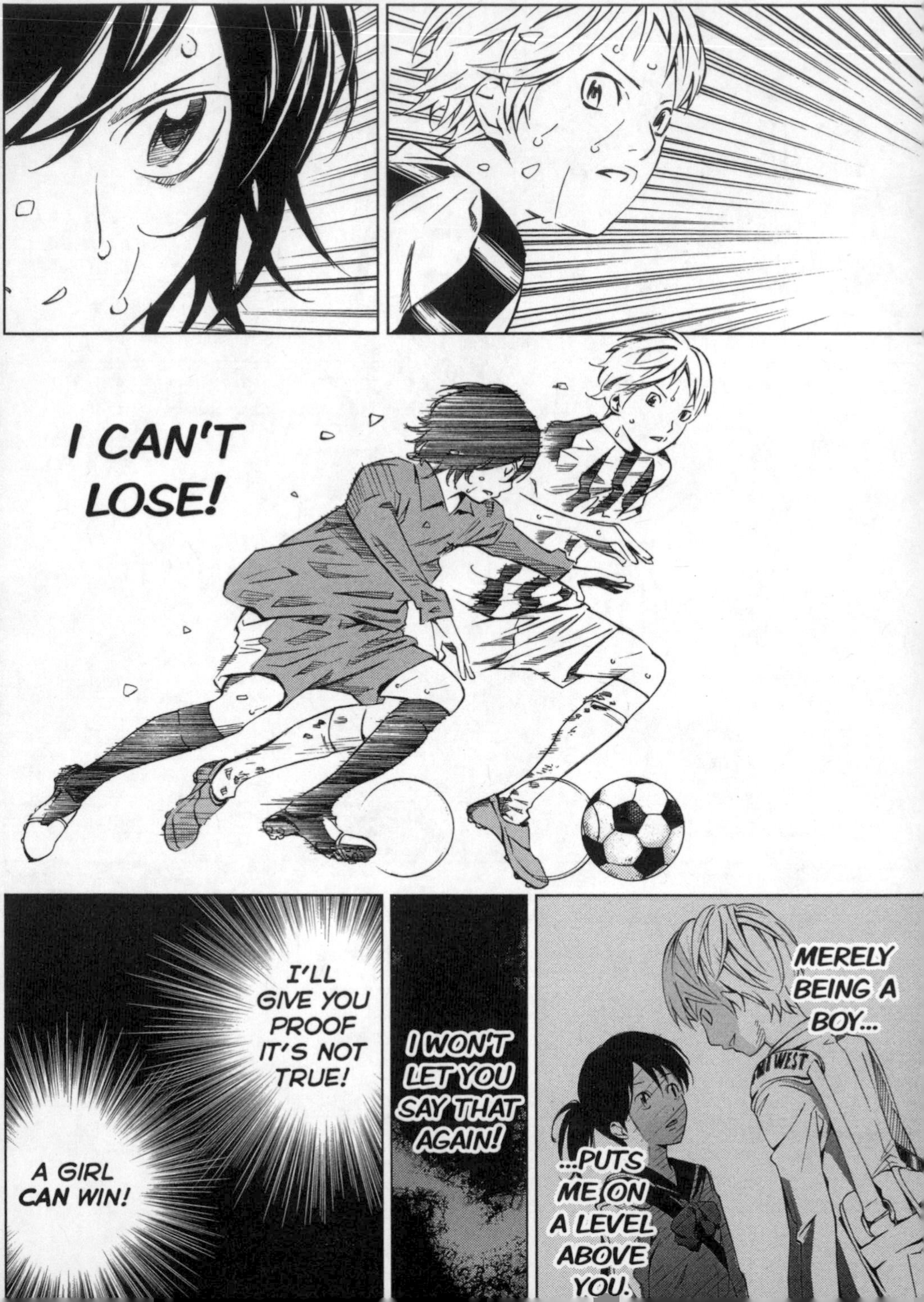
I CAN'T LOSE!
MERELY BEING A BOY...
...PUTS ME ON A LEVEL ABOVE YOU.
I WON'T LET YOU SAY THAT AGAIN!
I'LL GIVE YOU PROOF IT'S NOT TRUE!
A GIRL CAN WIN!

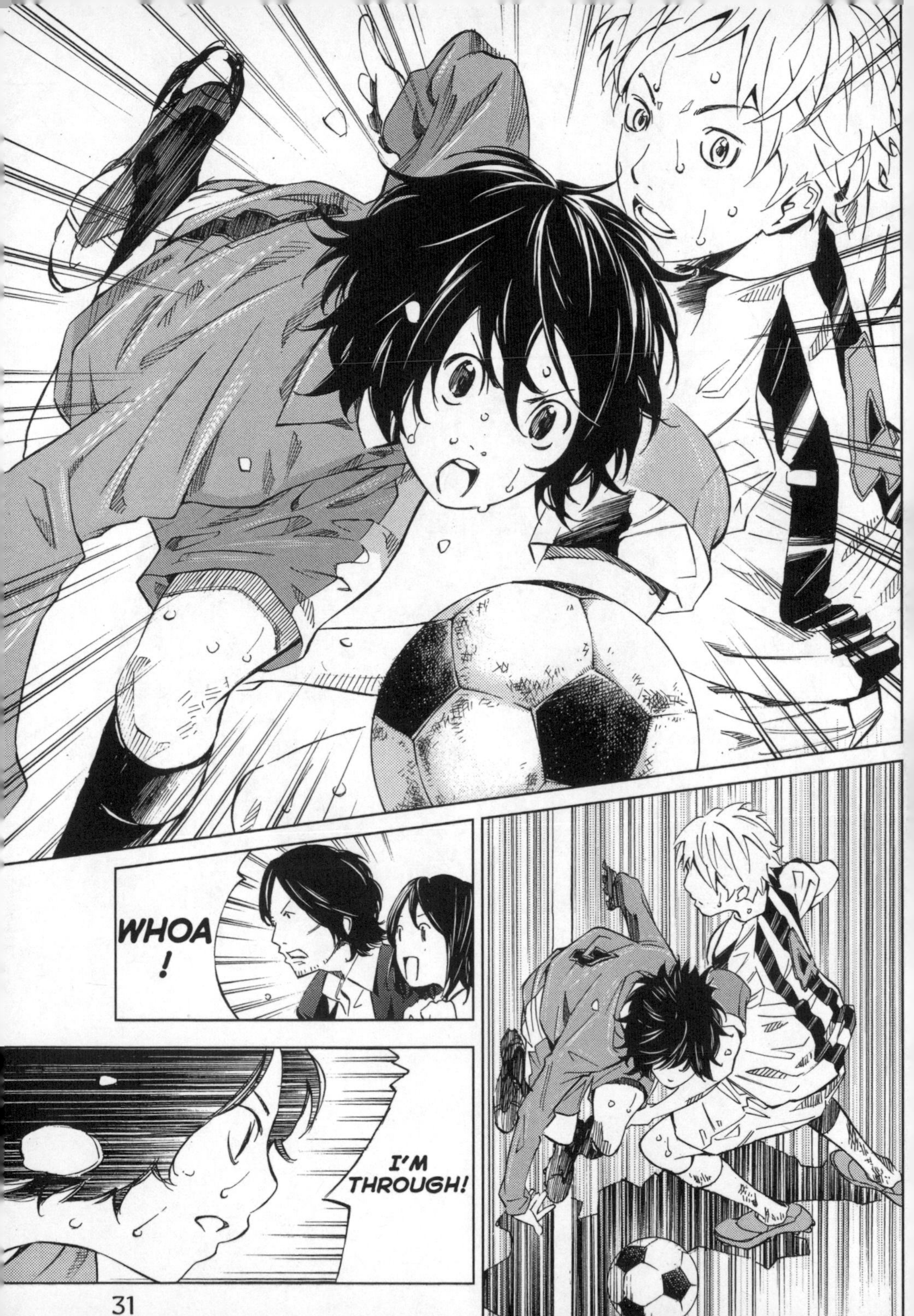
WHOA
!
I'M THROUGH!

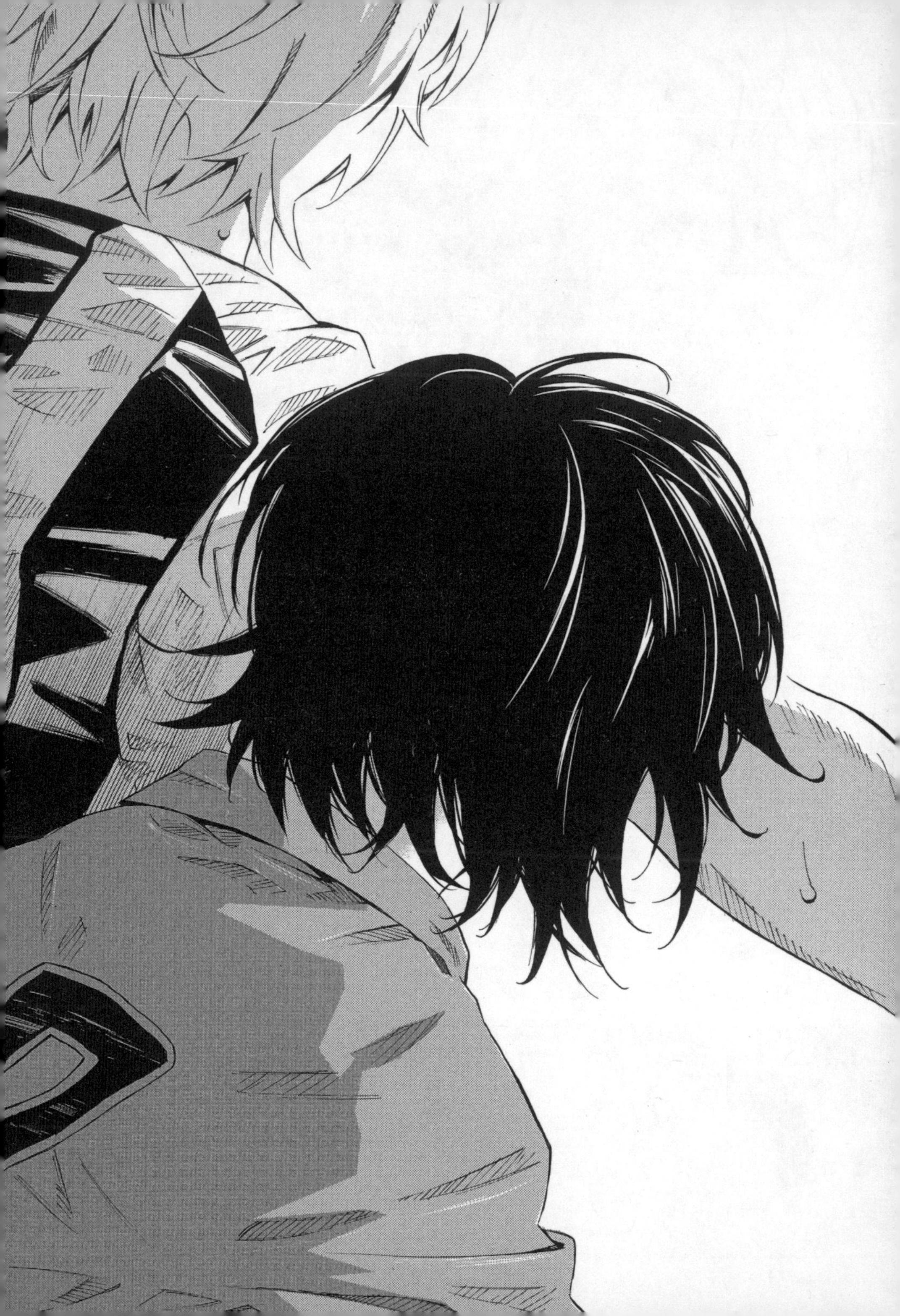

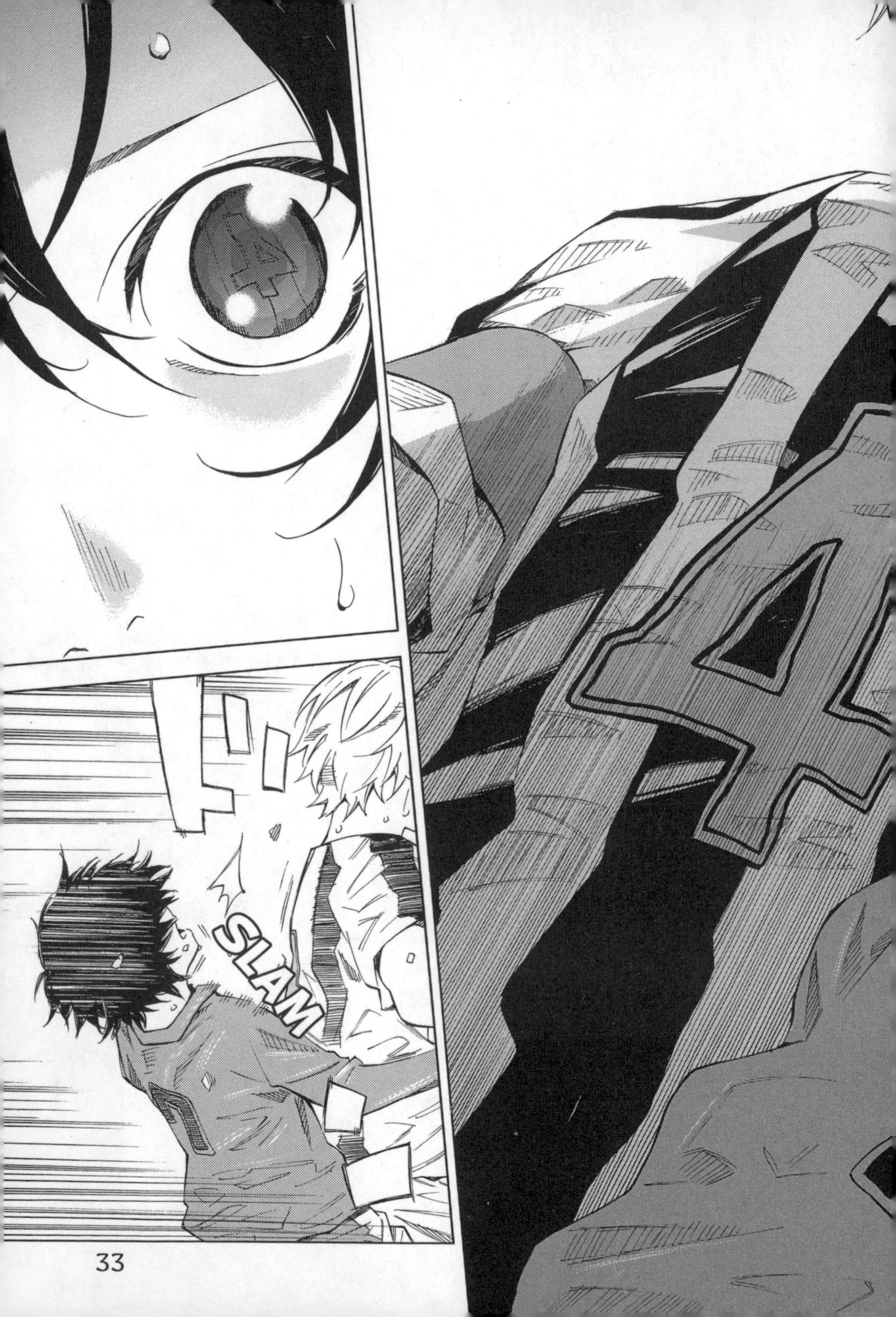
SLAM

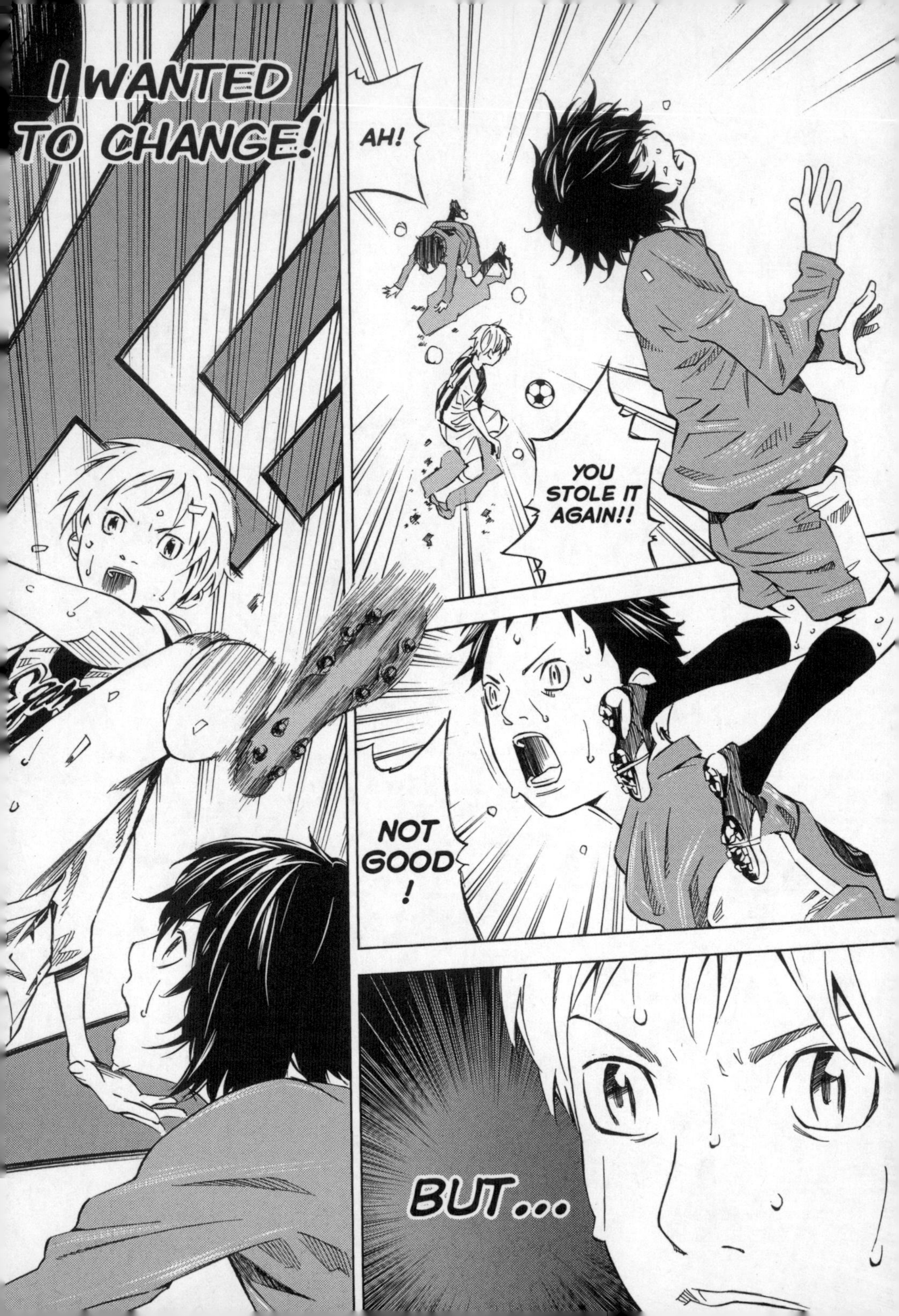
AH!
YOU STOLE IT AGAIN!!
NOT GOOD!
BUT...
I WANTED TO CHANGE!

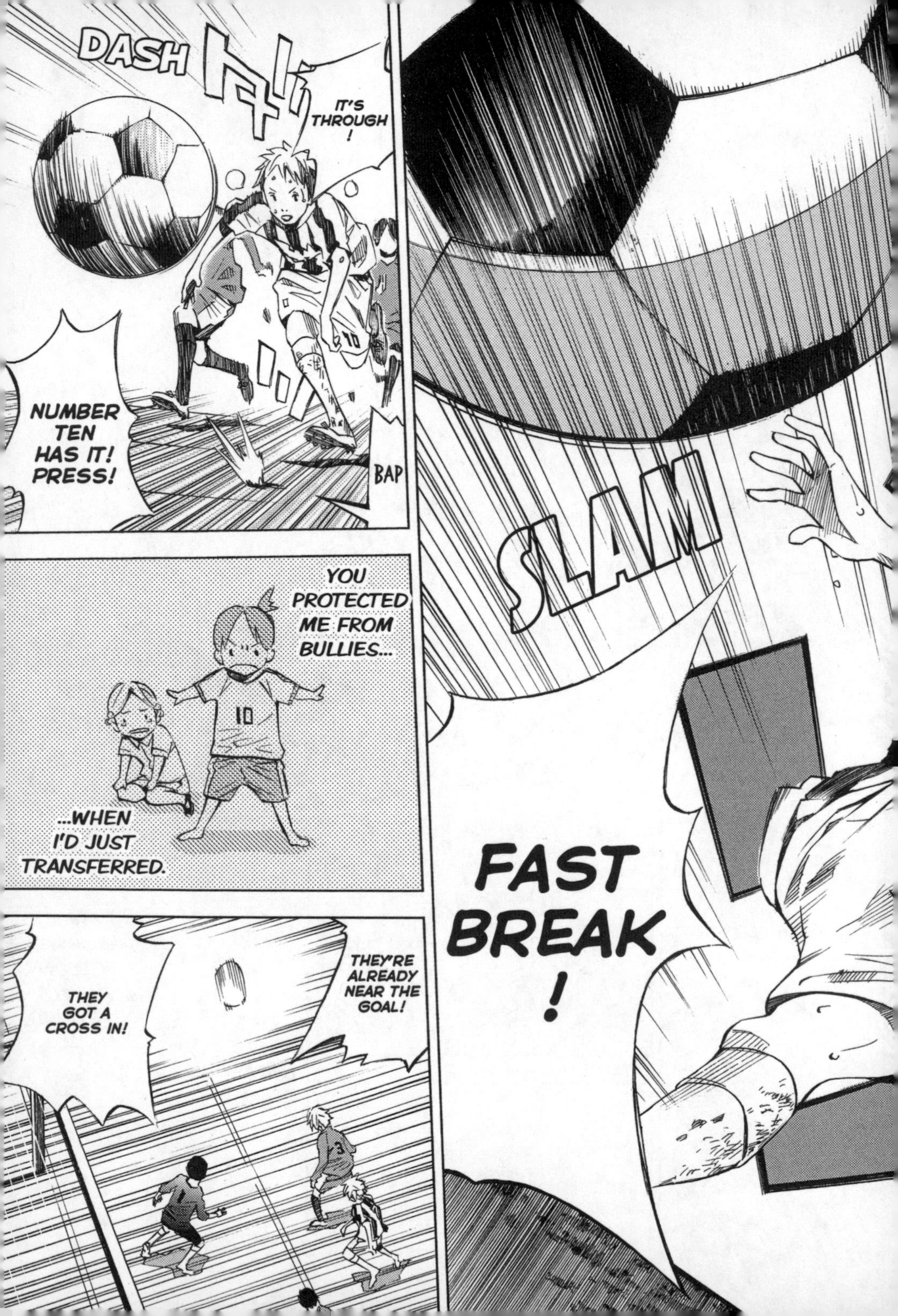
SLAM
FAST BREAK!
DASH
IT'S THROUGH!
NUMBER TEN HAS IT! PRESS!
BAP
YOU PROTECTED ME FROM BULLIES...
...WHEN I'D JUST TRANSFERRED.
THEY'RE ALREADY NEAR THE GOAL!
THEY GOT A CROSS IN!

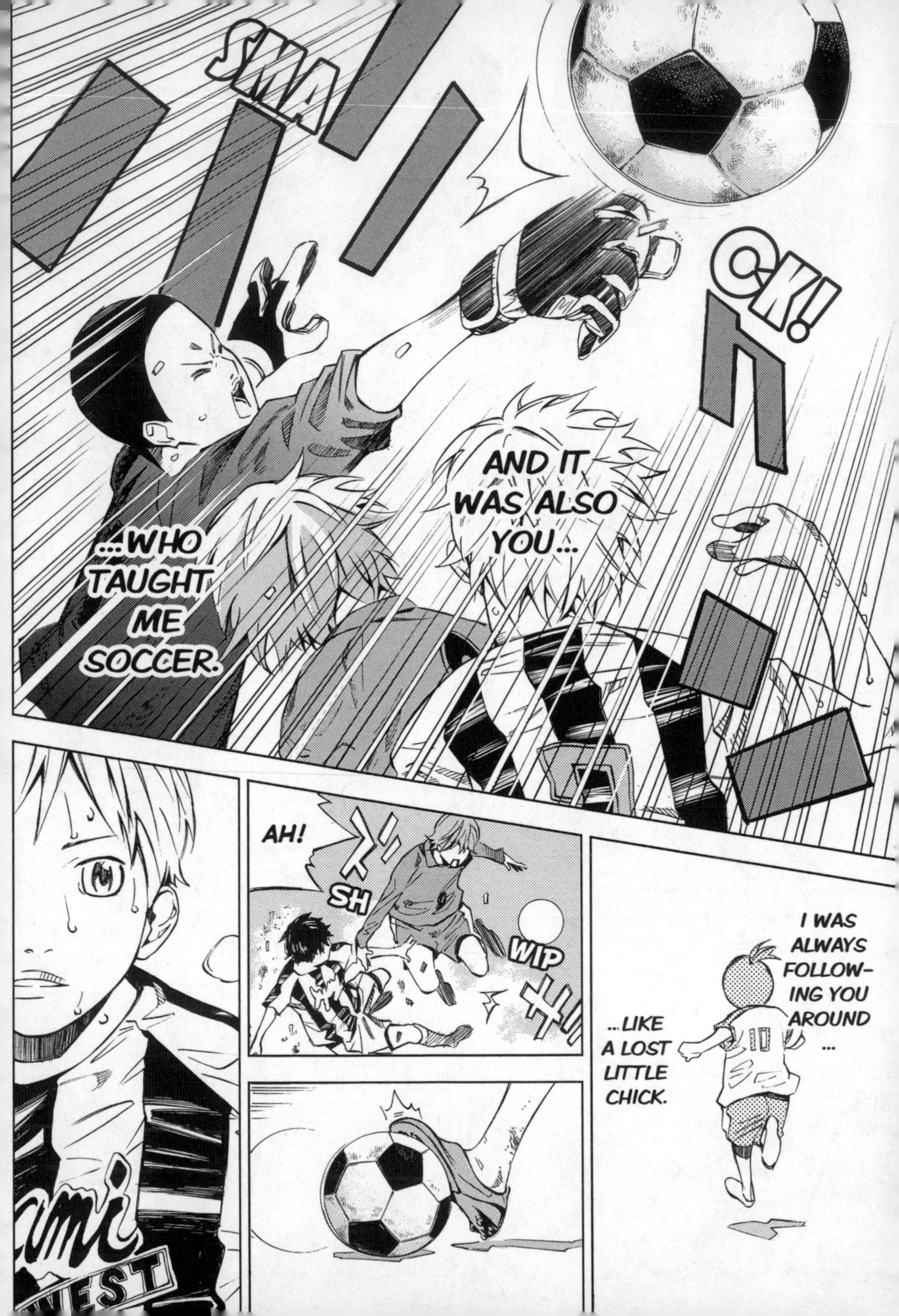
SHA
CK!
AND IT WAS ALSO YOU...
...WHO TAUGHT ME SOCCER.
I WAS ALWAYS FOLLOW-ING YOU AROUND ...
...LIKE A LOST LITTLE CHICK.
AH!
SH
WIP

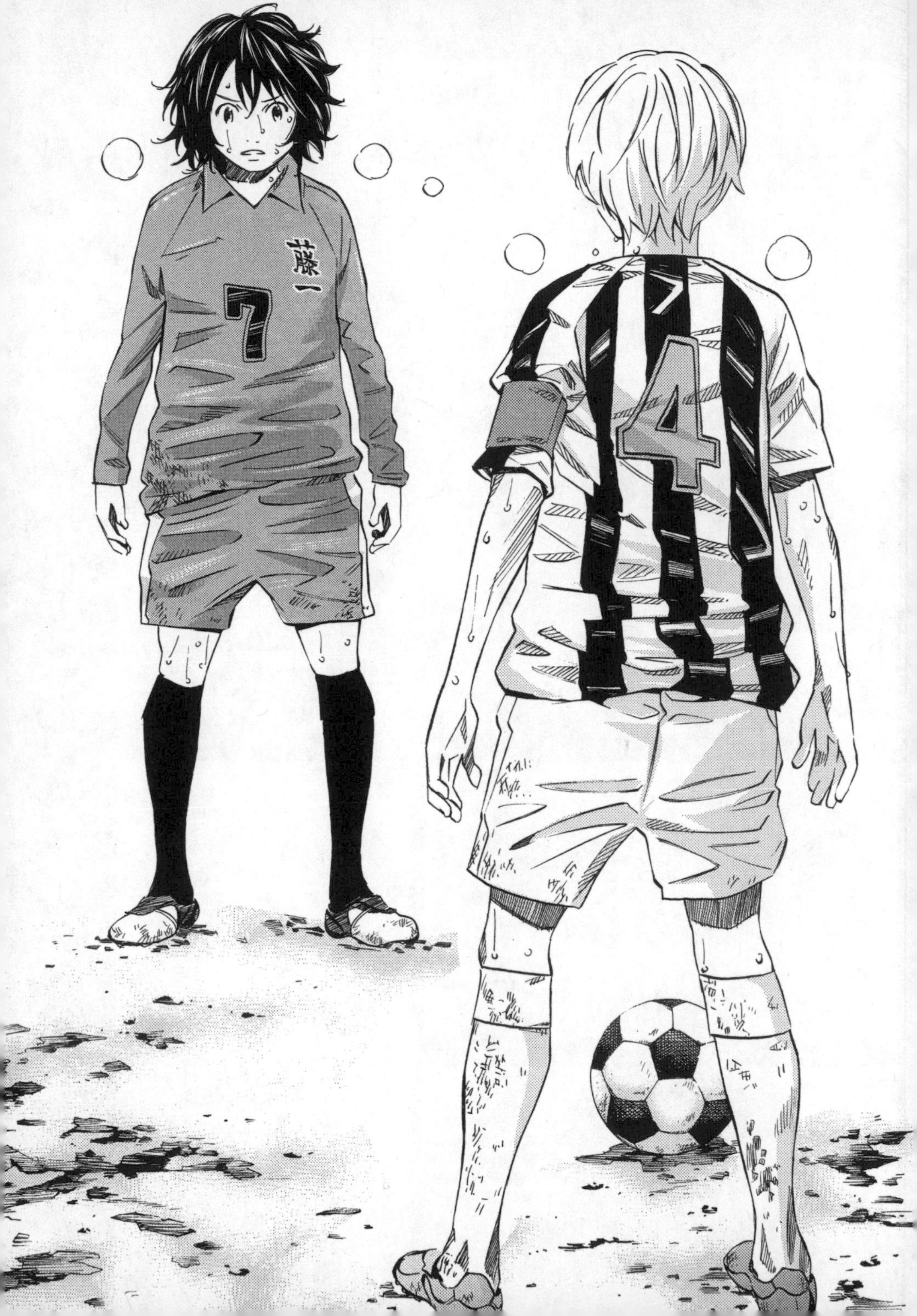
藤一
7
4

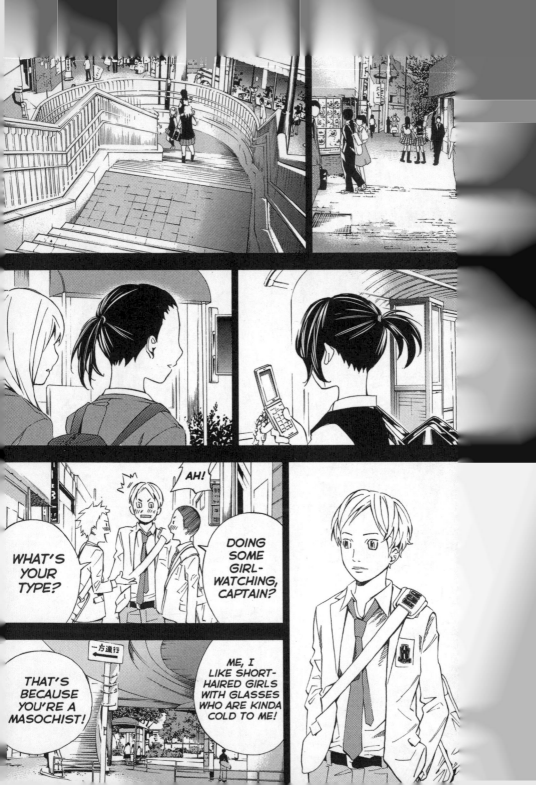

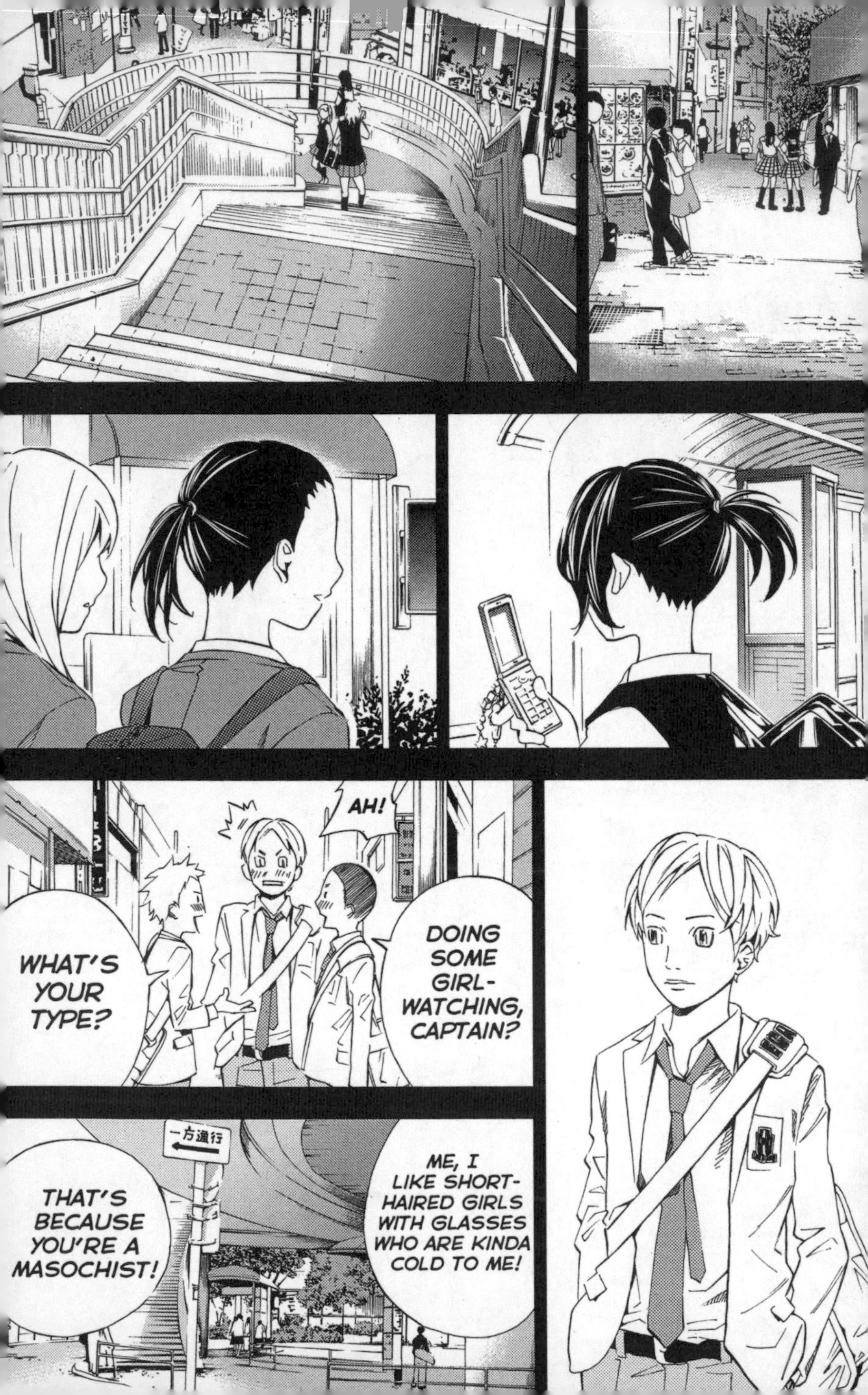
AH!
DOING SOME GIRL-WATCHING, CAPTAIN?
WHAT'S YOUR TYPE?
一方通行
ME, I LIKE SHORT-HAIRED GIRLS WITH GLASSES WHO ARE KINDA COLD TO ME!
THAT'S BECAUSE YOU'RE A MASOCHIST!

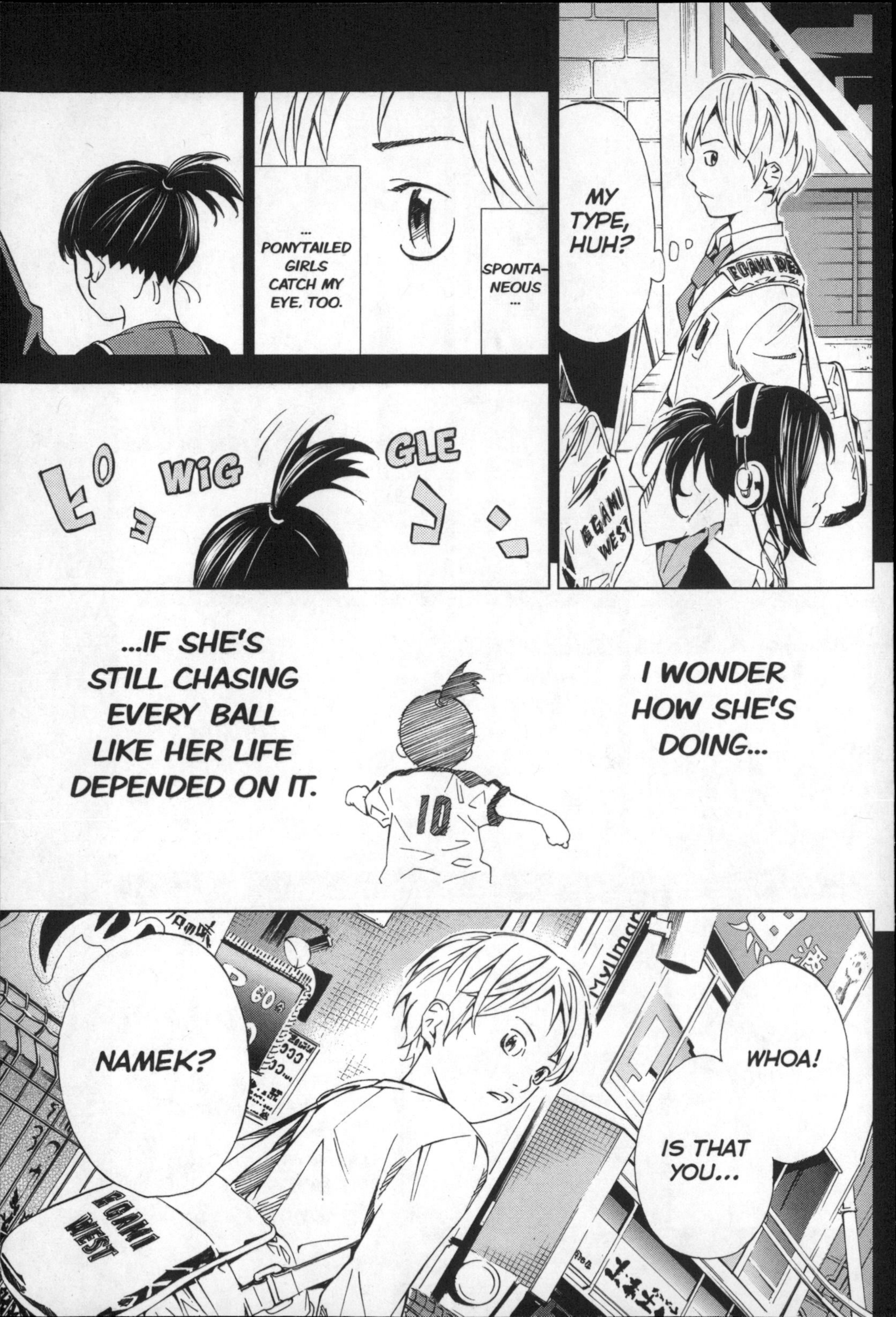
MY TYPE, HUH?
SPONTA-NEOUS ...
... PONYTAILED GIRLS CATCH MY EYE, TOO.
WIG GLE
I WONDER HOW SHE'S DOING...
...IF SHE'S STILL CHASING EVERY BALL LIKE HER LIFE DEPENDED ON IT.
WHOA!
IS THAT YOU...
NAMEK?

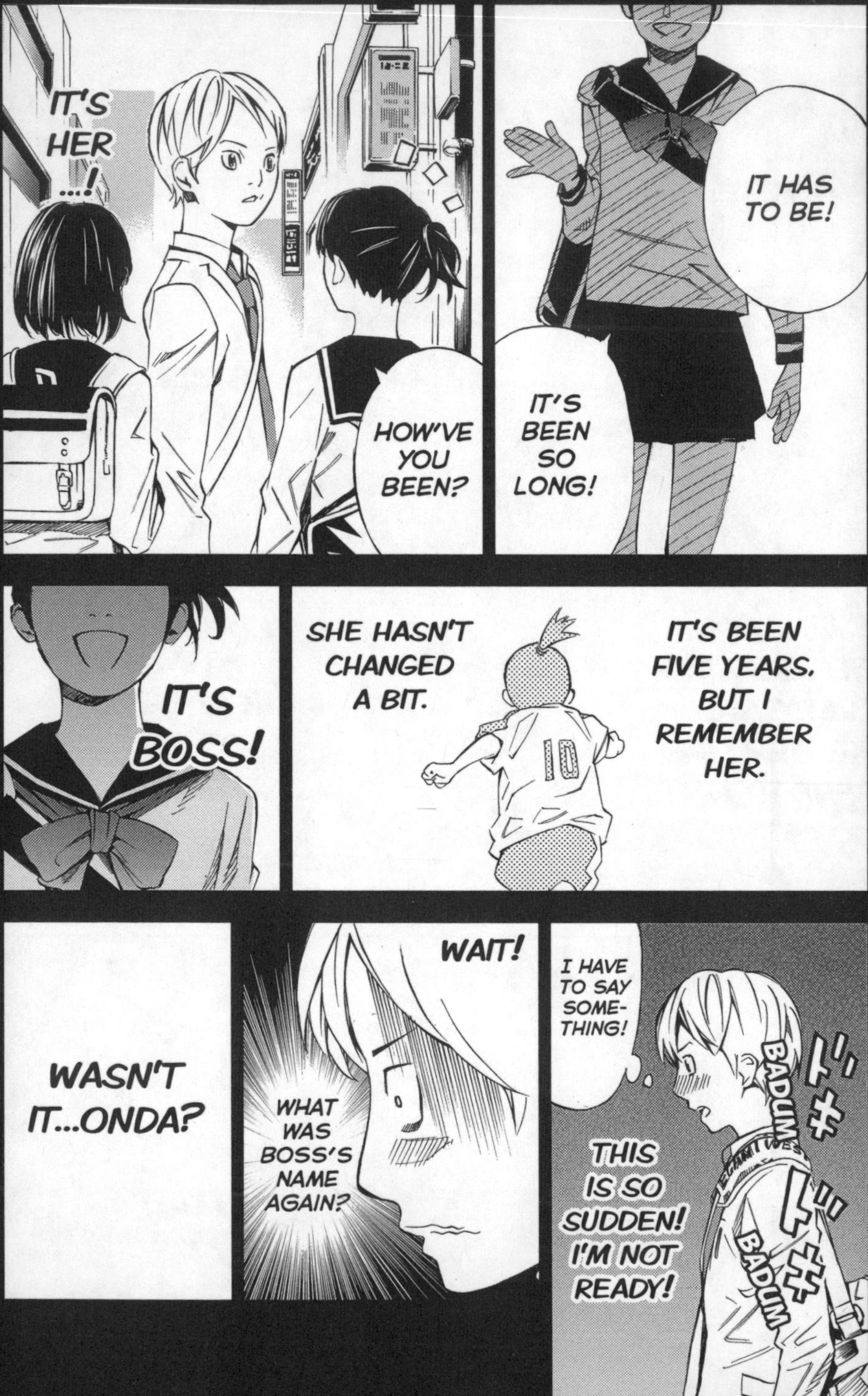
IT HAS TO BE!
IT'S BEEN SO LONG!
IT'S HER ...!
HOW'VE YOU BEEN?
IT'S BEEN FIVE YEARS, BUT I REMEMBER HER.
SHE HASN'T CHANGED A BIT.
IT'S BOSS!
I HAVE TO SAY SOME-THING!
BADUM
BADUM
THIS IS SO SUDDEN! I'M NOT READY!
WAIT!
WHAT WAS BOSS'S NAME AGAIN?
WASN'T IT...ONDA?

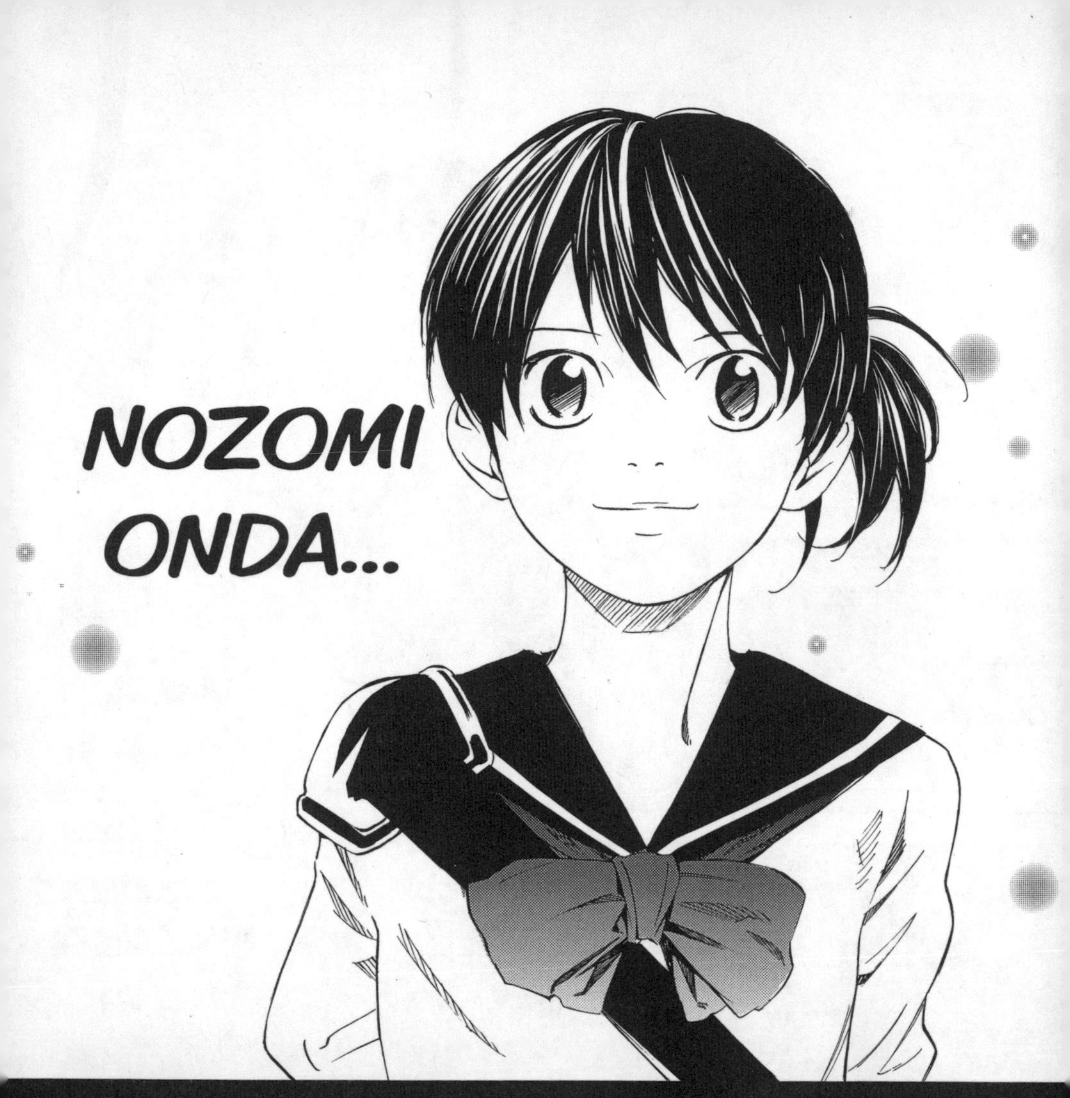
NOZOMI
ONDA...
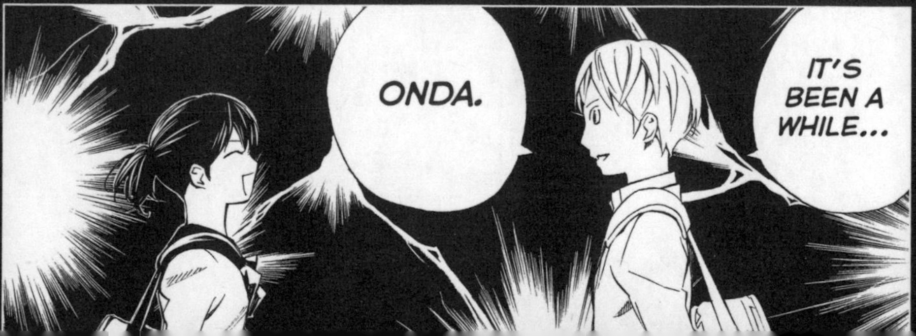
IT'S BEEN A WHILE...
ONDA.

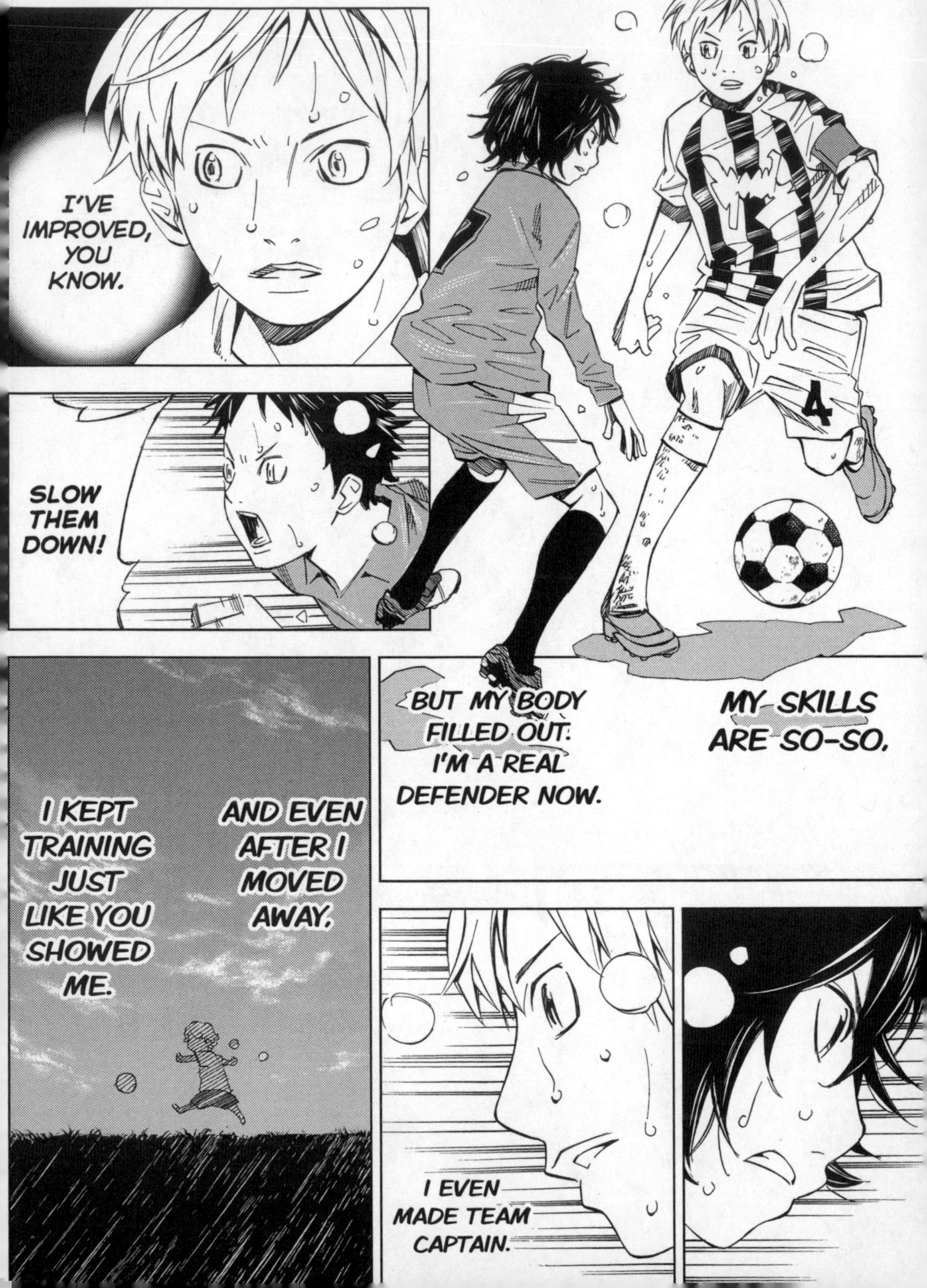
I'VE IMPROVED, YOU KNOW.
SLOW THEM DOWN!
MY SKILLS ARE SO-SO.
BUT MY BODY FILLED OUT. I'M A REAL DEFENDER NOW.
I EVEN MADE TEAM CAPTAIN.
AND EVEN AFTER I MOVED AWAY,
I KEPT TRAINING JUST LIKE YOU SHOWED ME.

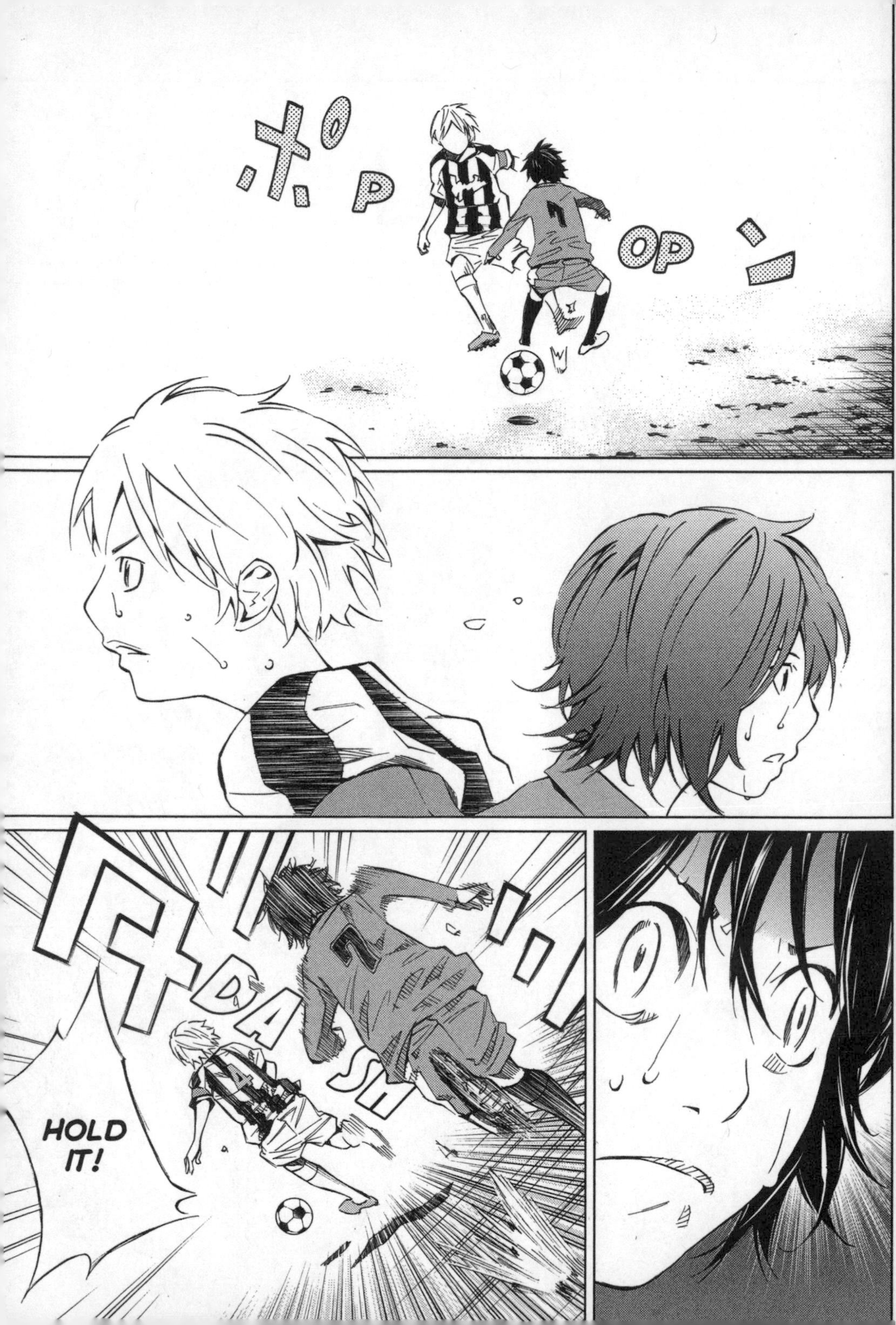
P
OP
DASH
HOLD IT!

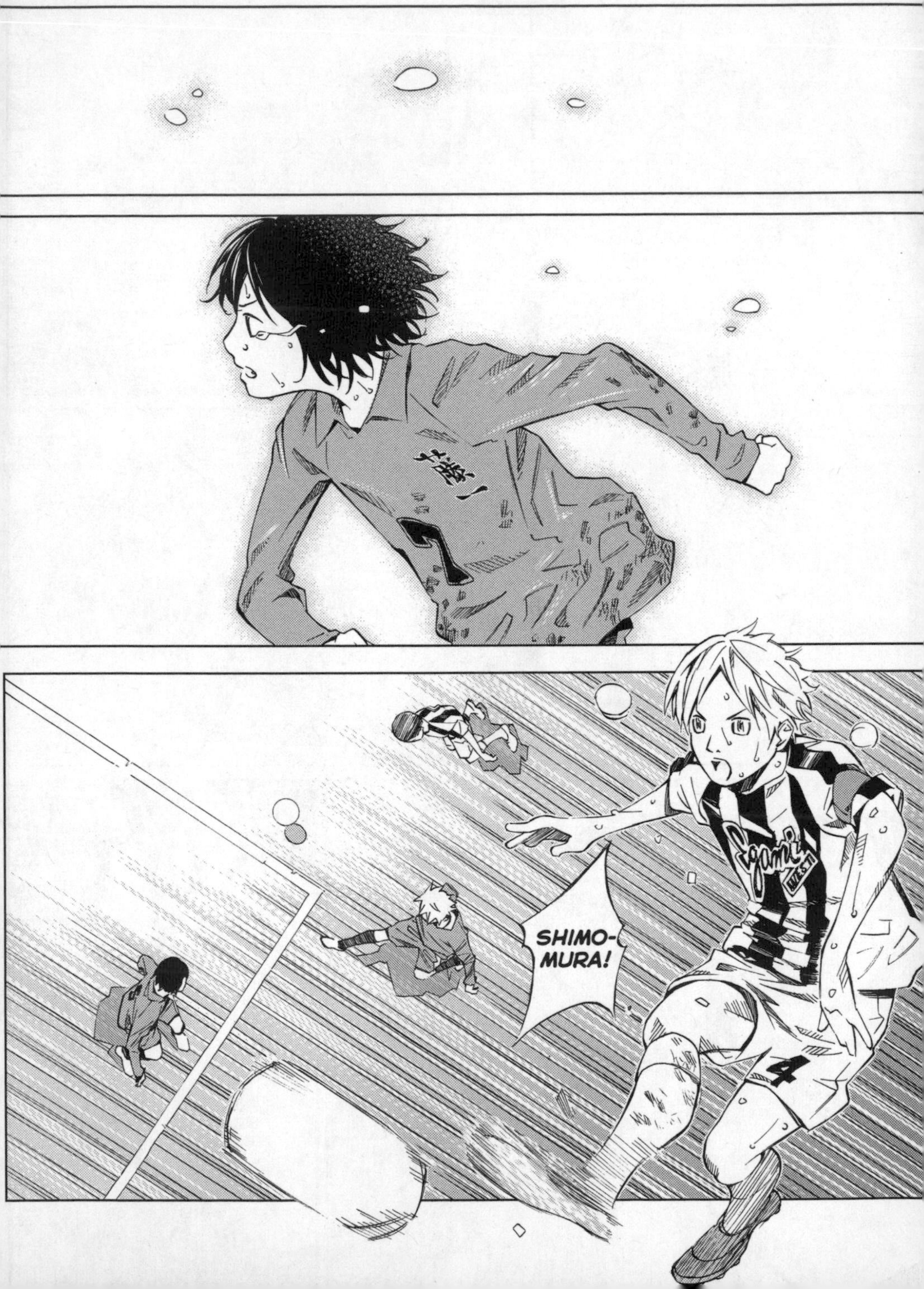
SHIMO-
MURA!

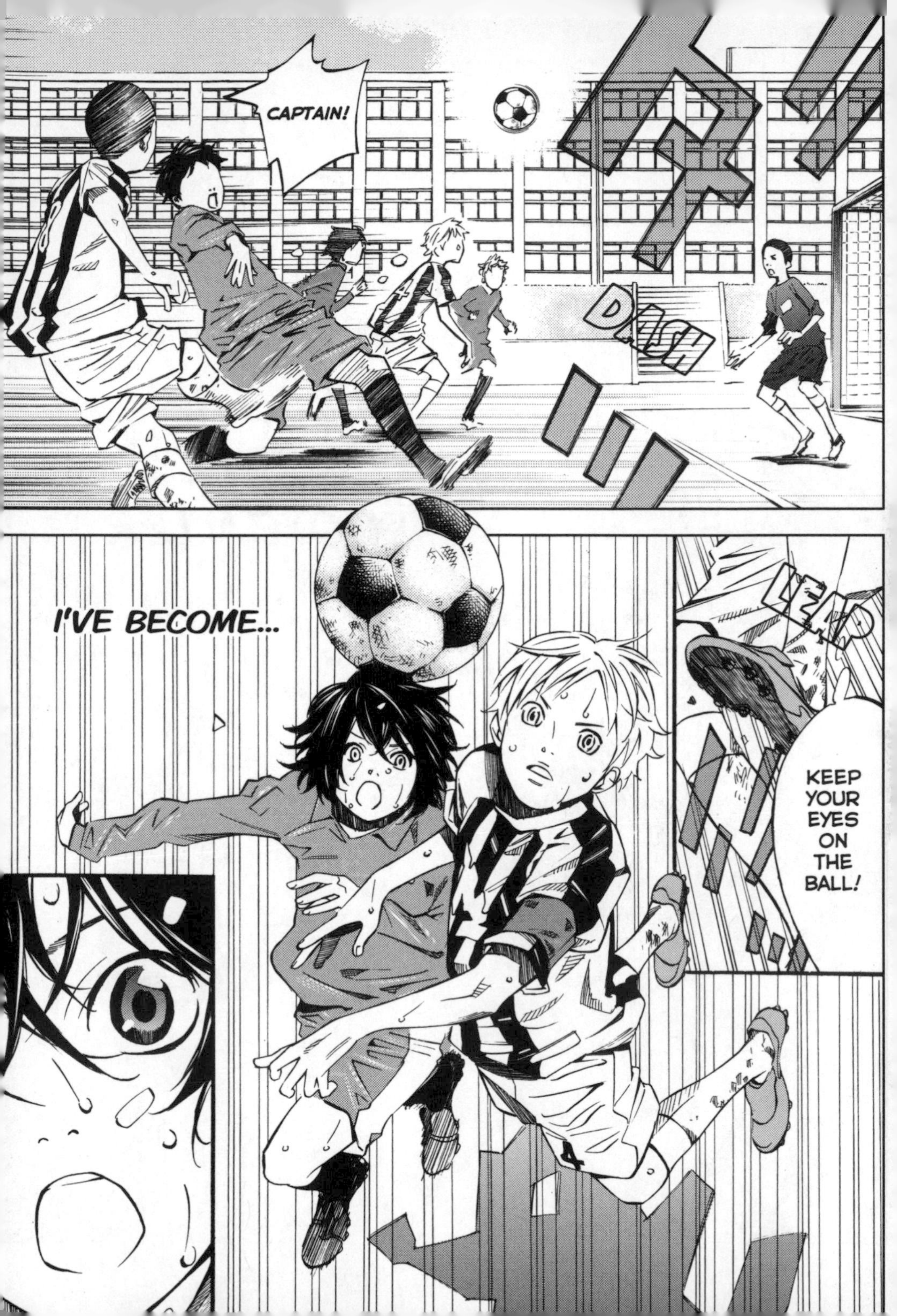
CAPTAIN!
DASH
LEAP
KEEP YOUR EYES ON THE BALL!
I'VE BECOME...

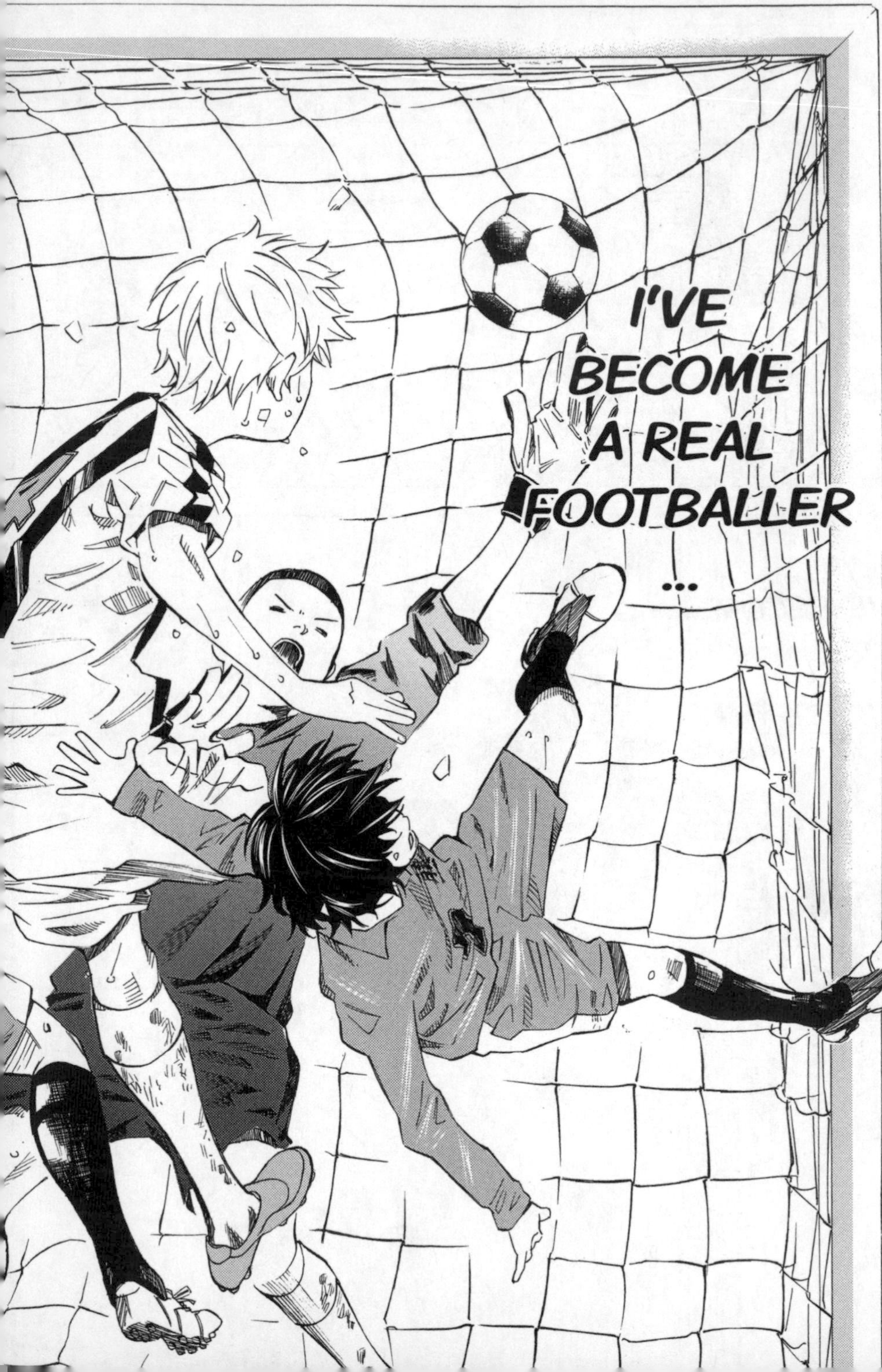
I'VE BECOME A REAL FOOTBALLER ...

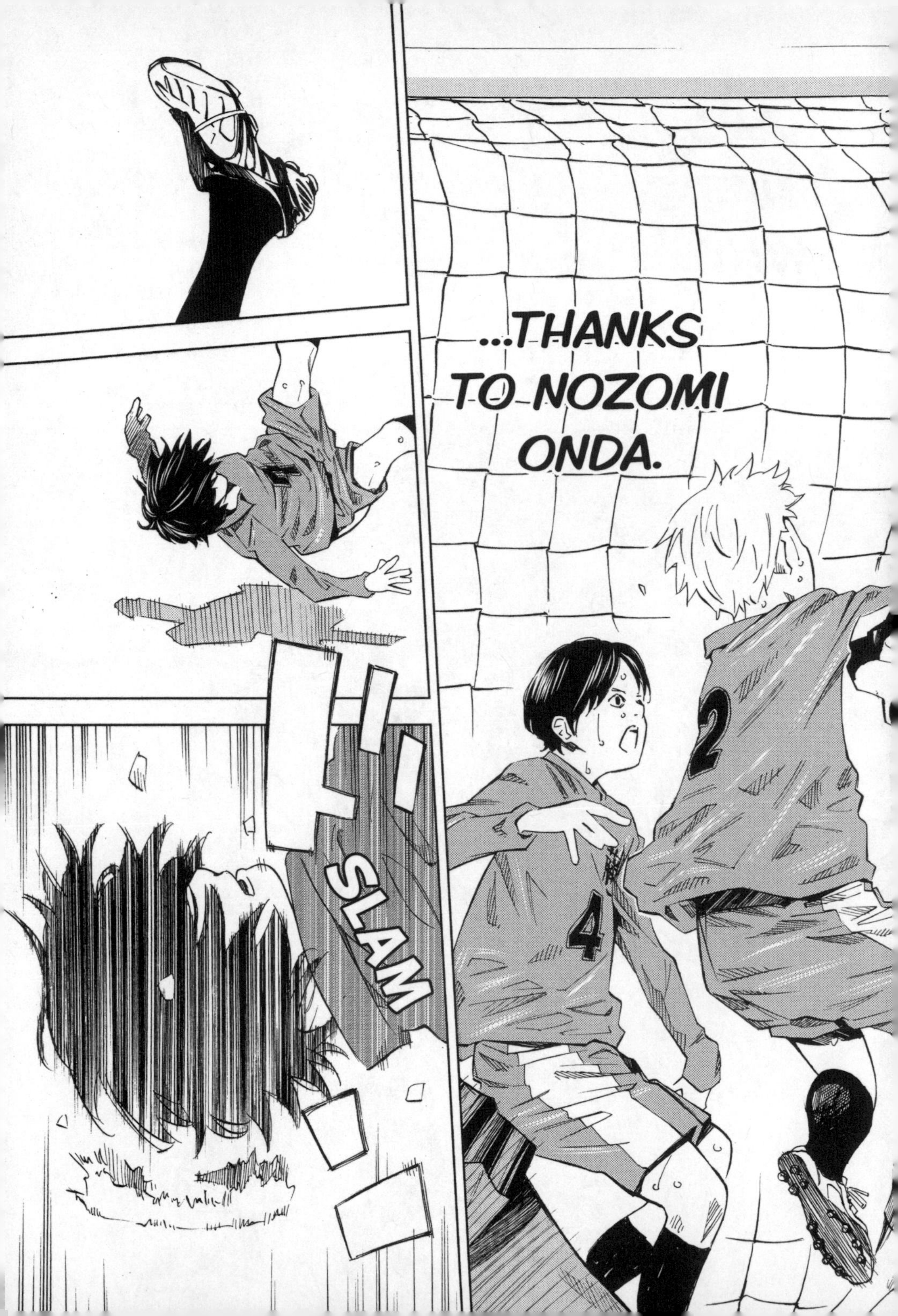
...THANKS TO NOZOMI ONDA.
SLAM

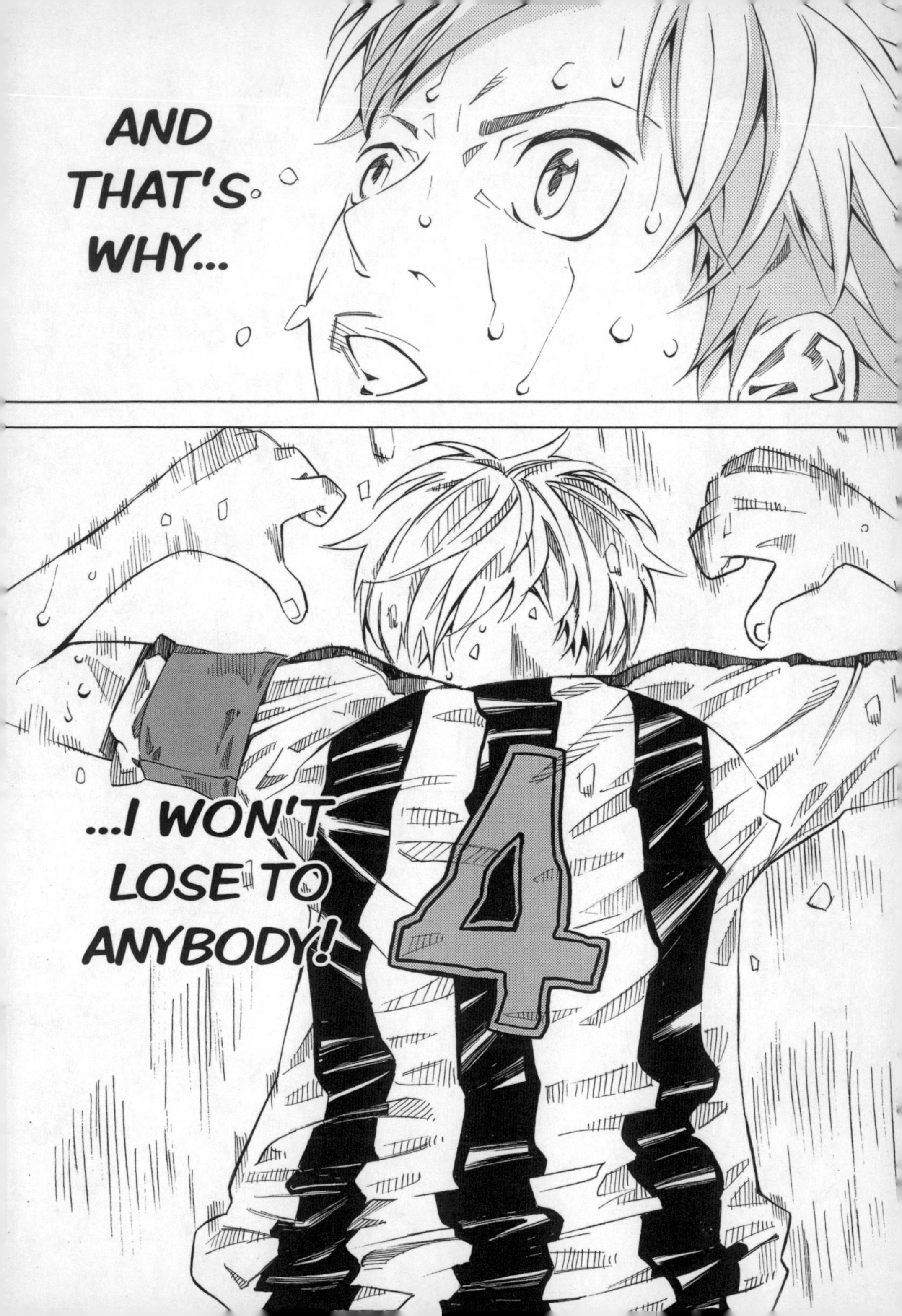
AND THAT'S WHY...
...I WON'T LOSE TO ANYBODY!

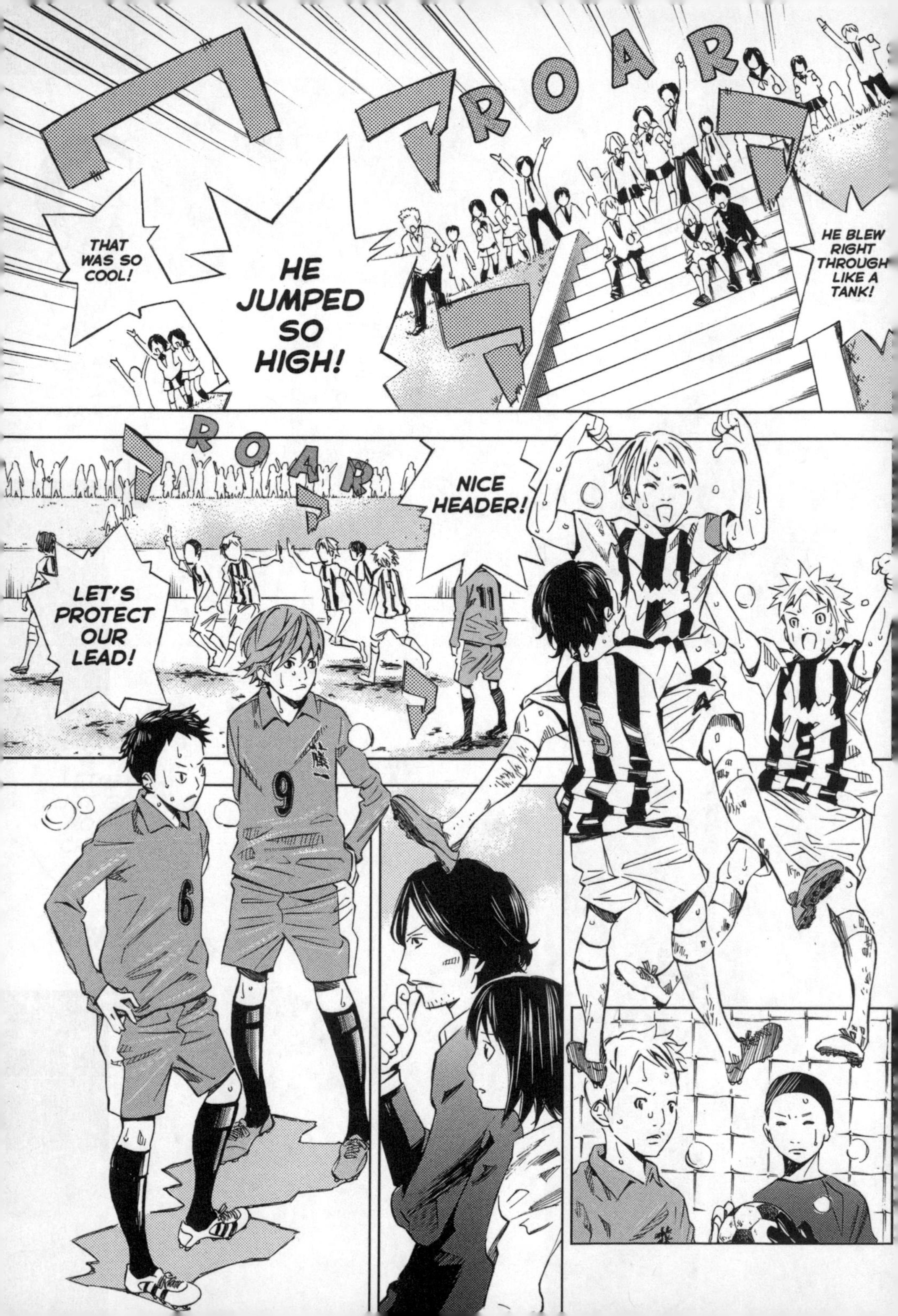
ROAR
HE BLEW RIGHT THROUGH LIKE A TANK!
HE JUMPED SO HIGH!
THAT WAS SO COOL!
ROAR
NICE HEADER!
LET'S PROTECT OUR LEAD!

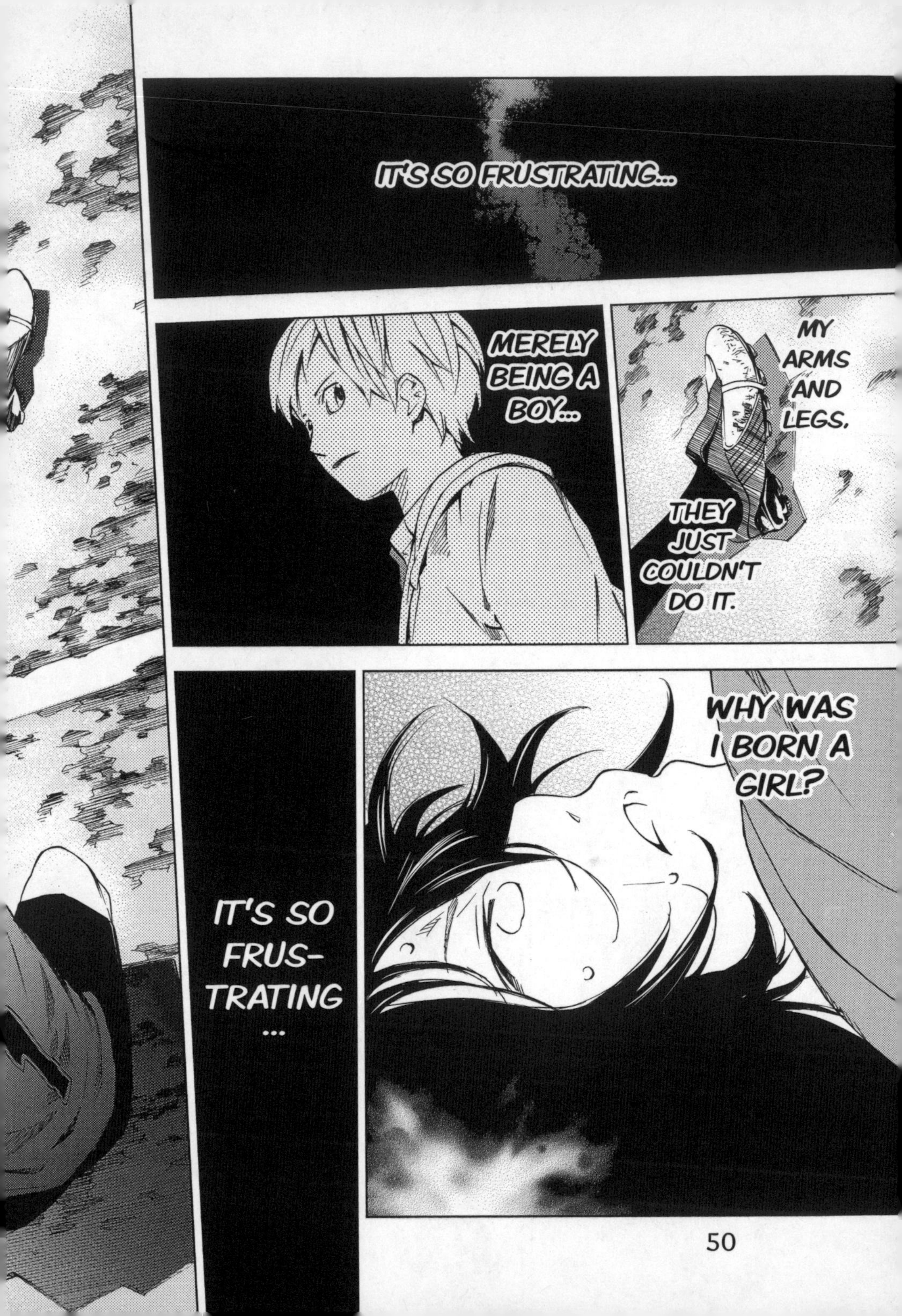
IT'S SO FRUSTRATING...
MY ARMS AND LEGS.
THEY JUST COULDN'T DO IT.
MERELY BEING A BOY...
WHY WAS I BORN A GIRL?
IT'S SO FRUSTRATING...

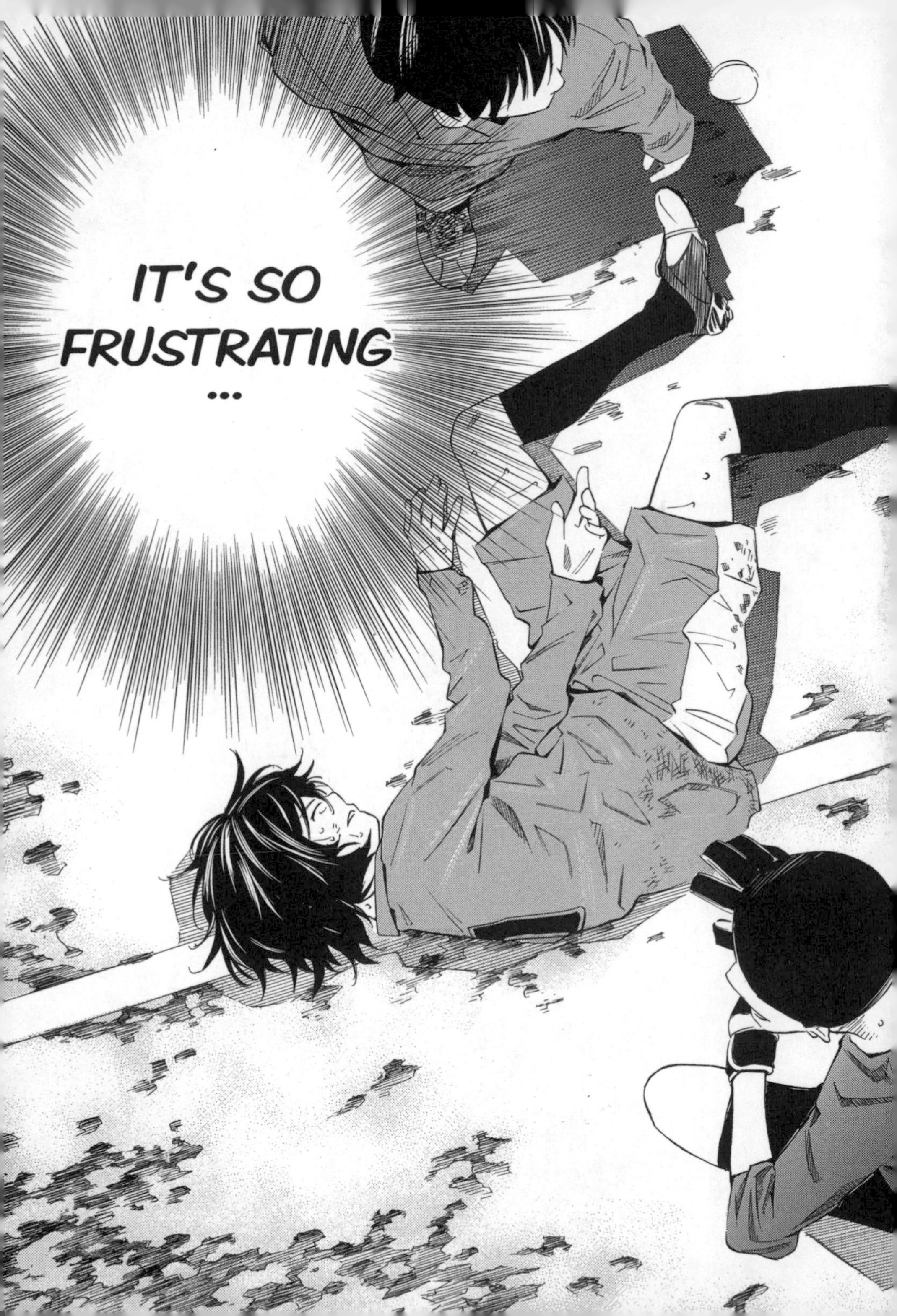
IT'S SO FRUSTRATING ...

SAYONARA FOOTBALL

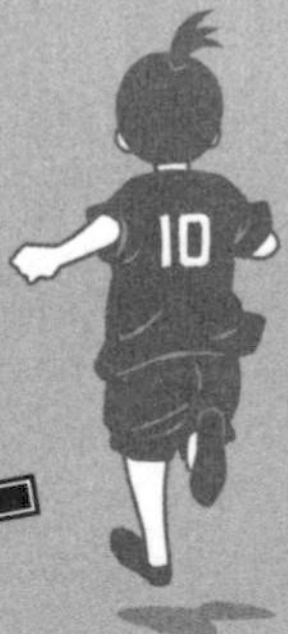
10

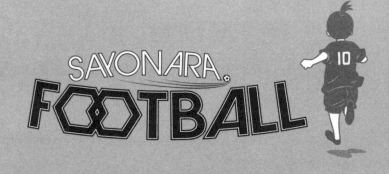

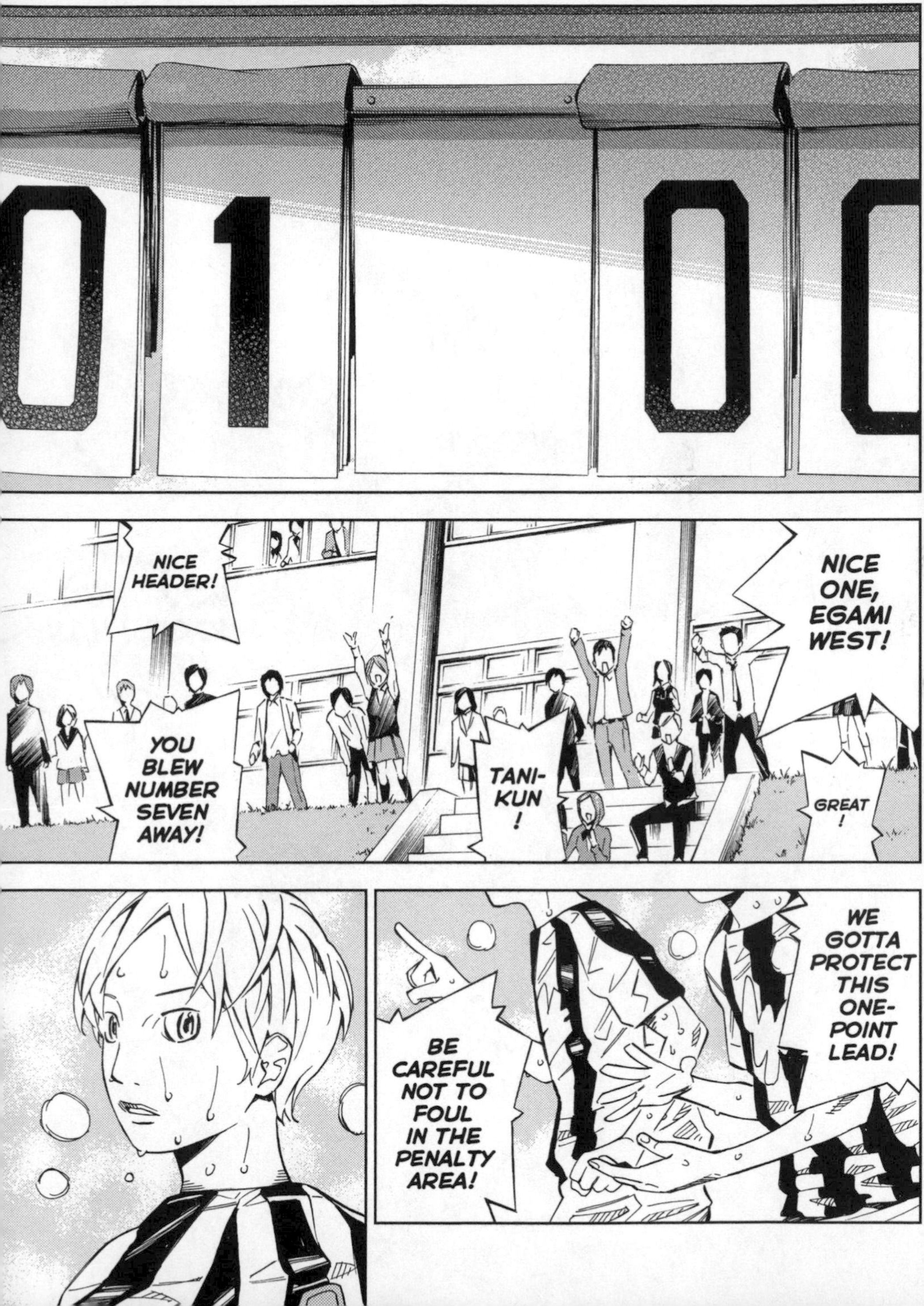
NICE ONE, EGAMI WEST!
NICE HEADER!
GREAT!
TANI-KUN!
YOU BLEW NUMBER SEVEN AWAY!
WE GOTTA PROTECT THIS ONE-POINT LEAD!
BE CAREFUL NOT TO FOUL IN THE PENALTY AREA!

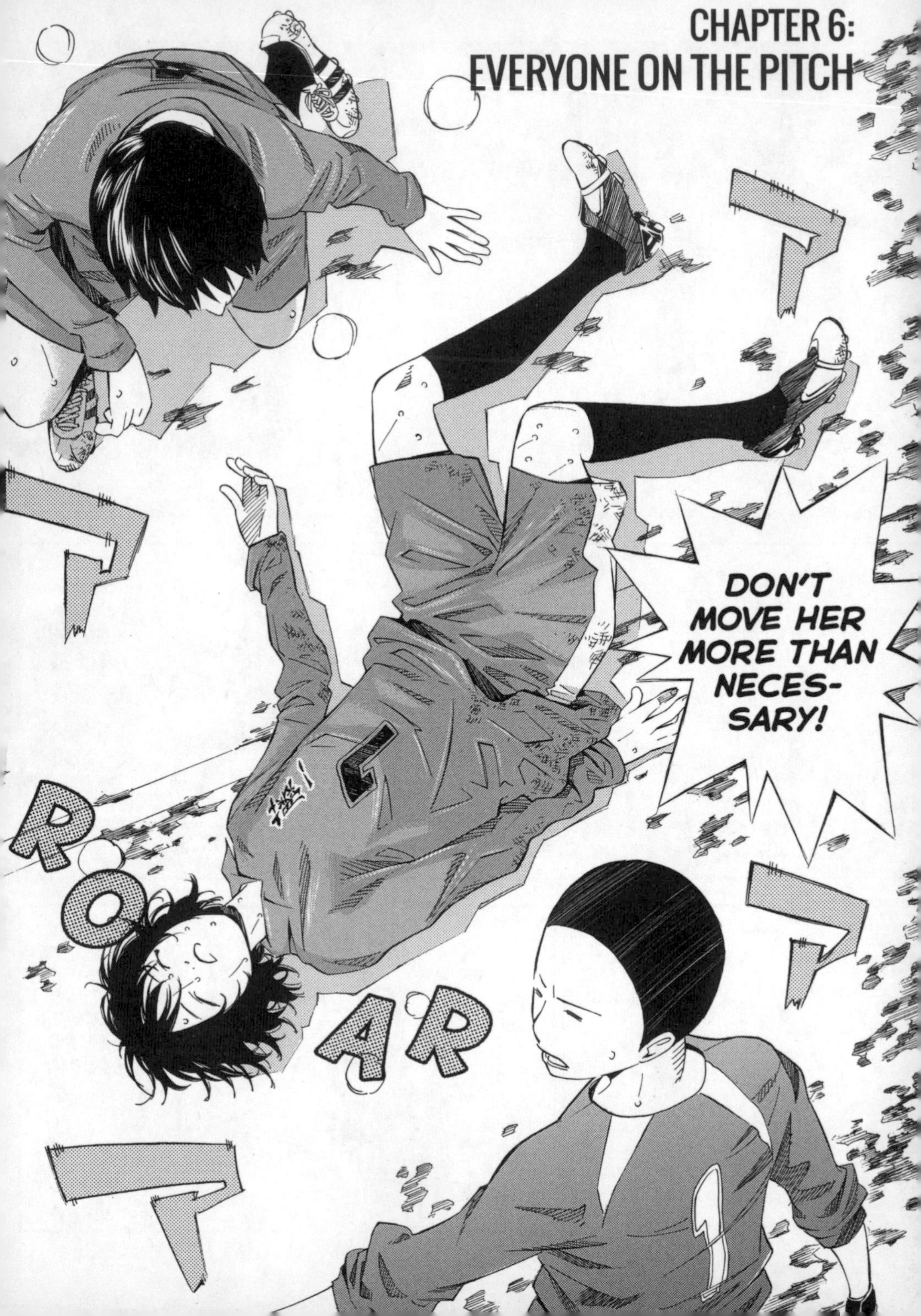
CHAPTER 6:
EVERYONE ON THE PITCH
DON'T MOVE HER MORE THAN NECES-SARY!
ROAR

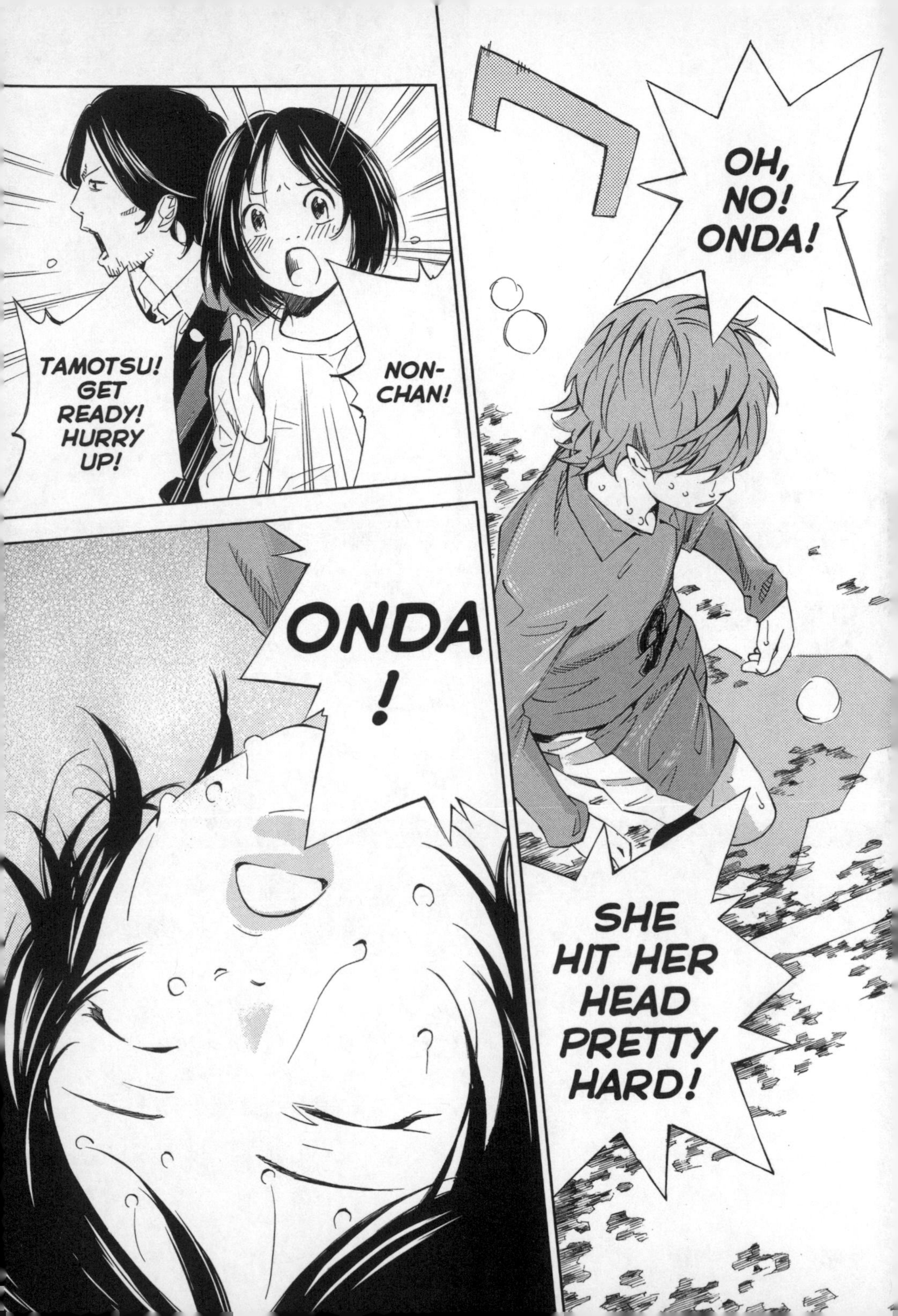
OH, NO! ONDA!
SHE HIT HER HEAD PRETTY HARD!
NON-CHAN!
TAMOTSU! GET READY! HURRY UP!
ONDA!

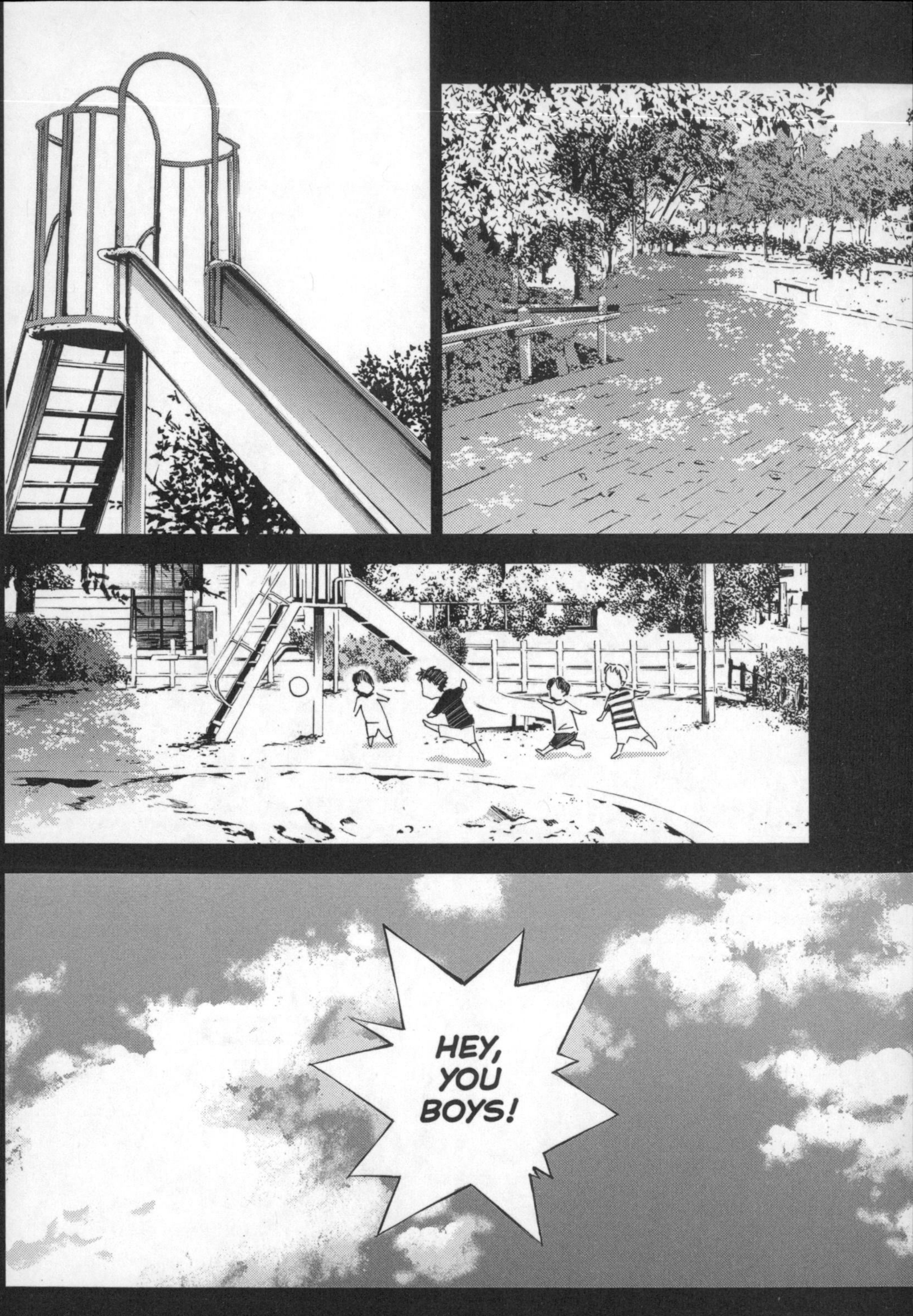
HEY, YOU BOYS!

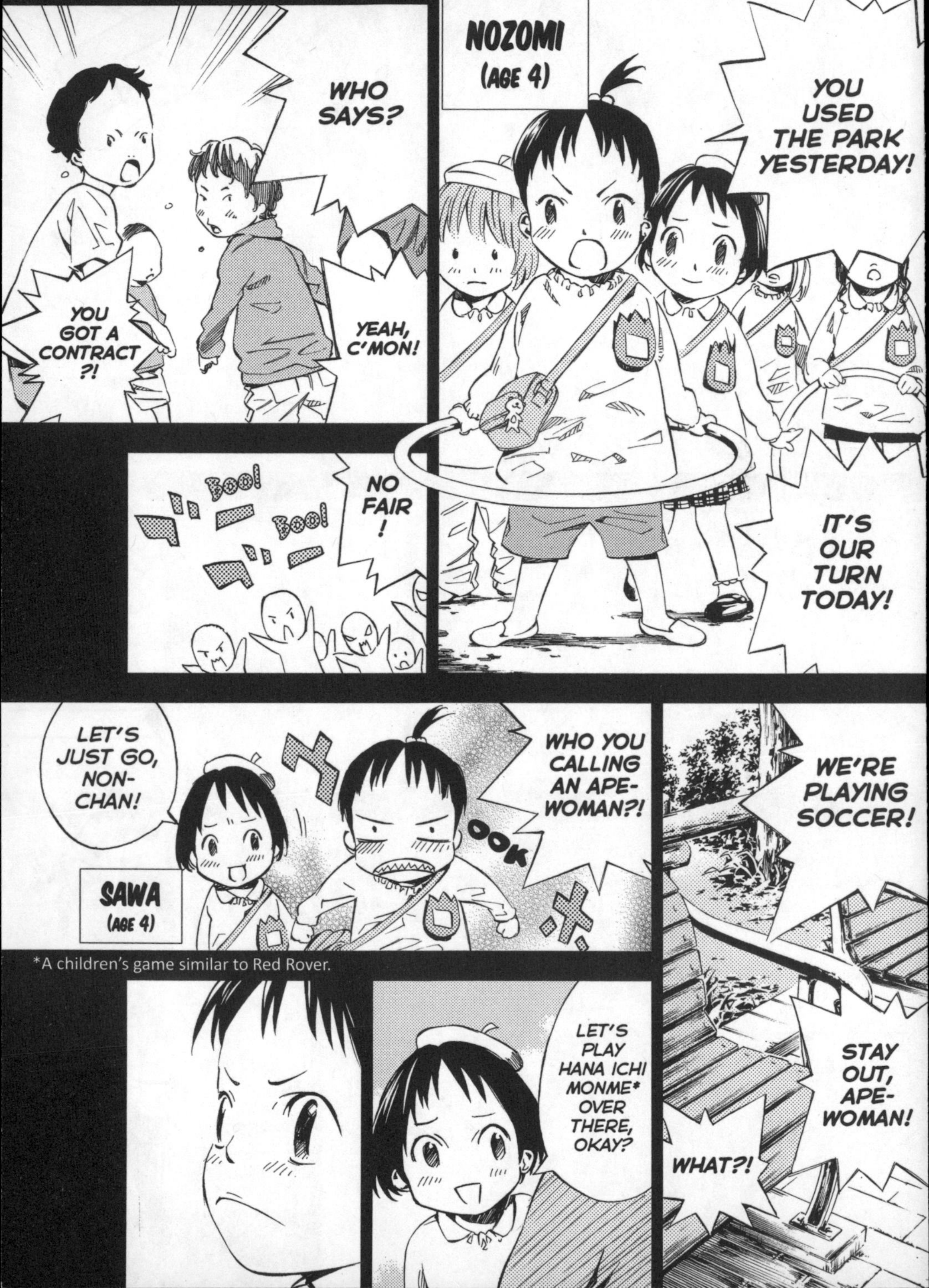
NOZOMI
(AGE 4)
YOU USED THE PARK YESTERDAY!
IT'S OUR TURN TODAY!
WHO SAYS?
YEAH, C'MON!
YOU GOT A CONTRACT?!
NO FAIR!
BOO!
BOO!
WE'RE PLAYING SOCCER!
STAY OUT, APE-WOMAN!
WHAT?!
WHO YOU CALLING AN APE-WOMAN?!
OOK
LET'S JUST GO, NON-CHAN!
SAWA
(AGE 4)
LET'S PLAY HANA ICHI MONME* OVER THERE, OKAY?

*A children's game similar to Red Rover.

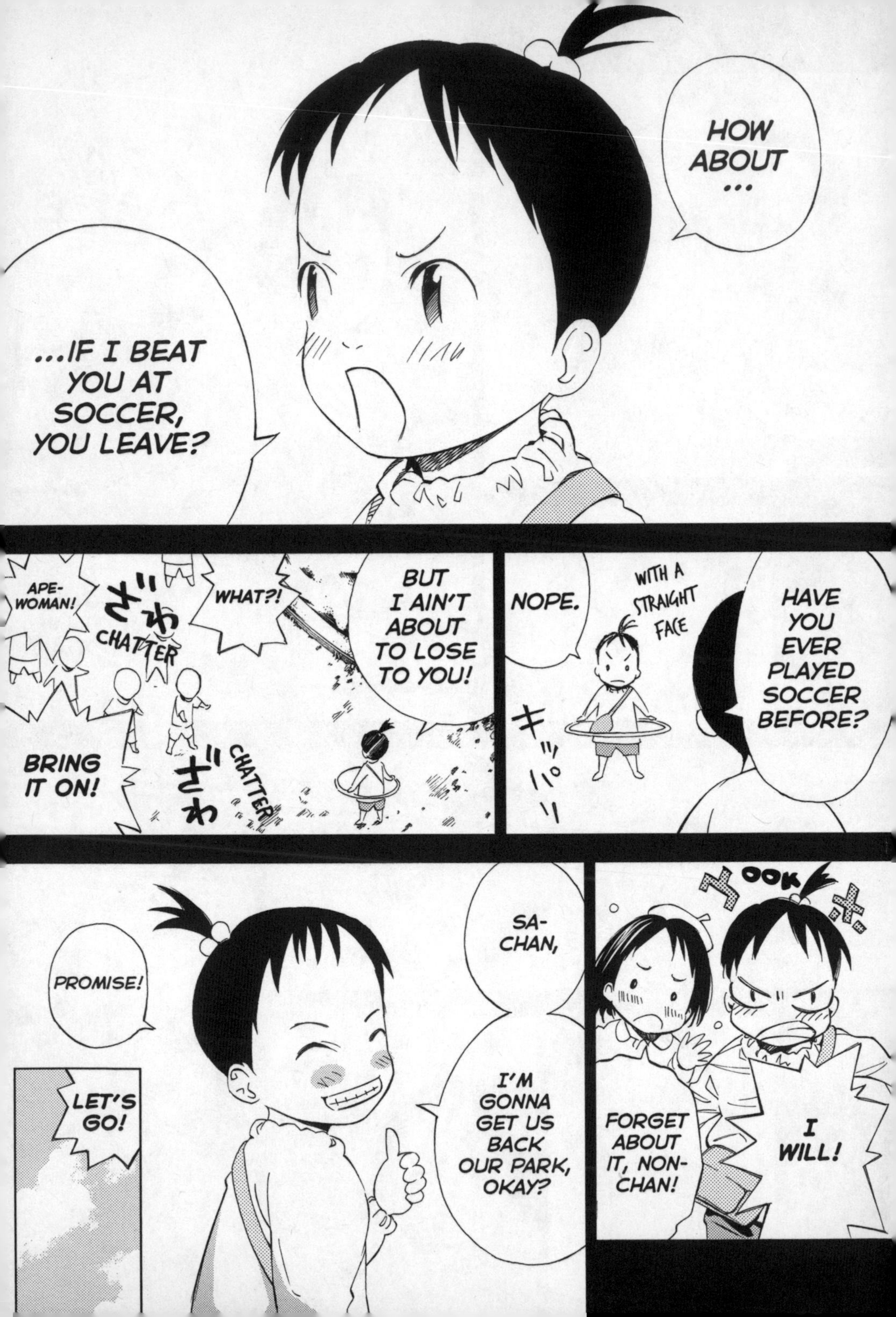
HOW ABOUT ...
...IF I BEAT YOU AT SOCCER, YOU LEAVE?
HAVE YOU EVER PLAYED SOCCER BEFORE?
NOPE.
WITH A STRAIGHT FACE
キッパリ
BUT I AIN'T ABOUT TO LOSE TO YOU!
WHAT?!
ざわ
CHATTER
APE-WOMAN!
BRING IT ON!
ざわ
CHATTER
OOK
I WILL!
FORGET ABOUT IT, NON-CHAN!
SA-CHAN,
I'M GONNA GET US BACK OUR PARK, OKAY?
PROMISE!
LET'S GO!

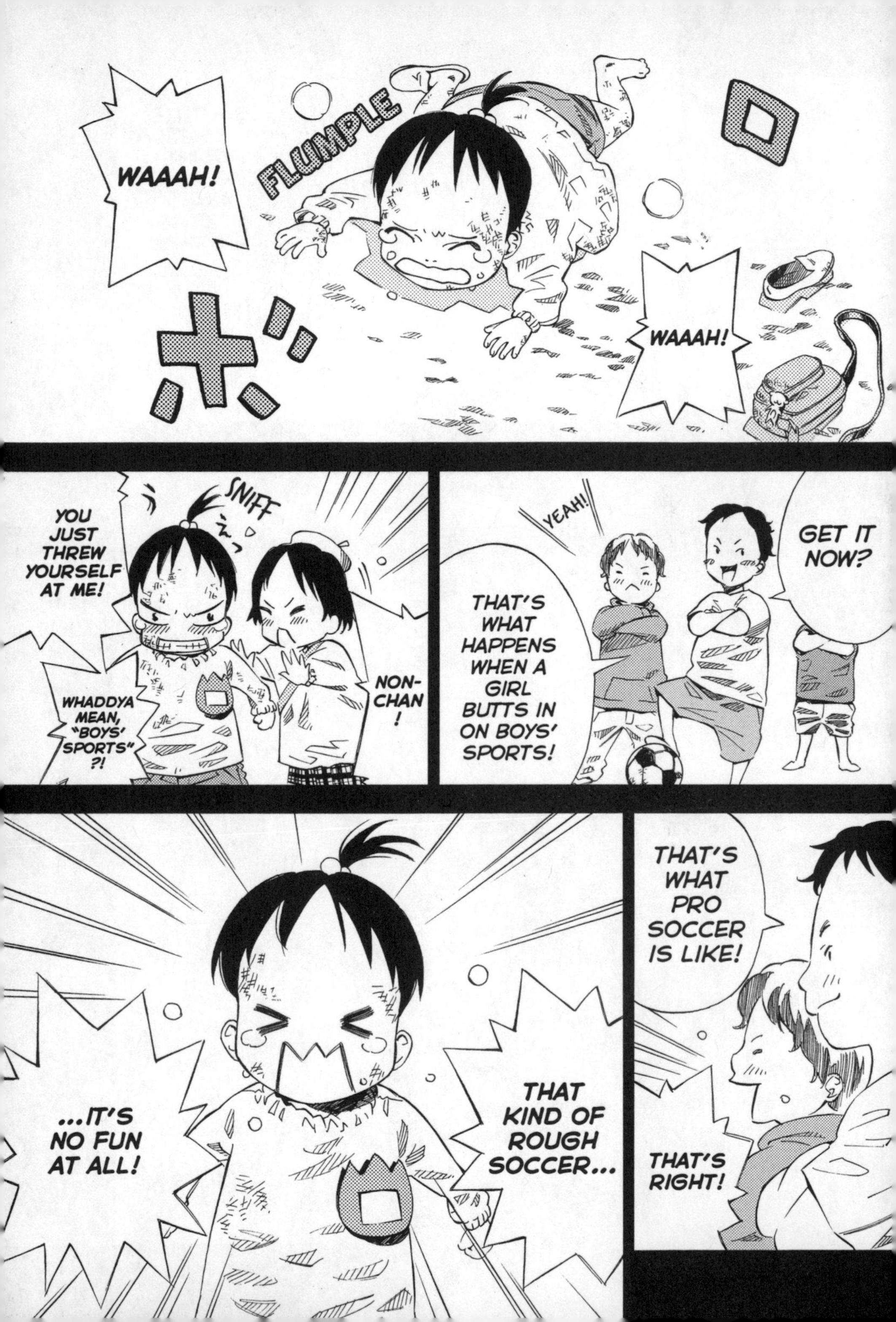
FLUMPLE
WAAAH!
WAAAH!
GET IT NOW?
YEAH!
THAT'S WHAT HAPPENS WHEN A GIRL BUTTS IN ON BOYS' SPORTS!
SNIFF
NON-CHAN!
YOU JUST THREW YOURSELF AT ME!
WHADDYA MEAN, "BOYS' SPORTS"?!
THAT'S WHAT PRO SOCCER IS LIKE!
THAT'S RIGHT!
THAT KIND OF ROUGH SOCCER...
...IT'S NO FUN AT ALL!

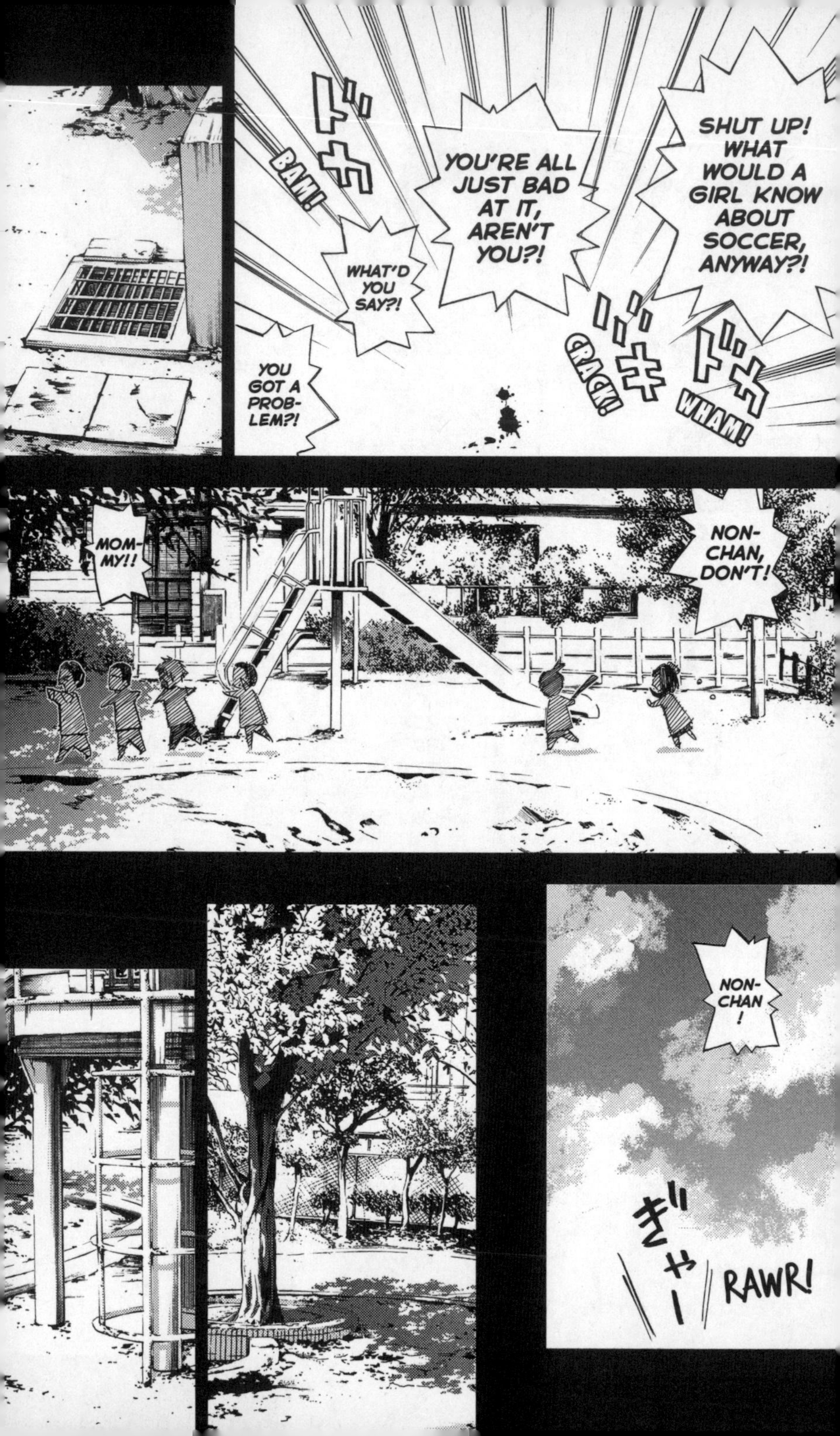
SHUT UP! WHAT WOULD A GIRL KNOW ABOUT SOCCER, ANYWAY?!
YOU'RE ALL JUST BAD AT IT, AREN'T YOU?!
BAM!
WHAT'D YOU SAY?!
WHAM!
CRACK!
YOU GOT A PROB-LEM?!
NON-CHAN, DON'T!
MOMMY!!
NON-CHAN!
ぎゃー
RAWR!

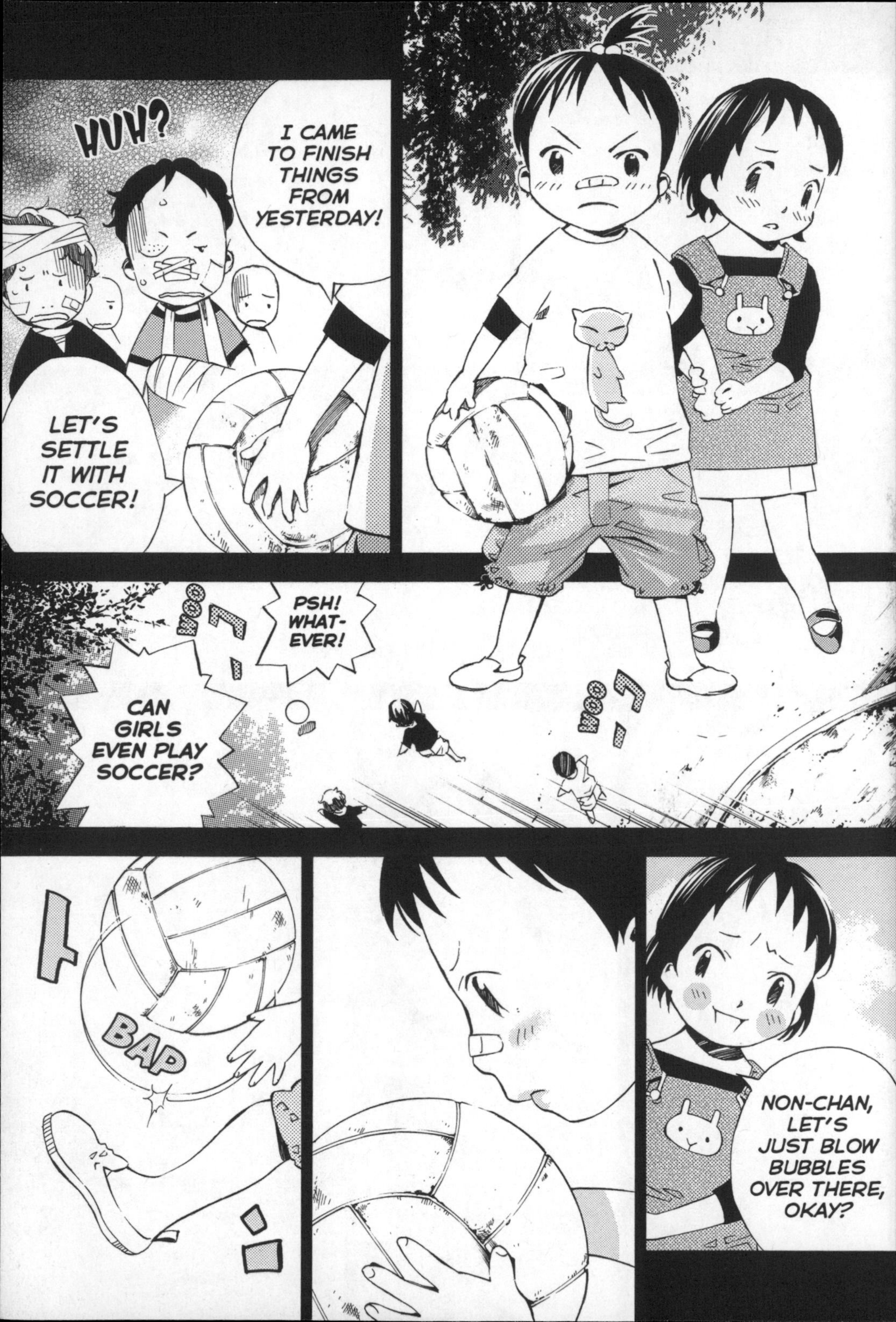
I CAME TO FINISH THINGS FROM YESTERDAY!
HUH?
LET'S SETTLE IT WITH SOCCER!
PSH! WHAT-EVER!
CAN GIRLS EVEN PLAY SOCCER?
NON-CHAN, LET'S JUST BLOW BUBBLES OVER THERE, OKAY?
BAP

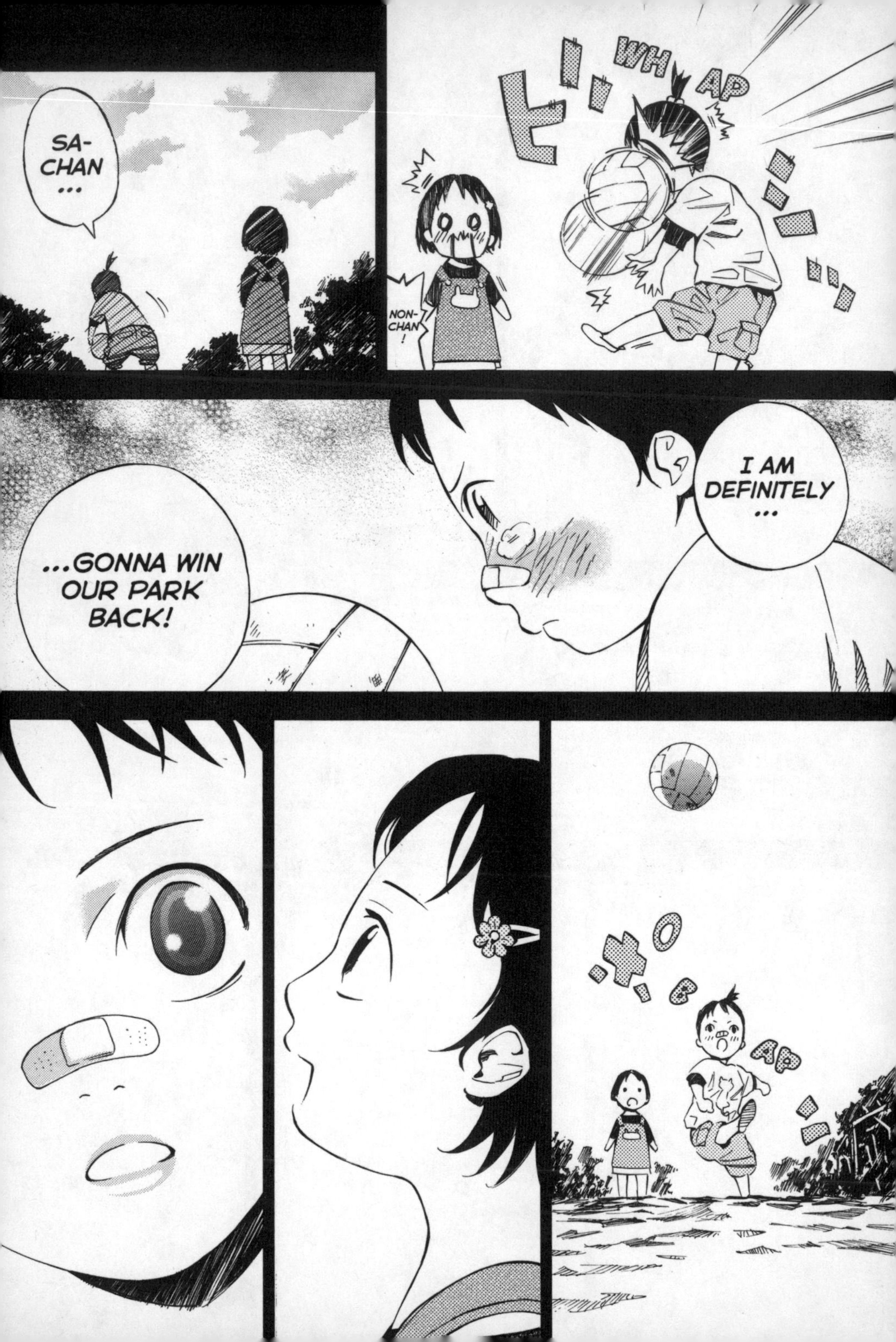
WHAP
NON-CHAN!
SA-CHAN...
I AM DEFINITELY...
...GONNA WIN OUR PARK BACK!

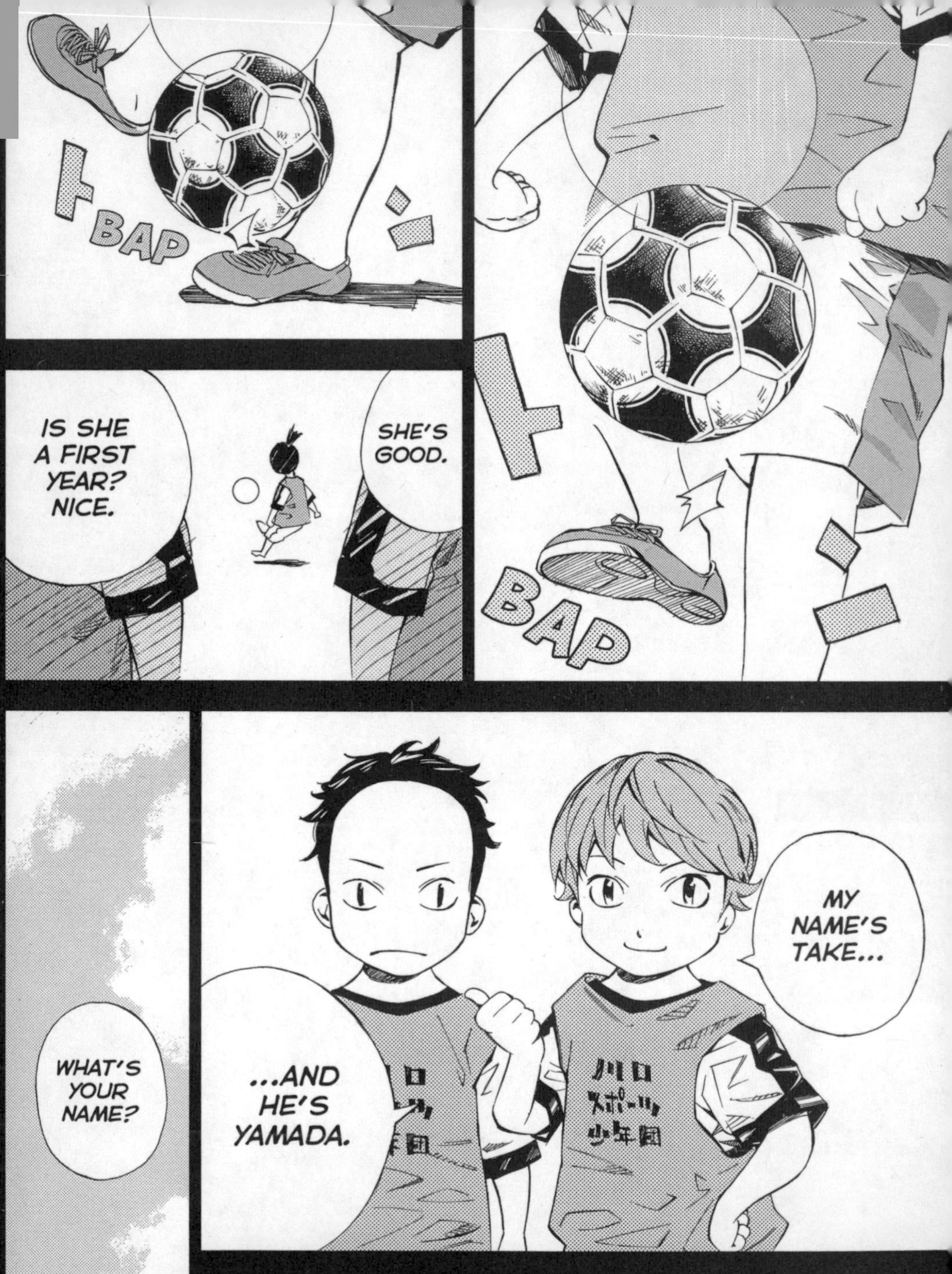
ト
BAP
ト
BAP
SHE'S GOOD.
IS SHE A FIRST YEAR? NICE.
MY NAME'S TAKE...
...AND HE'S YAMADA.
WHAT'S YOUR NAME?

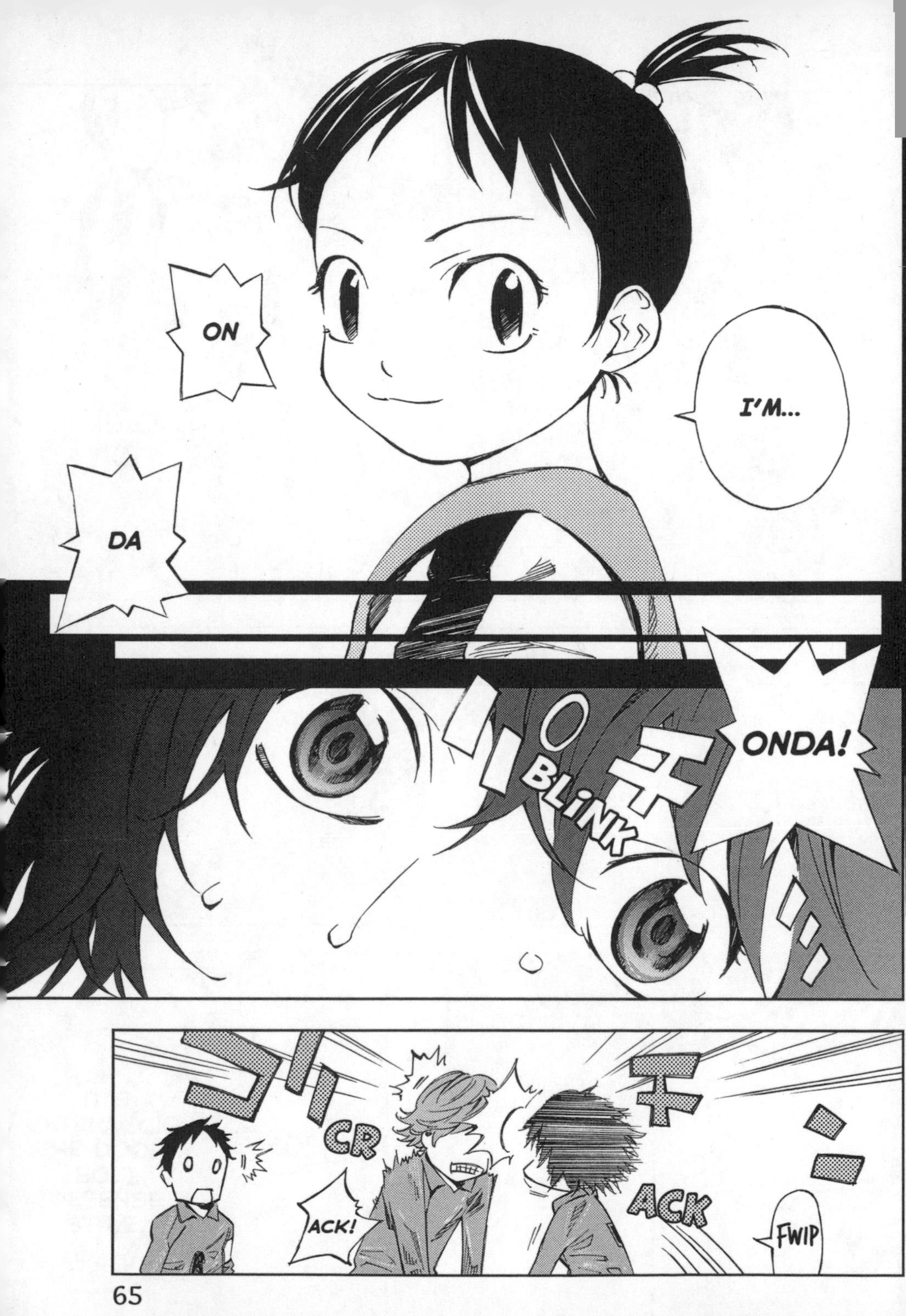
I'M...
ON
DA
ONDA!
BLINK
CR
ACK
FWIP
ACK!

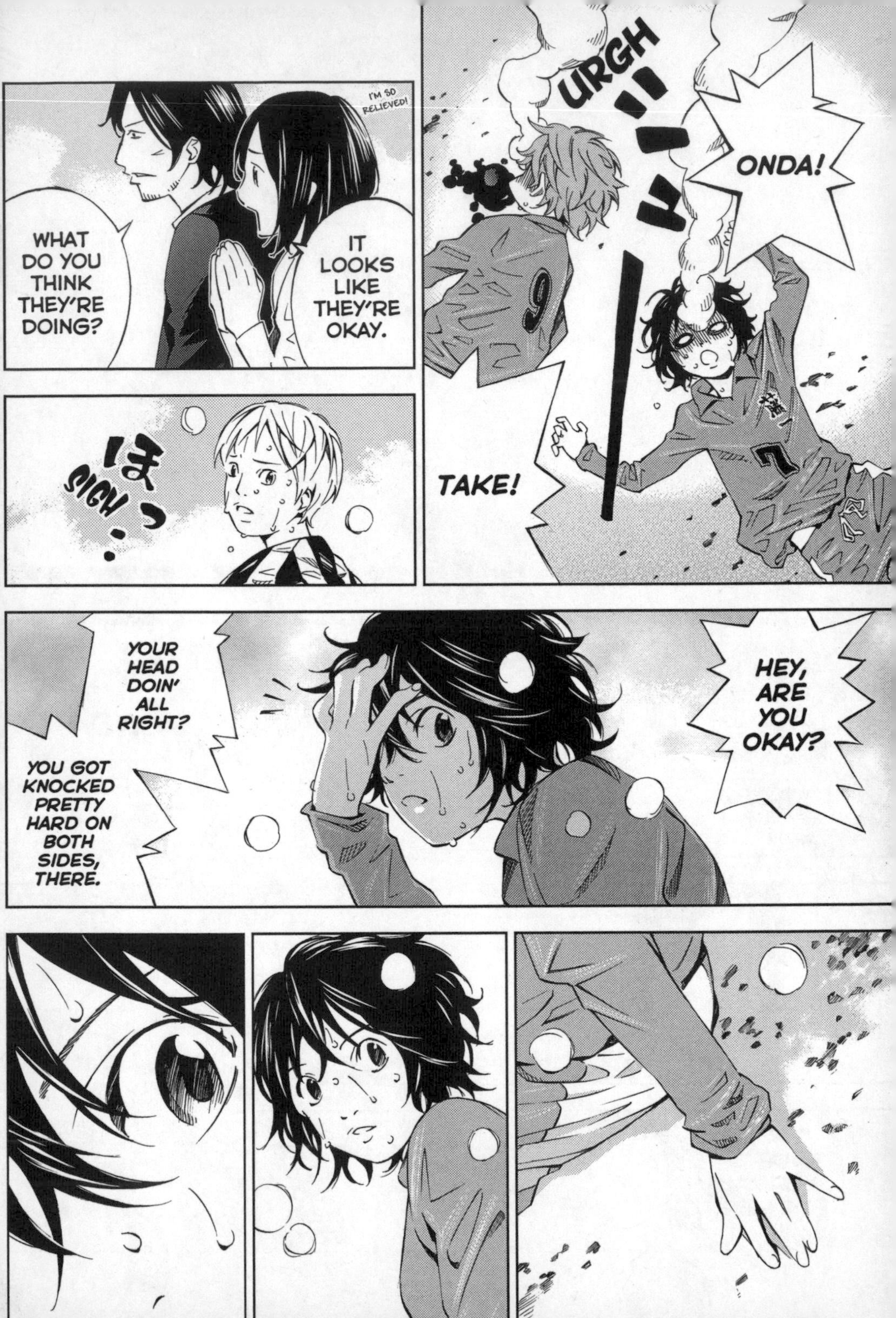
URGH
ONDA!
TAKE!
I'M SO RELIEVED!
IT LOOKS LIKE THEY'RE OKAY.
WHAT DO YOU THINK THEY'RE DOING?
ほっ
SIGH
HEY, ARE YOU OKAY?
YOUR HEAD DOIN' ALL RIGHT?
YOU GOT KNOCKED PRETTY HARD ON BOTH SIDES, THERE.

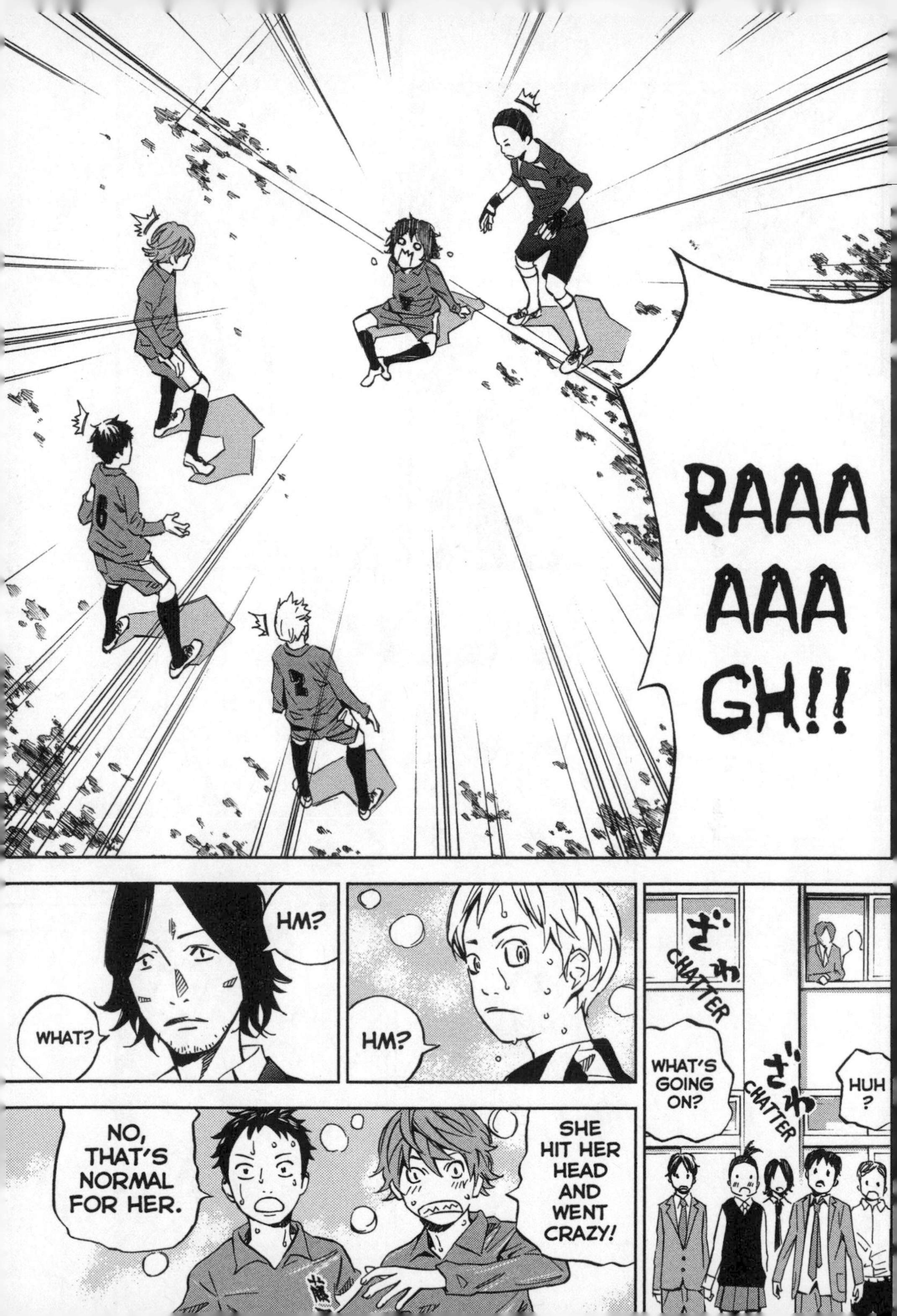
RAAA
AAA
GH!!
ざわ
CHATTER
HUH
?
ざわ
CHATTER
WHAT'S
GOING
ON?
HM?
HM?
WHAT?
SHE
HIT HER
HEAD
AND
WENT
CRAZY!
NO,
THAT'S
NORMAL
FOR HER.

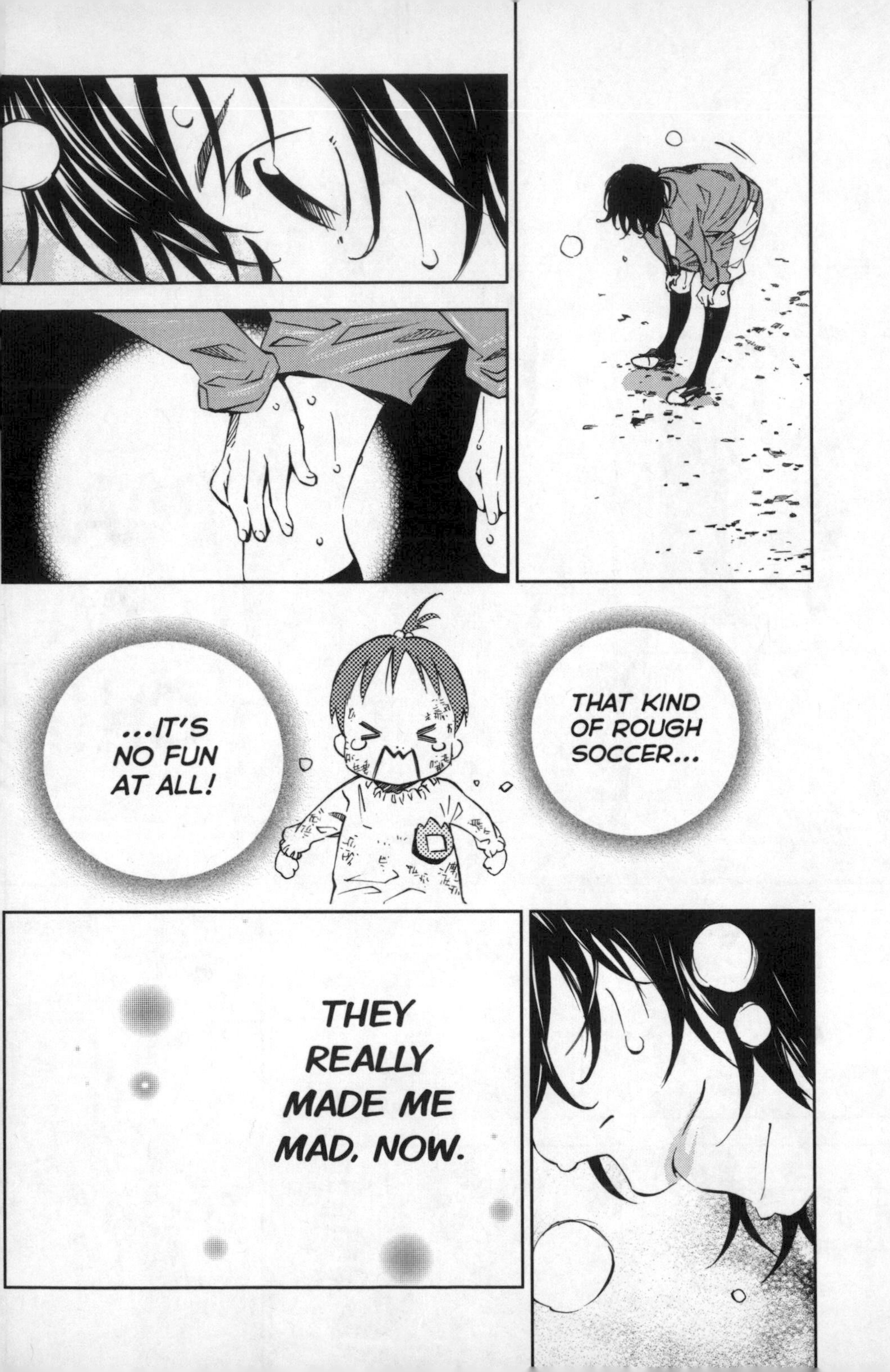
THAT KIND OF ROUGH SOCCER...
...IT'S NO FUN AT ALL!
THEY REALLY MADE ME MAD, NOW.

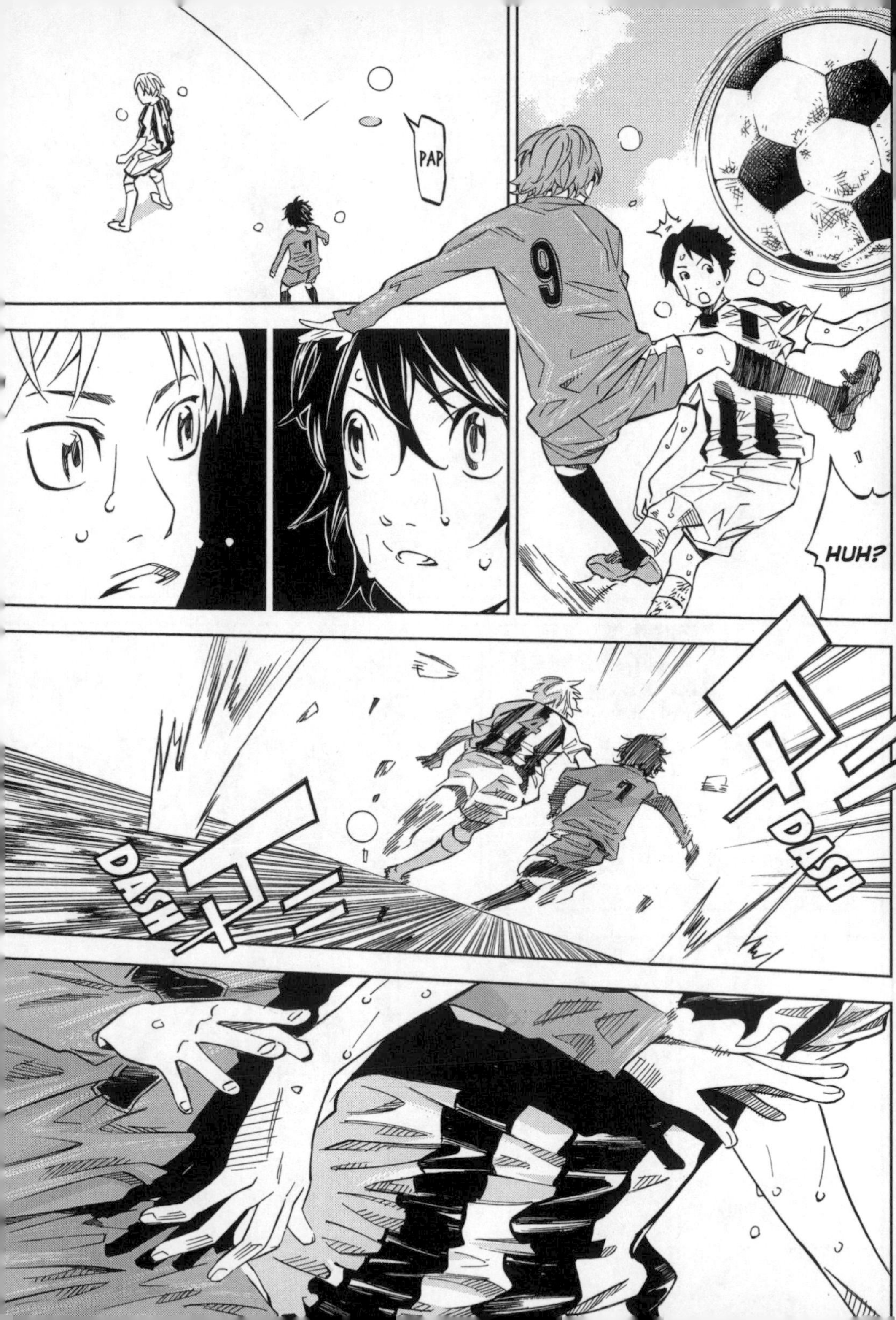
HUH?
PAP
DASH
DASH

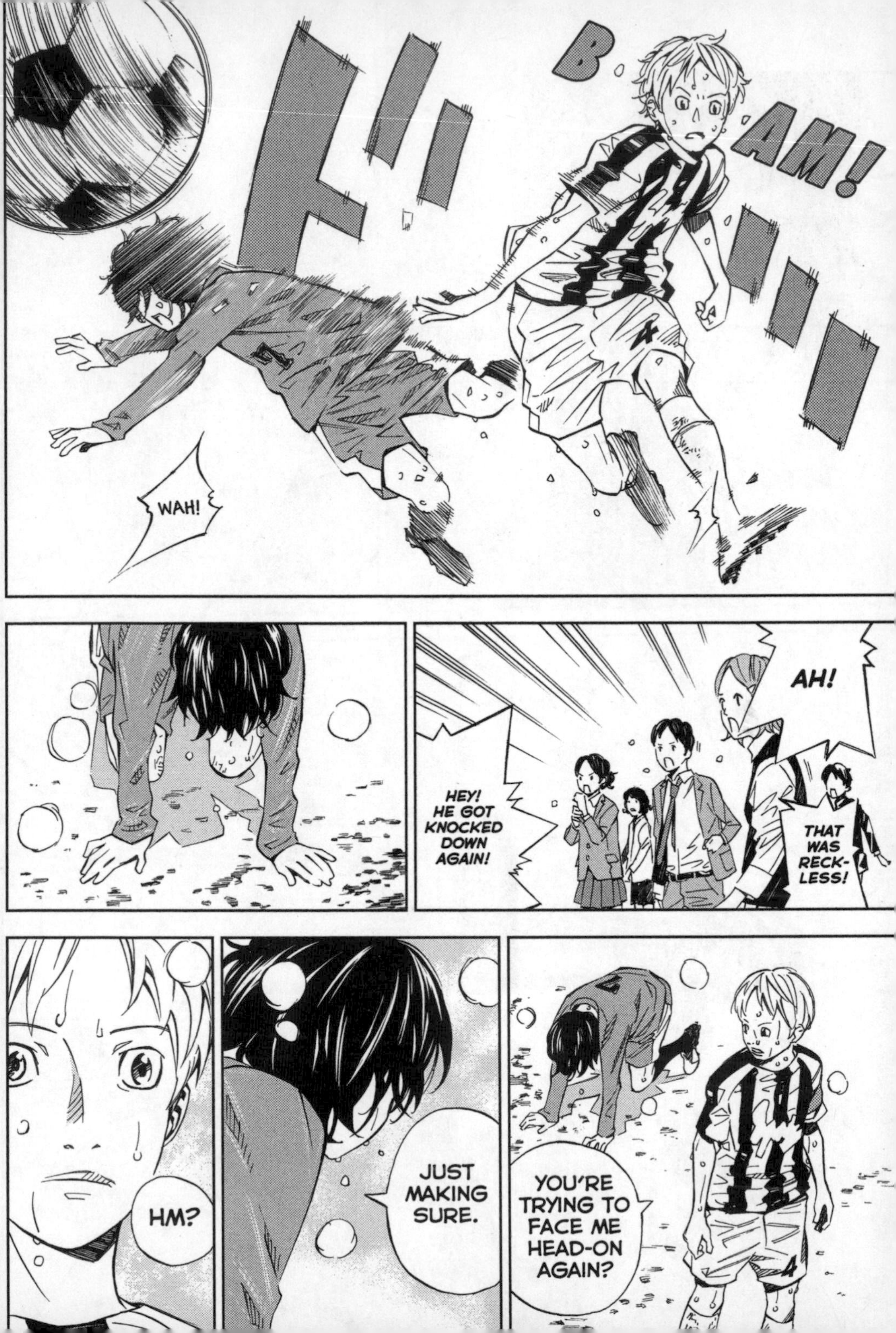
BAM!
WAH!
AH!
THAT WAS RECKLESS!
HEY! HE GOT KNOCKED DOWN AGAIN!
YOU'RE TRYING TO FACE ME HEAD-ON AGAIN?
JUST MAKING SURE.
HM?

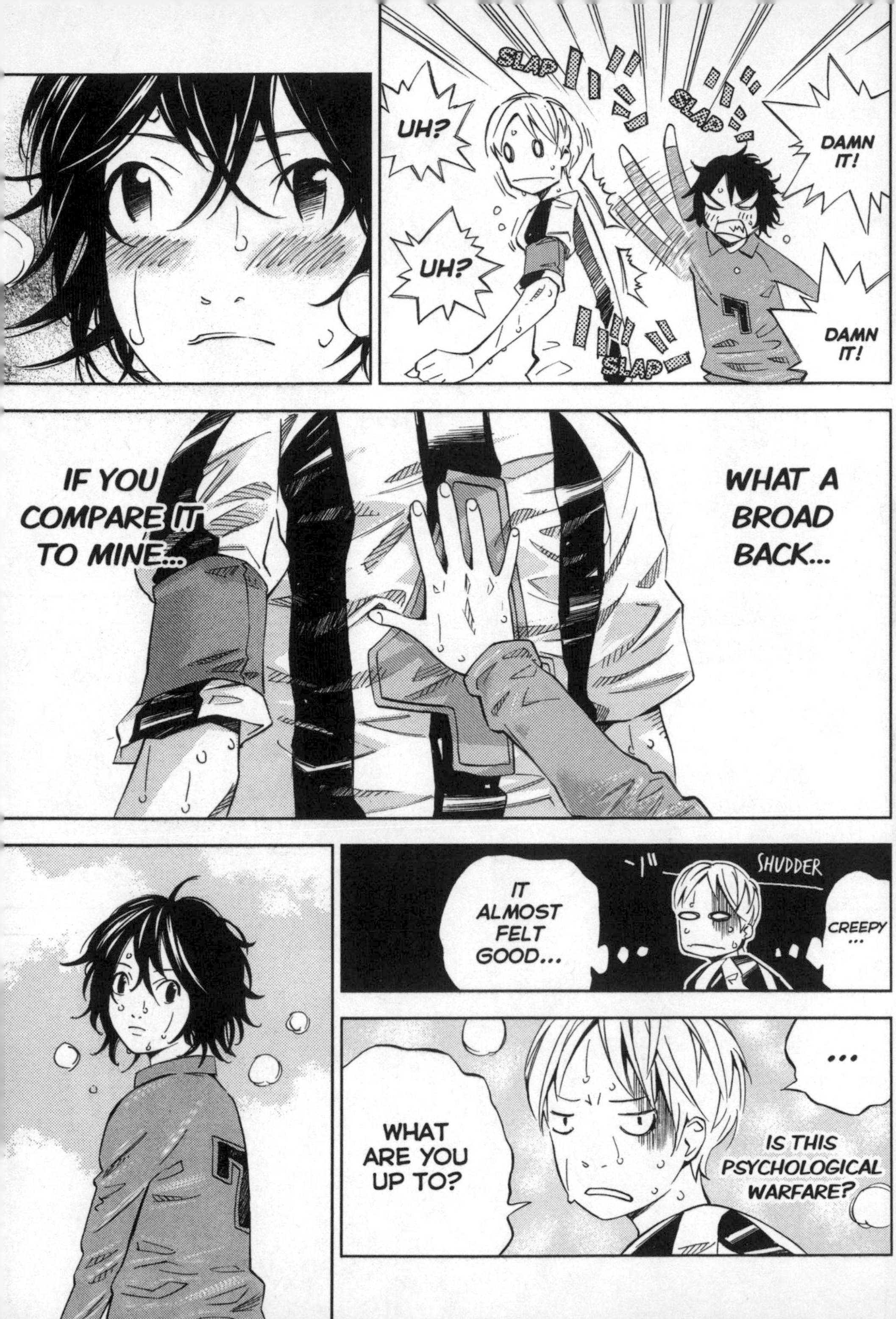
DAMN IT!
SLAP
SLAP
UH?
UH?
DAMN IT!
SLAP
WHAT A BROAD BACK...
IF YOU COMPARE IT TO MINE...
CREEPY...
SHUDDER
IT ALMOST FELT GOOD...
...
IS THIS PSYCHOLOGICAL WARFARE?
WHAT ARE YOU UP TO?

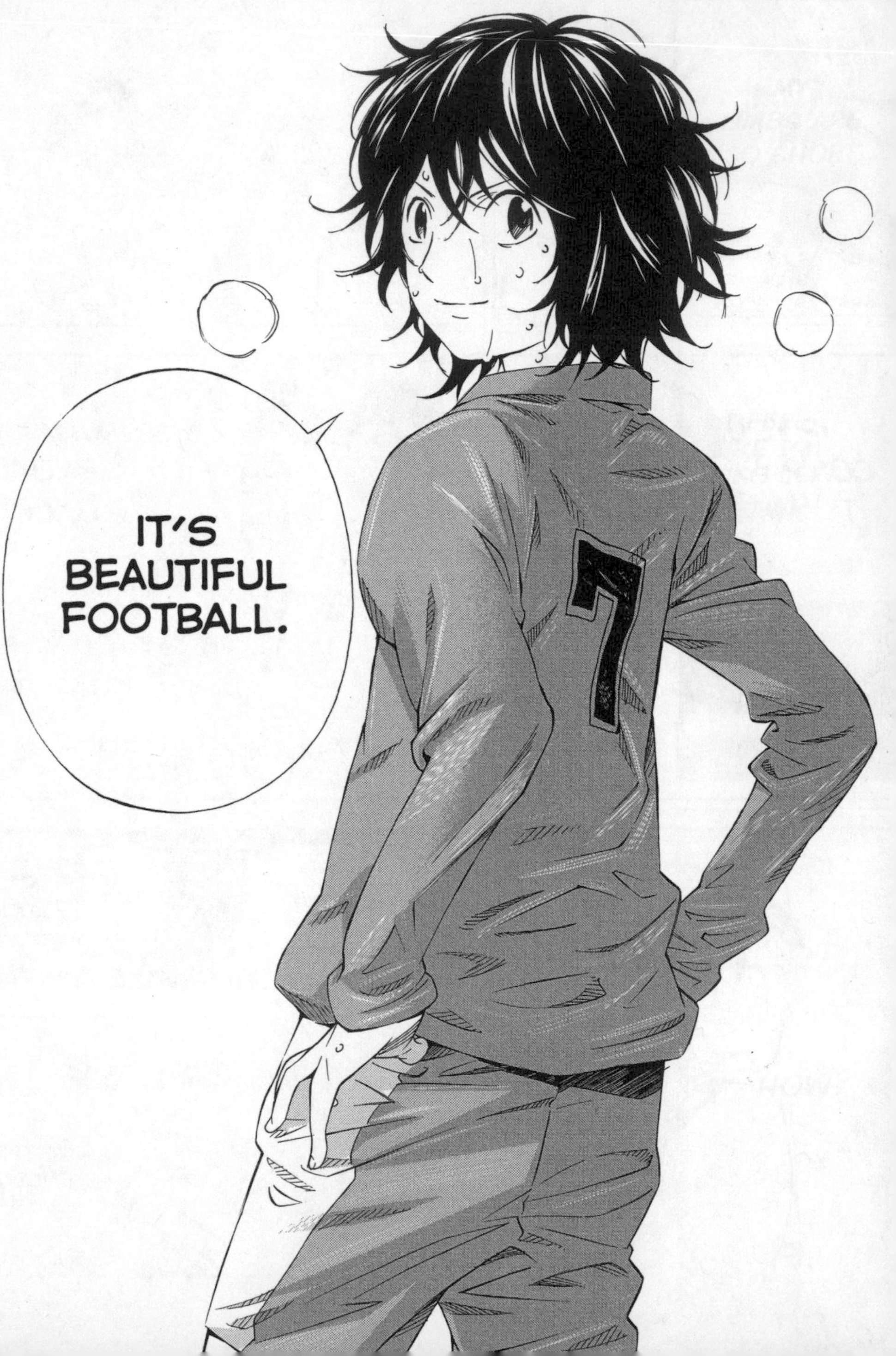
IT'S BEAUTIFUL FOOTBALL.

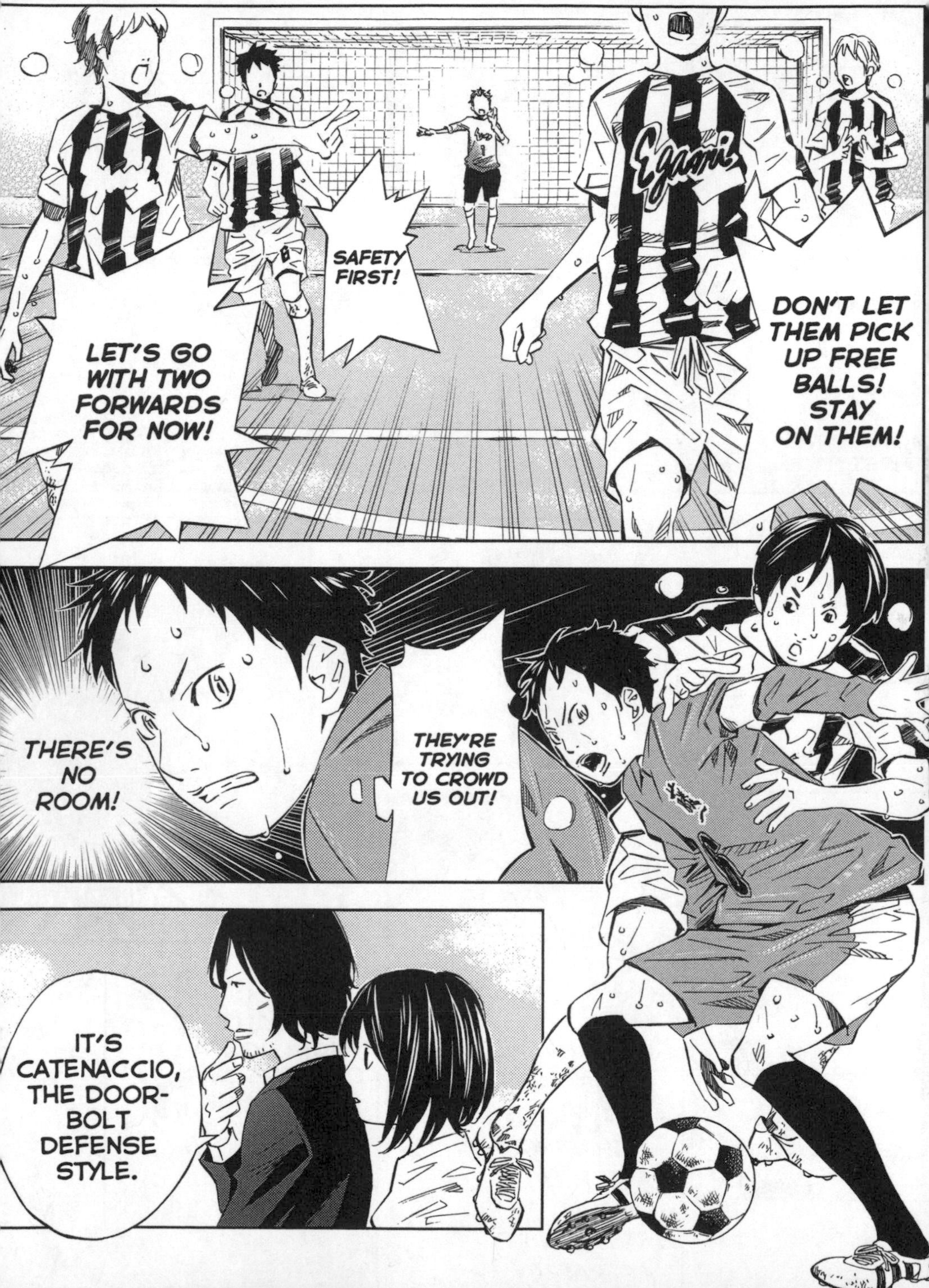
DON'T LET THEM PICK UP FREE BALLS! STAY ON THEM!
SAFETY FIRST!
LET'S GO WITH TWO FORWARDS FOR NOW!
THEY'RE TRYING TO CROWD US OUT!
THERE'S NO ROOM!
IT'S CATENACCIO, THE DOOR-BOLT DEFENSE STYLE.

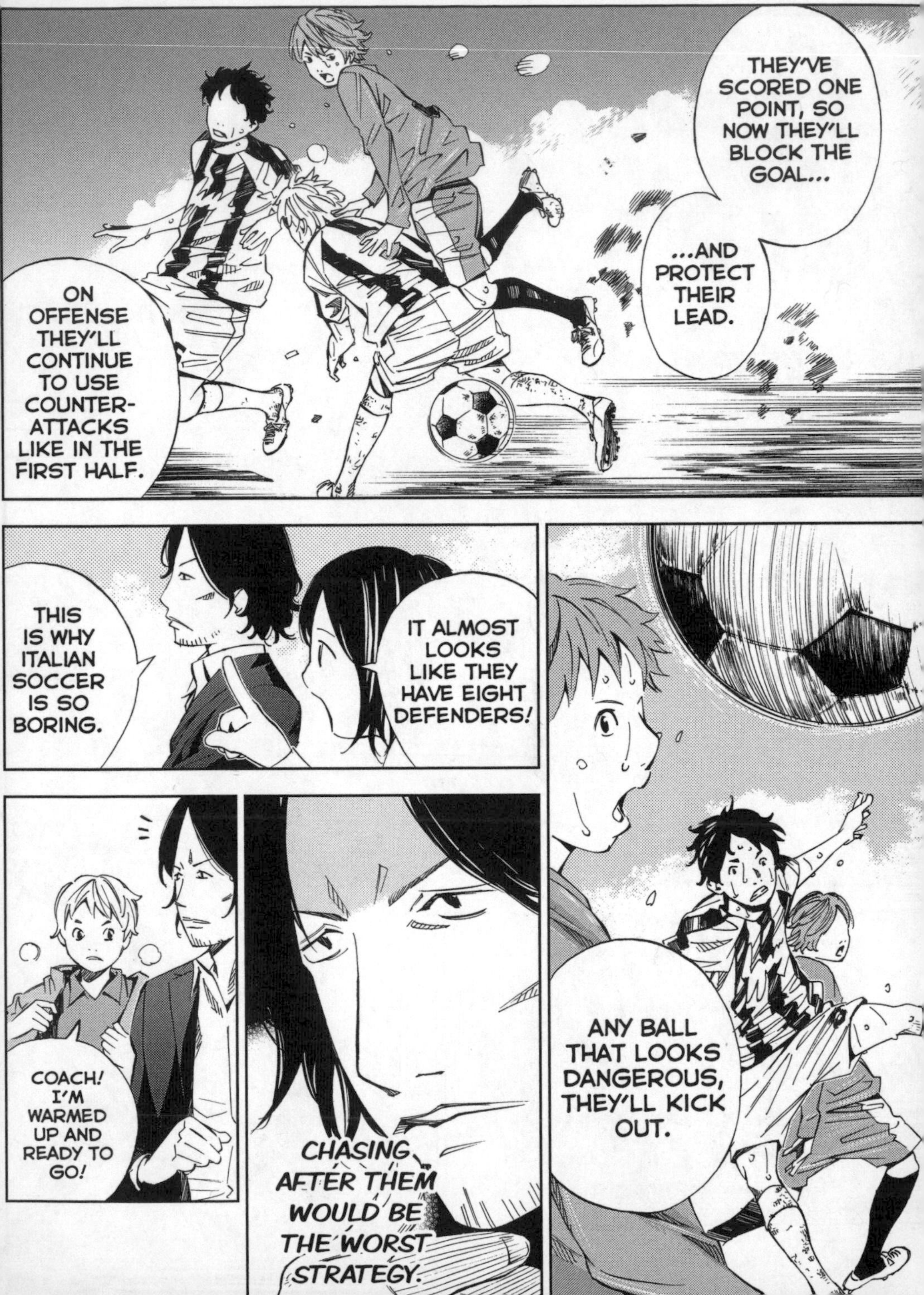
THEY'VE SCORED ONE POINT, SO NOW THEY'LL BLOCK THE GOAL...
...AND PROTECT THEIR LEAD.
ON OFFENSE THEY'LL CONTINUE TO USE COUNTER-ATTACKS LIKE IN THE FIRST HALF.
ANY BALL THAT LOOKS DANGEROUS, THEY'LL KICK OUT.
IT ALMOST LOOKS LIKE THEY HAVE EIGHT DEFENDERS!
THIS IS WHY ITALIAN SOCCER IS SO BORING.
CHASING AFTER THEM WOULD BE THE WORST STRATEGY.
COACH! I'M WARMED UP AND READY TO GO!

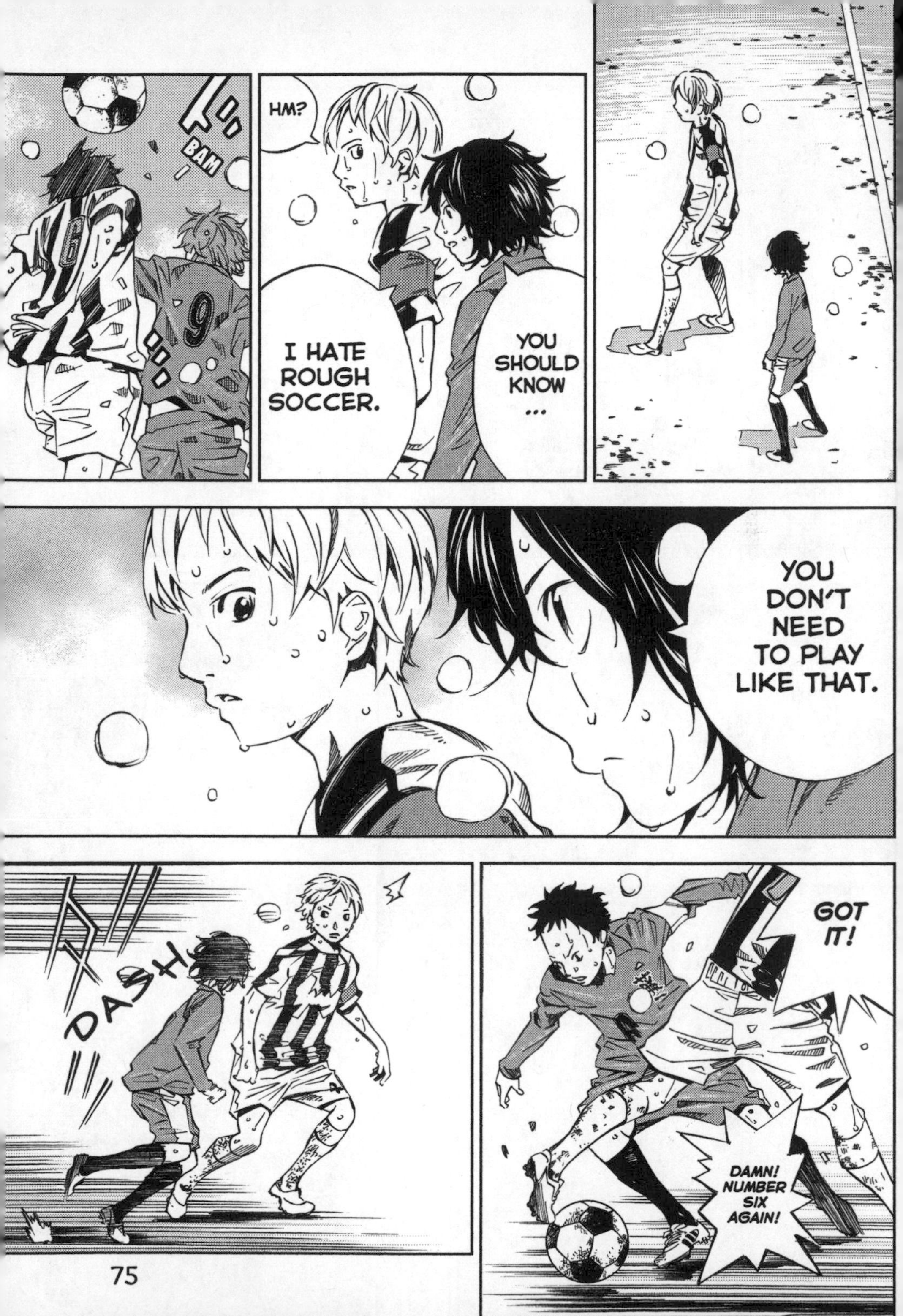
HM?
YOU SHOULD KNOW ...
I HATE ROUGH SOCCER.
BAM
YOU DON'T NEED TO PLAY LIKE THAT.
GOT IT!
DAMN! NUMBER SIX AGAIN!
DASH

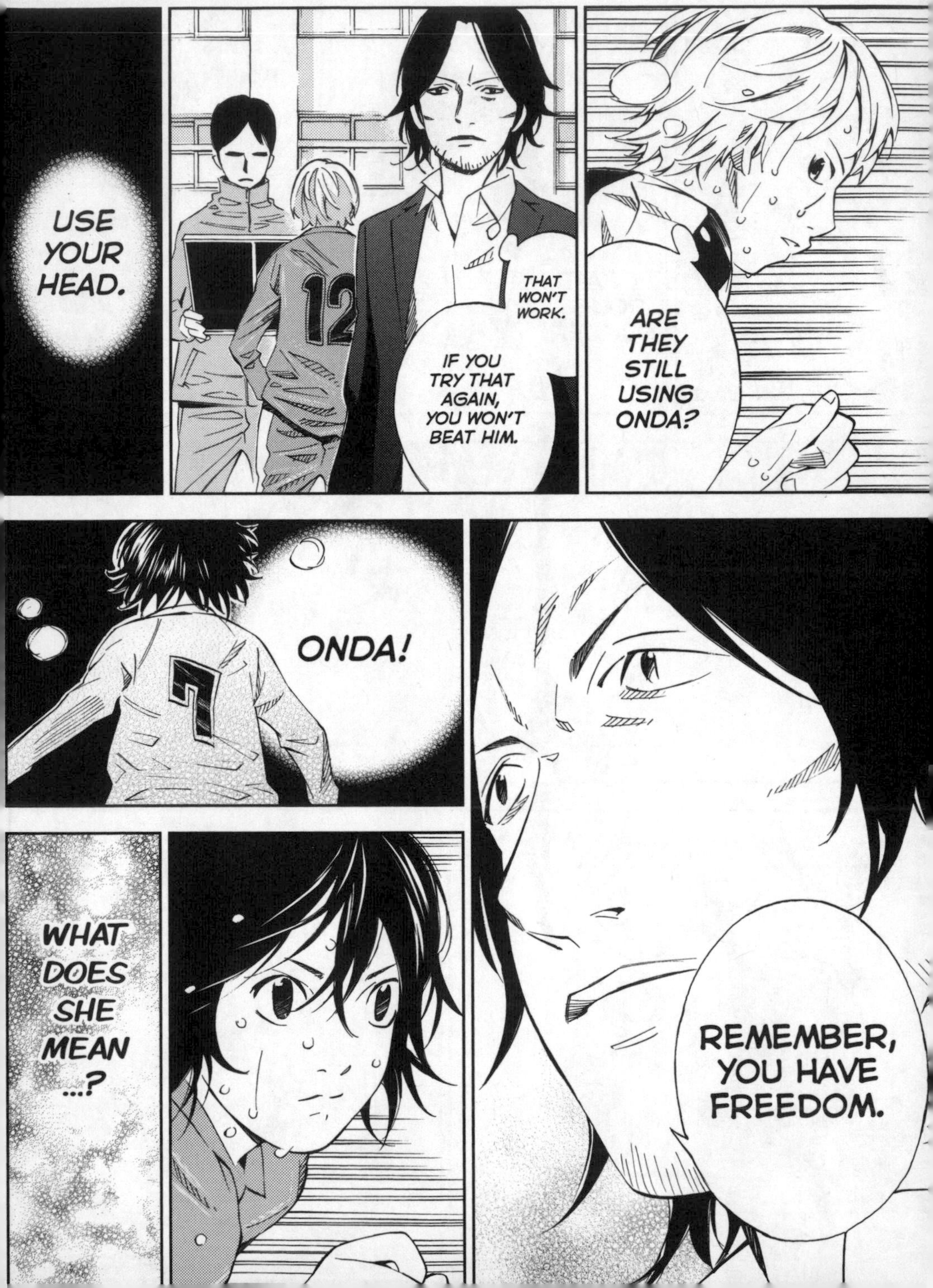
ARE THEY STILL USING ONDA?
THAT WON'T WORK.
IF YOU TRY THAT AGAIN, YOU WON'T BEAT HIM.
USE YOUR HEAD.
REMEMBER, YOU HAVE FREEDOM.
ONDA!
WHAT DOES SHE MEAN ...?

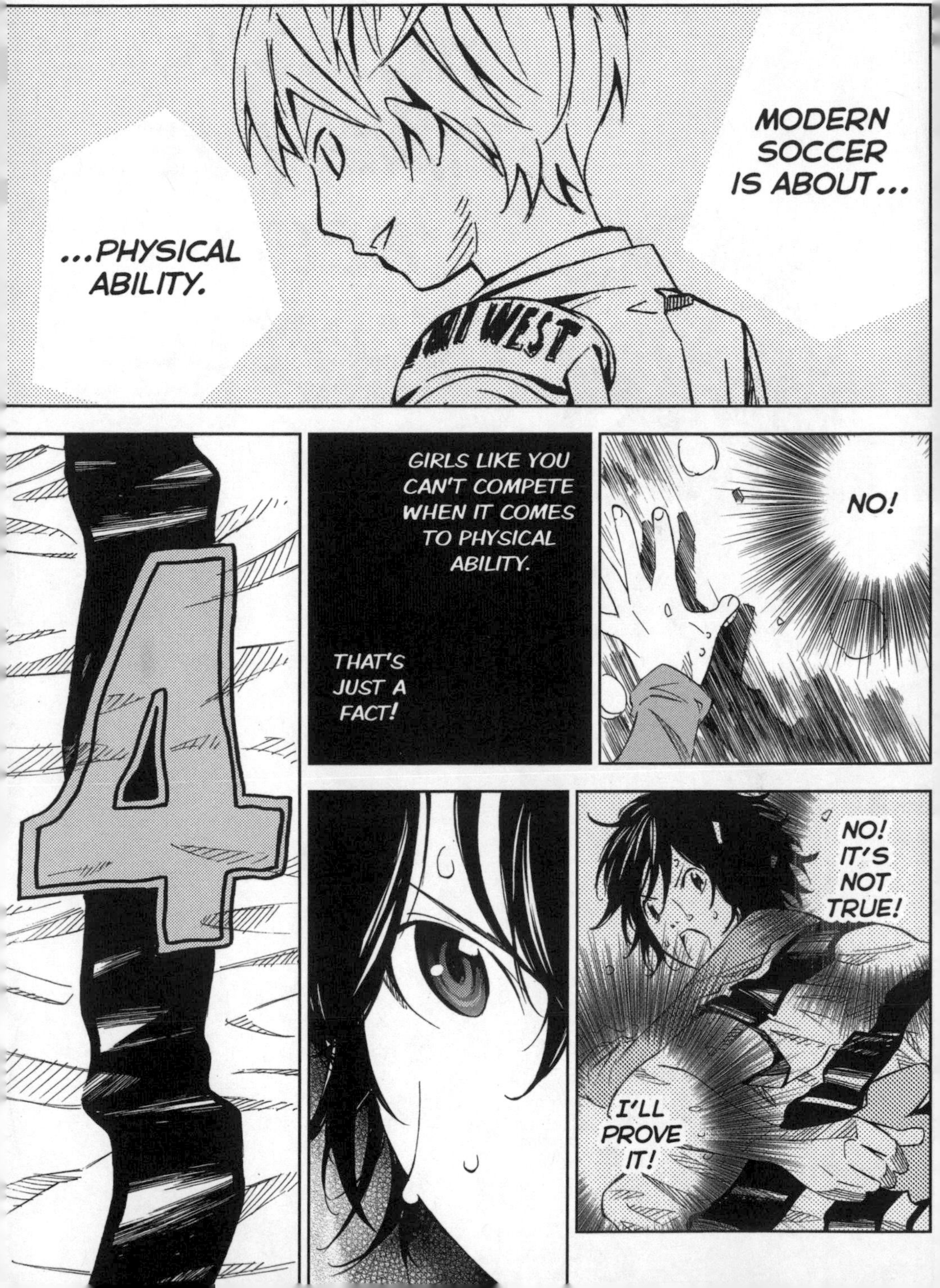
MODERN SOCCER IS ABOUT...
...PHYSICAL ABILITY.
NO!
GIRLS LIKE YOU CAN'T COMPETE WHEN IT COMES TO PHYSICAL ABILITY.
THAT'S JUST A FACT!
NO! IT'S NOT TRUE!
I'LL PROVE IT!
4

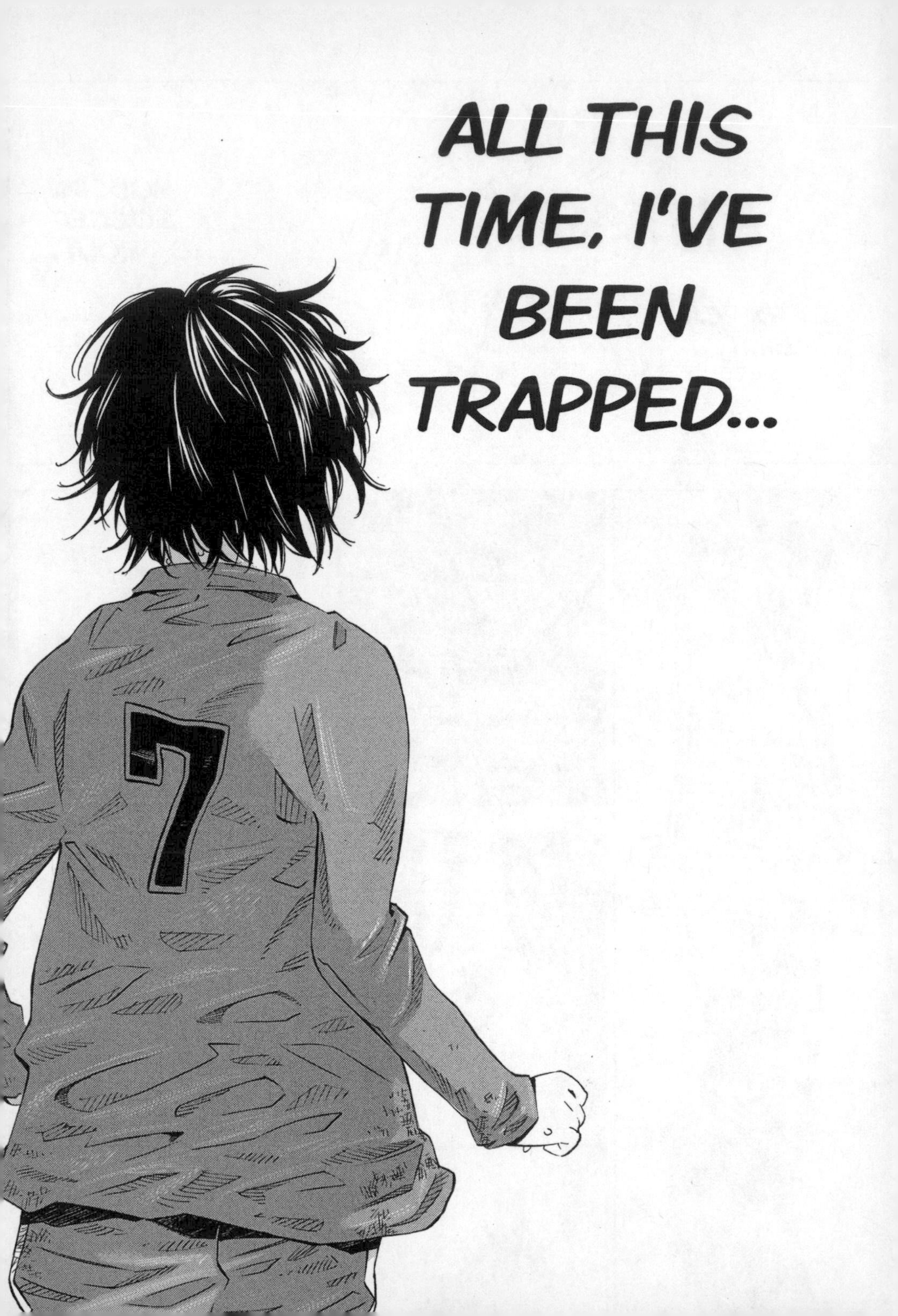
ALL THIS TIME, I'VE BEEN TRAPPED...

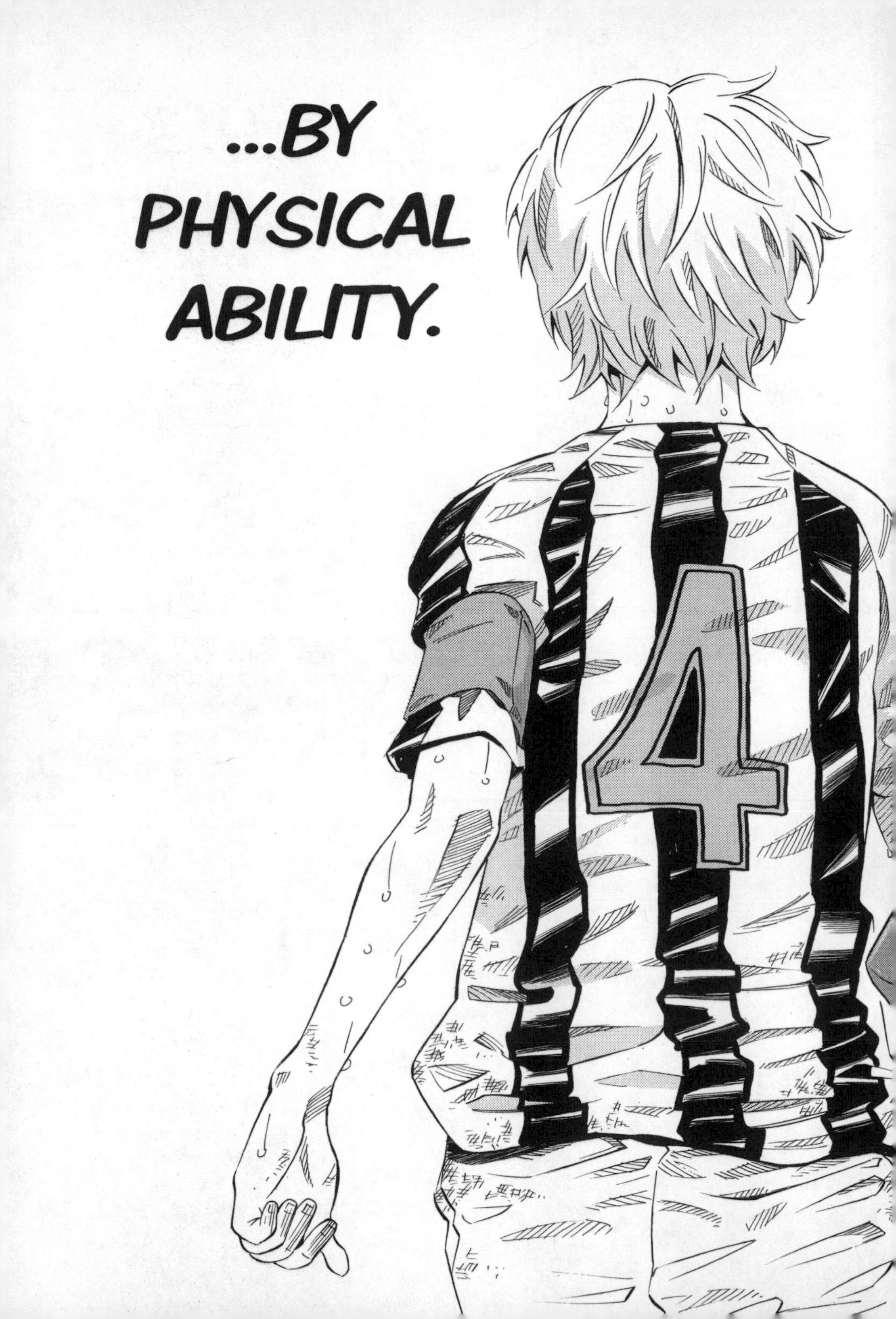
...BY PHYSICAL ABILITY.

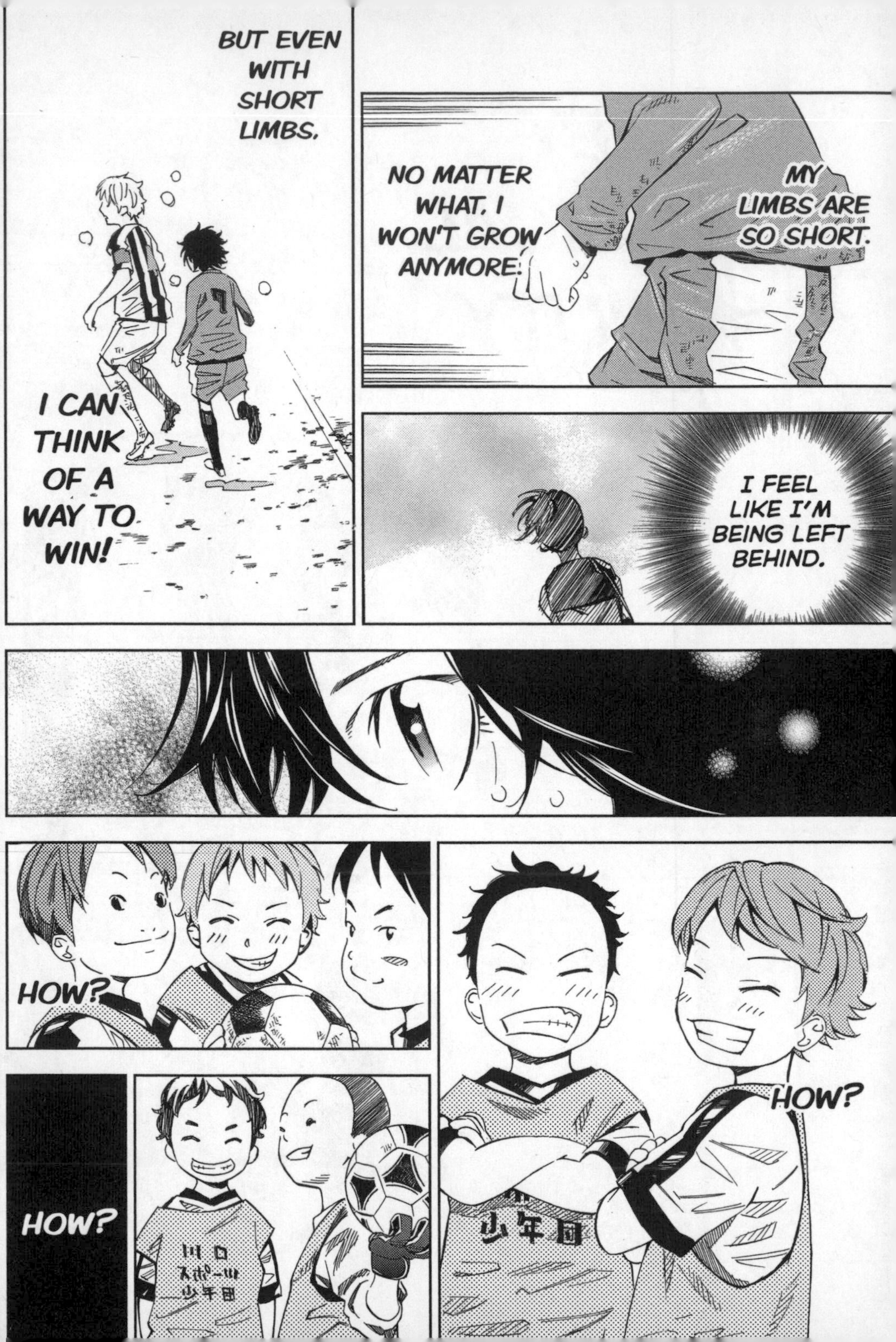
MY LIMBS ARE SO SHORT.
NO MATTER WHAT, I WON'T GROW ANYMORE.
I FEEL LIKE I'M BEING LEFT BEHIND.
BUT EVEN WITH SHORT LIMBS,
I CAN THINK OF A WAY TO WIN!
HOW?
少年団
HOW?
HOW?
川口 スポーツ 少年団

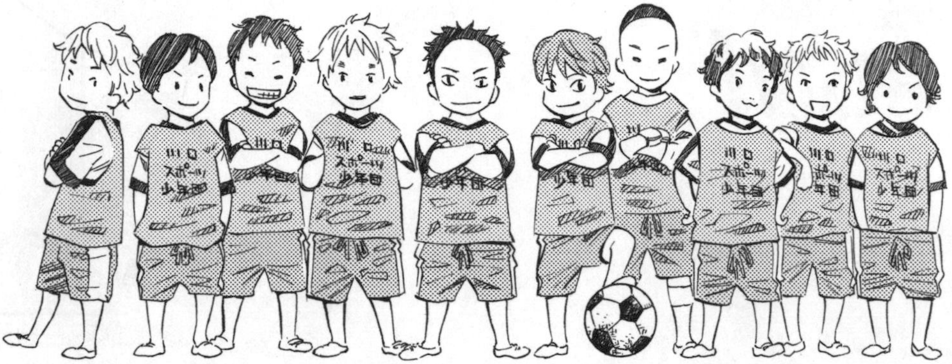

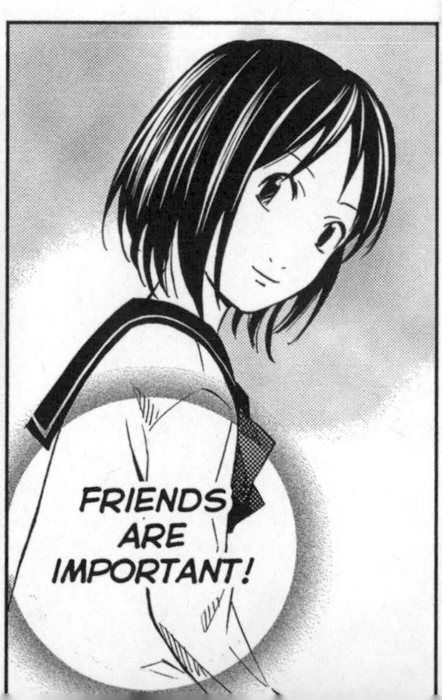
FRIENDS ARE IMPORTANT!

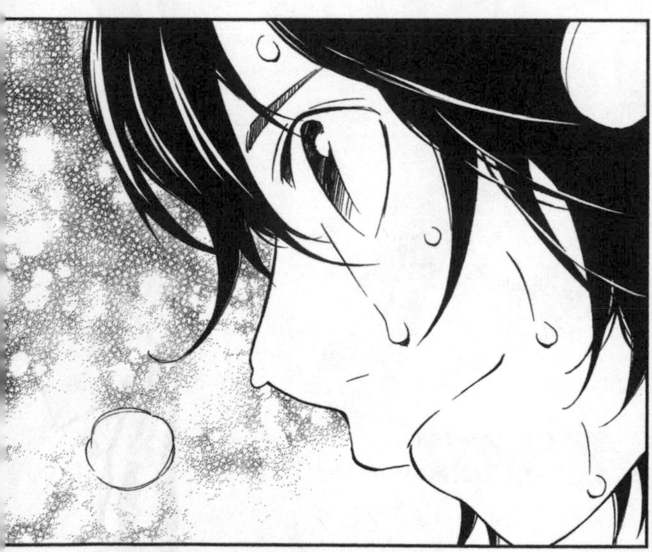

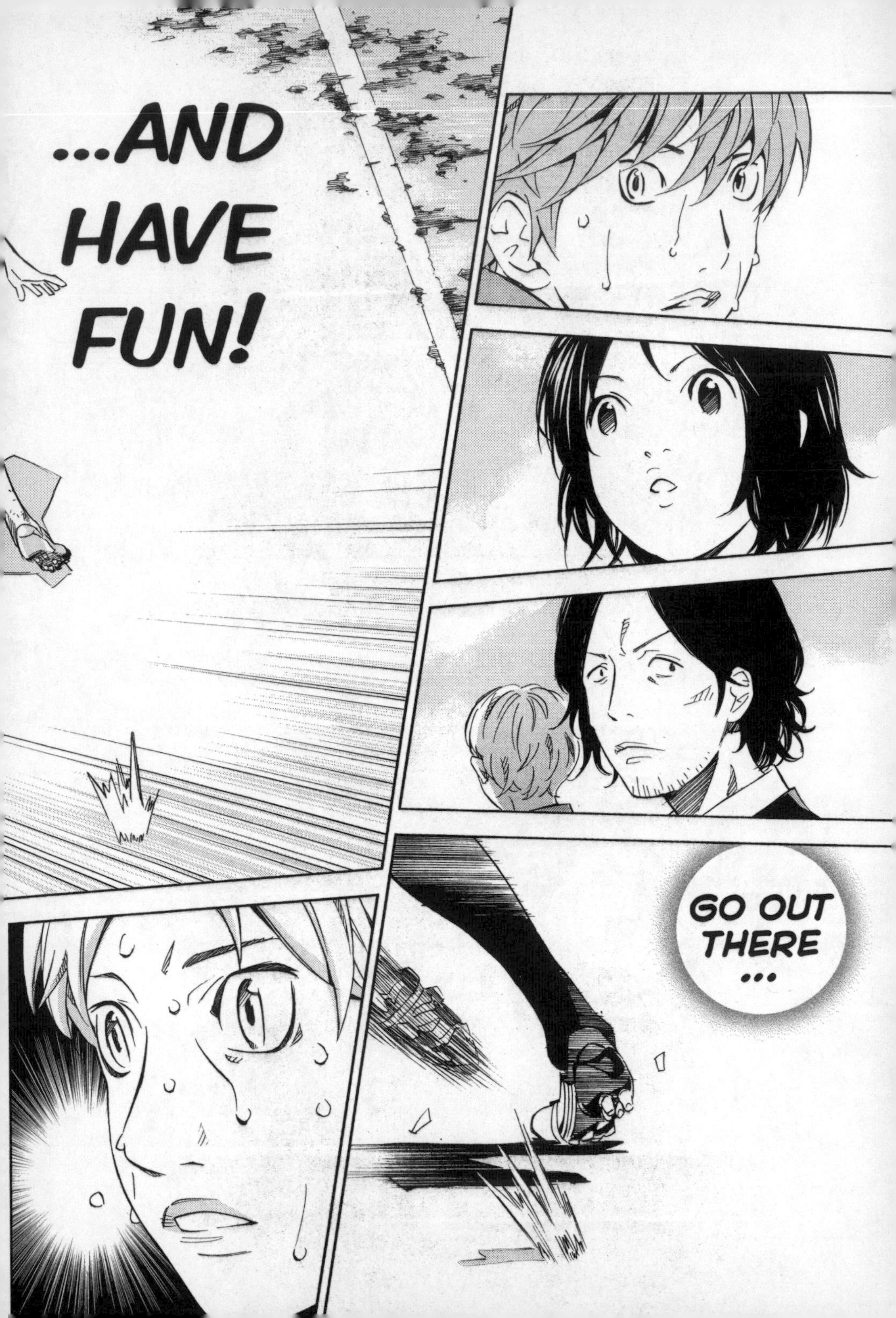
...AND HAVE FUN!
GO OUT THERE ...

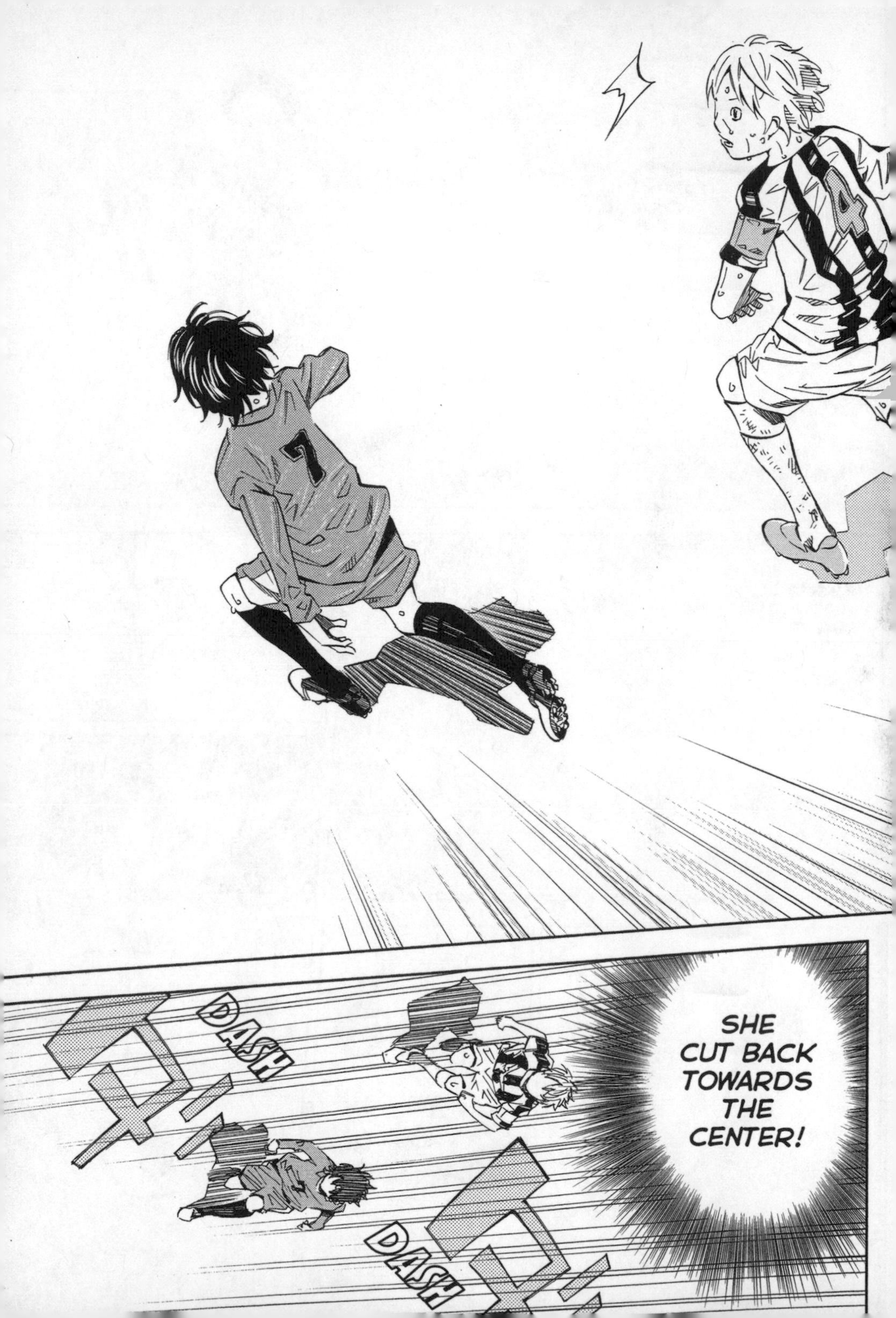
SHE CUT BACK TOWARDS THE CENTER!
DASH
DASH

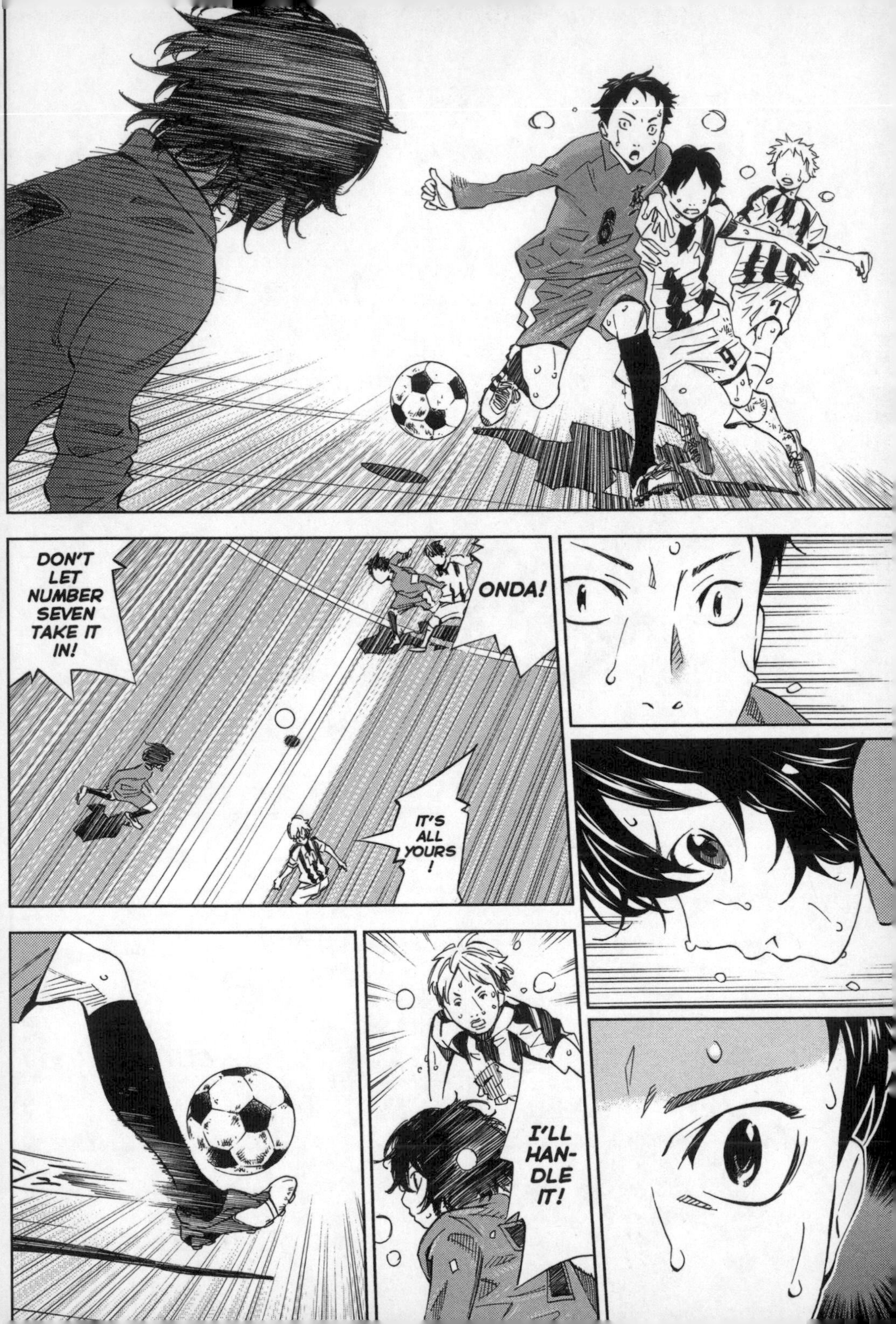
ONDA!
DON'T LET NUMBER SEVEN TAKE IT IN!
IT'S ALL YOURS!
I'LL HANDLE IT!

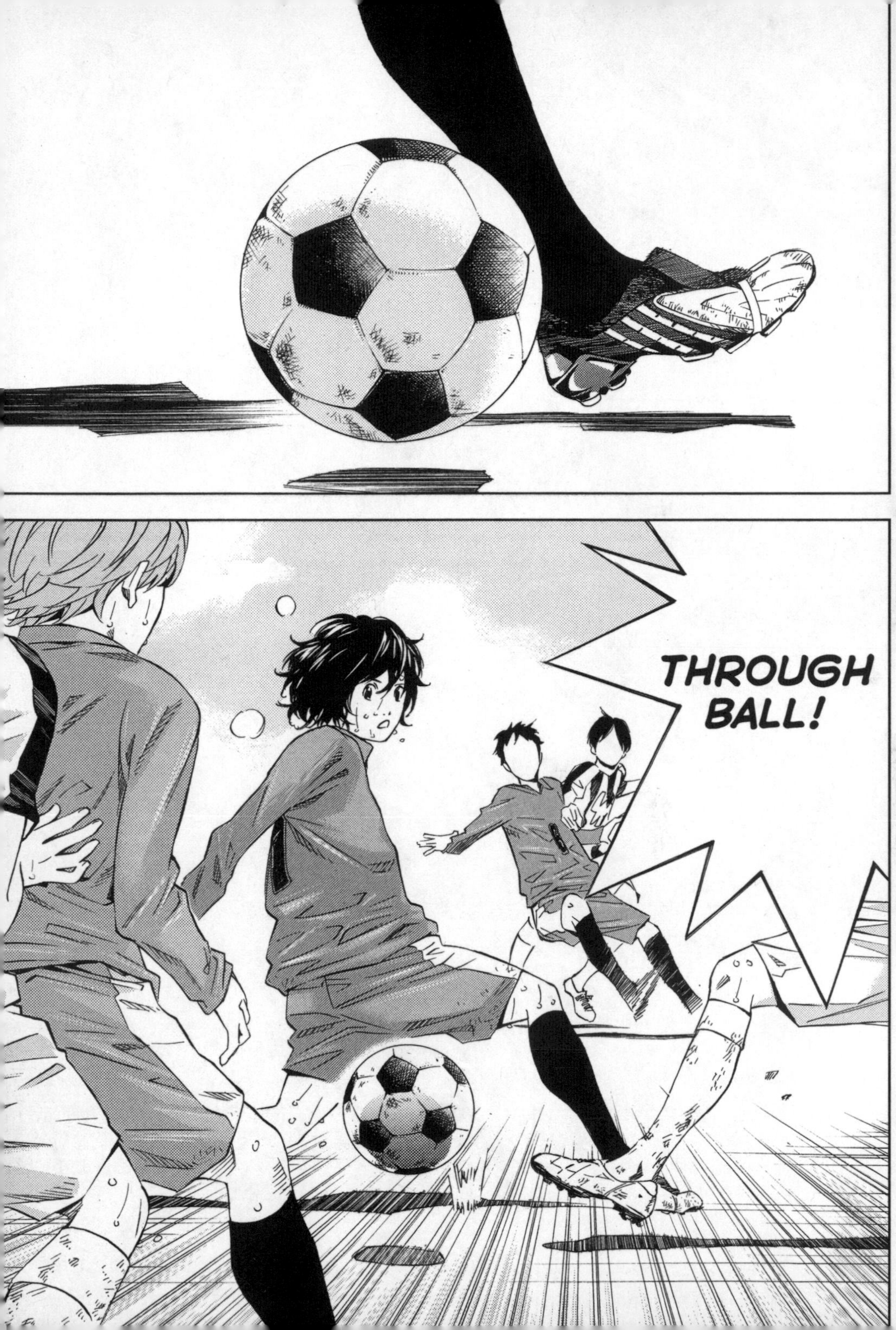
THROUGH BALL!

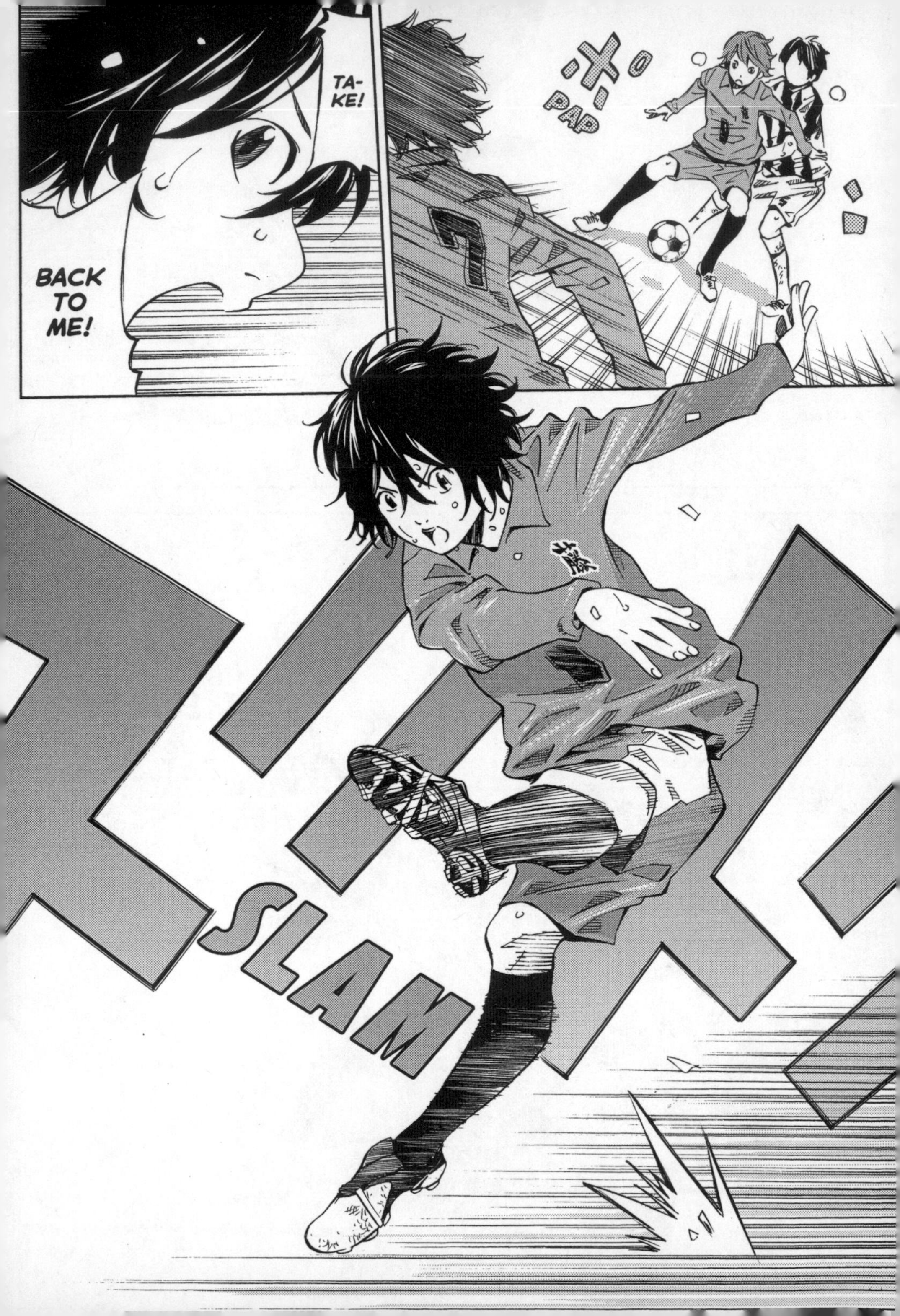
PAP
TA-KE!
BACK TO ME!
SLAM

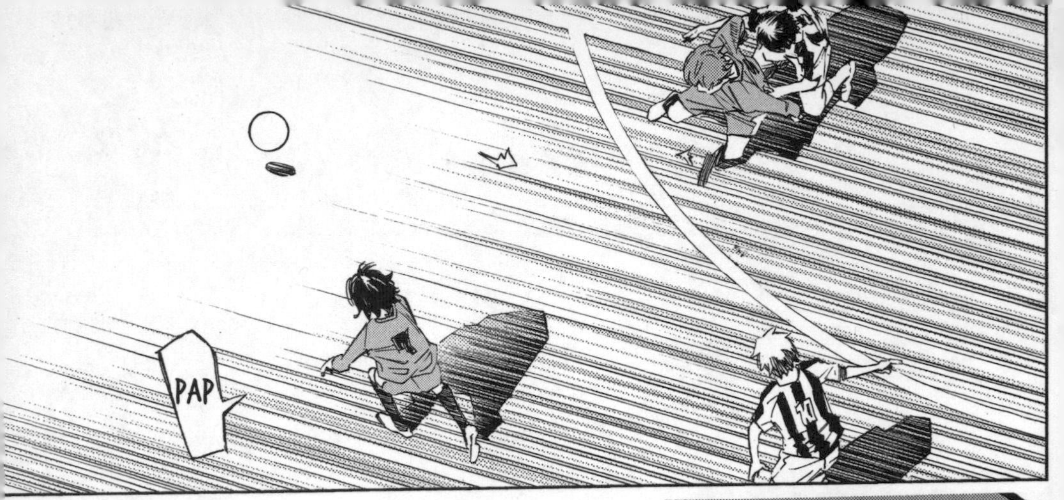
PAP
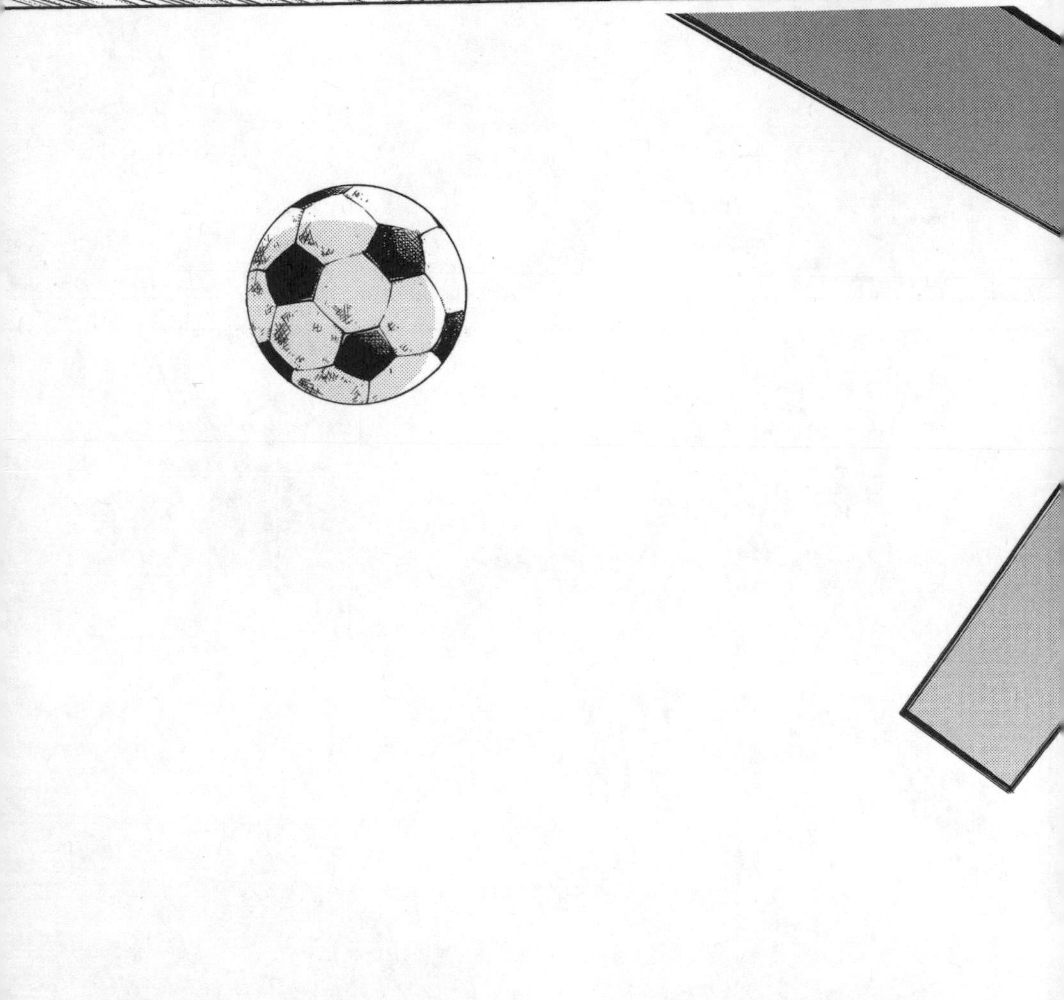

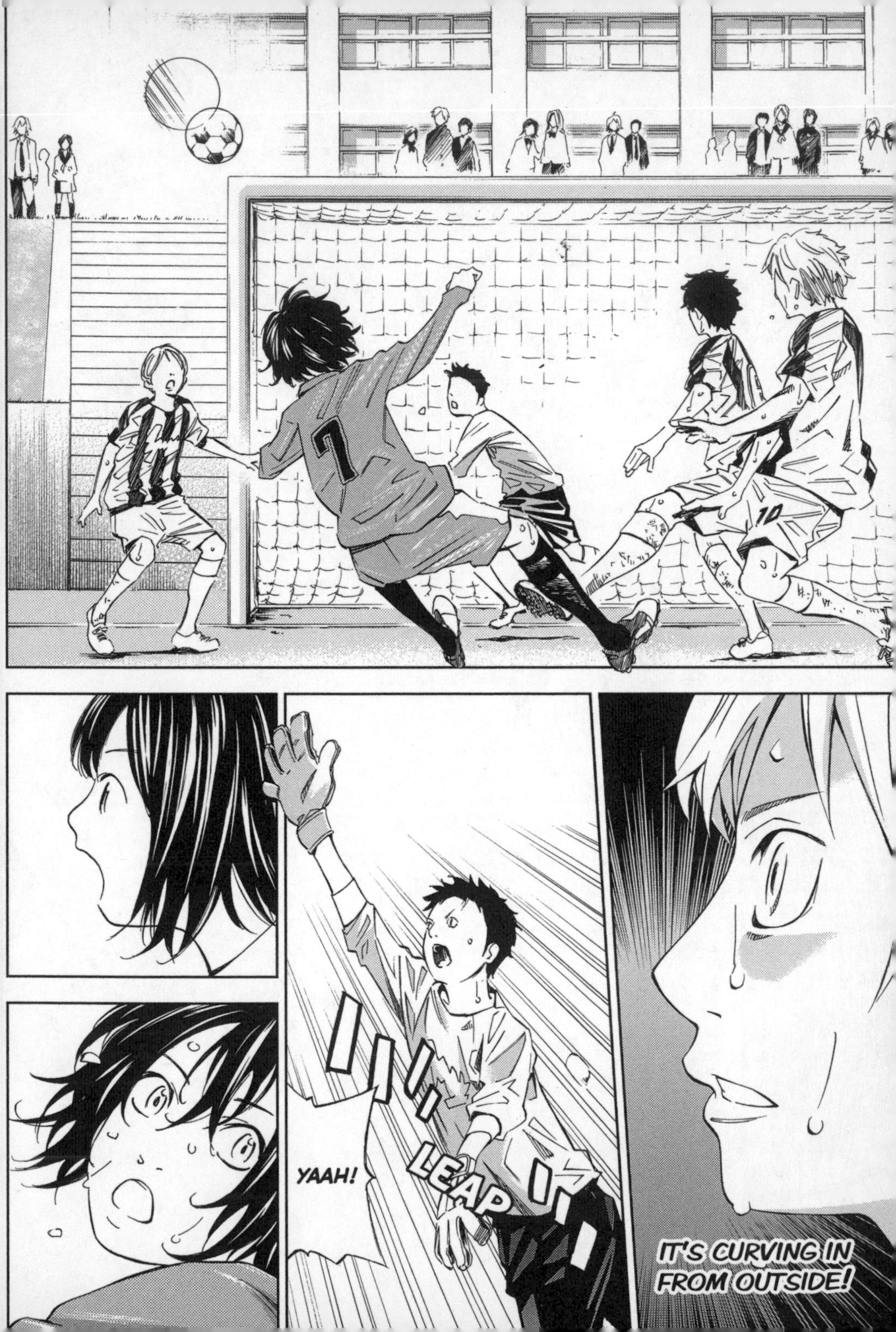
IT'S CURVING IN FROM OUTSIDE!
LEAP
YAAH!

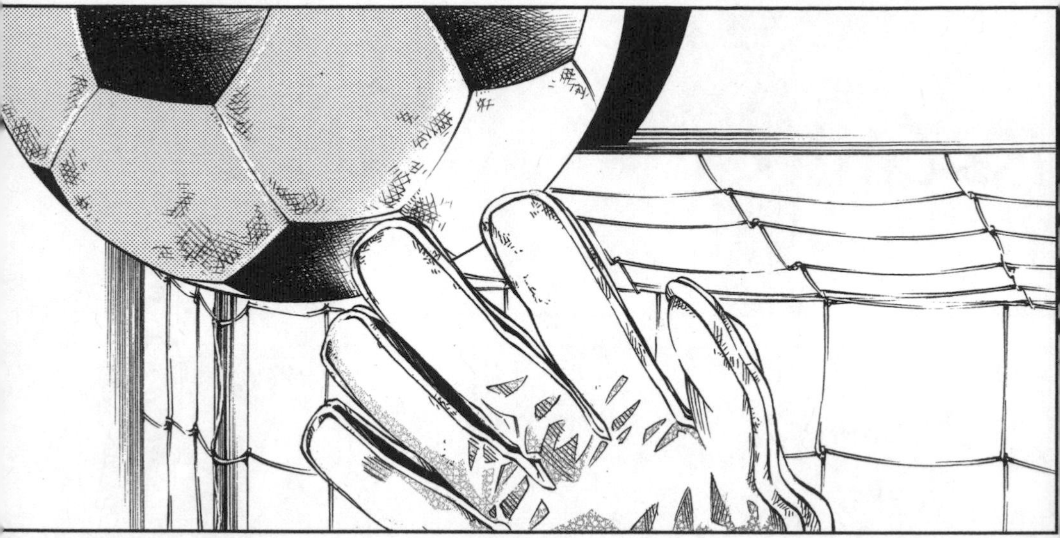
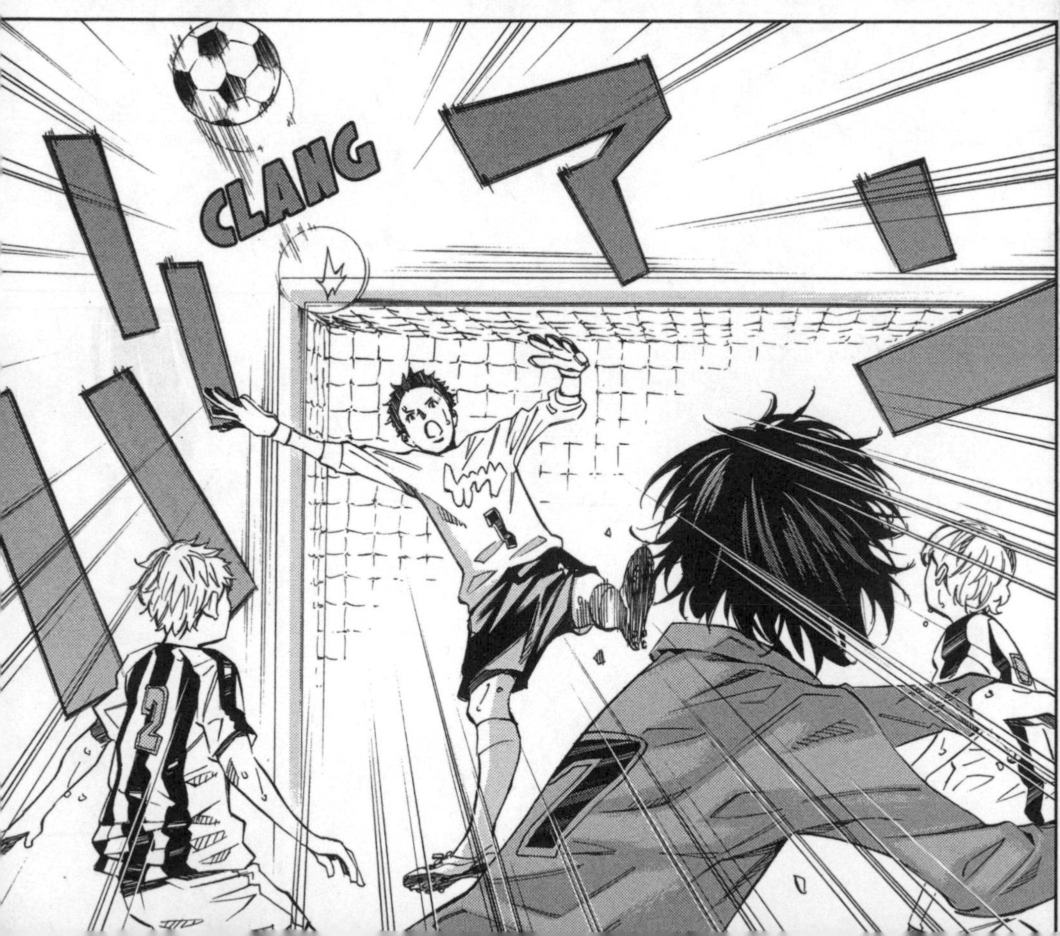
CLANG

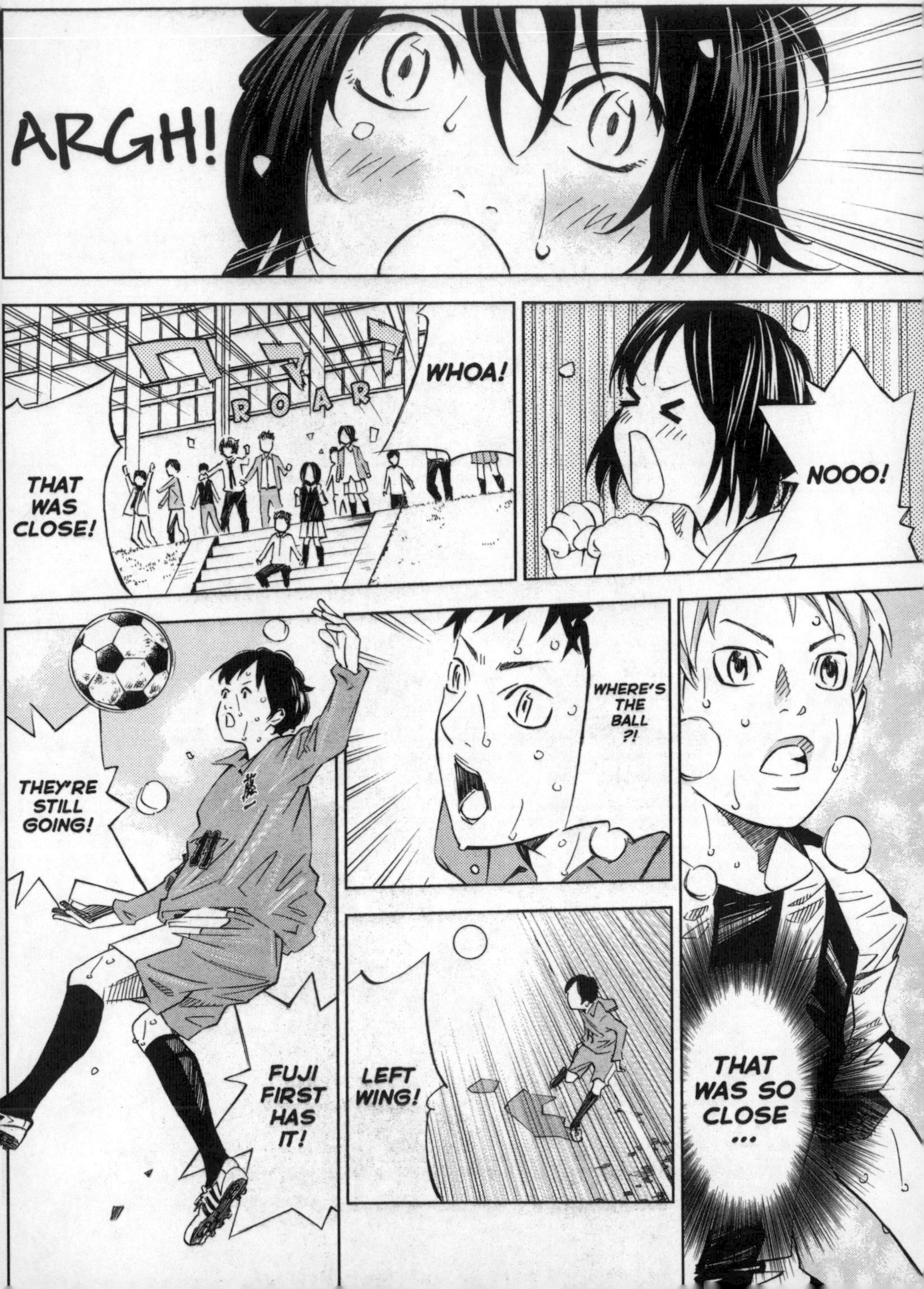
ARGH!
NOOO!
ROAR
WHOA!
THAT WAS CLOSE!
THAT WAS SO CLOSE...
WHERE'S THE BALL ?!
LEFT WING!
THEY'RE STILL GOING!
FUJI FIRST HAS IT!

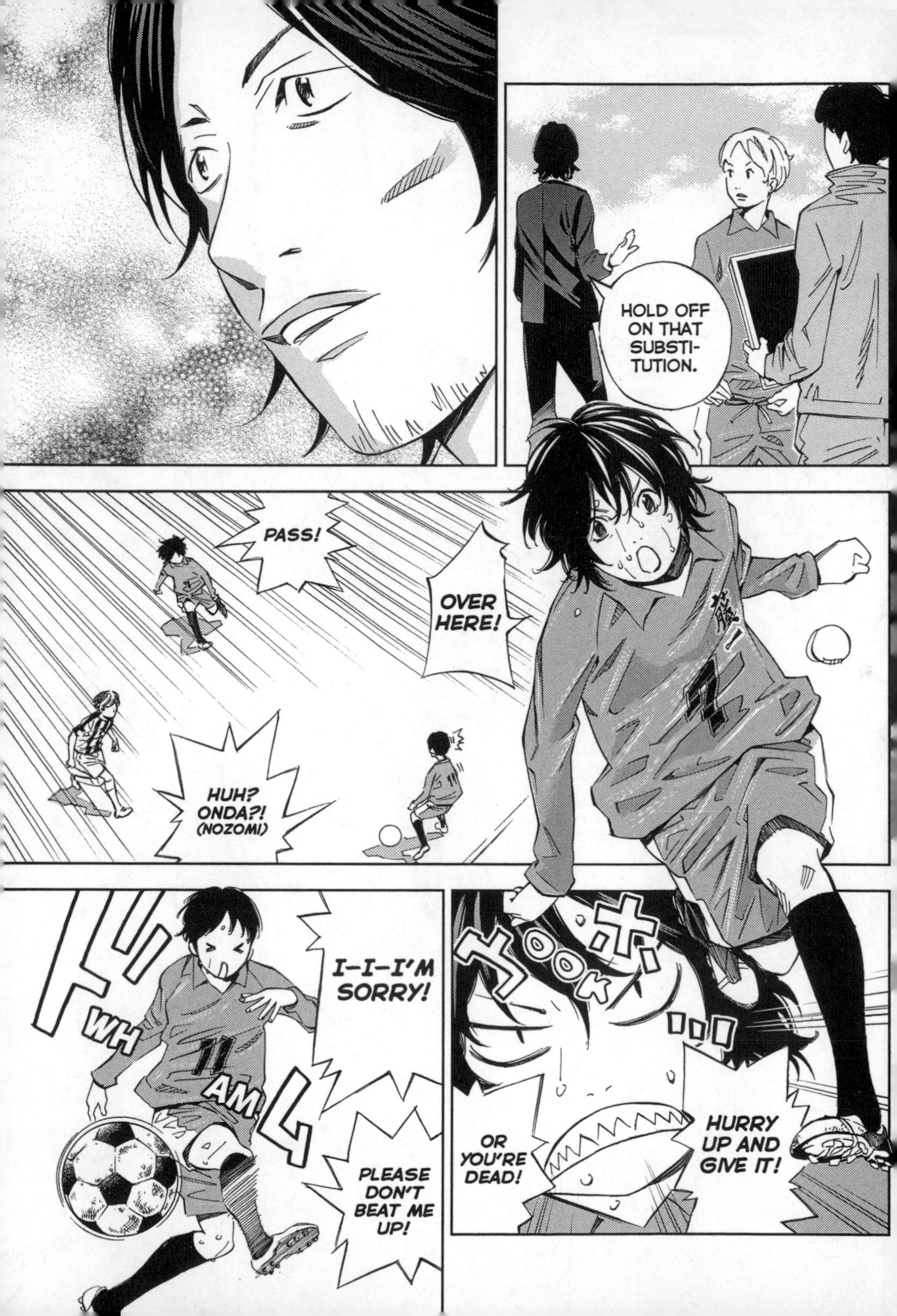
HOLD OFF ON THAT SUBSTI-TUTION.
PASS!
OVER HERE!
HUH? ONDA?! (NOZOMI)
OOOK!!!
HURRY UP AND GIVE IT!
OR YOU'RE DEAD!
WHAM
I-I-I'M SORRY!
PLEASE DON'T BEAT ME UP!

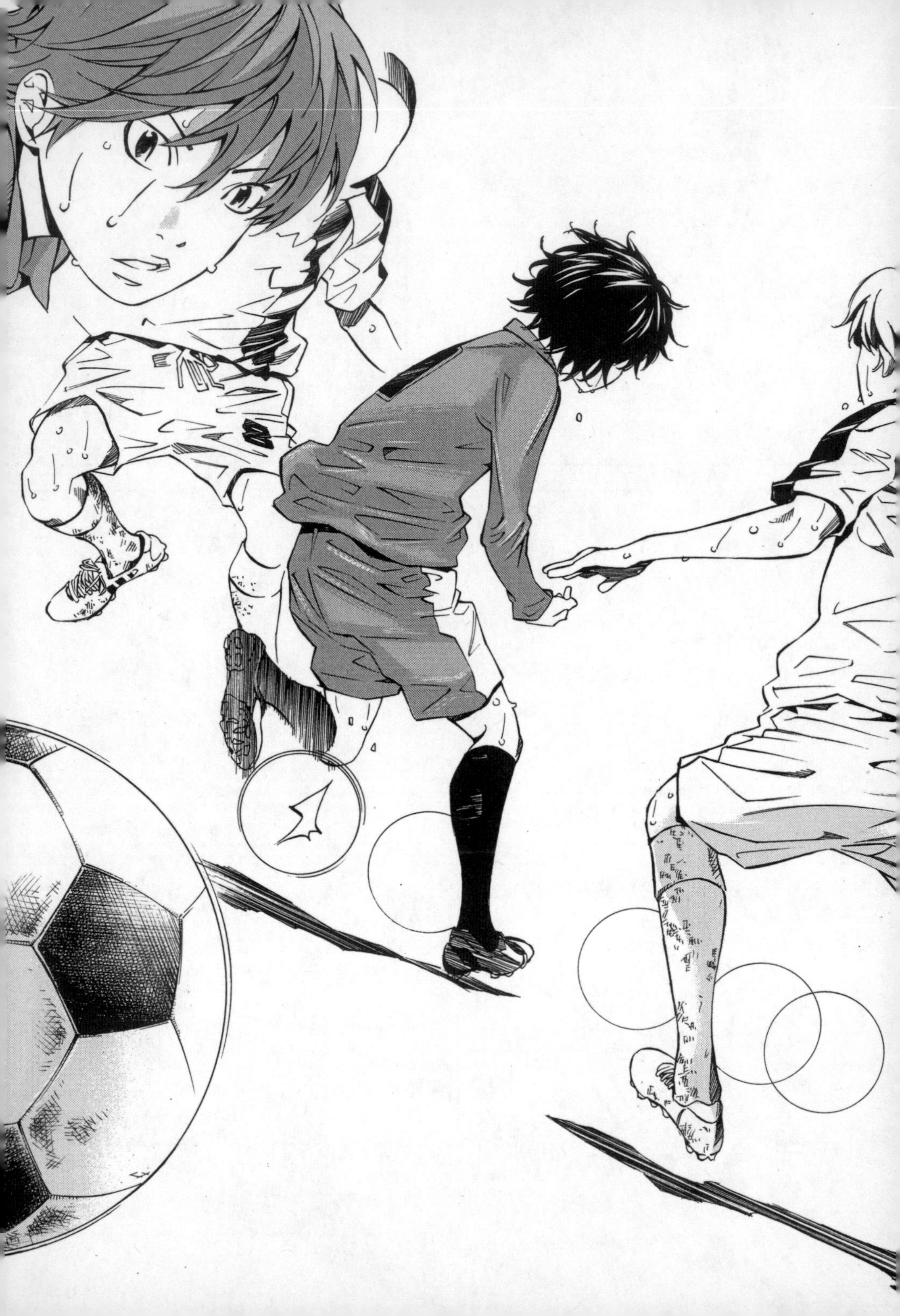

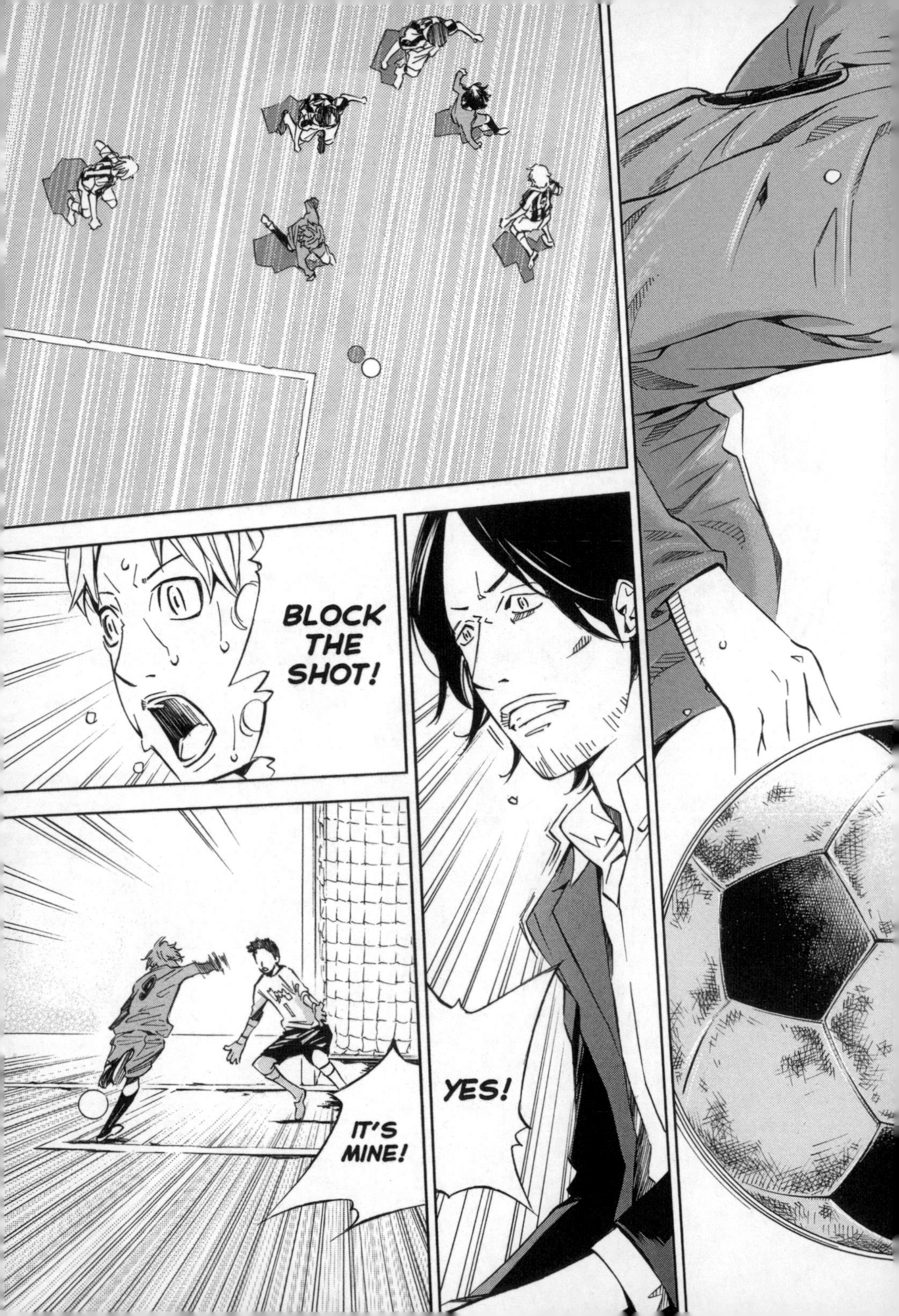
YES!
BLOCK THE SHOT!
IT'S MINE!

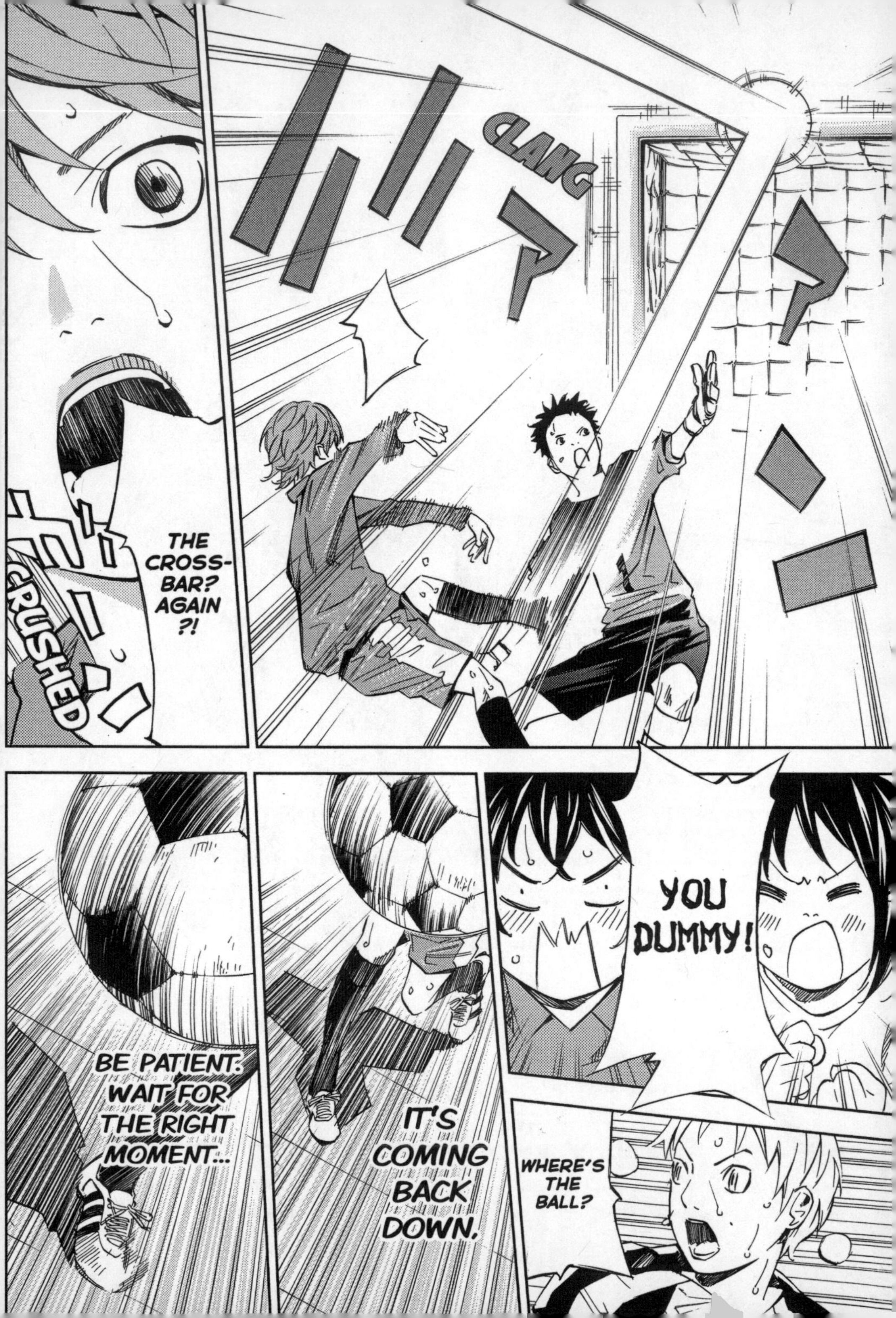
CLANG
THE CROSS-BAR? AGAIN ?!
CRUSHED
YOU DUMMY!
WHERE'S THE BALL?
IT'S COMING BACK DOWN.
BE PATIENT. WAIT FOR THE RIGHT MOMENT...

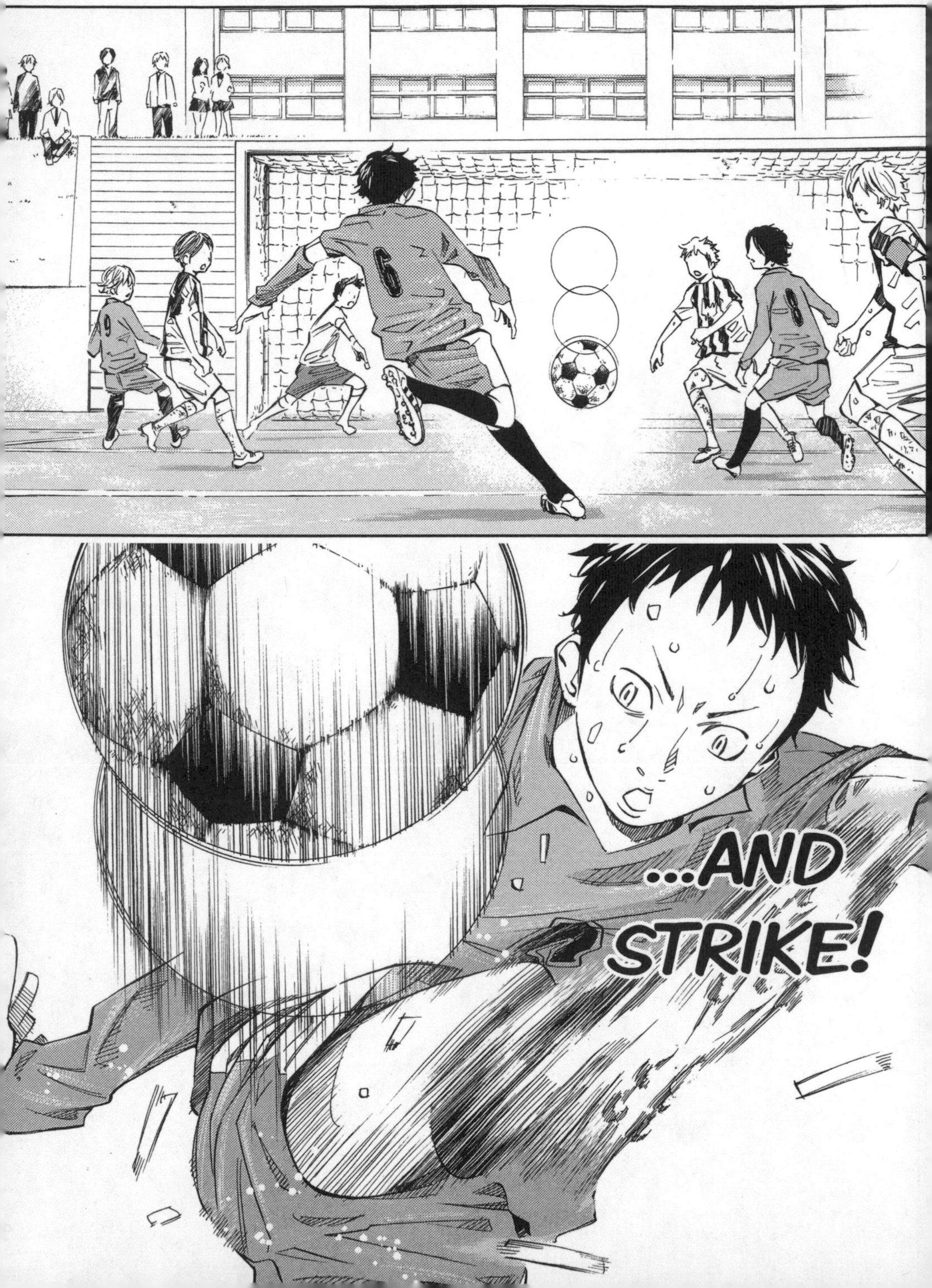
...AND STRIKE!

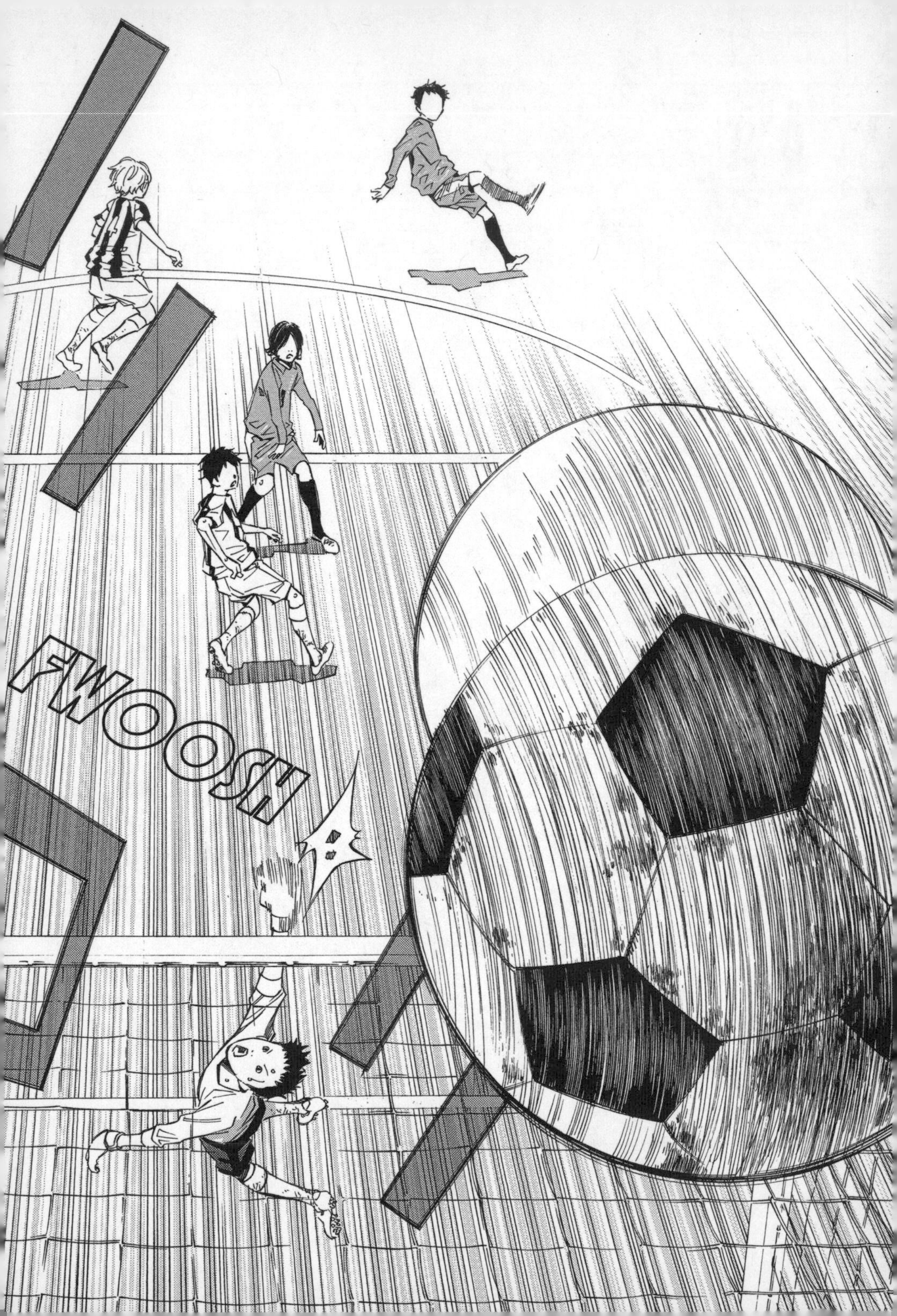
FWOOSH

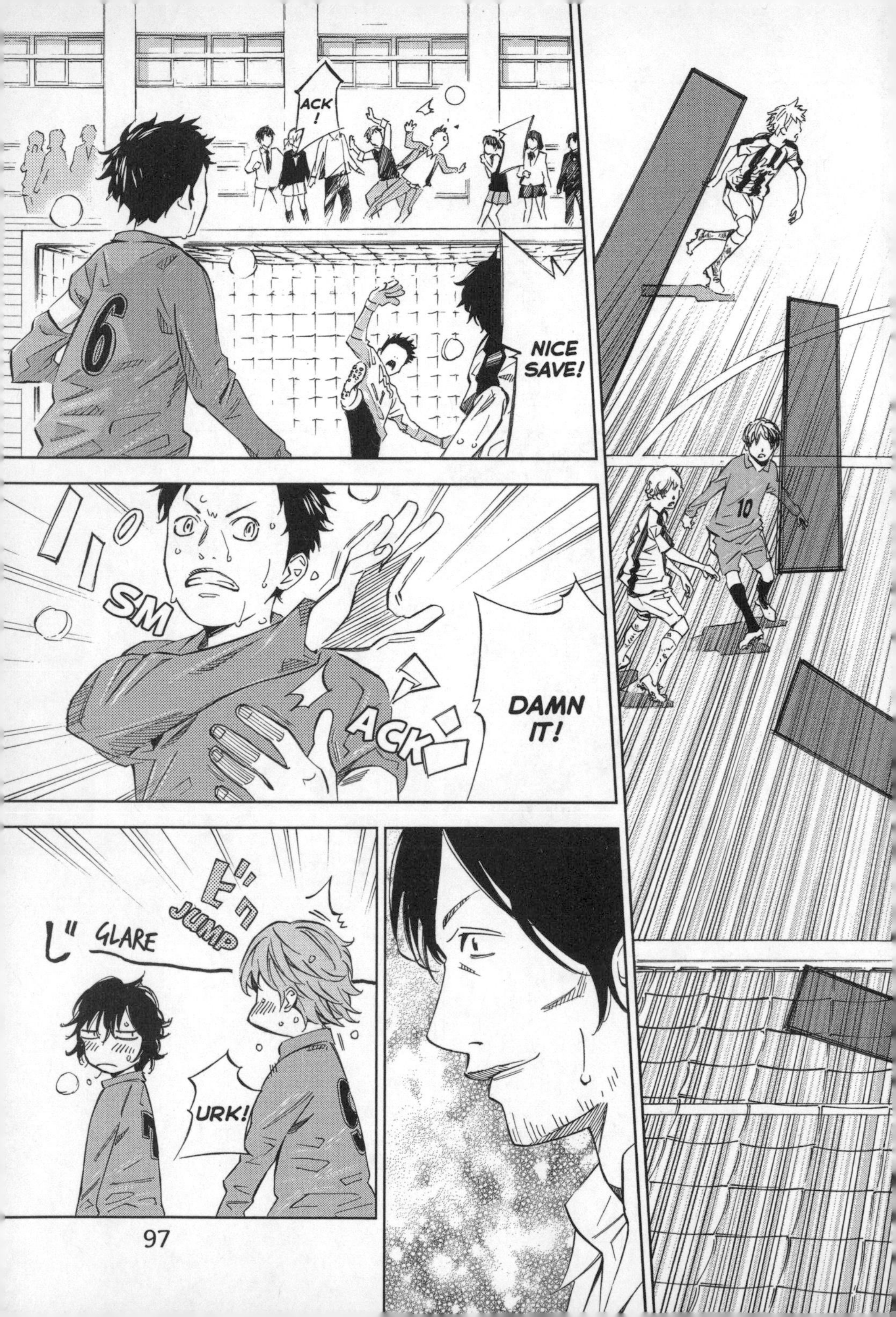
ACK!
NICE SAVE!
SM
ACK
DAMN IT!
JUMP
GLARE
URK!

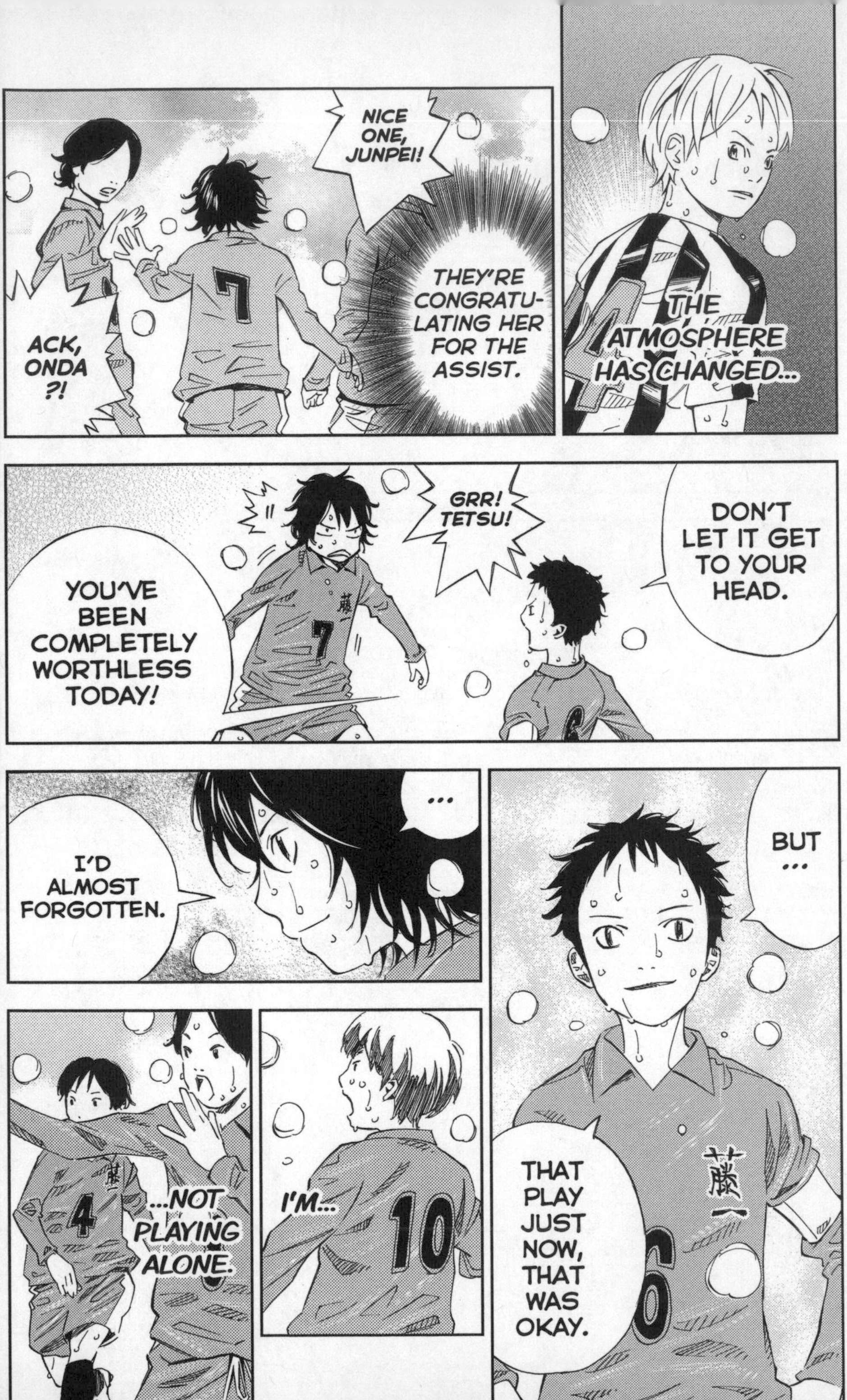
THE ATMOSPHERE HAS CHANGED...
NICE ONE, JUNPEI!
THEY'RE CONGRATU-LATING HER FOR THE ASSIST.
ACK, ONDA ?!
DON'T LET IT GET TO YOUR HEAD.
GRR! TETSU!
YOU'VE BEEN COMPLETELY WORTHLESS TODAY!
BUT ...
THAT PLAY JUST NOW, THAT WAS OKAY.
...
I'D ALMOST FORGOTTEN.
I'M...
...NOT PLAYING ALONE.

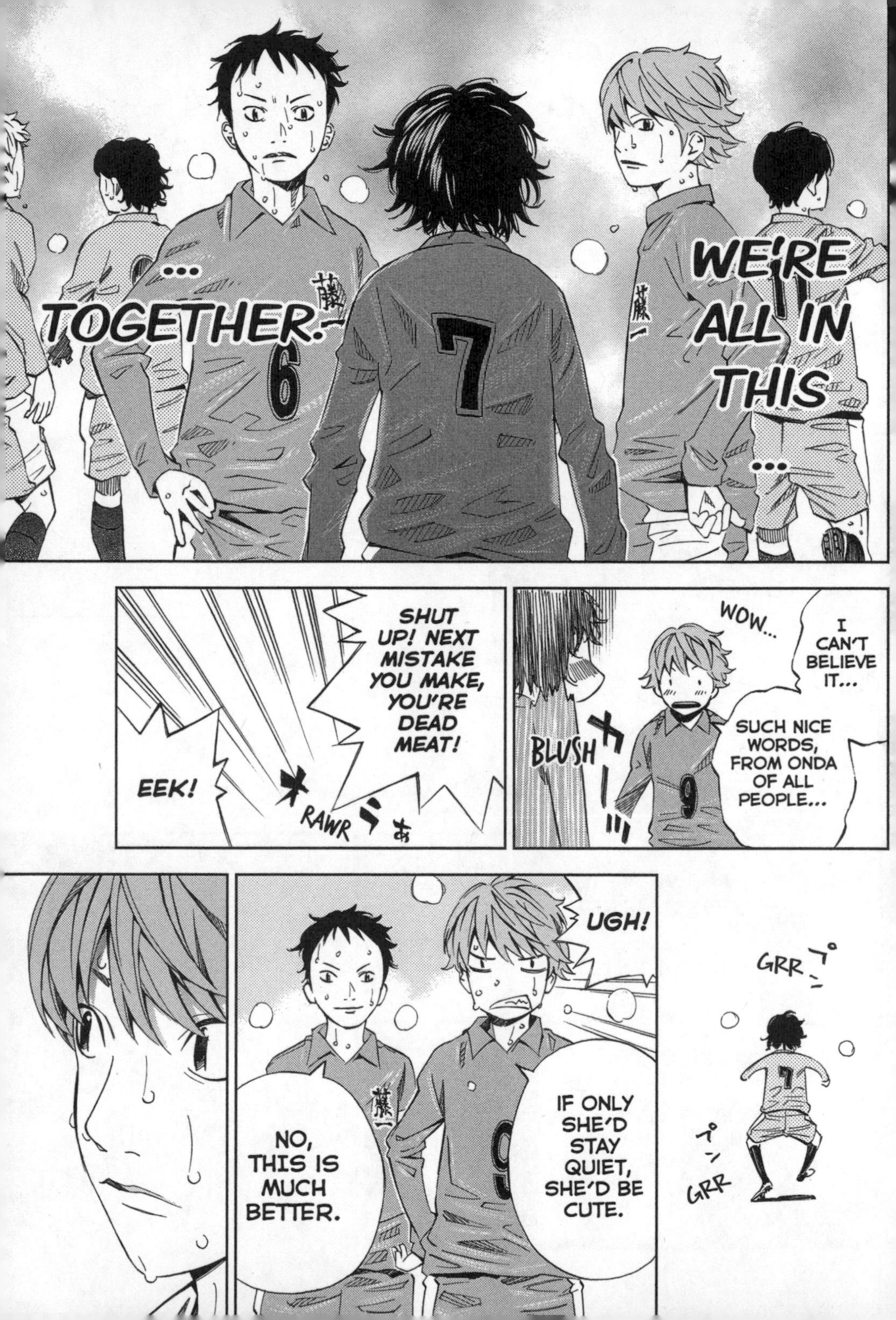
WE'RE ALL IN THIS ...
... TOGETHER.
WOW...
I CAN'T BELIEVE IT...
SUCH NICE WORDS, FROM ONDA OF ALL PEOPLE...
BLUSH
SHUT UP! NEXT MISTAKE YOU MAKE, YOU'RE DEAD MEAT!
RAWR
EEK!
GRR
GRR
UGH!
IF ONLY SHE'D STAY QUIET, SHE'D BE CUTE.
NO, THIS IS MUCH BETTER.

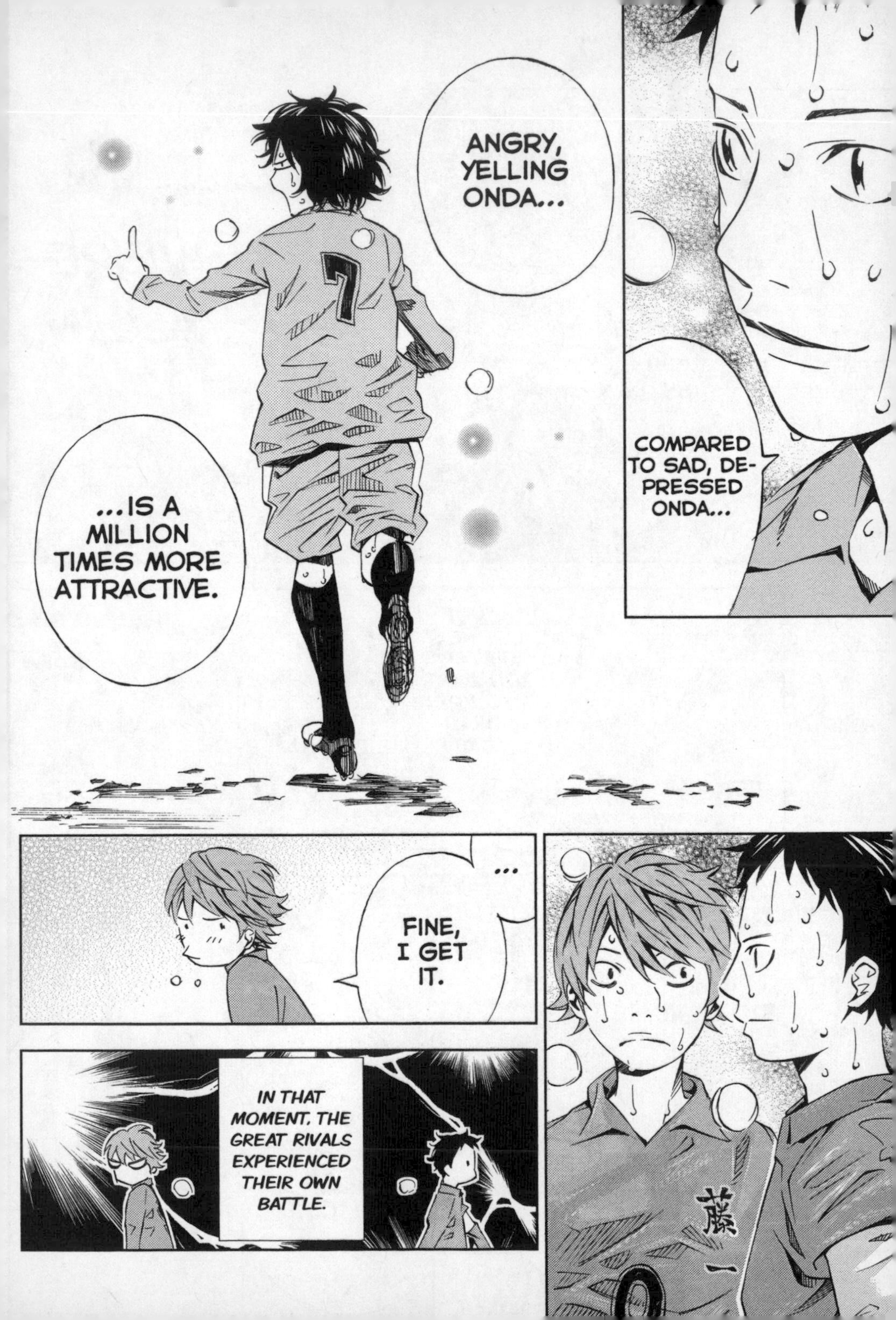
COMPARED TO SAD, DE-PRESSED ONDA...
ANGRY, YELLING ONDA...
...IS A MILLION TIMES MORE ATTRACTIVE.
藤
...
FINE, I GET IT.
IN THAT MOMENT. THE GREAT RIVALS EXPERIENCED THEIR OWN BATTLE.

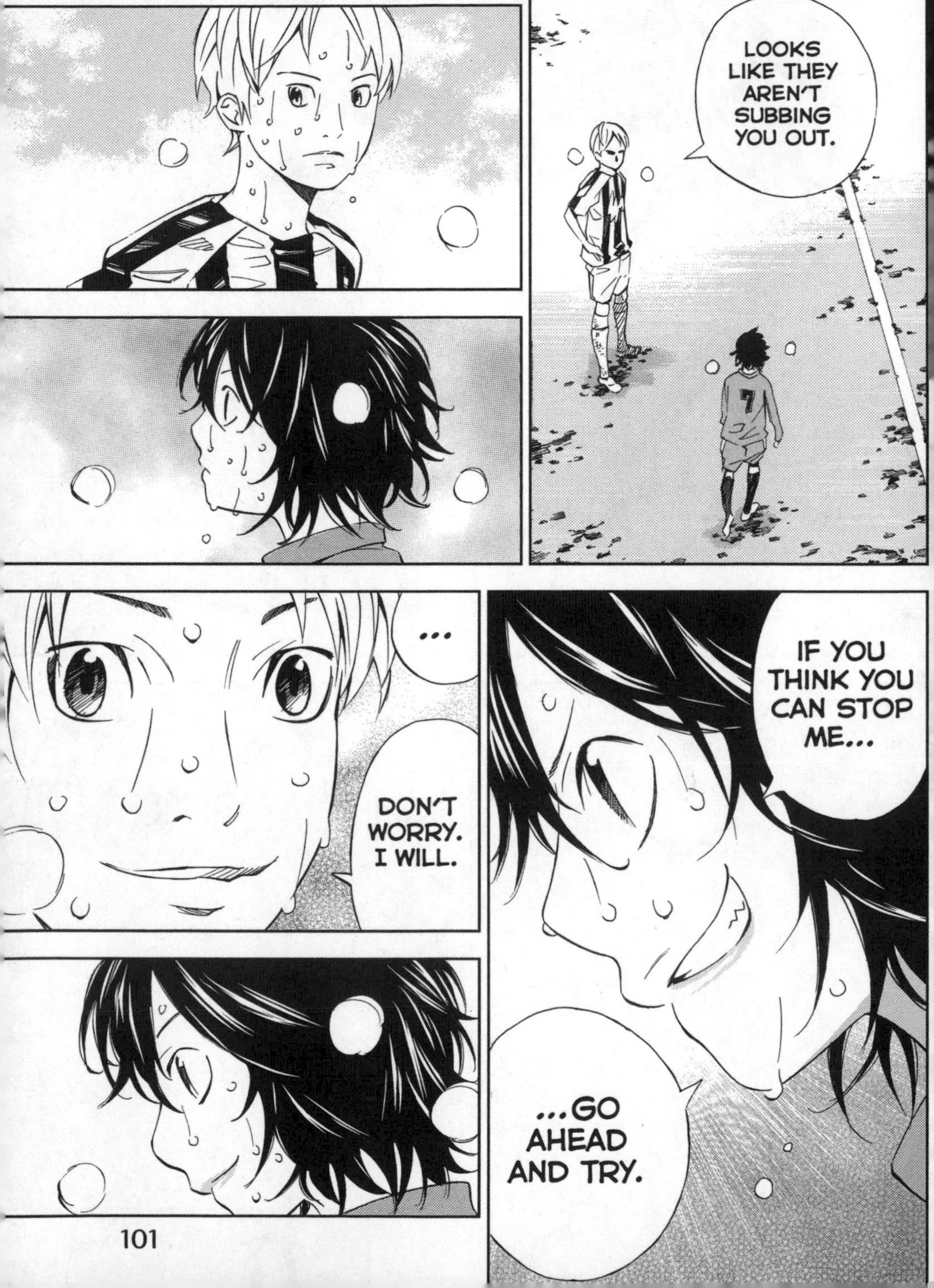
LOOKS LIKE THEY AREN'T SUBBING YOU OUT.
IF YOU THINK YOU CAN STOP ME...
...GO AHEAD AND TRY.
...
DON'T WORRY. I WILL.

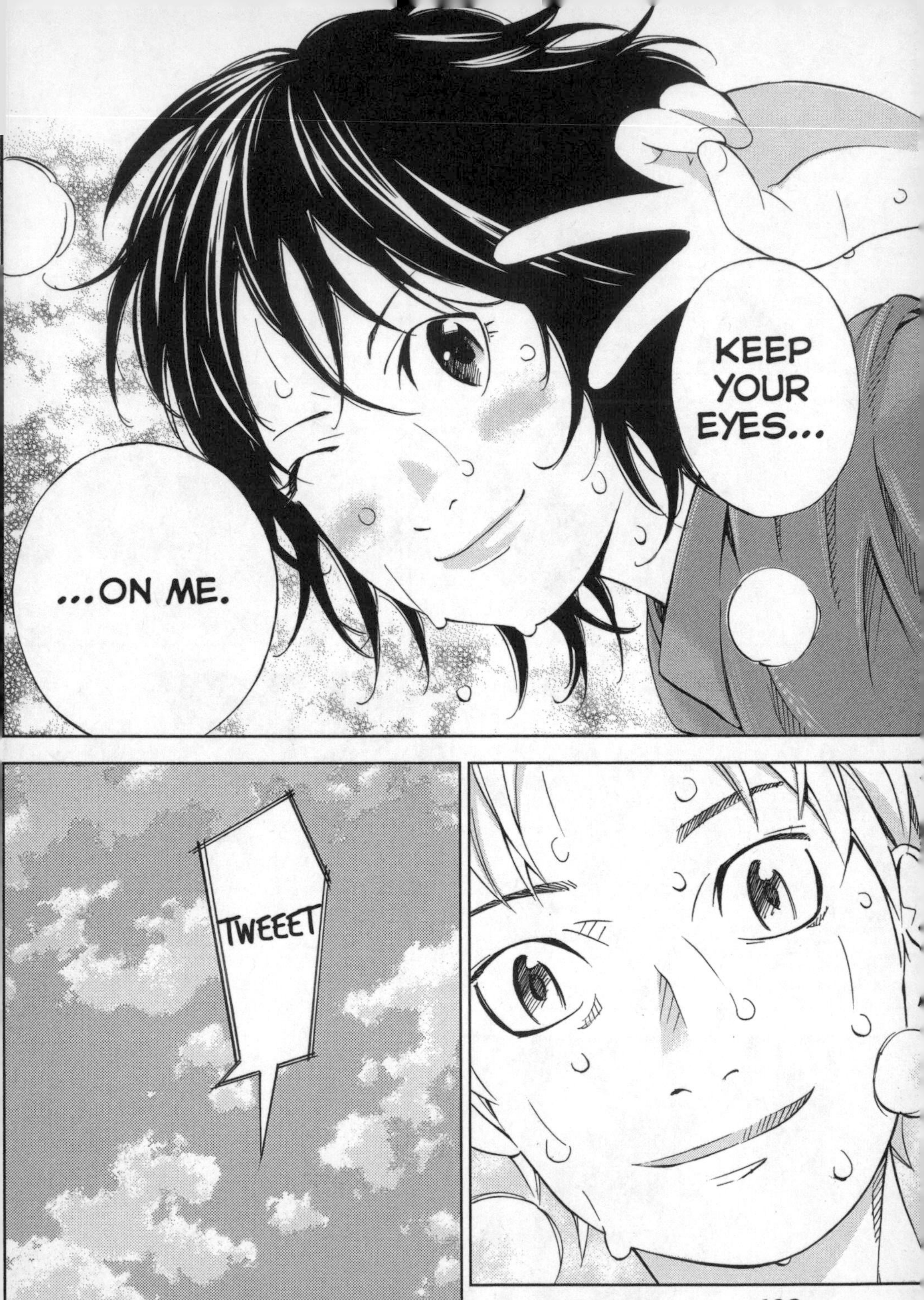
KEEP YOUR EYES...
...ON ME.
TWEEET

SAYONARA,
FOOTBALL

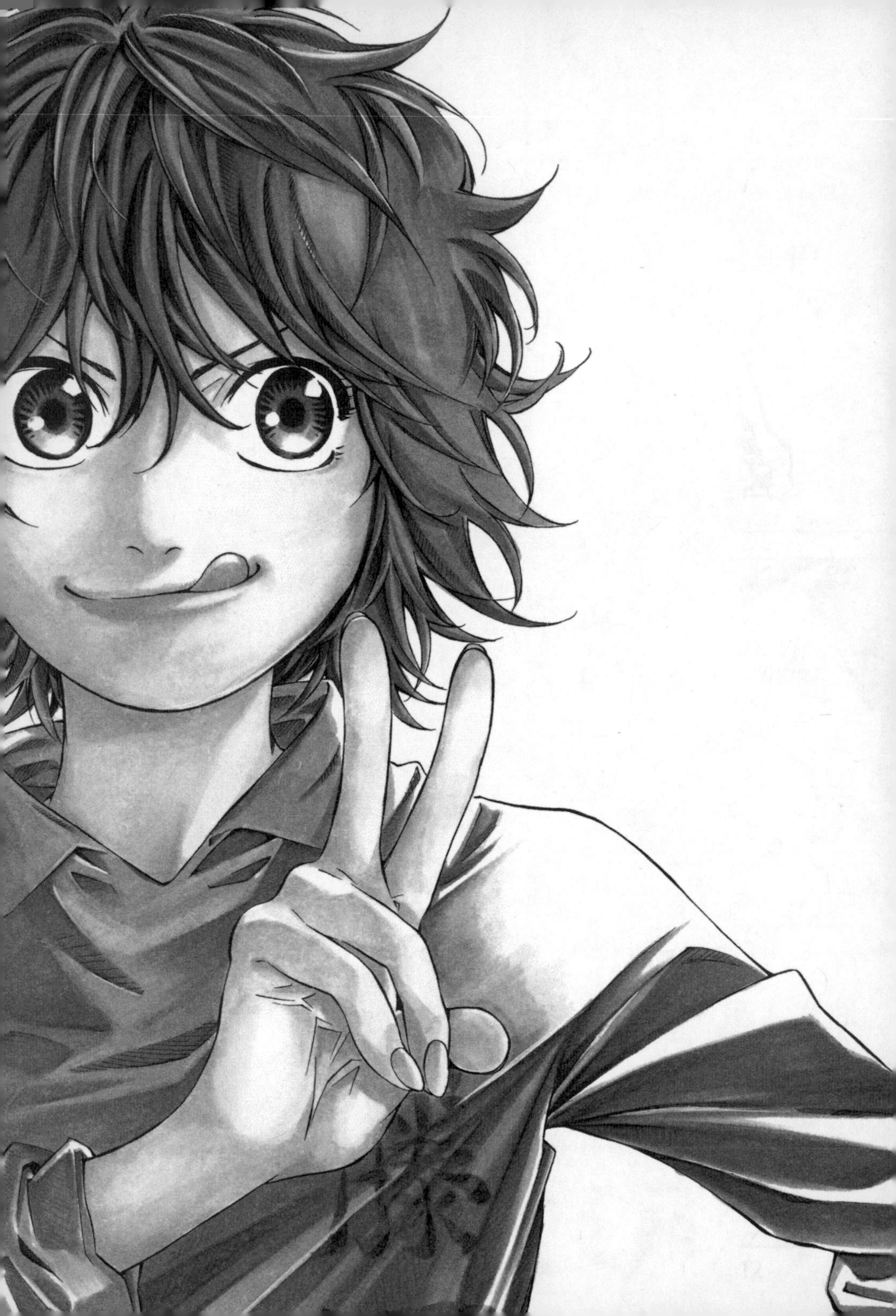

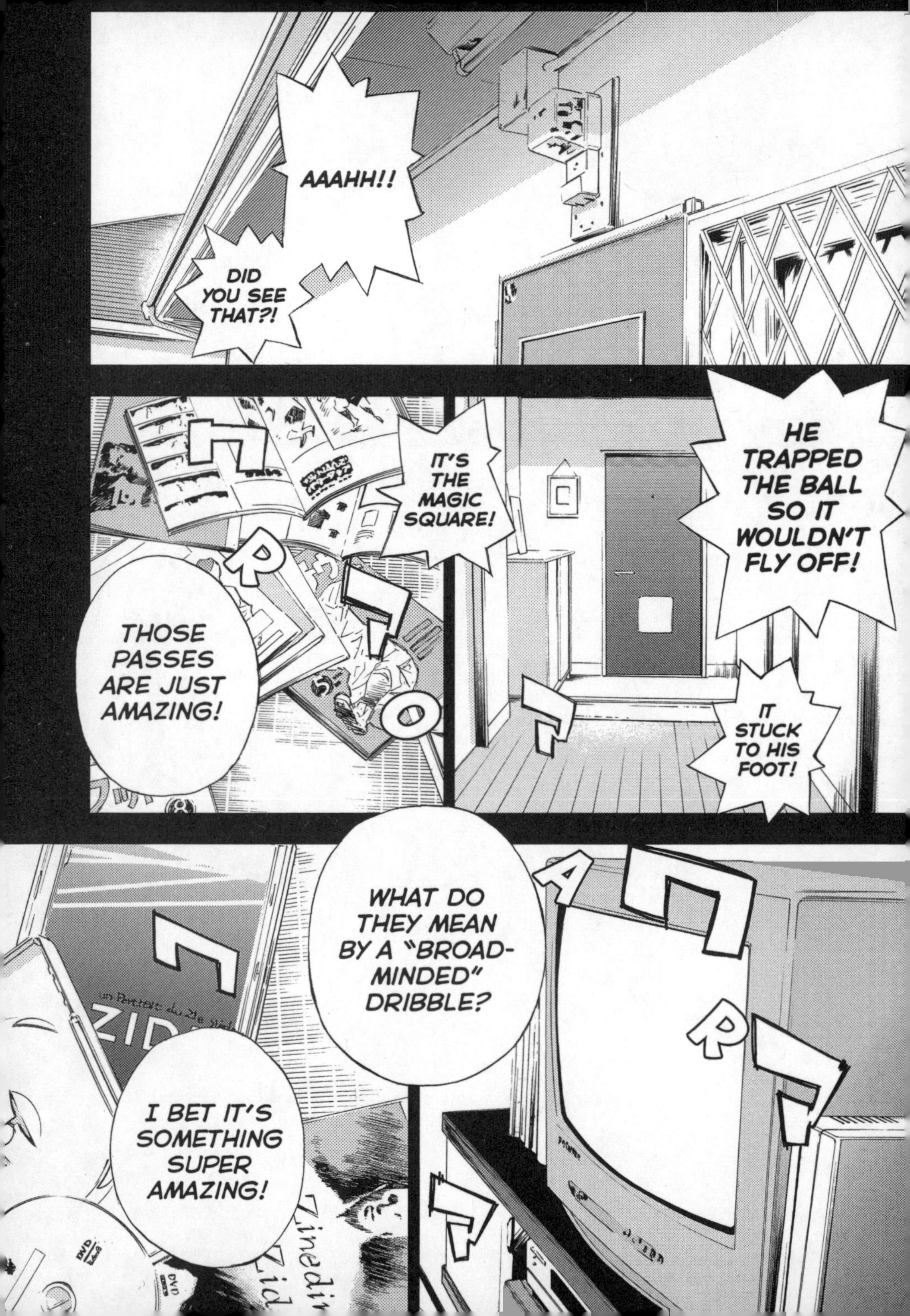
AAAHH!!
DID YOU SEE THAT?!
HE TRAPPED THE BALL SO IT WOULDN'T FLY OFF!
IT STUCK TO HIS FOOT!
IT'S THE MAGIC SQUARE!
THOSE PASSES ARE JUST AMAZING!
WHAT DO THEY MEAN BY A "BROAD-MINDED" DRIBBLE?
I BET IT'S SOMETHING SUPER AMAZING!

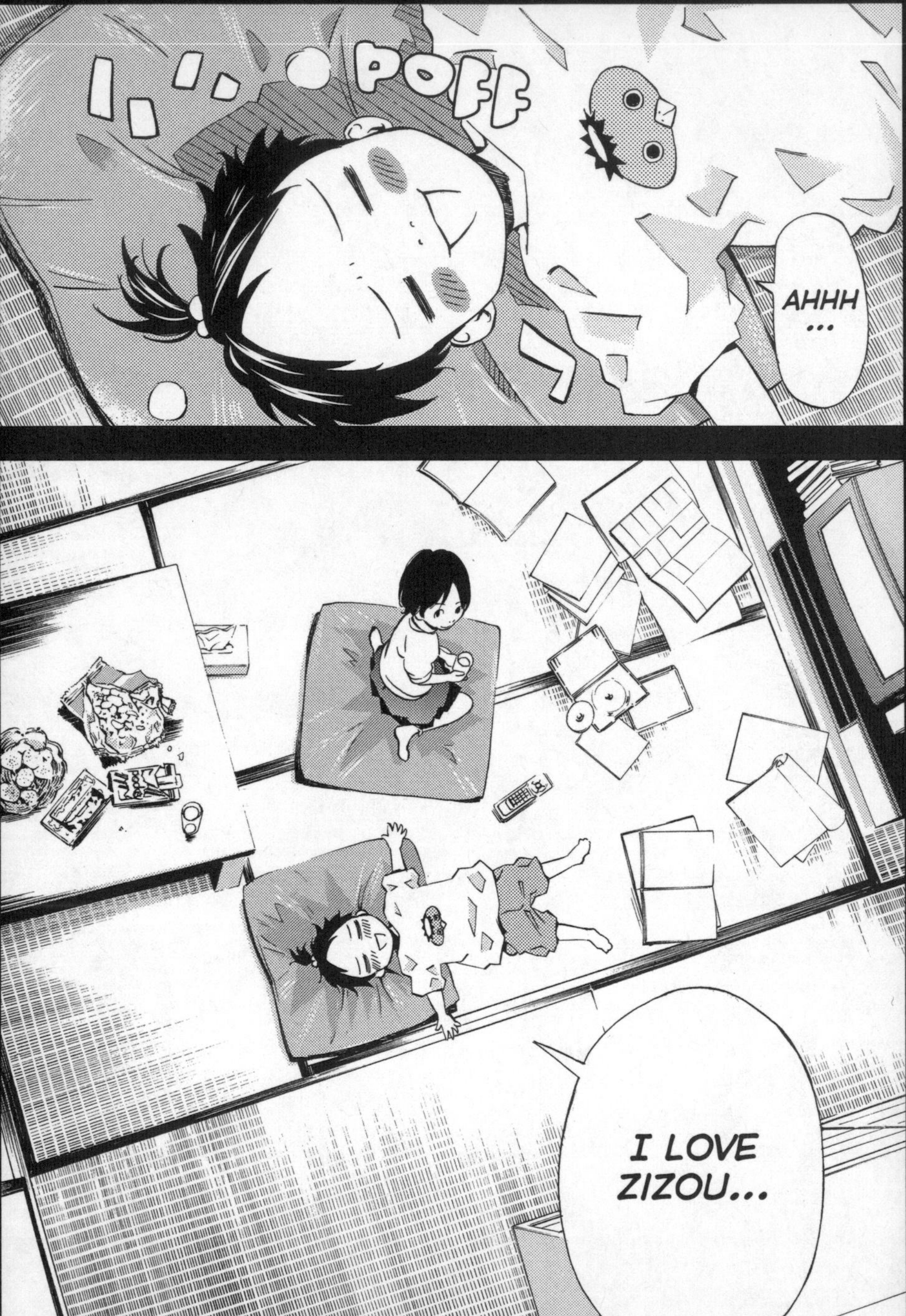
POFF
AHHH ...
I LOVE ZIZOU...

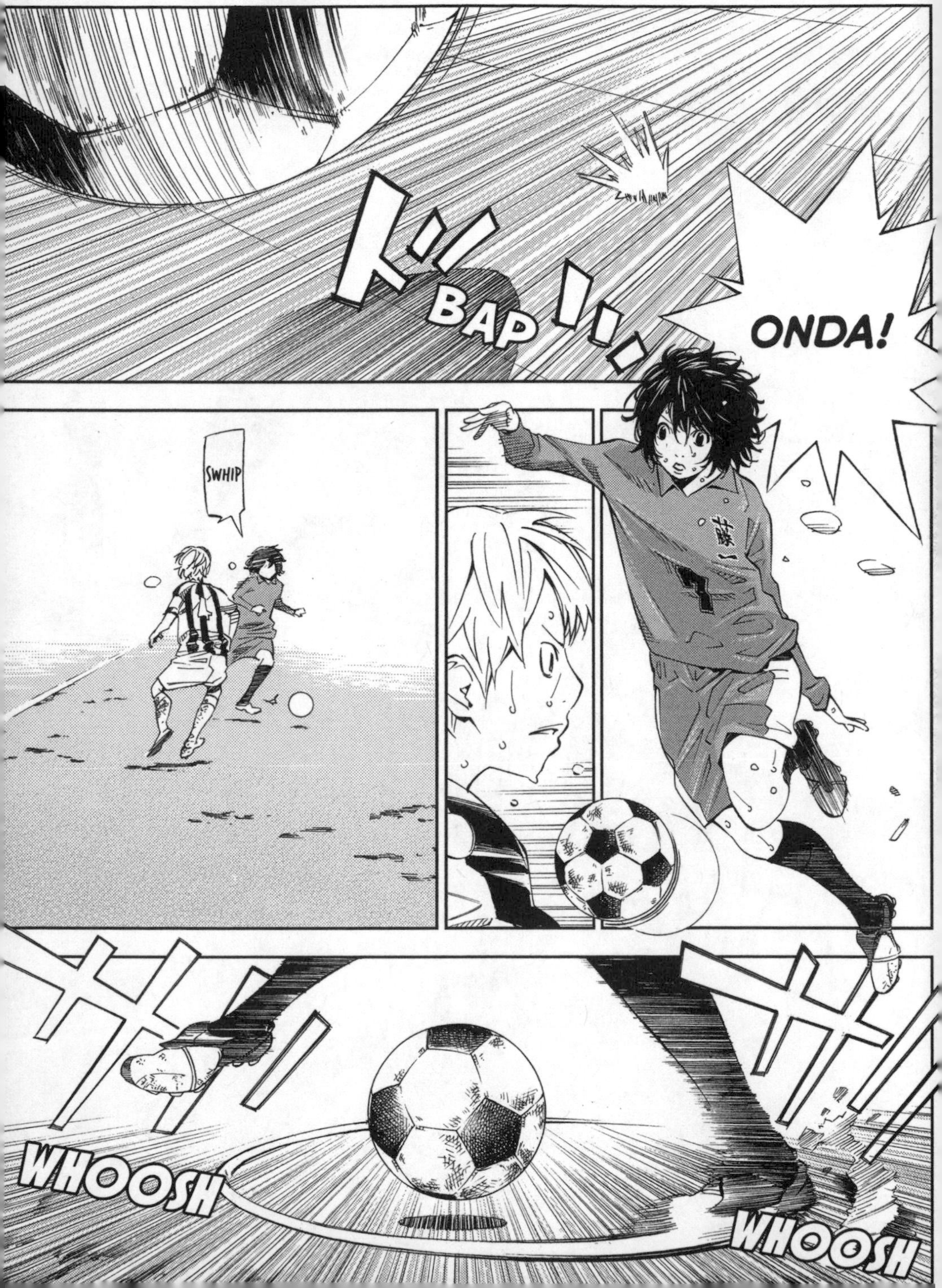
BAP
ONDA!
SWHIP
WHOOSH
WHOOSH

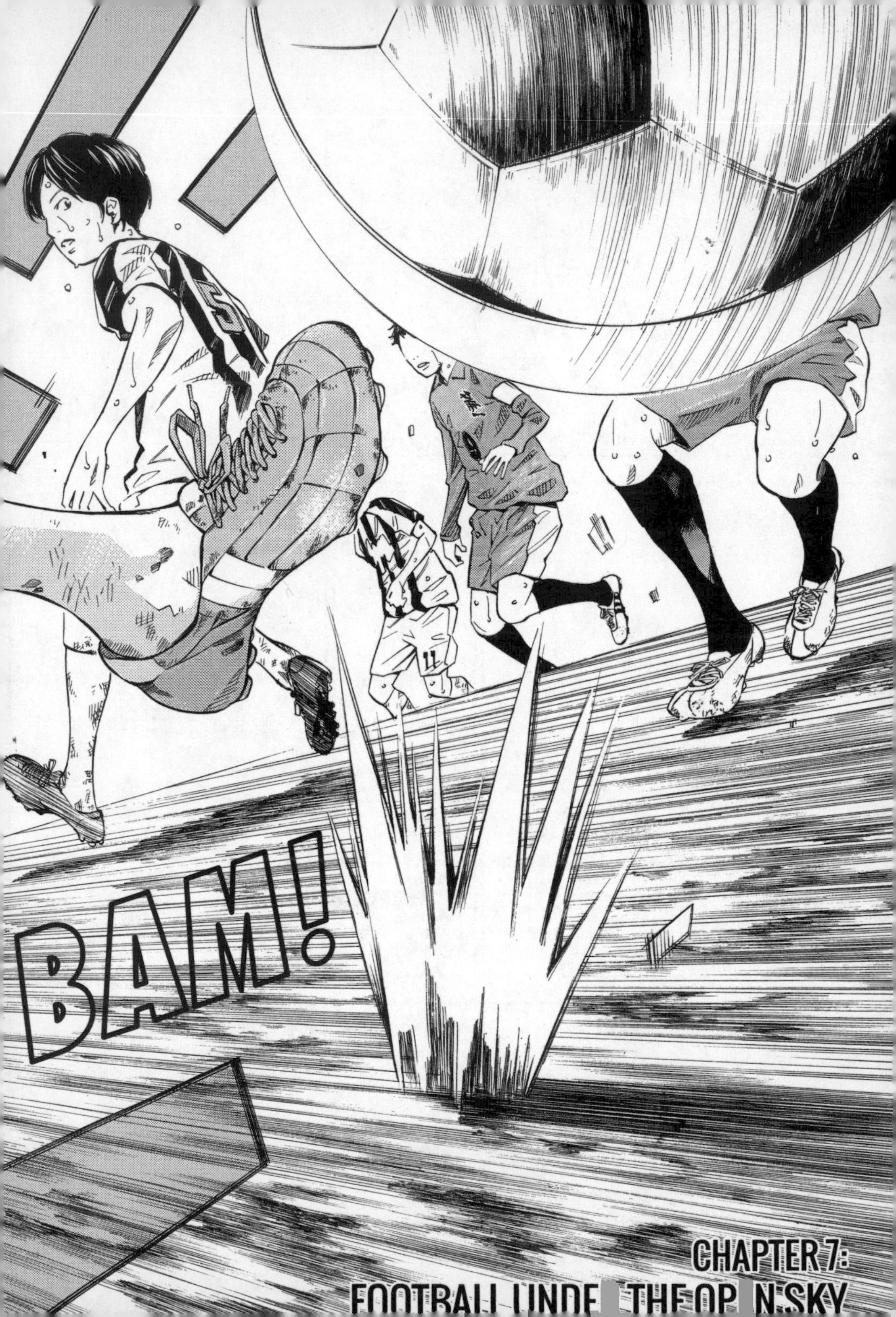
BAM!

CHAPTER 7: FOOTBALL UNDER THE OPEN SKY

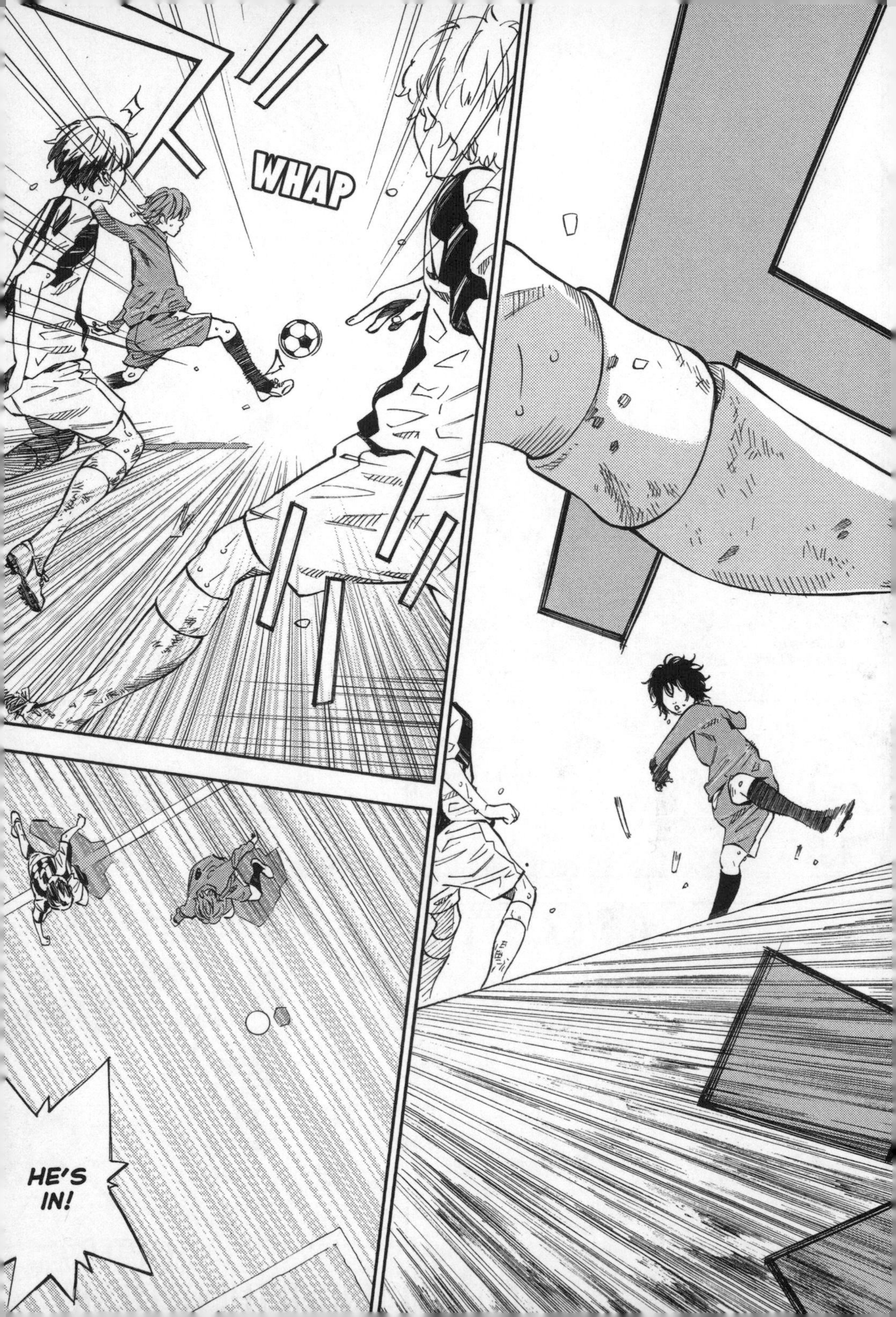
WHAP
HE'S IN!

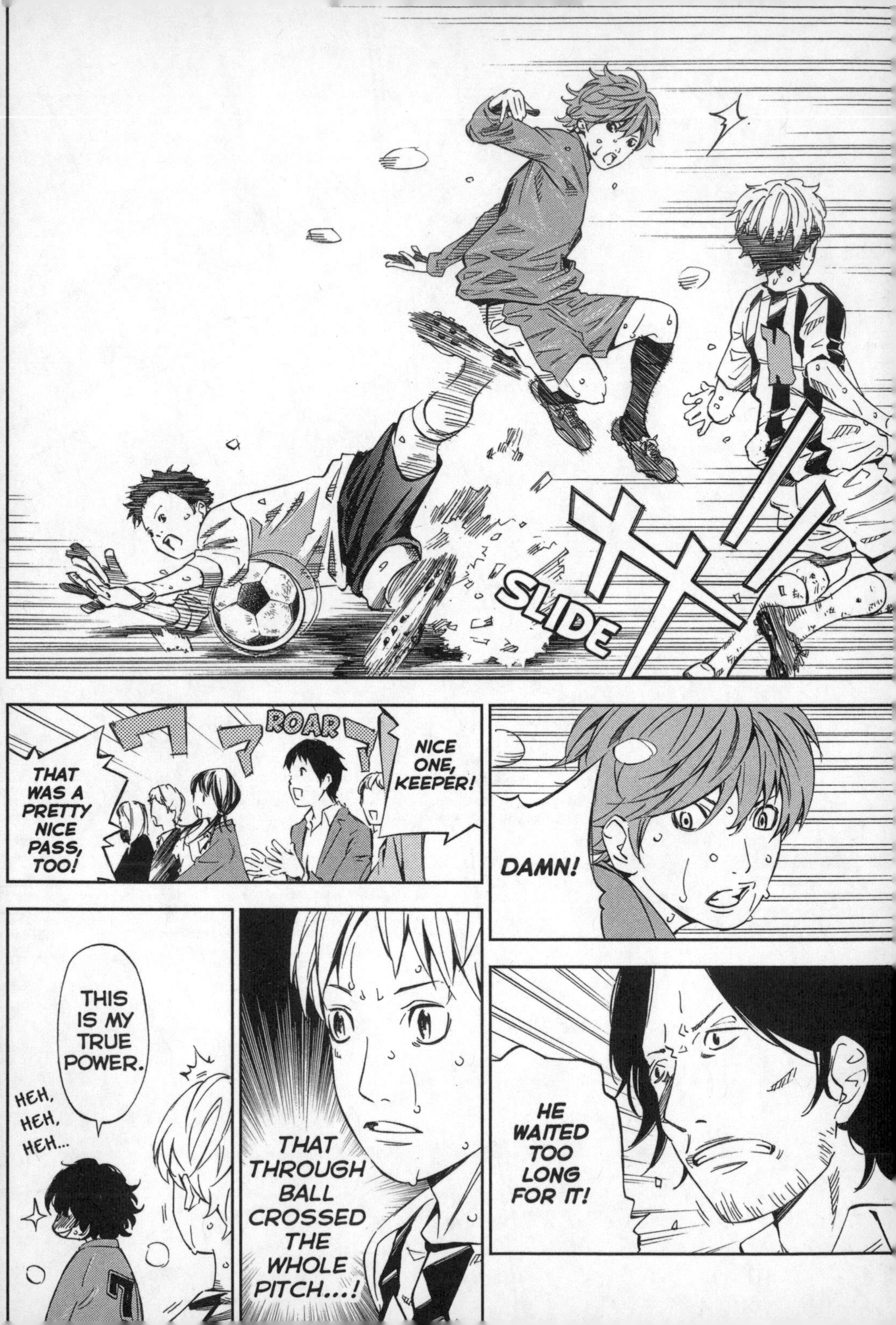
SLIDE
DAMN!
ROAR
NICE ONE, KEEPER!
THAT WAS A PRETTY NICE PASS, TOO!
HE WAITED TOO LONG FOR IT!
THAT THROUGH BALL CROSSED THE WHOLE PITCH...!
THIS IS MY TRUE POWER.
HEH, HEH, HEH...

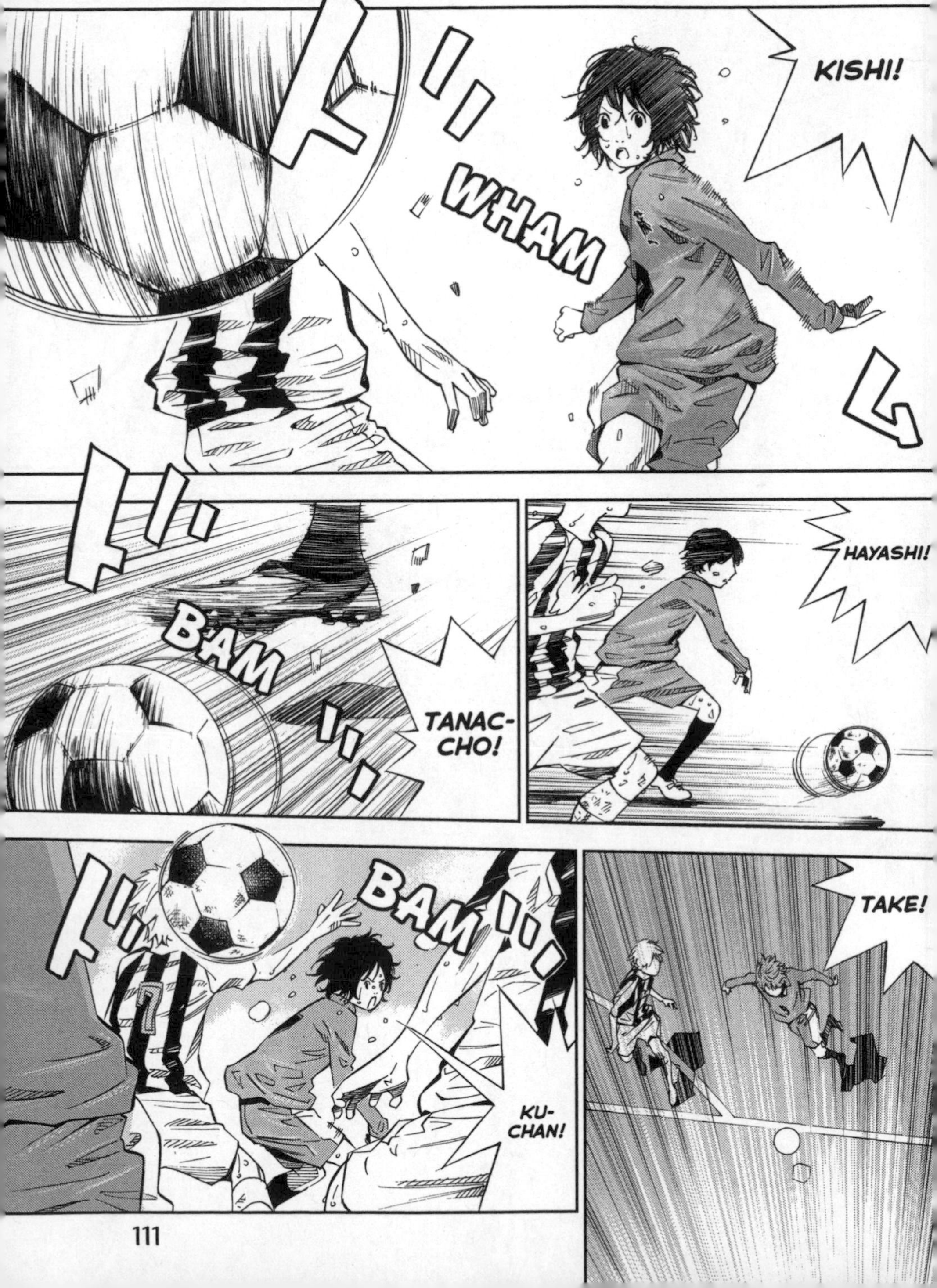
KISHI!
WHAM
HAYASHI!
BAM
TANAC-
CHO!
TAKE!
BAM
KU-
CHAN!

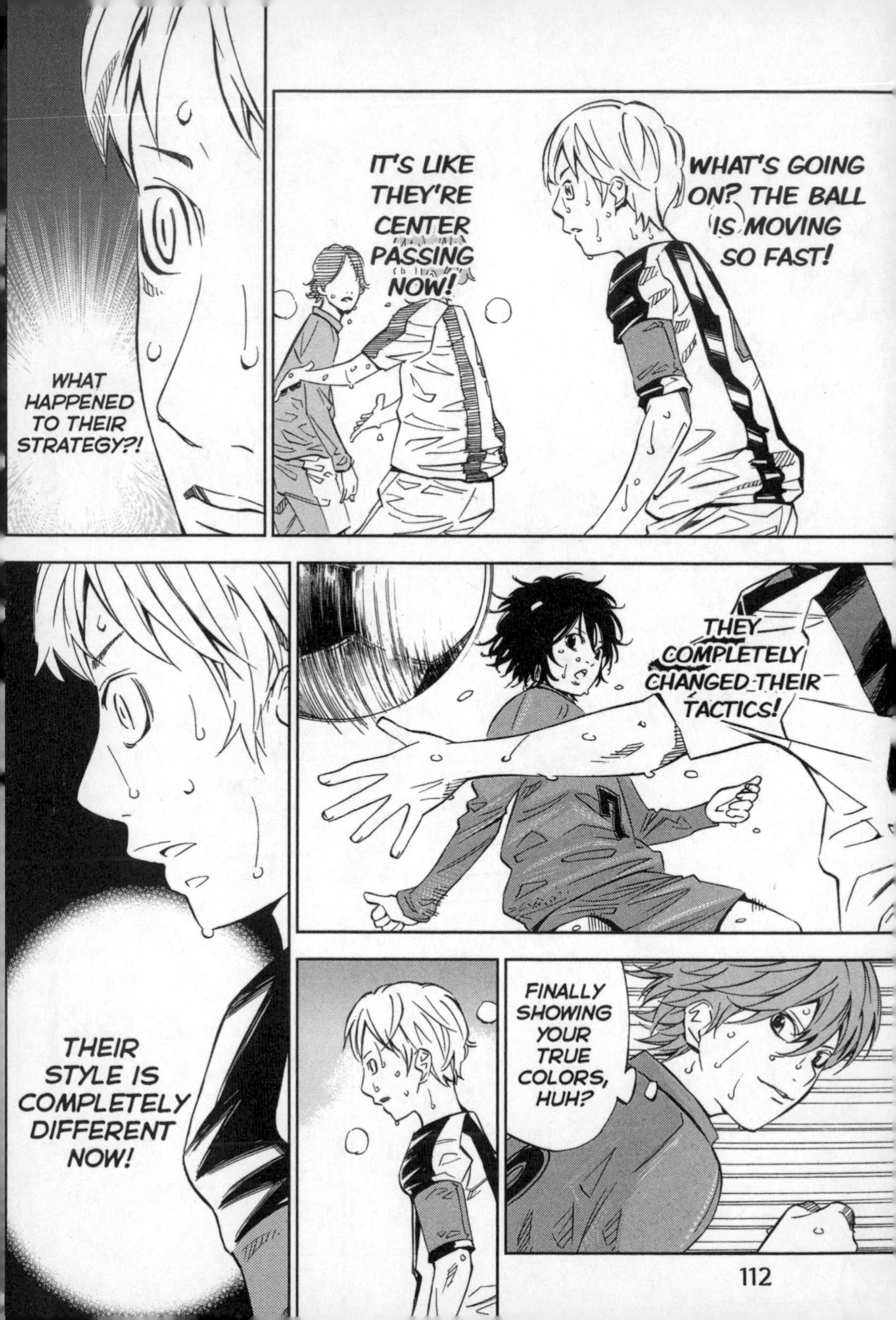
WHAT'S GOING ON? THE BALL IS MOVING SO FAST!
IT'S LIKE THEY'RE CENTER PASSING NOW!
WHAT HAPPENED TO THEIR STRATEGY?!
THEY COMPLETELY CHANGED THEIR TACTICS!
FINALLY SHOWING YOUR TRUE COLORS, HUH?
THEIR STYLE IS COMPLETELY DIFFERENT NOW!

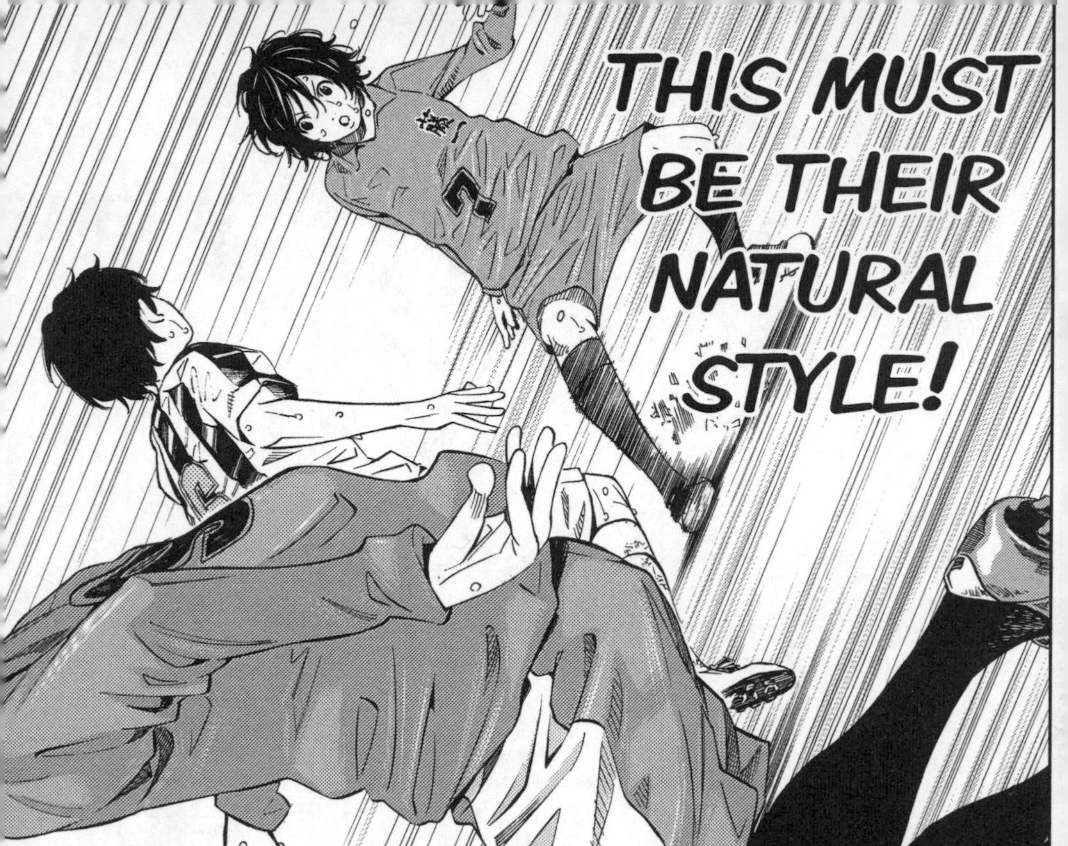
THIS MUST BE THEIR NATURAL STYLE!

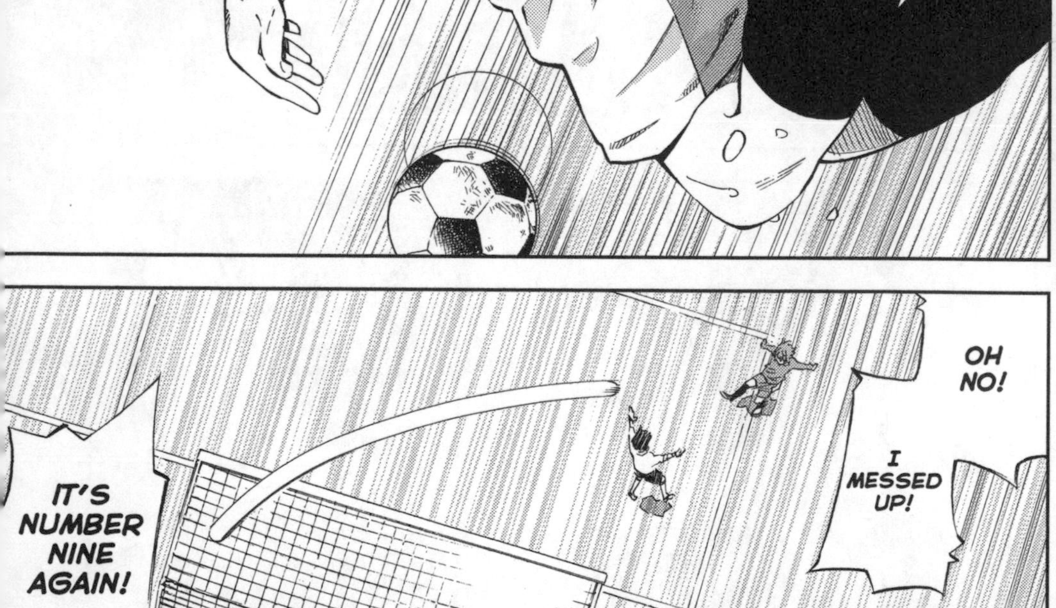
OH NO!
I MESSED UP!
IT'S NUMBER NINE AGAIN!

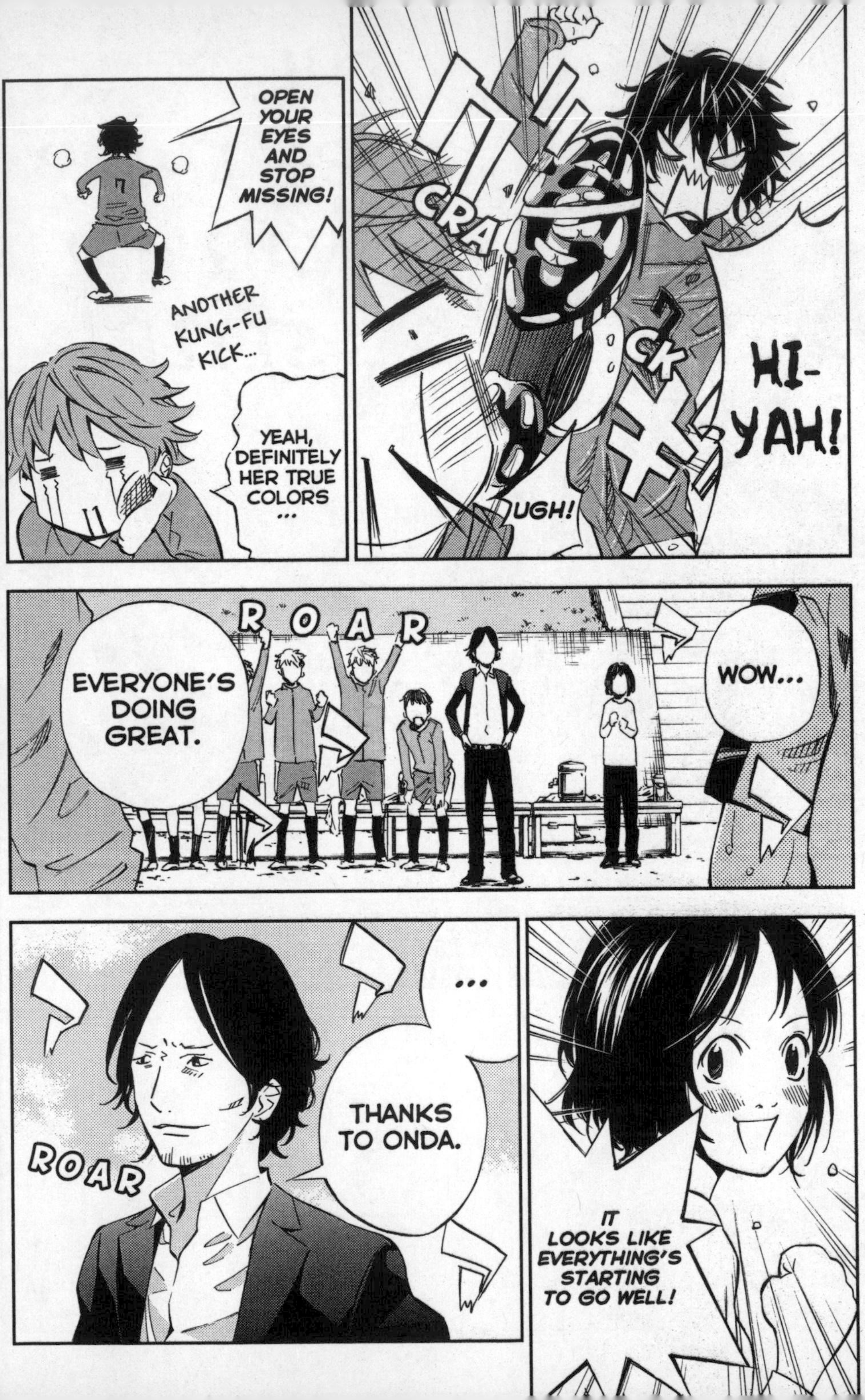
HI-YAH!
CRA
CK
UGH!
OPEN YOUR EYES AND STOP MISSING!
ANOTHER KUNG-FU KICK...
YEAH, DEFINITELY HER TRUE COLORS ...
WOW...
ROAR
EVERYONE'S DOING GREAT.
IT LOOKS LIKE EVERYTHING'S STARTING TO GO WELL!
...
THANKS TO ONDA.
ROAR

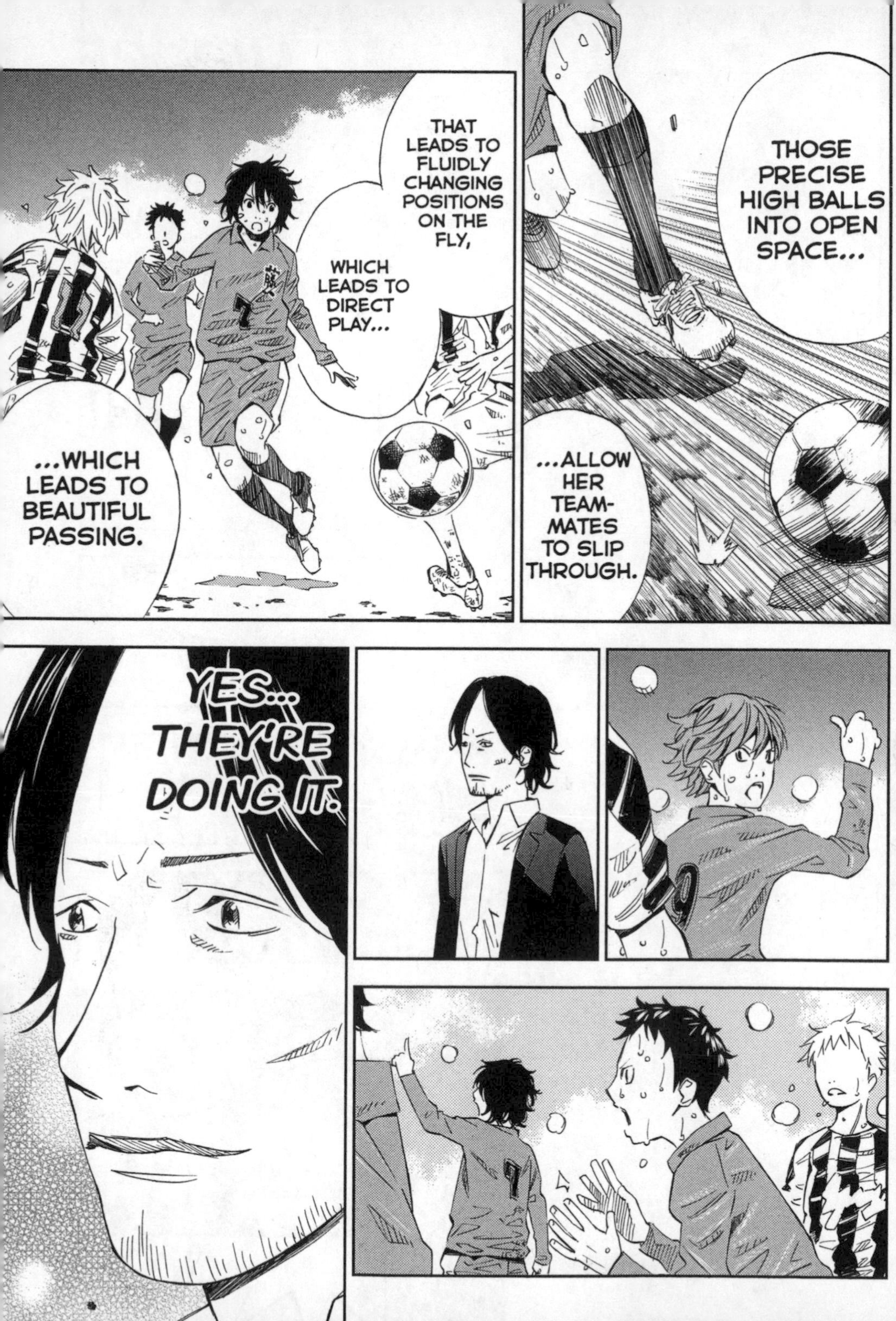
THOSE PRECISE HIGH BALLS INTO OPEN SPACE...
...ALLOW HER TEAM-MATES TO SLIP THROUGH.
THAT LEADS TO FLUIDLY CHANGING POSITIONS ON THE FLY,
WHICH LEADS TO DIRECT PLAY...
...WHICH LEADS TO BEAUTIFUL PASSING.
YES... THEY'RE DOING IT.

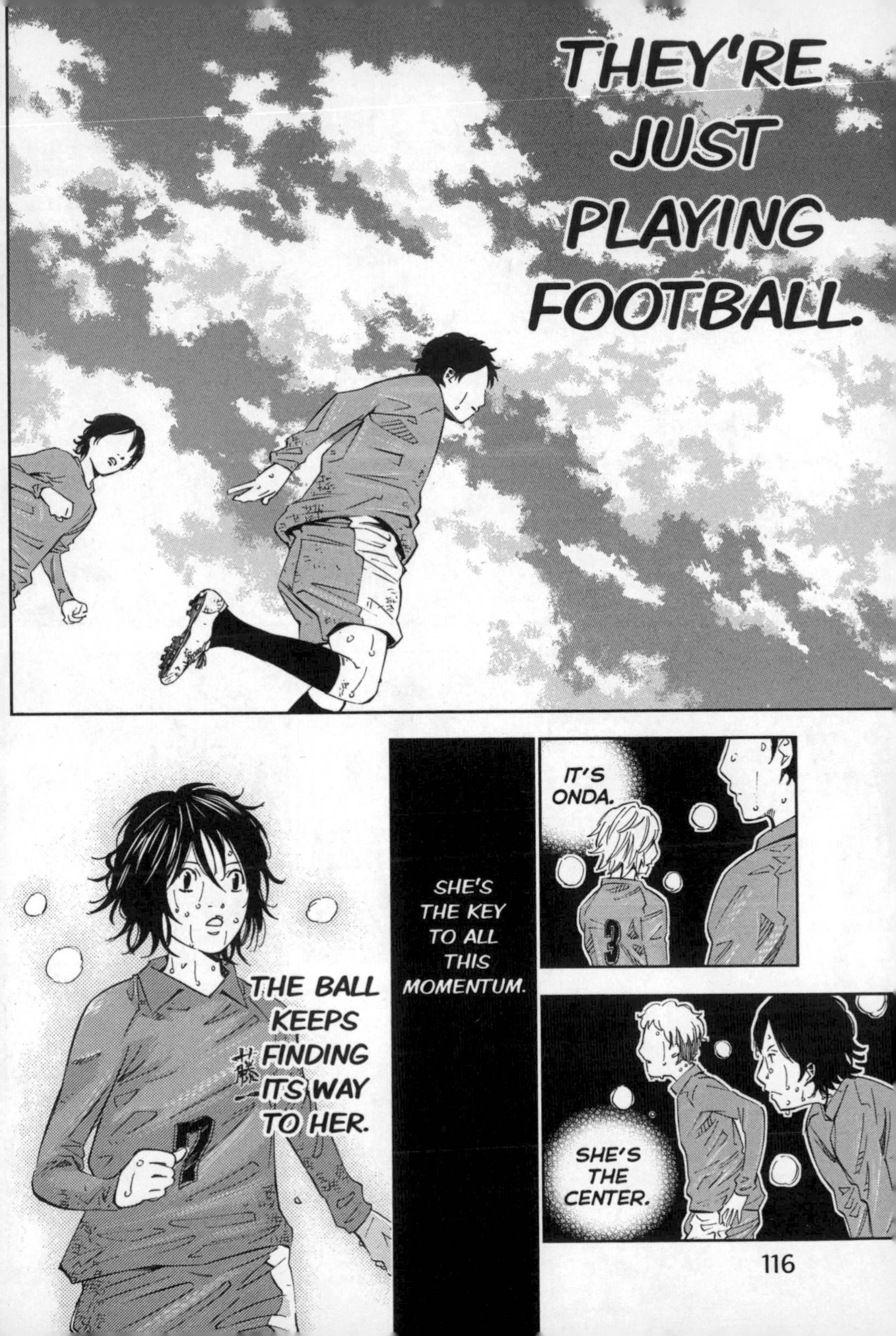
THEY'RE JUST PLAYING FOOTBALL.
IT'S ONDA.
SHE'S THE CENTER.
SHE'S THE KEY TO ALL THIS MOMENTUM.
THE BALL KEEPS FINDING ITS WAY TO HER.

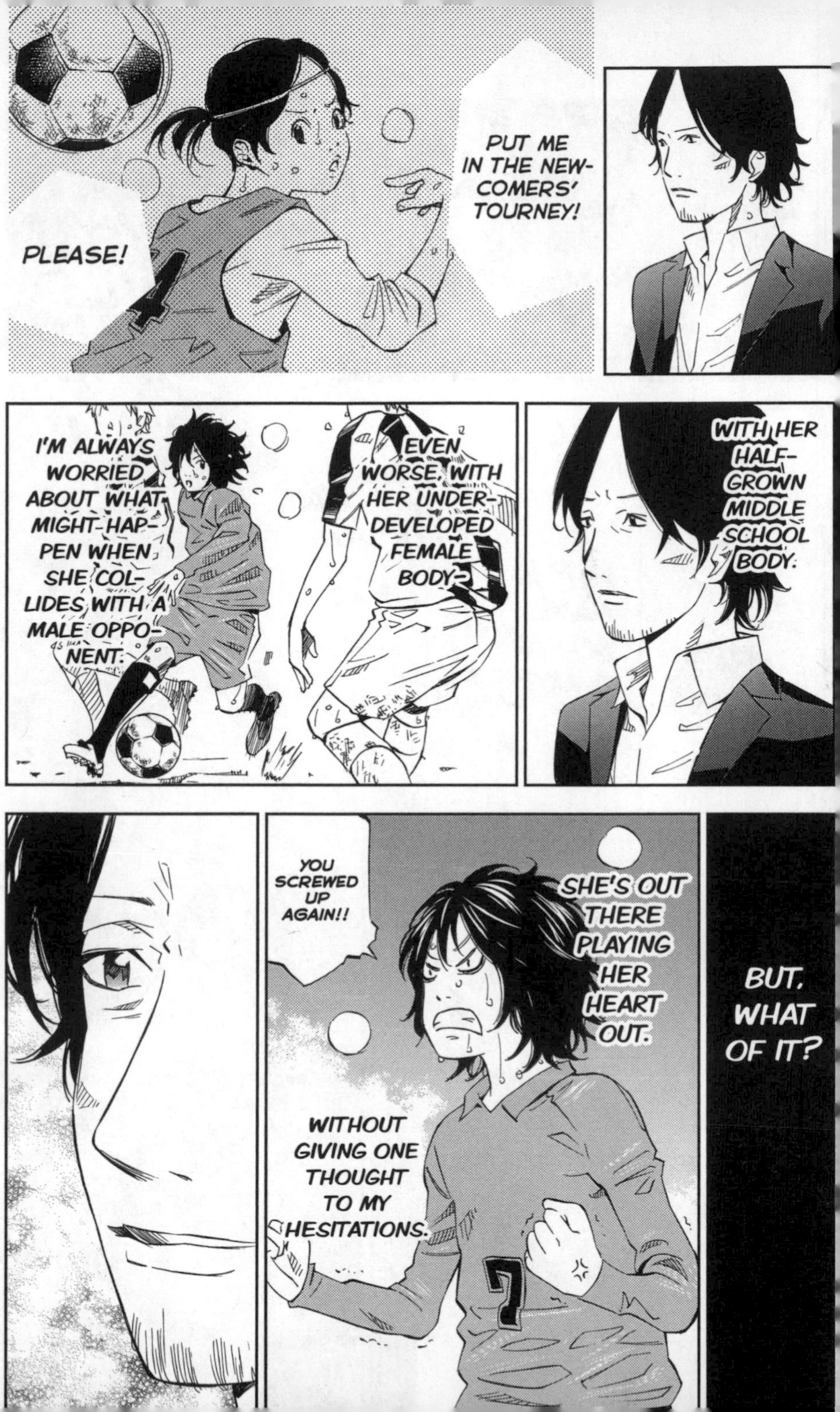
PUT ME IN THE NEW-COMERS' TOURNEY!
PLEASE!
WITH HER HALF-GROWN MIDDLE SCHOOL BODY.
EVEN WORSE, WITH HER UNDER-DEVELOPED FEMALE BODY,
I'M ALWAYS WORRIED ABOUT WHAT MIGHT HAP-PEN WHEN SHE COL-LIDES WITH A MALE OPPO-NENT.
BUT, WHAT OF IT?
SHE'S OUT THERE PLAYING HER HEART OUT.
YOU SCREWED UP AGAIN!!
WITHOUT GIVING ONE THOUGHT TO MY HESITATIONS.

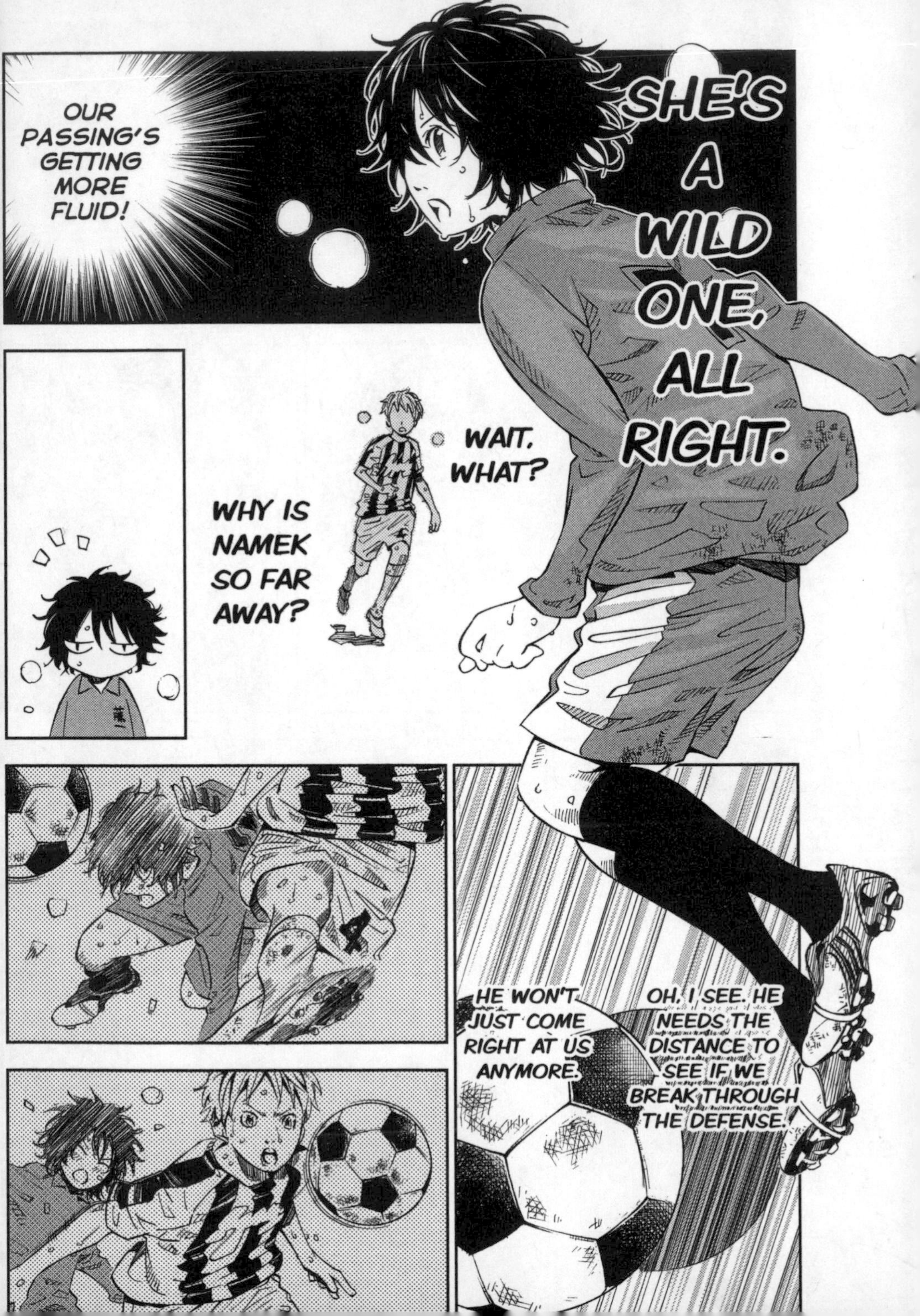
SHE'S A WILD ONE, ALL RIGHT.
OUR PASSING'S GETTING MORE FLUID!
WAIT, WHAT?
WHY IS NAMEK SO FAR AWAY?
OH, I SEE. HE NEEDS THE DISTANCE TO SEE IF WE BREAK THROUGH THE DEFENSE.
HE WON'T JUST COME RIGHT AT US ANYMORE.

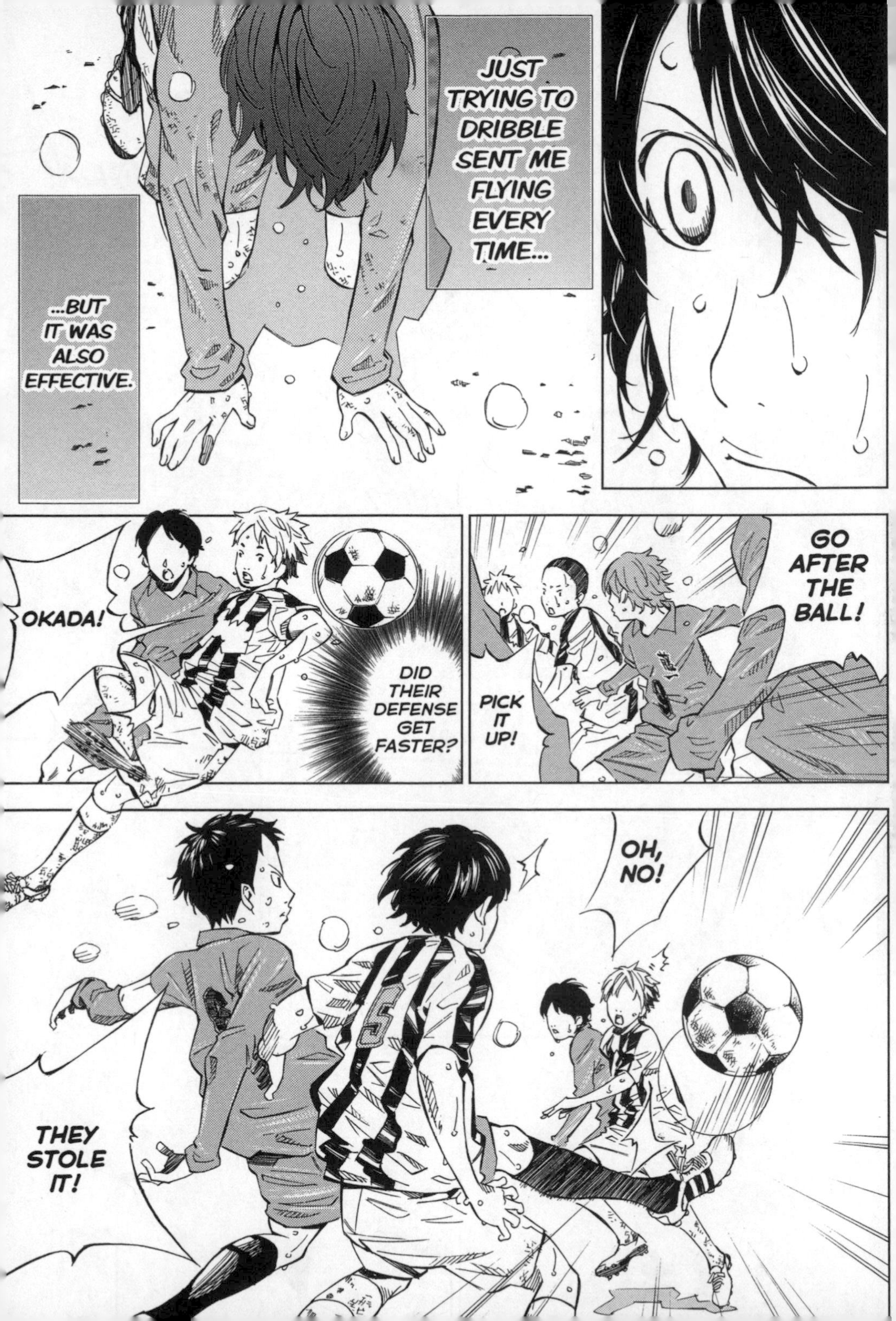
JUST TRYING TO DRIBBLE SENT ME FLYING EVERY TIME...
...BUT IT WAS ALSO EFFECTIVE.
GO AFTER THE BALL!
PICK IT UP!
DID THEIR DEFENSE GET FASTER?
OKADA!
OH, NO!
THEY STOLE IT!

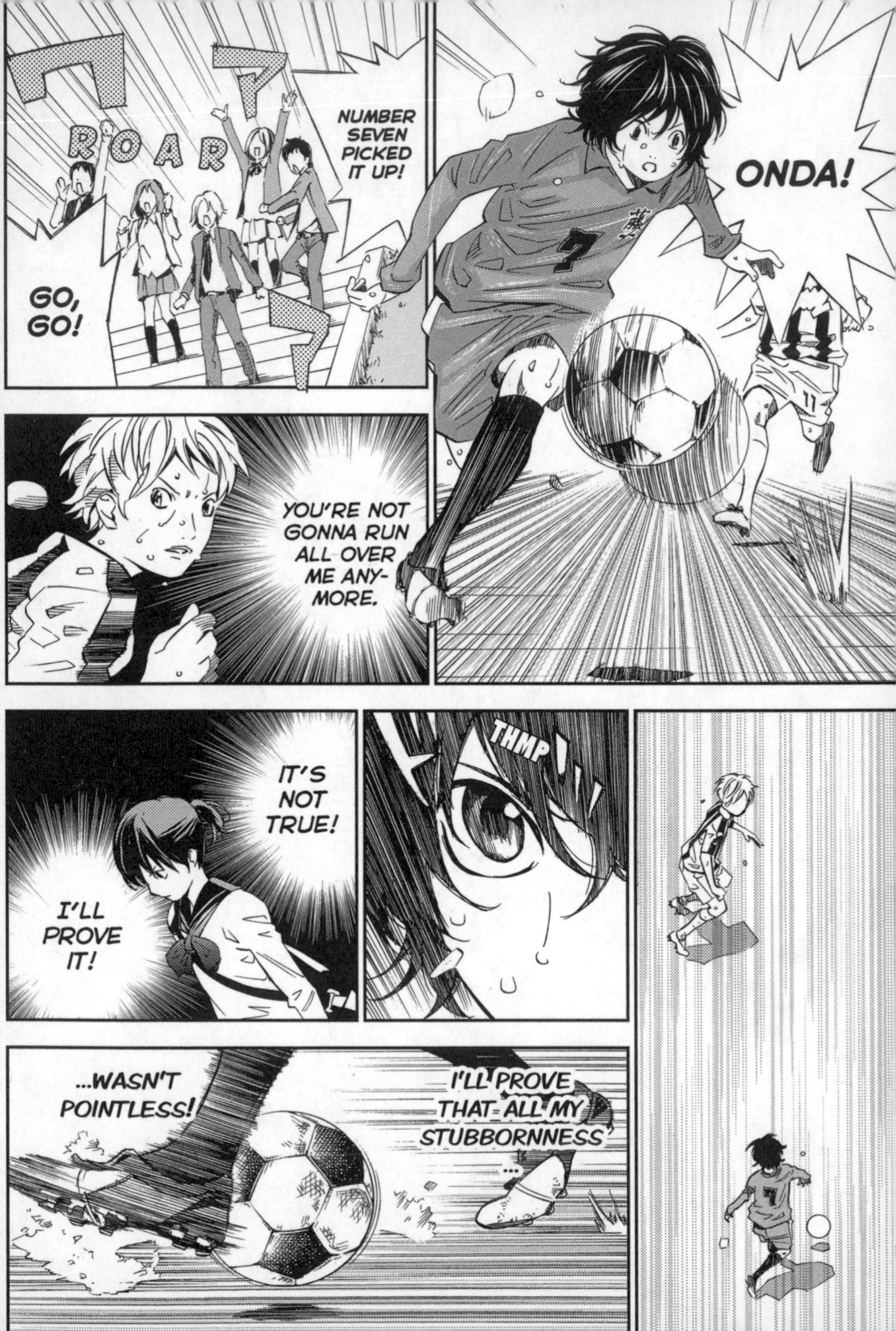
ONDA!
NUMBER SEVEN PICKED IT UP!
ROAR
GO, GO!
YOU'RE NOT GONNA RUN ALL OVER ME ANY-MORE.
THMP
IT'S NOT TRUE!
I'LL PROVE IT!
I'LL PROVE THAT ALL MY STUBBORNNESS
...
...WASN'T POINTLESS!

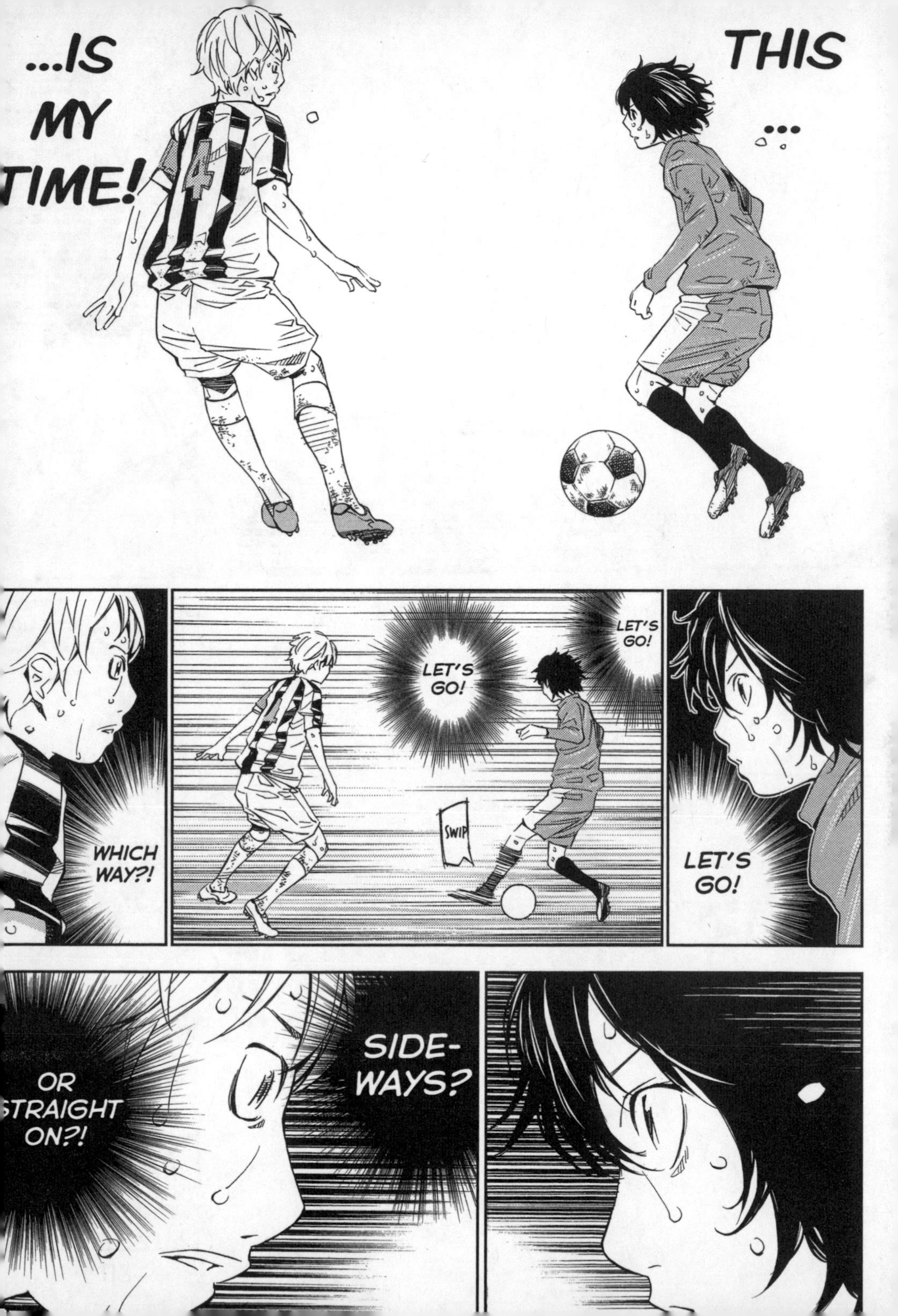

THIS
...
...IS MY TIME!
LET'S GO!
LET'S GO!
LET'S GO!
SWIP
WHICH WAY?!
SIDE-WAYS?
OR STRAIGHT ON?!

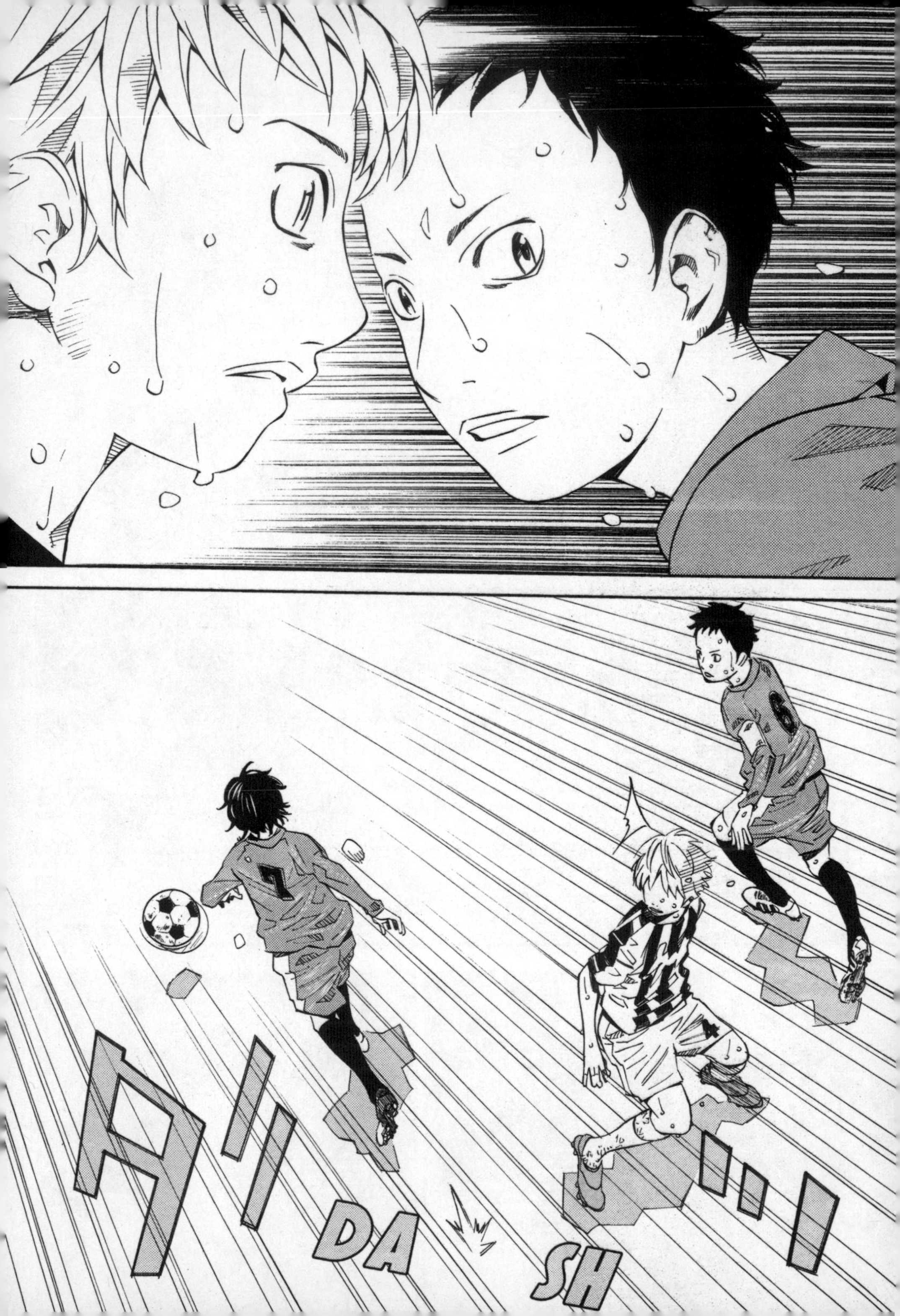
DASH

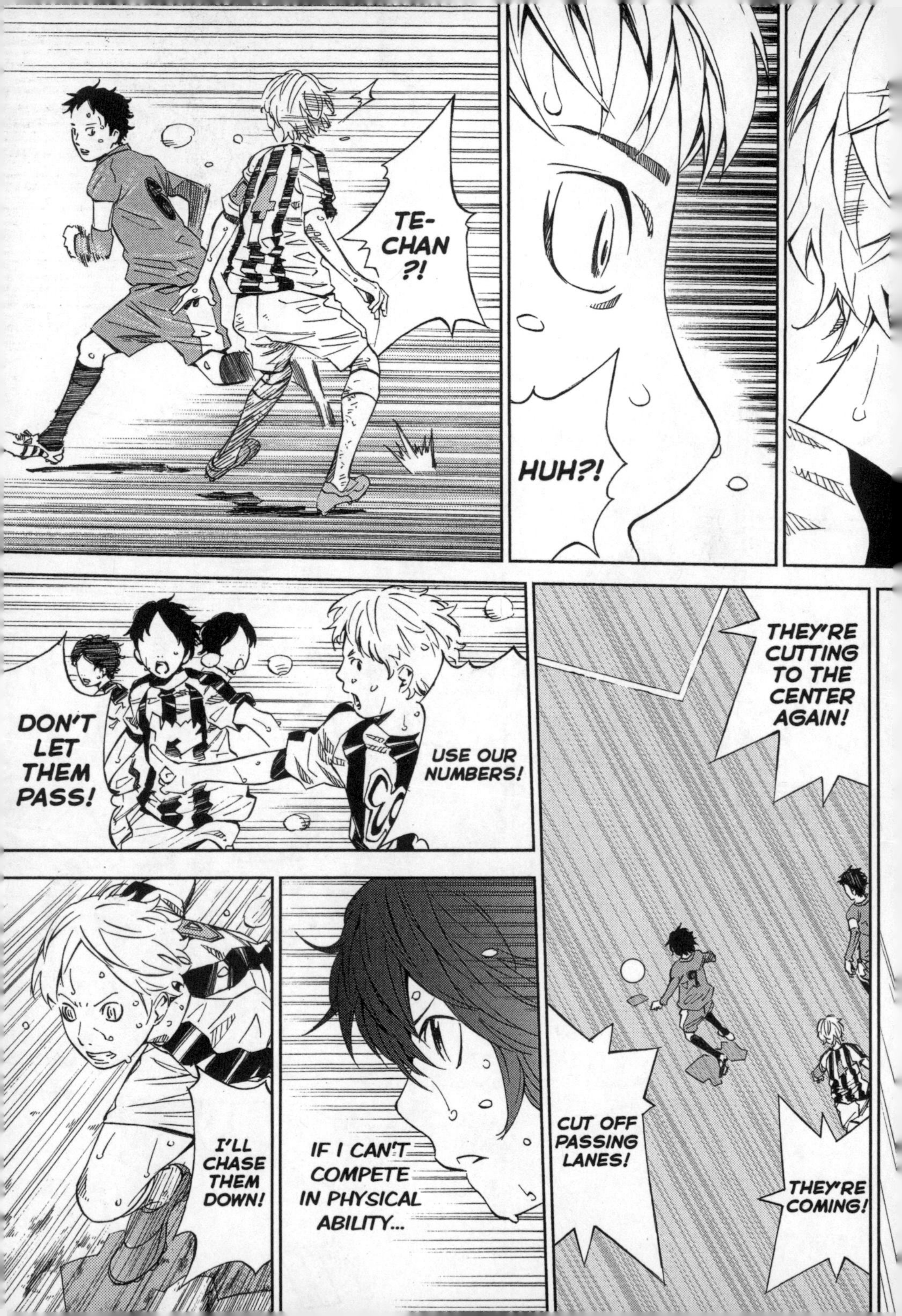
HUH?!
TE-CHAN?!
THEY'RE CUTTING TO THE CENTER AGAIN!
CUT OFF PASSING LANES!
THEY'RE COMING!
USE OUR NUMBERS!
DON'T LET THEM PASS!
IF I CAN'T COMPETE IN PHYSICAL ABILITY...
I'LL CHASE THEM DOWN!

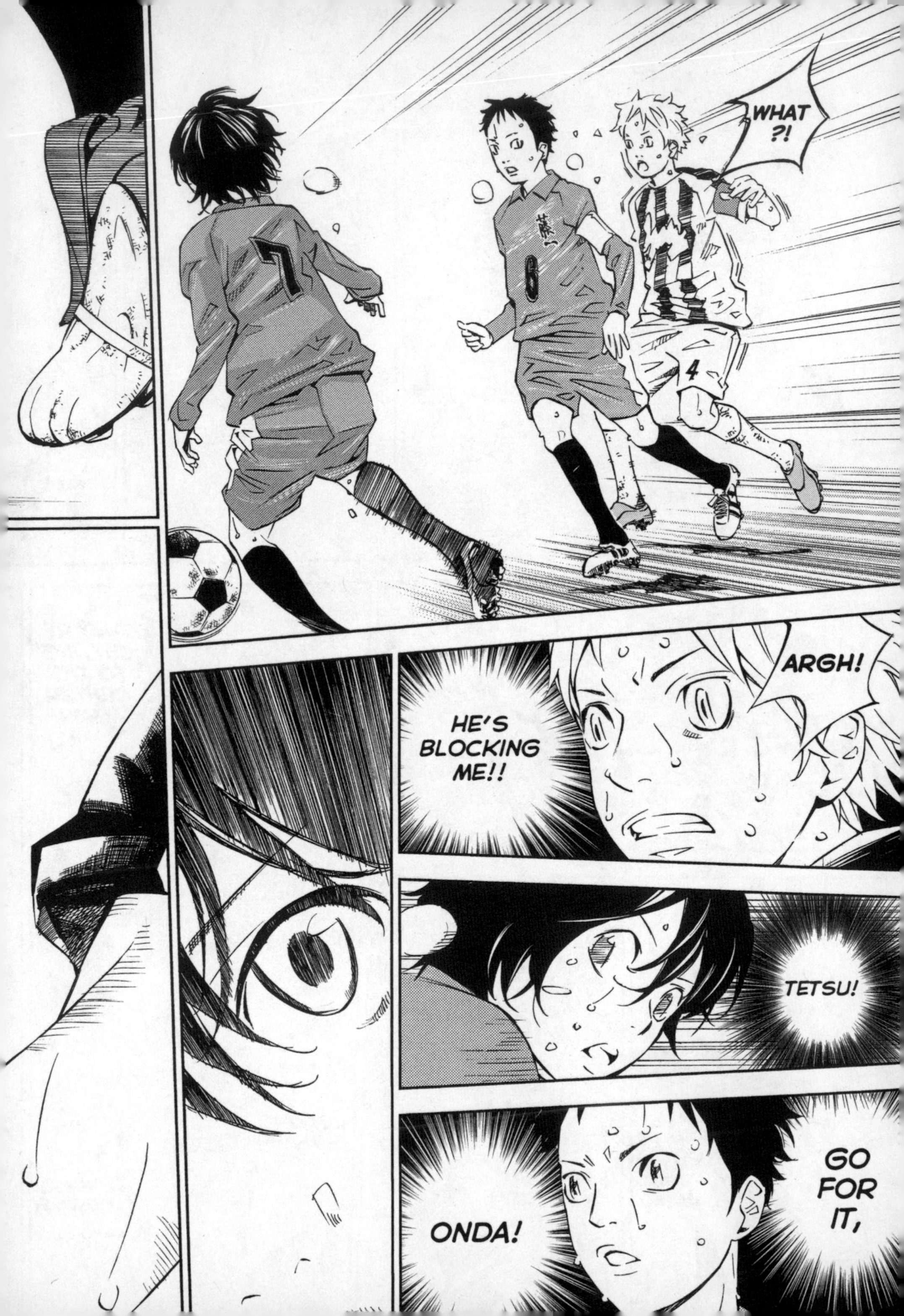
WHAT ?!
ARGH!
HE'S BLOCKING ME!!
TETSU!
GO FOR IT,
ONDA!

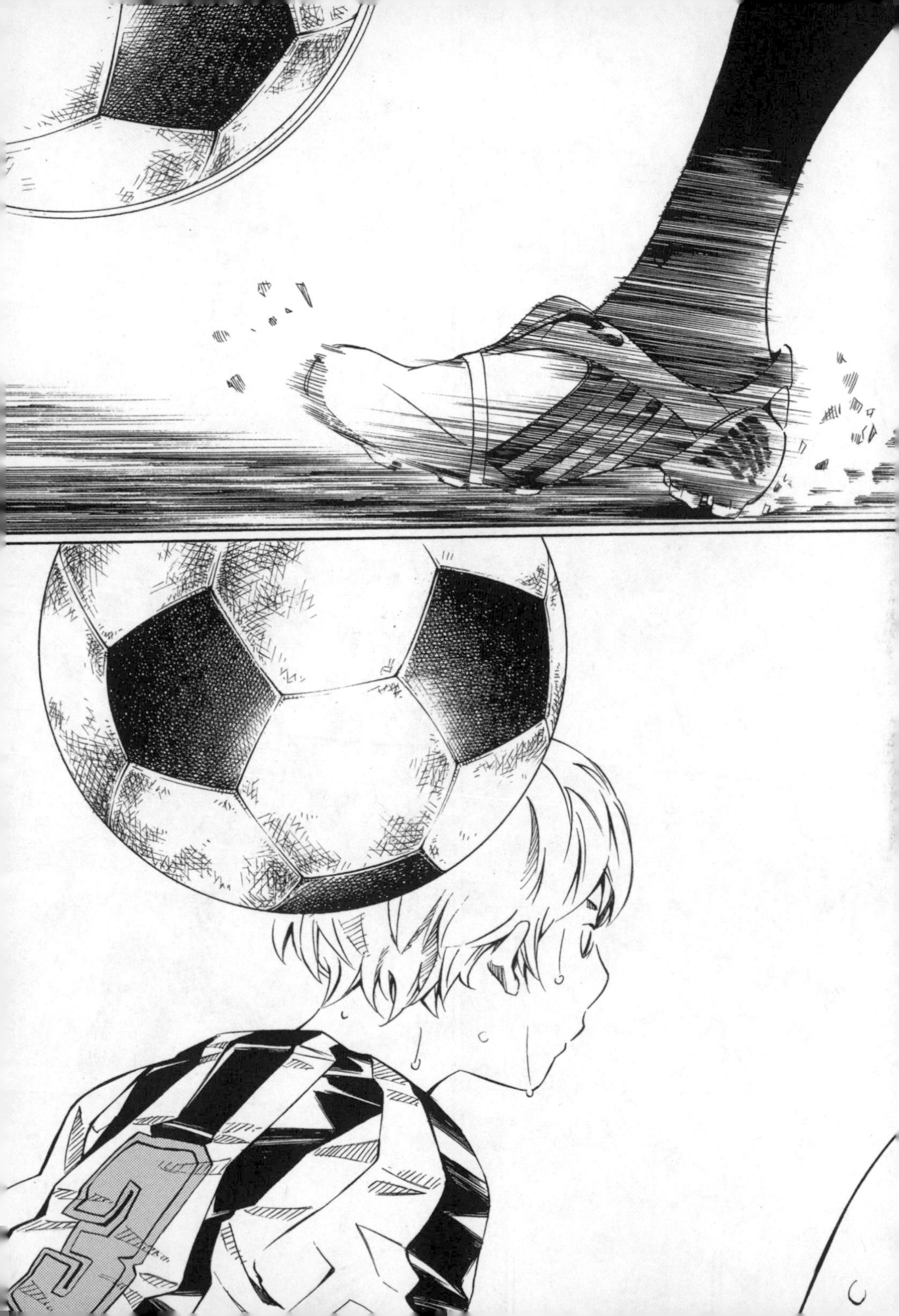

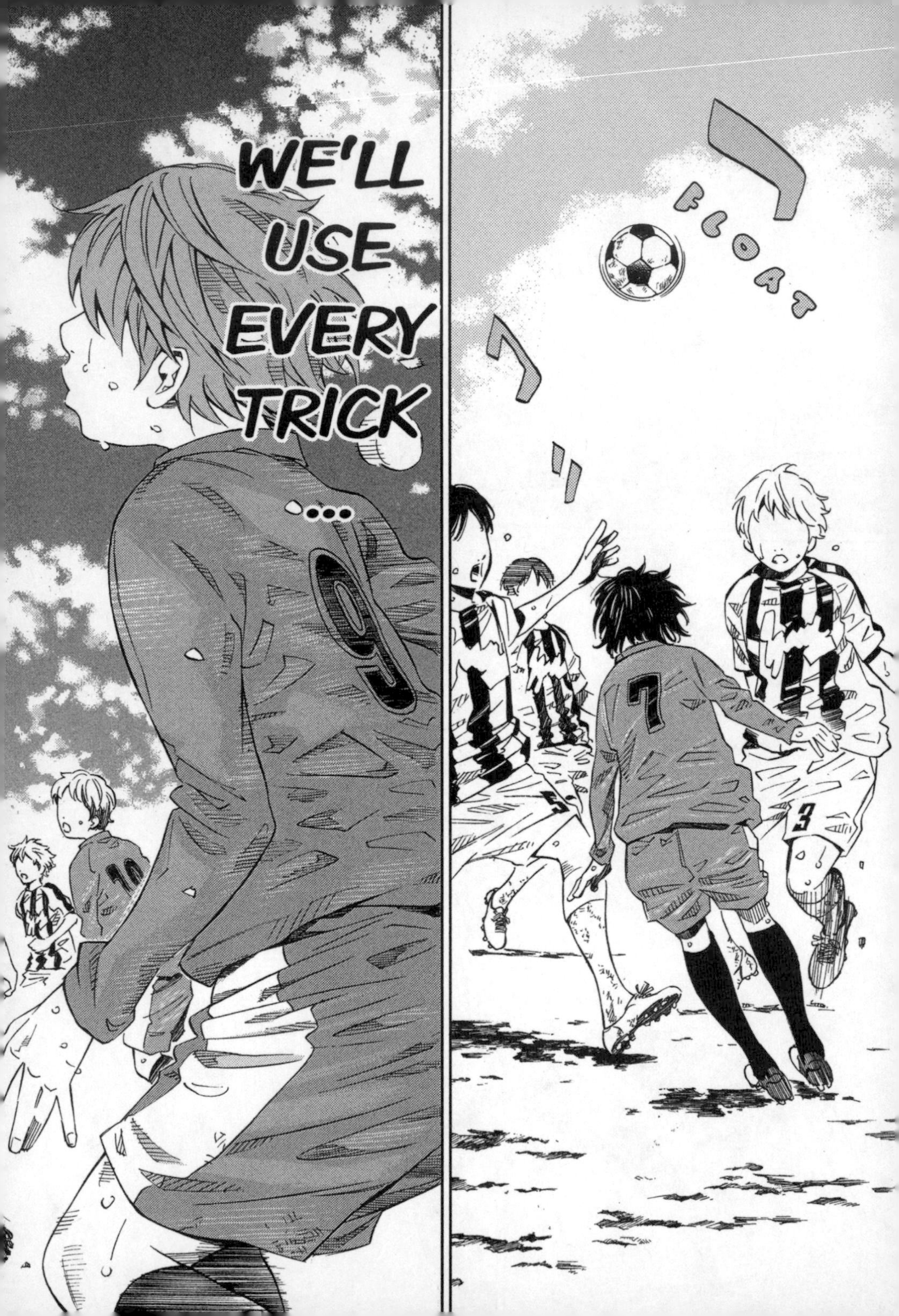
FLOAT
WE'LL USE EVERY TRICK
...

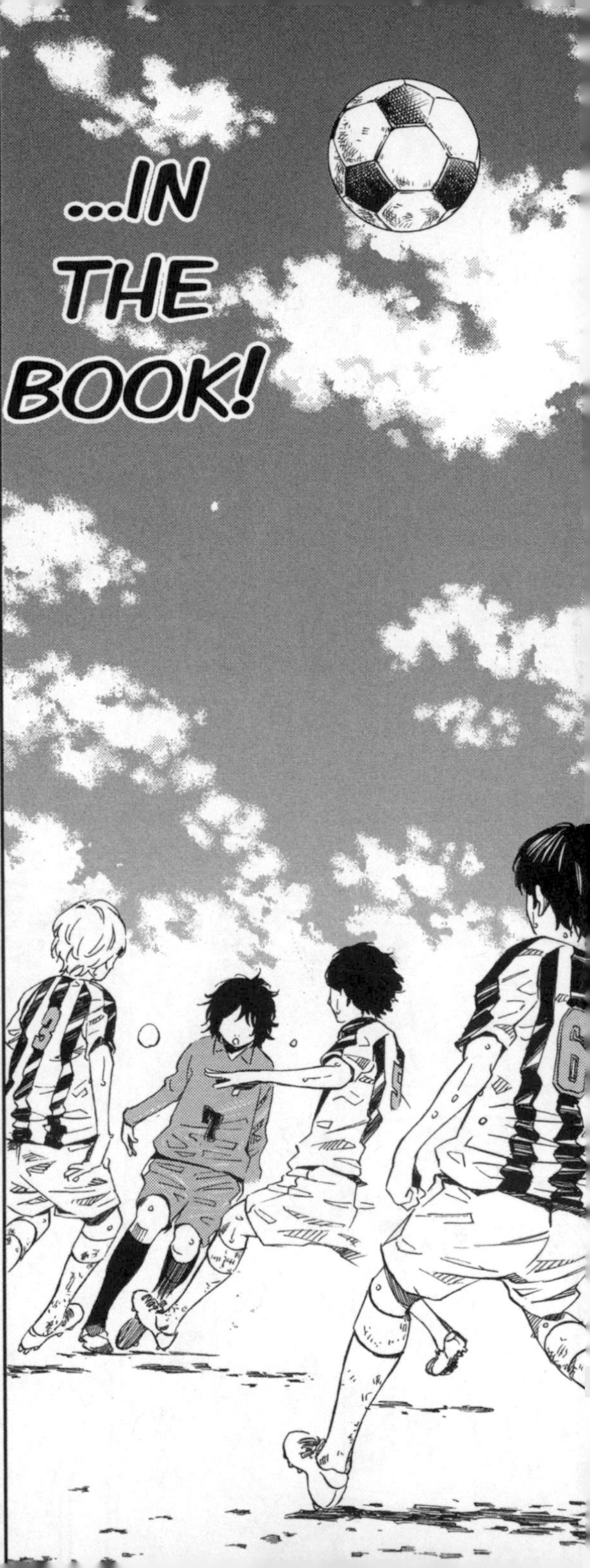
...IN THE BOOK!
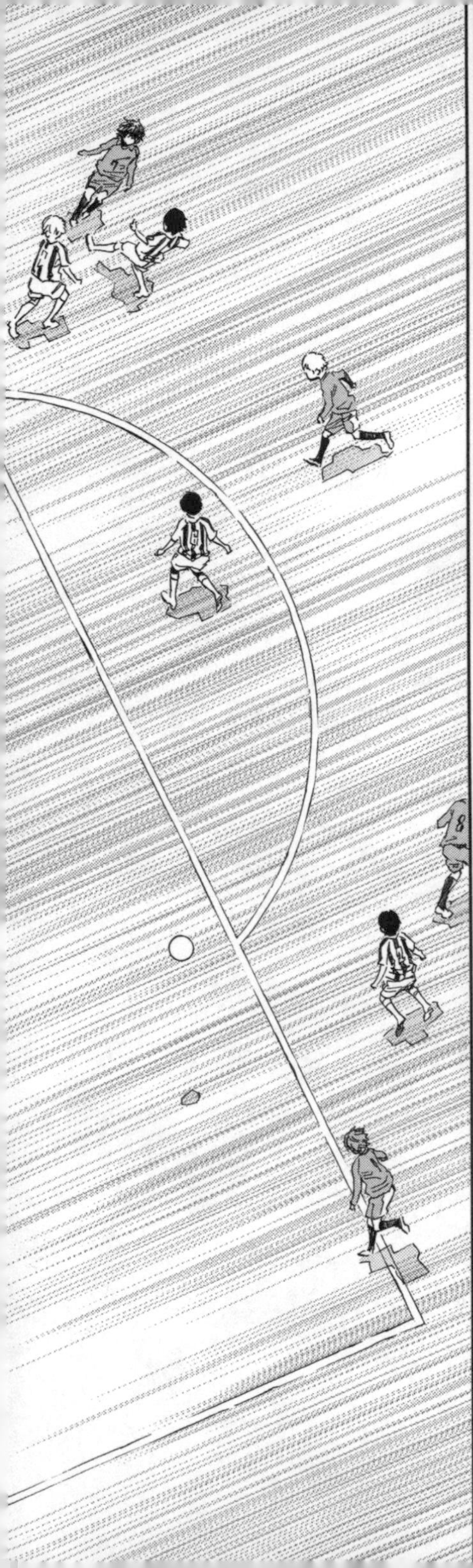

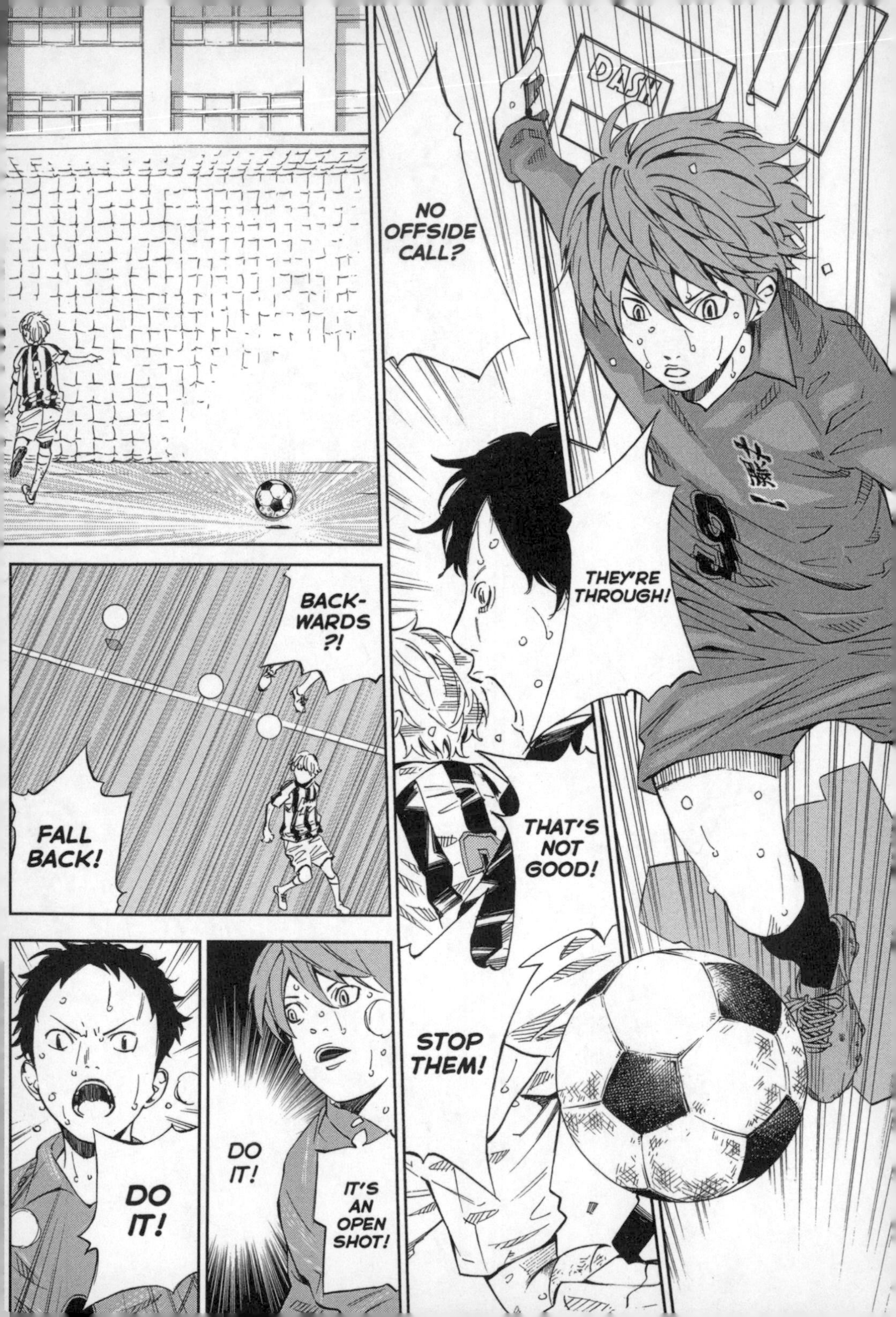

NO OFFSIDE CALL?
THEY'RE THROUGH!
THAT'S NOT GOOD!
STOP THEM!
BACK-WARDS ?!
FALL BACK!
DO IT!
IT'S AN OPEN SHOT!
DO IT!

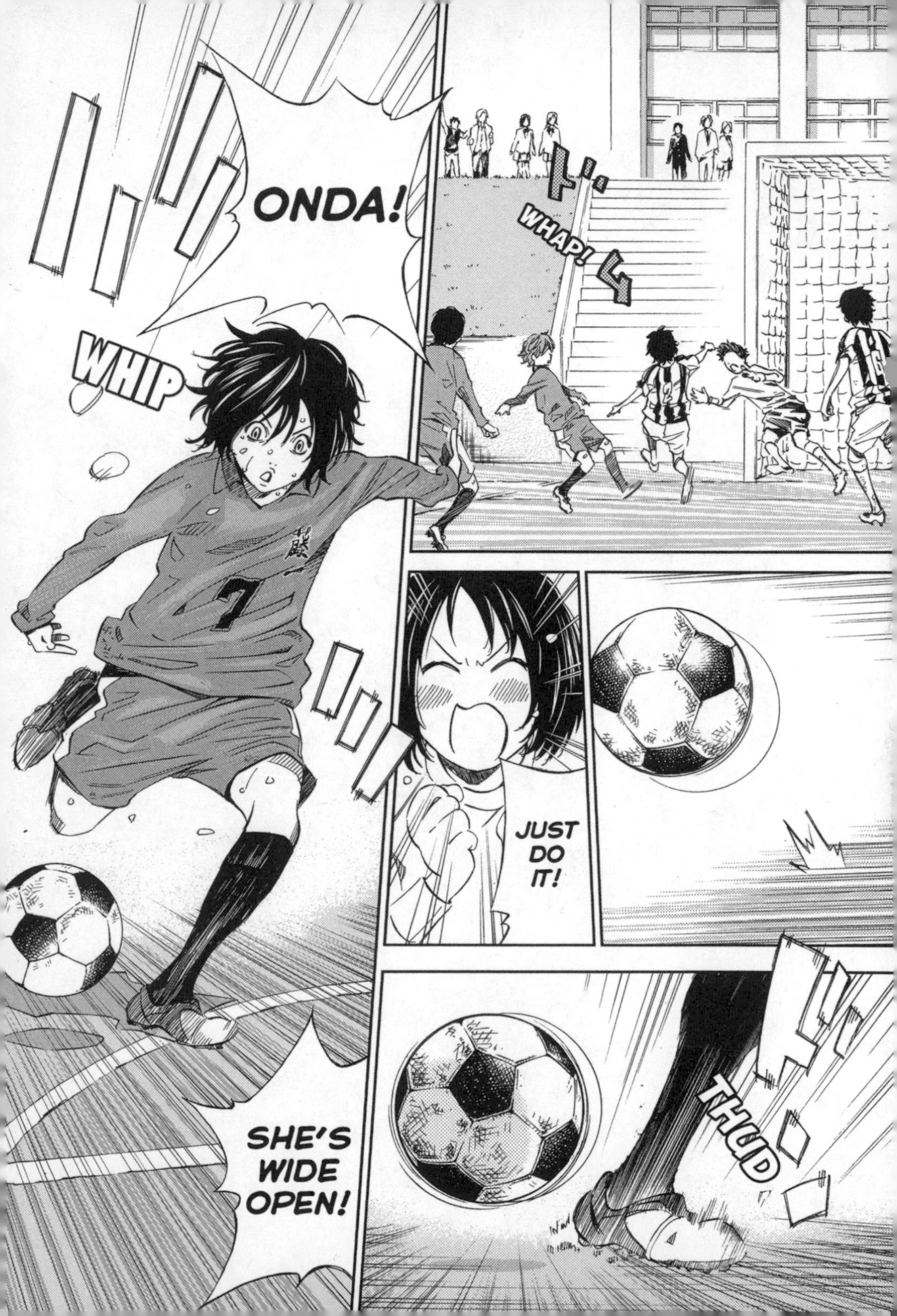
WHAP!
JUST DO IT!
THUD
ONDA!
WHIP
SHE'S WIDE OPEN!

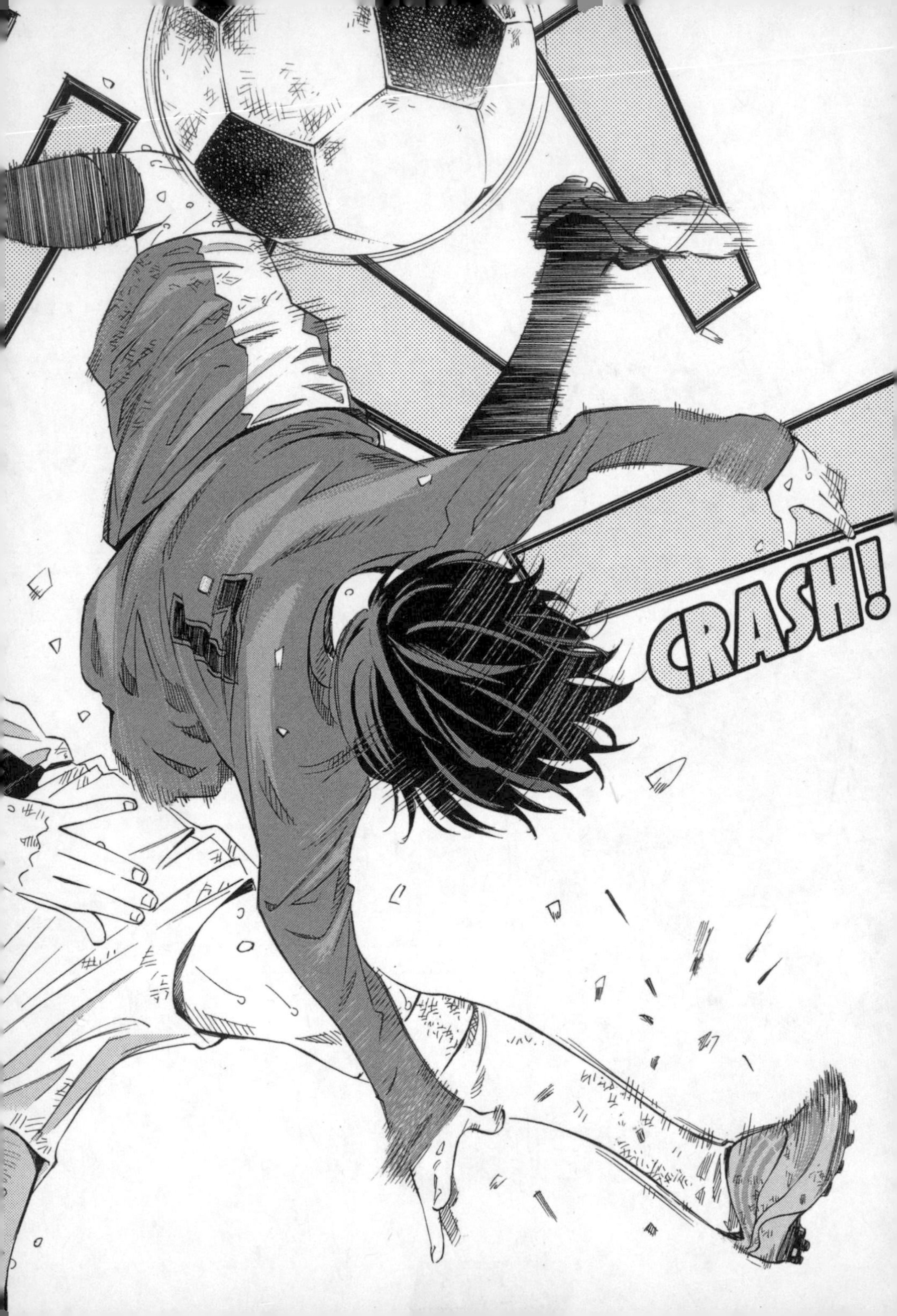
CRASH!

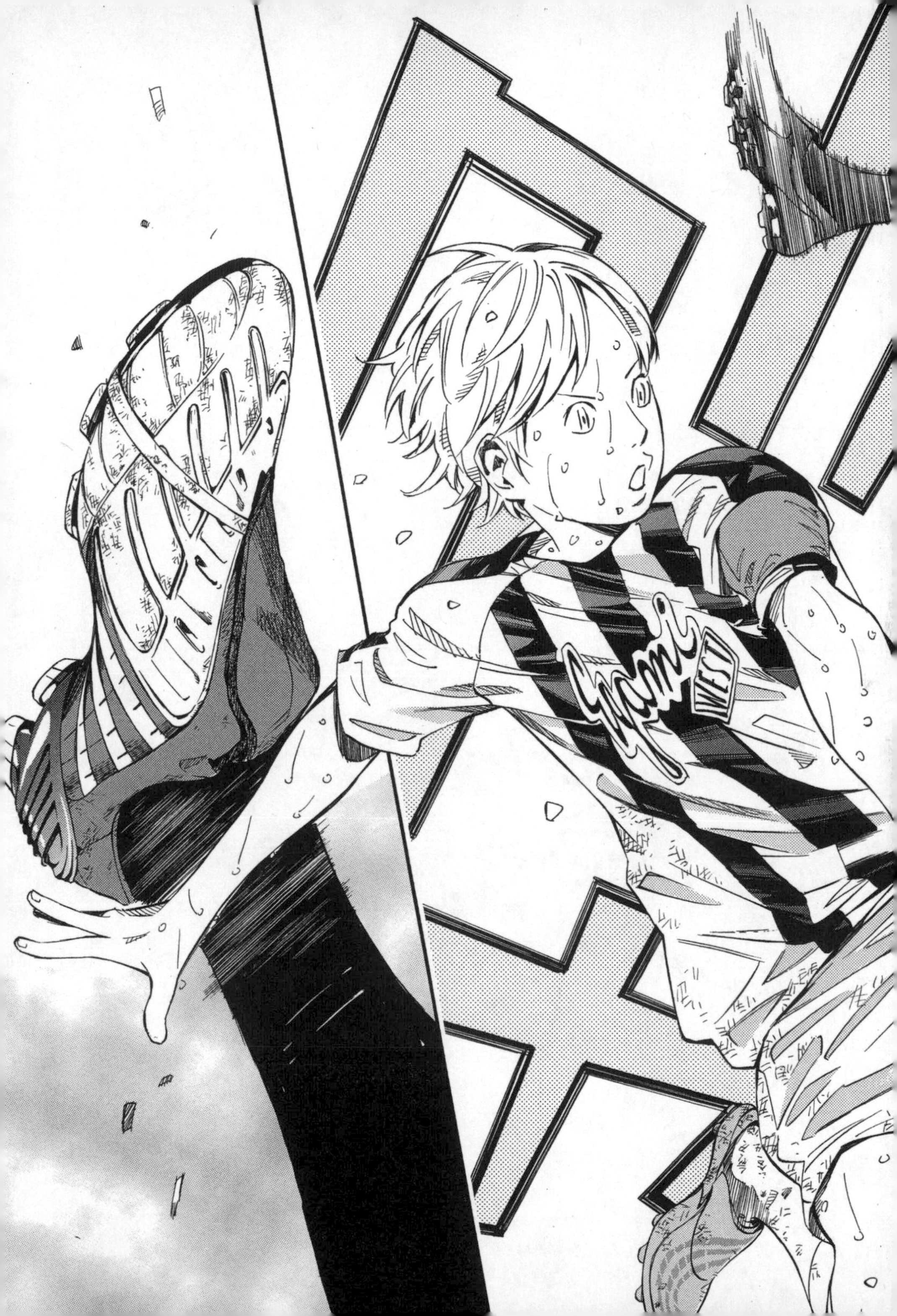
WEST

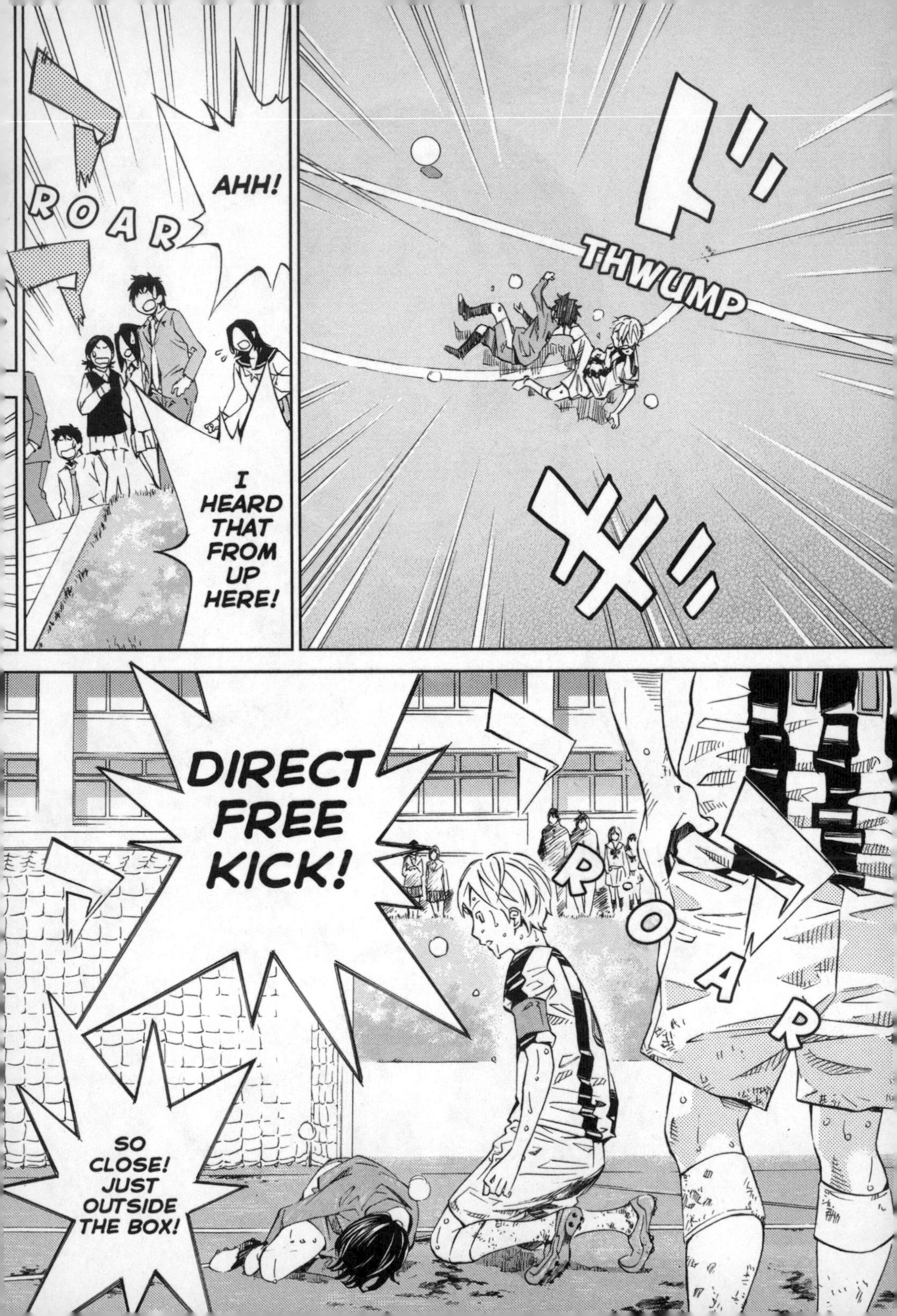
THWUMP
ROAR
AHH!
I HEARD THAT FROM UP HERE!
ROAR
DIRECT FREE KICK!
SO CLOSE! JUST OUTSIDE THE BOX!

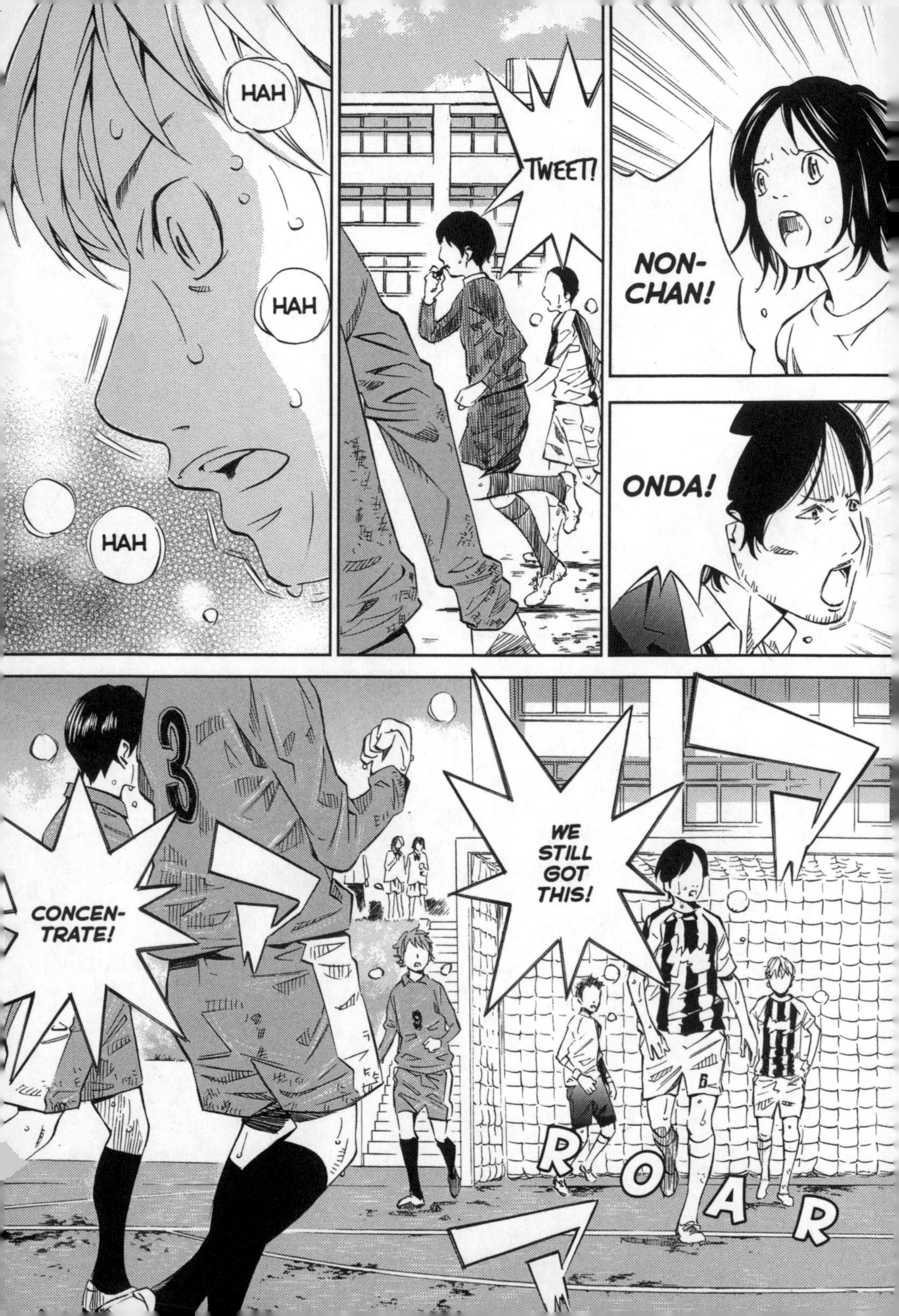
NON-CHAN!
ONDA!
TWEET!
HAH
HAH
HAH
WE STILL GOT THIS!
CONCENTRATE!
ROAR

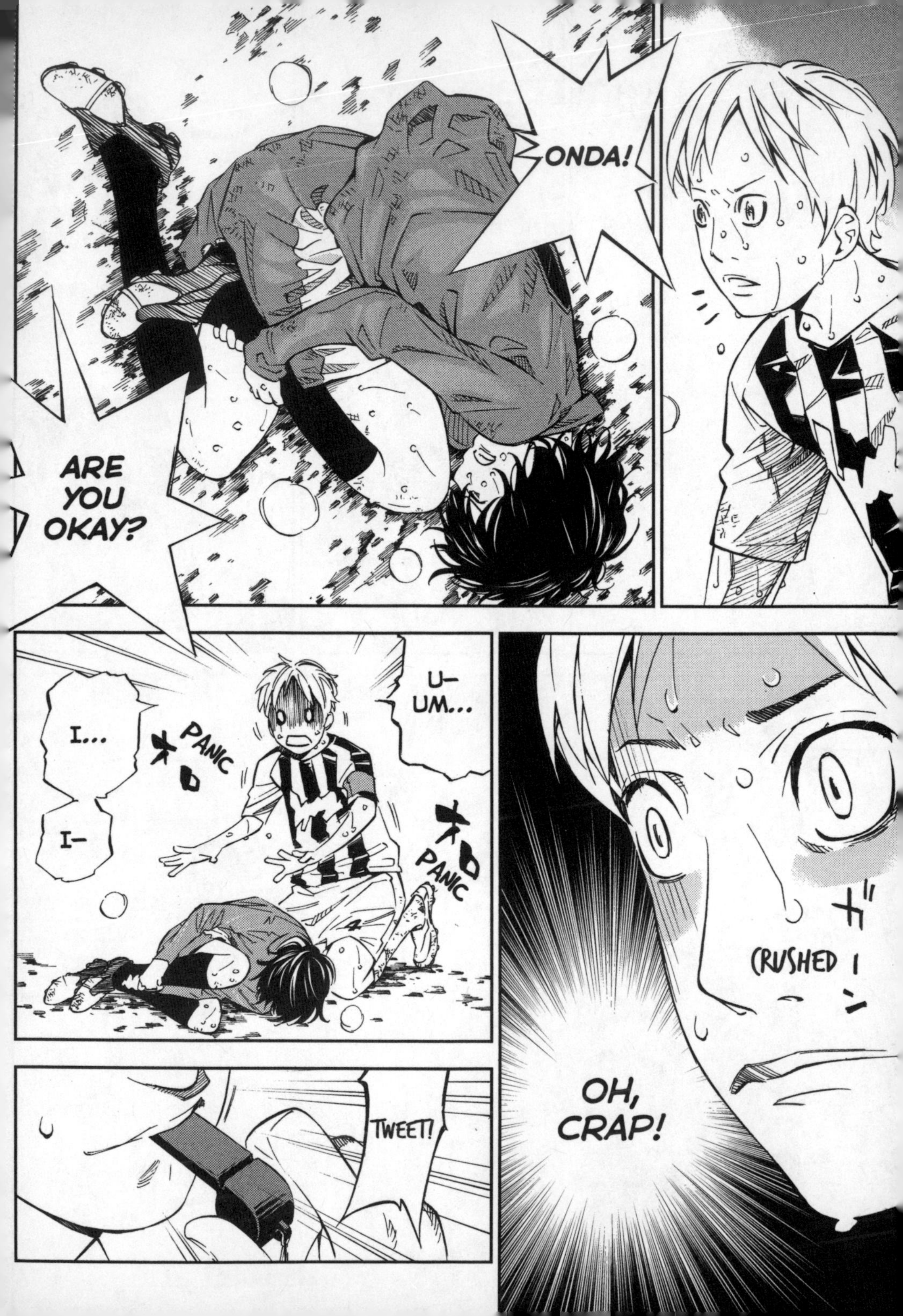
ONDA!
ARE YOU OKAY?
CRUSHED
OH, CRAP!
U-UM...
PANIC
PANIC
I...
I-
TWEET!

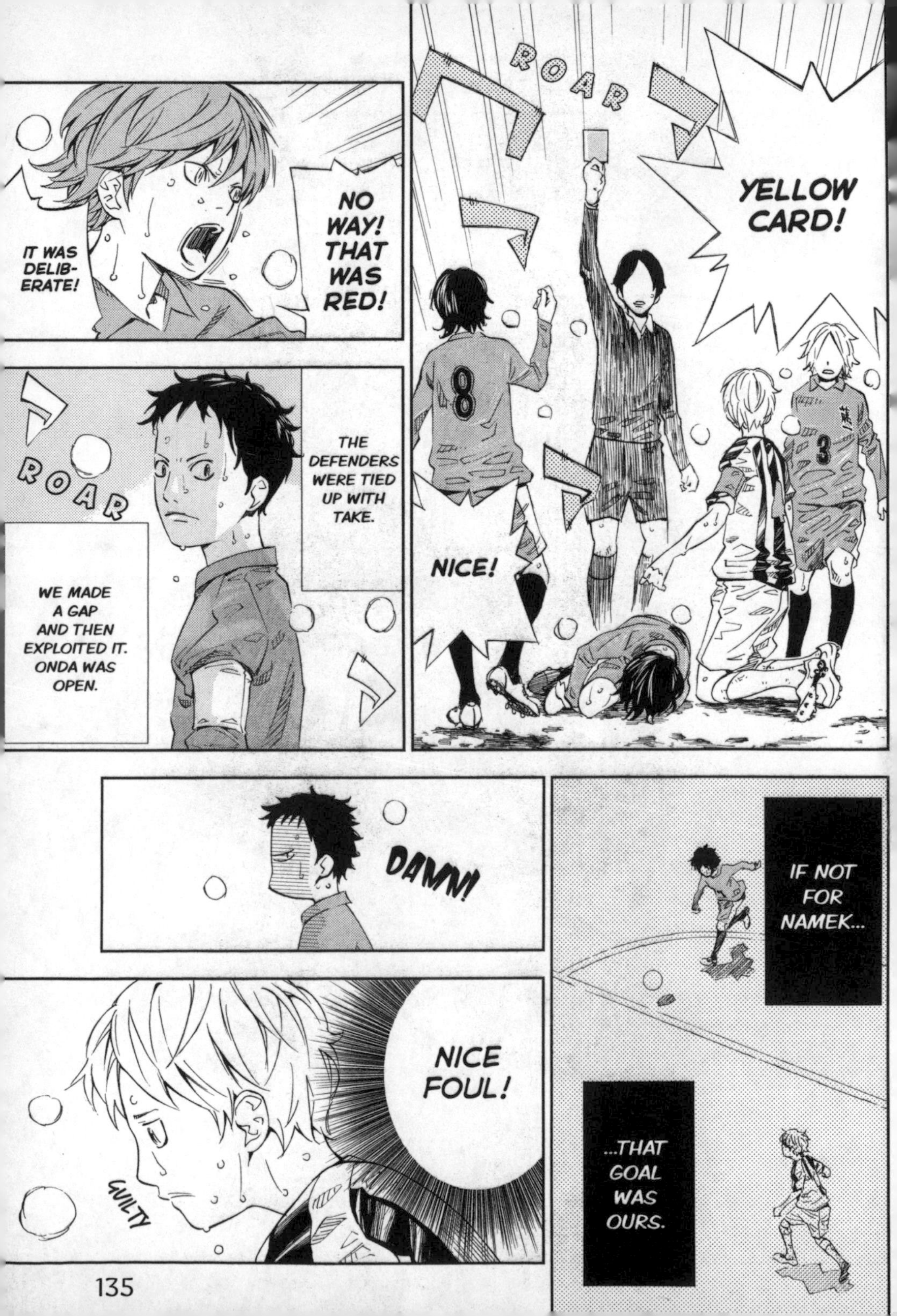
ROAR
YELLOW CARD!
NICE!
NO WAY! THAT WAS RED!
IT WAS DELIBERATE!
ROAR
THE DEFENDERS WERE TIED UP WITH TAKE.
WE MADE A GAP AND THEN EXPLOITED IT. ONDA WAS OPEN.
IF NOT FOR NAMEK...
...THAT GOAL WAS OURS.
DAMN!
NICE FOUL!
GUILTY

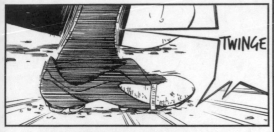

TWINGE

NAMEK, THAT LOSER!

YOU OKAY, ONDA?

TRYIN' TO UPSTAGE ME...

...URK!

WHIP

REF

I-I-I-I'M FINE!

ARE YOU ALL RIGHT?

ROAR

THEY HAVE A FREE KICK!

NOW'S THEIR CHANCE!

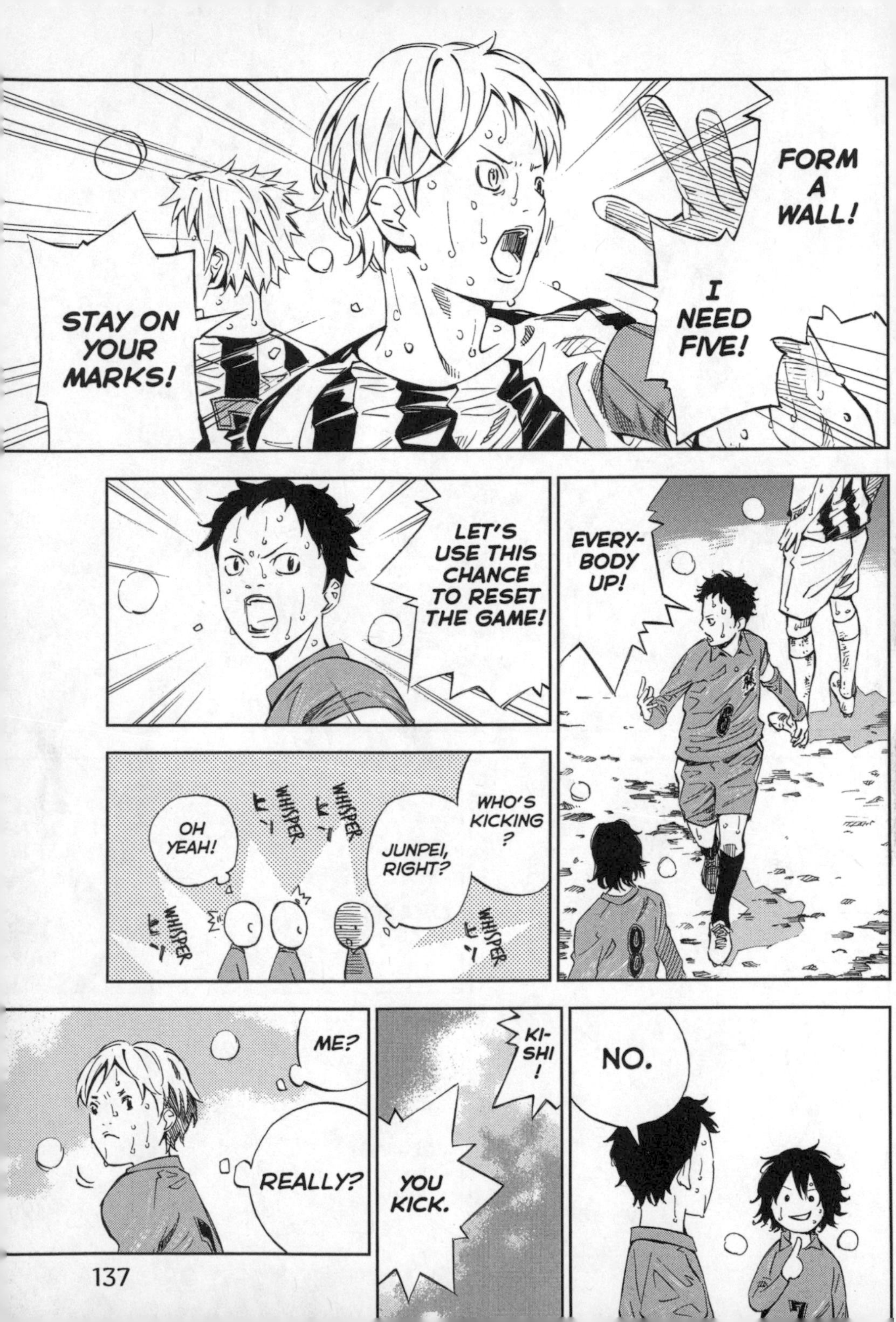
FORM A WALL!
I NEED FIVE!
STAY ON YOUR MARKS!
EVERY-BODY UP!
LET'S USE THIS CHANCE TO RESET THE GAME!
WHO'S KICKING?
WHISPER
JUNPEI, RIGHT?
WHISPER
WHISPER
OH YEAH!
WHISPER
NO.
KI-SHI!
YOU KICK.
ME?
REALLY?

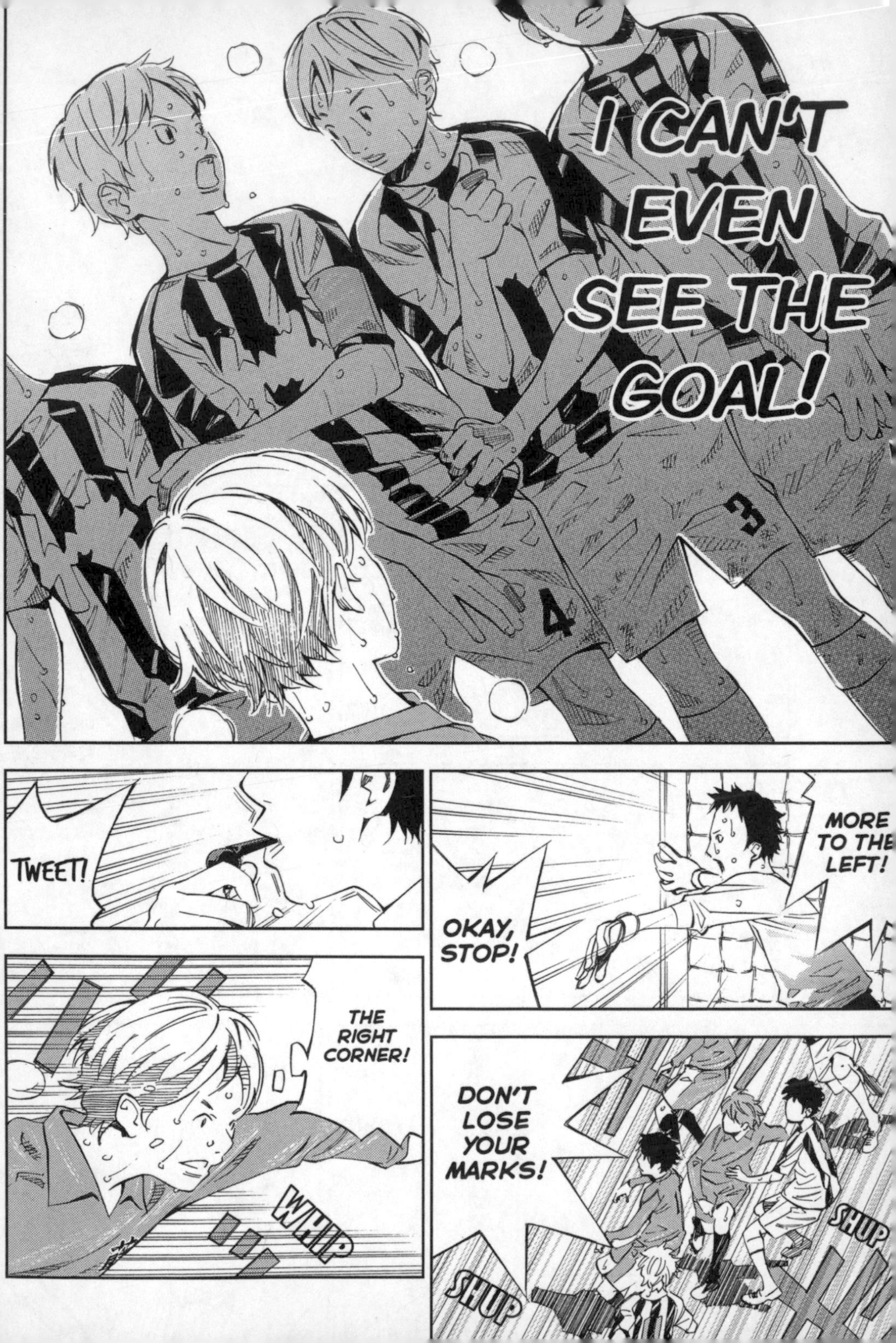
I CAN'T EVEN SEE THE GOAL!
MORE TO THE LEFT!
OKAY, STOP!
TWEET!
DON'T LOSE YOUR MARKS!
SHUP
SHUP
THE RIGHT CORNER!
WHIP

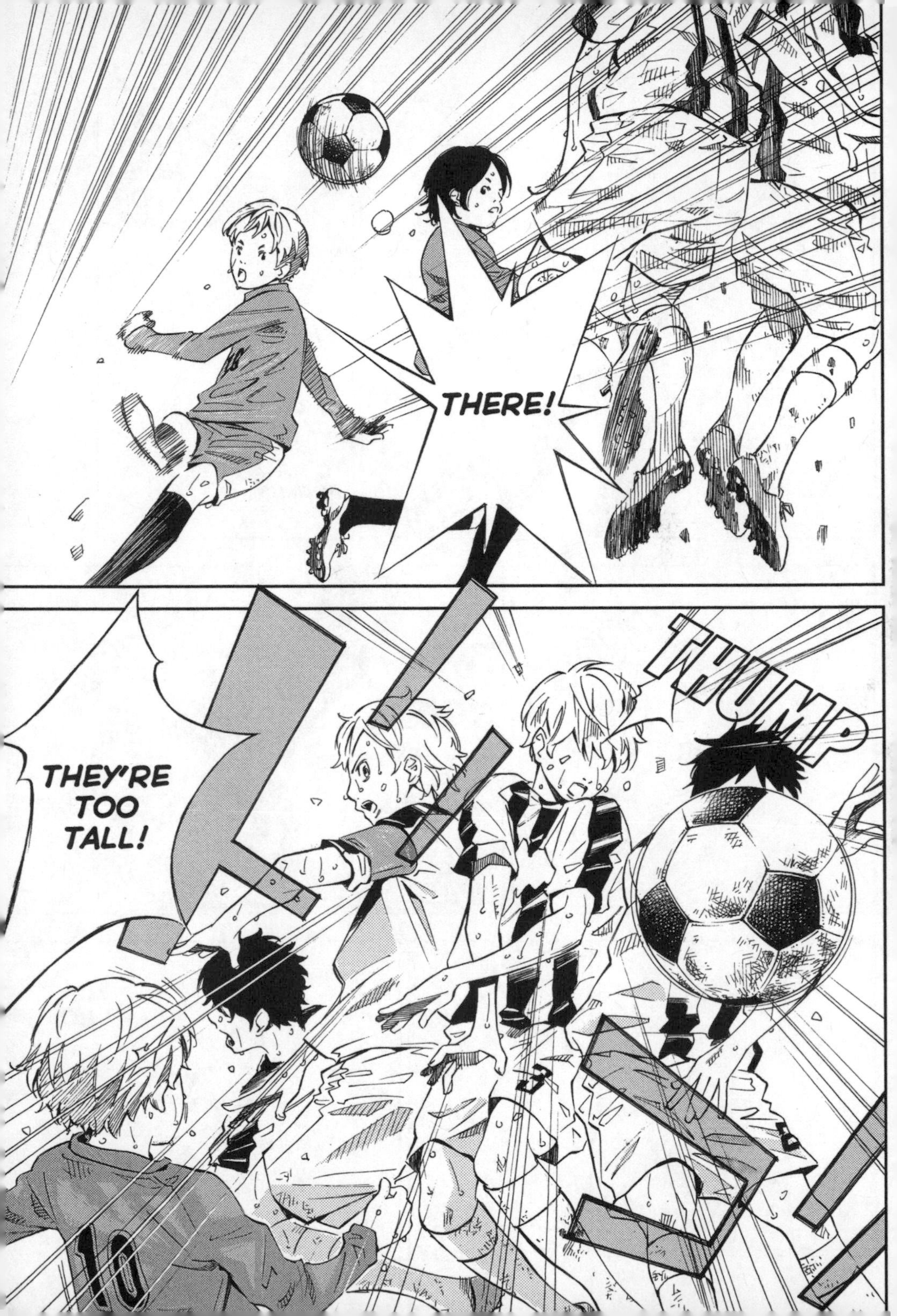
THERE!
THUMP
THEY'RE TOO TALL!

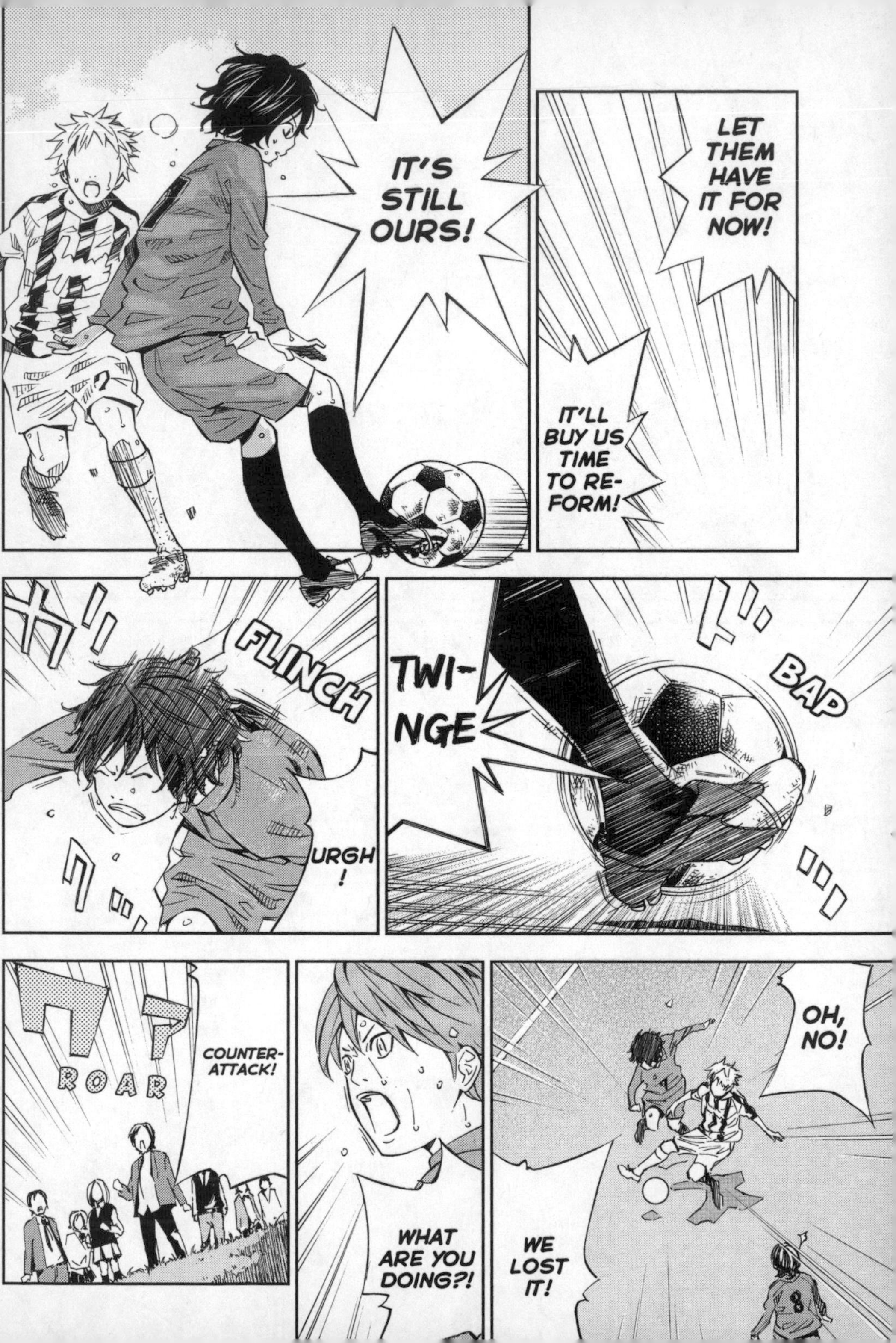

LET THEM HAVE IT FOR NOW!
IT'LL BUY US TIME TO RE-FORM!
IT'S STILL OURS!
BAP
TWI-NGE
FLINCH
URGH!
OH, NO!
WE LOST IT!
WHAT ARE YOU DOING?!
ROAR
COUNTER-ATTACK!

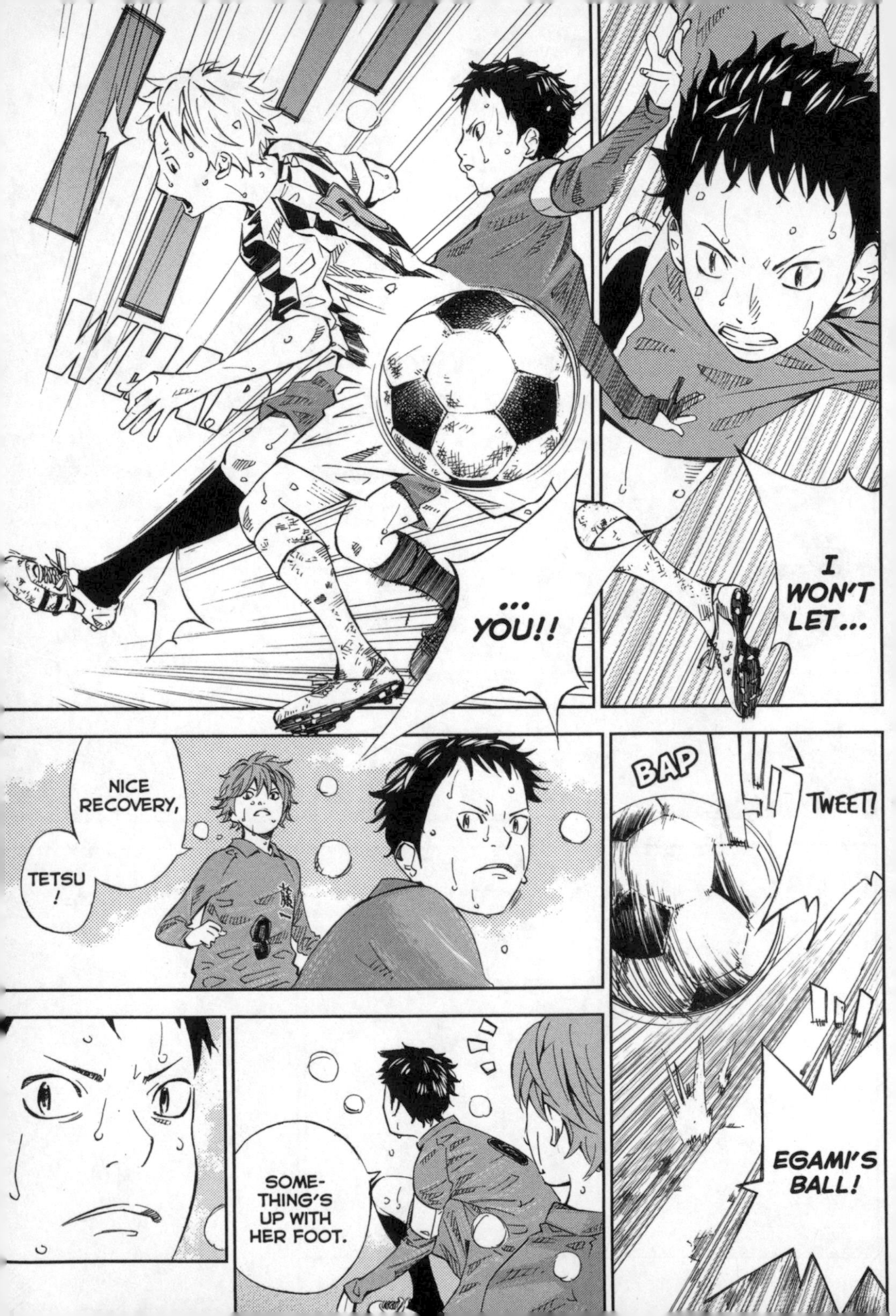
I WON'T LET...
...YOU!!
WHA...
BAP
TWEET!
EGAMI'S BALL!
NICE RECOVERY,
TETSU!
SOMETHING'S UP WITH HER FOOT.

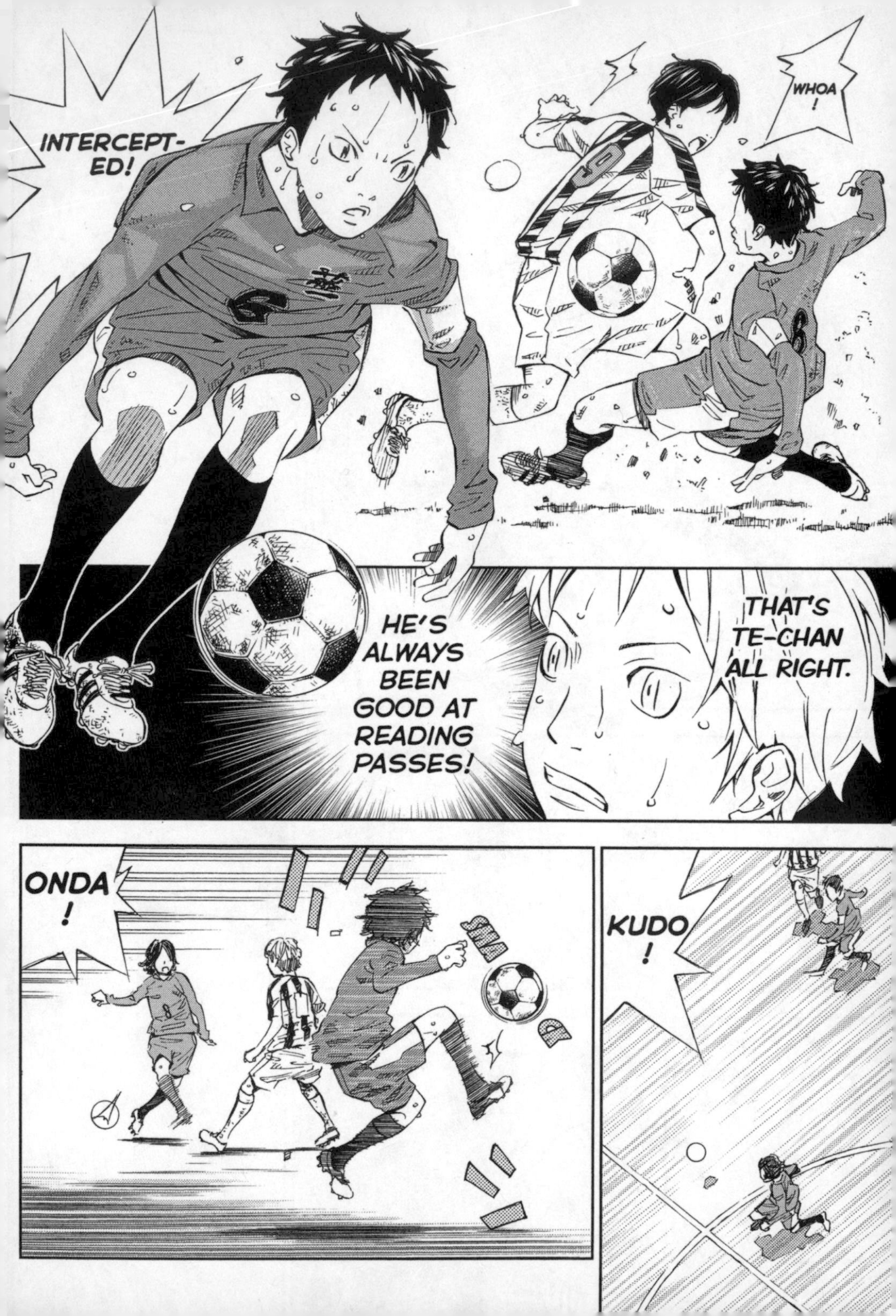
WHOA!
INTERCEPT-ED!
THAT'S TE-CHAN ALL RIGHT.
HE'S ALWAYS BEEN GOOD AT READING PASSES!
KUDO!
ONDA!

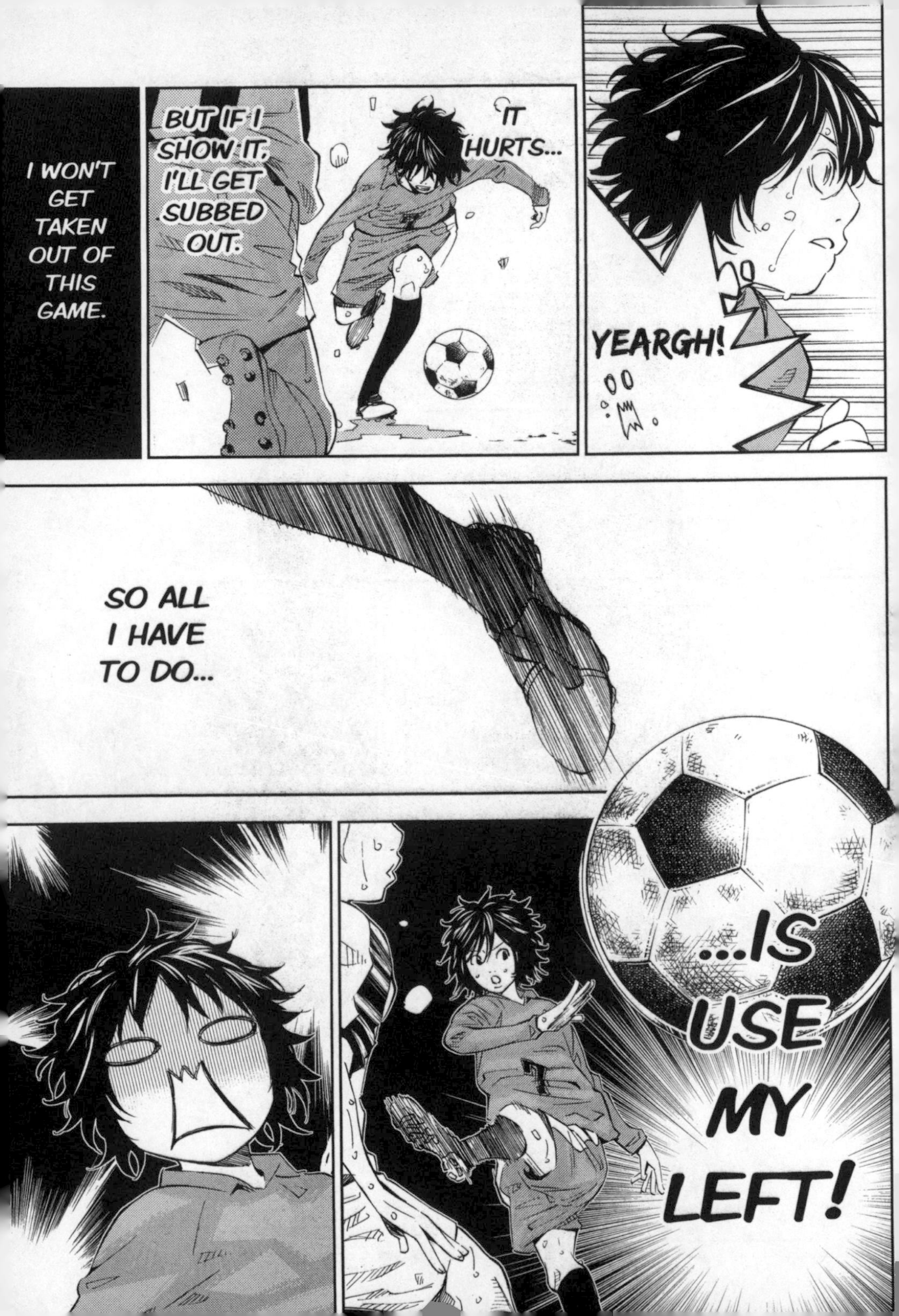
YEARGH!
IT HURTS...
BUT IF I SHOW IT, I'LL GET SUBBED OUT.
I WON'T GET TAKEN OUT OF THIS GAME.
SO ALL I HAVE TO DO...
...IS USE MY LEFT!

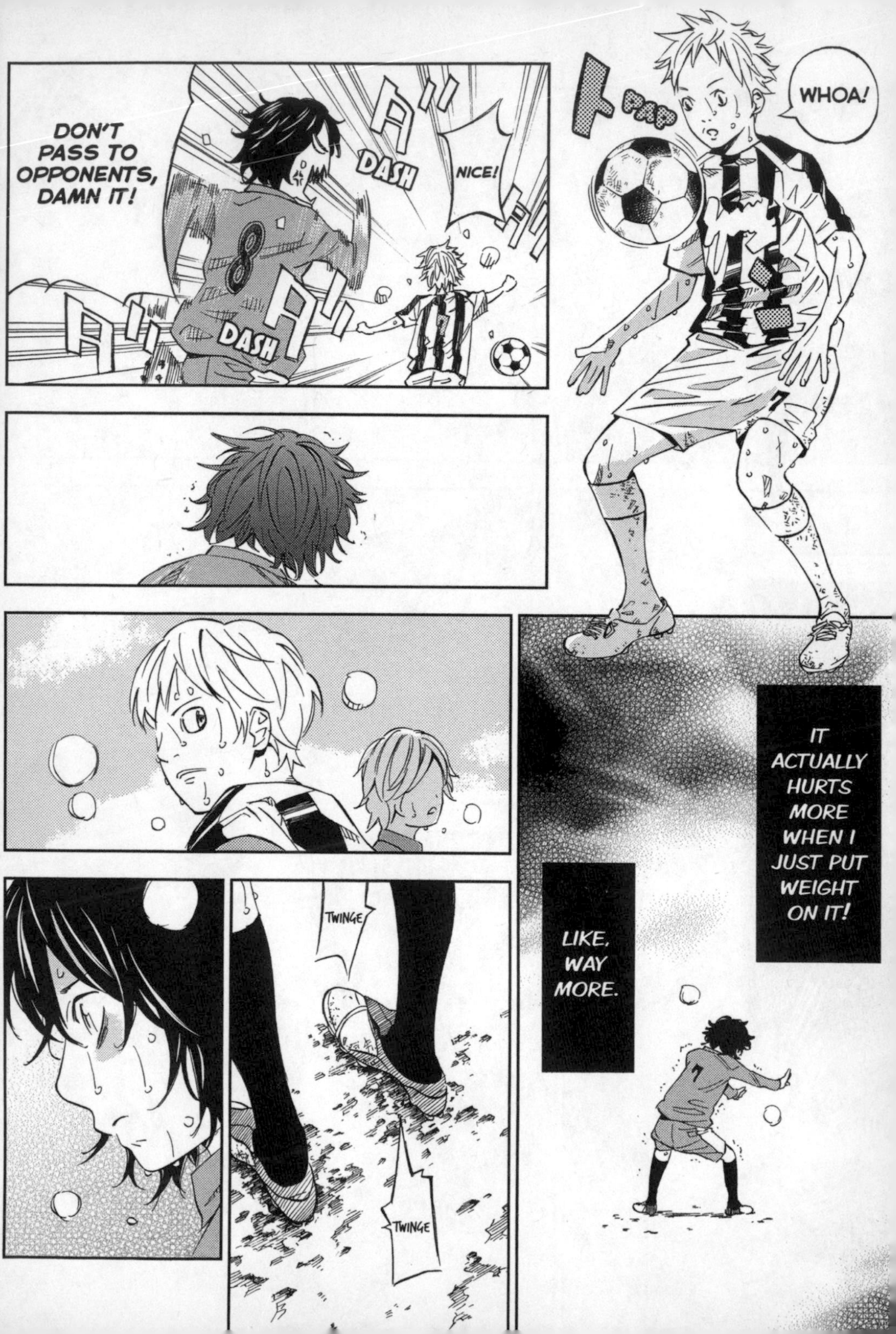
PAP
WHOA!
NICE!
DASH
DON'T PASS TO OPPONENTS, DAMN IT!
DASH
IT ACTUALLY HURTS MORE WHEN I JUST PUT WEIGHT ON IT!
LIKE, WAY MORE.
TWINGE
TWINGE

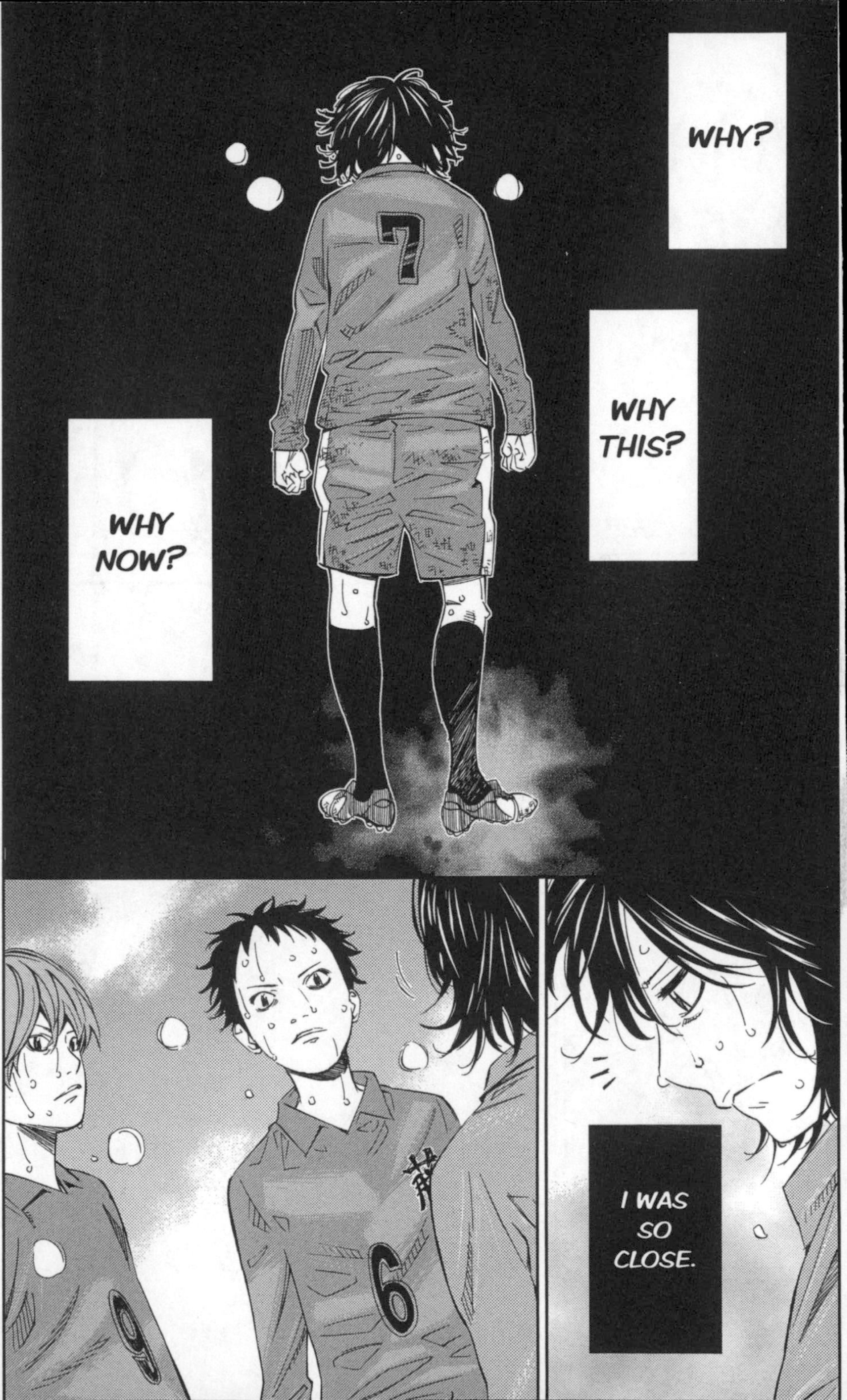
WHY?
WHY THIS?
WHY NOW?
I WAS SO CLOSE.

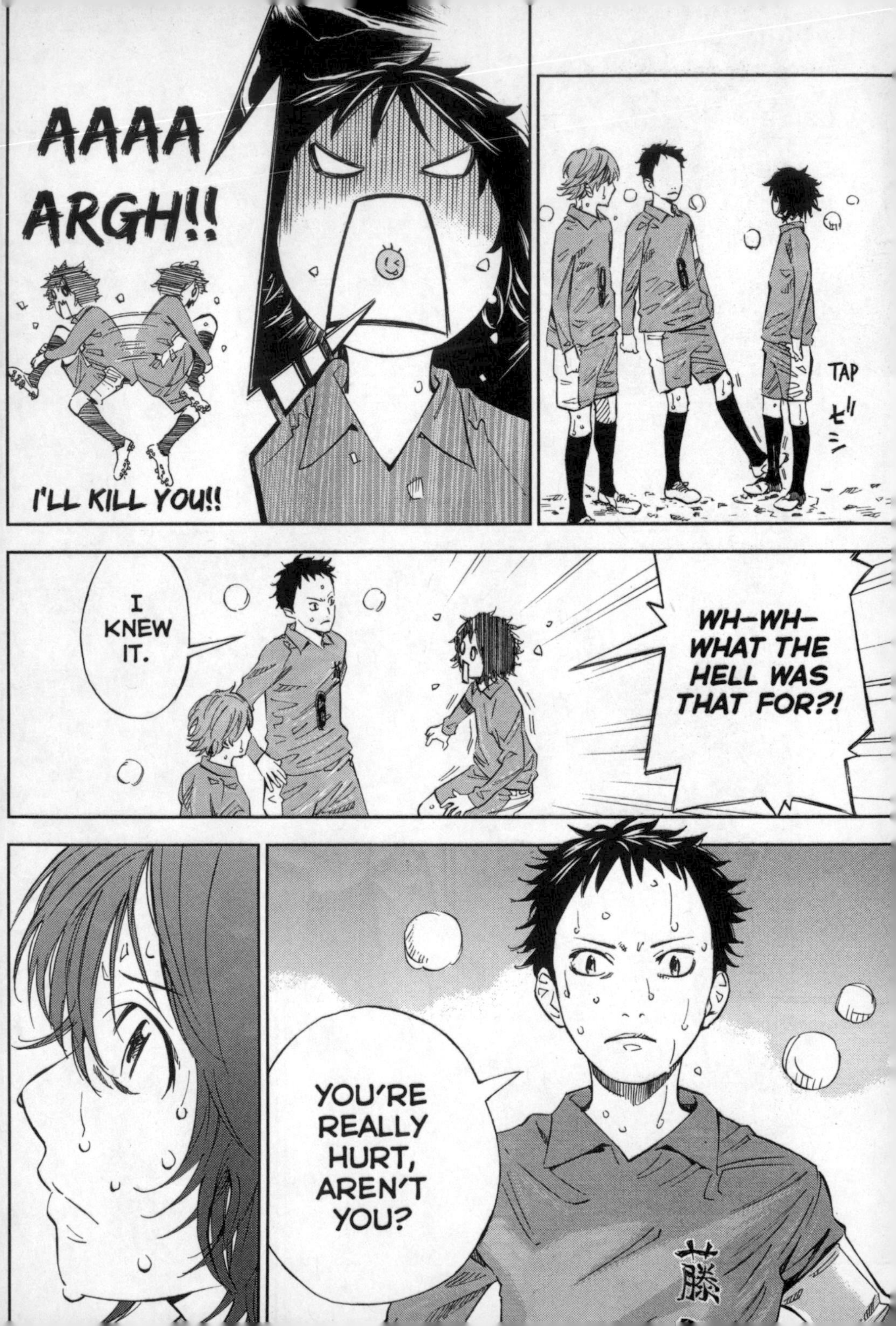
TAP
ビシ
AAAA ARGH!!
I'LL KILL YOU!!
WH-WH-WHAT THE HELL WAS THAT FOR?!
I KNEW IT.
YOU'RE REALLY HURT, AREN'T YOU?

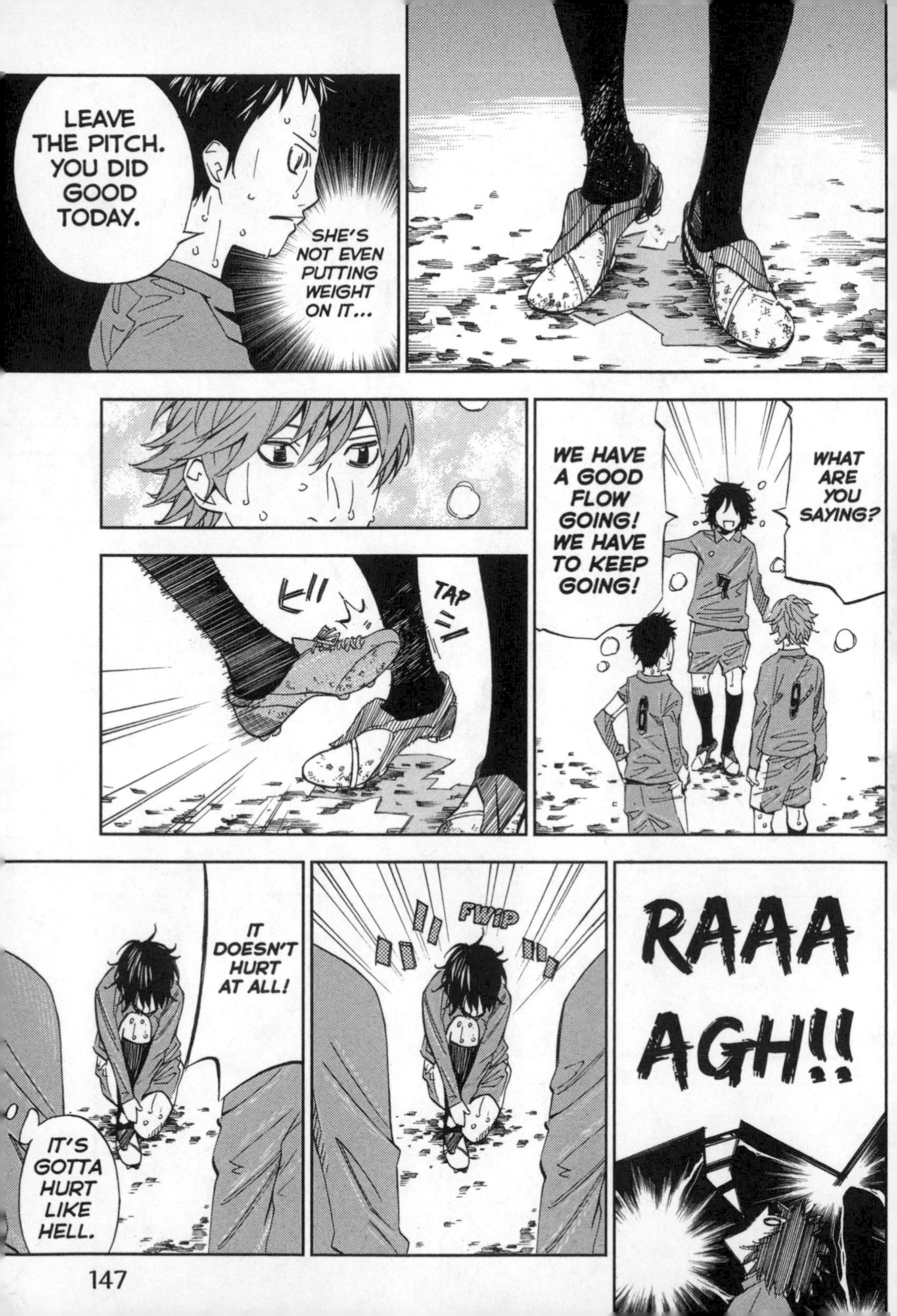
LEAVE THE PITCH. YOU DID GOOD TODAY.
SHE'S NOT EVEN PUTTING WEIGHT ON IT...
WHAT ARE YOU SAYING?
WE HAVE A GOOD FLOW GOING! WE HAVE TO KEEP GOING!
ヒリ
TAP
RAAA AGH!!
FWIP
IT DOESN'T HURT AT ALL!
IT'S GOTTA HURT LIKE HELL.

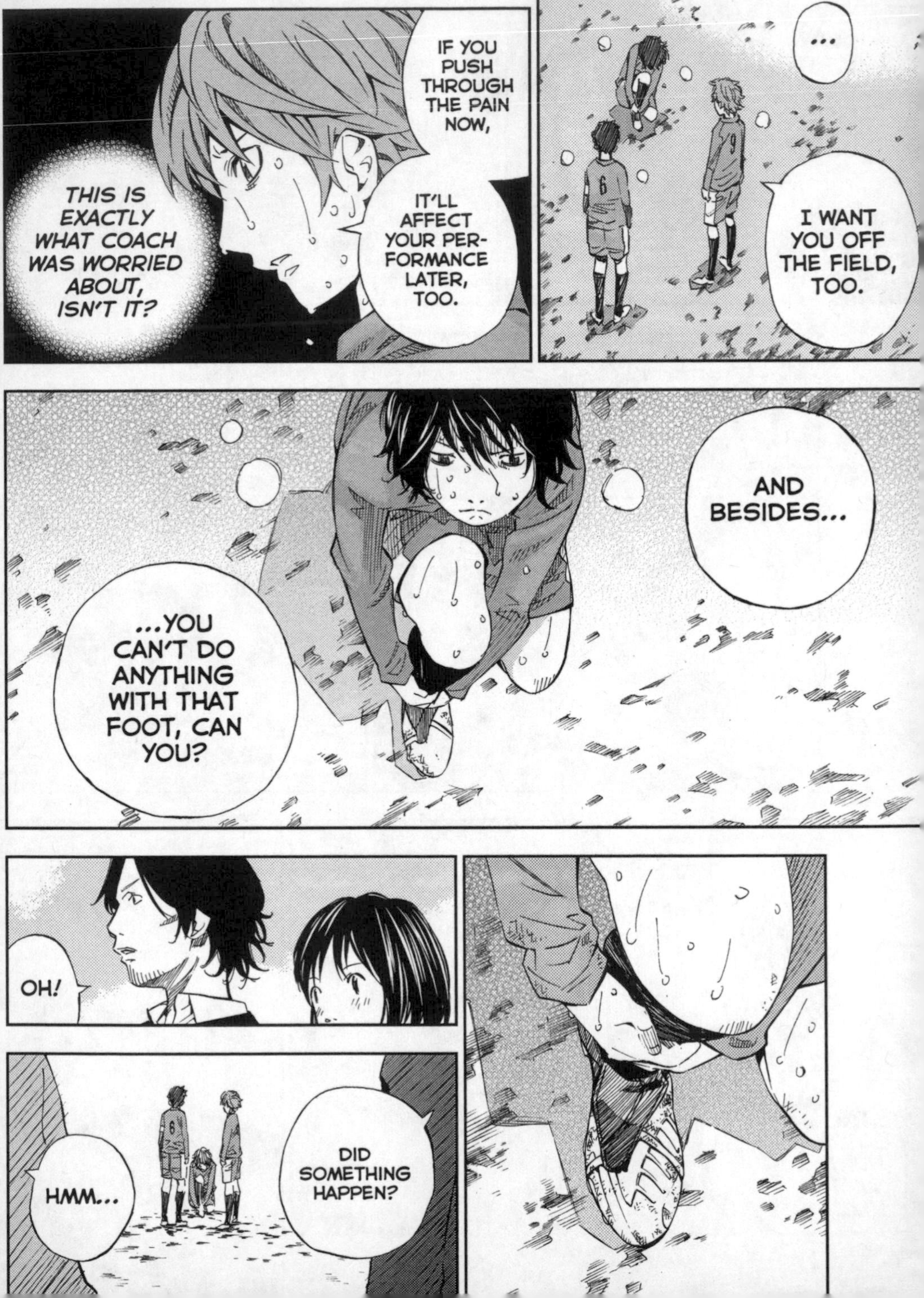
...
I WANT YOU OFF THE FIELD, TOO.
IF YOU PUSH THROUGH THE PAIN NOW,
IT'LL AFFECT YOUR PER-FORMANCE LATER, TOO.
THIS IS EXACTLY WHAT COACH WAS WORRIED ABOUT, ISN'T IT?
AND BESIDES...
...YOU CAN'T DO ANYTHING WITH THAT FOOT, CAN YOU?
OH!
DID SOMETHING HAPPEN?
HMM...

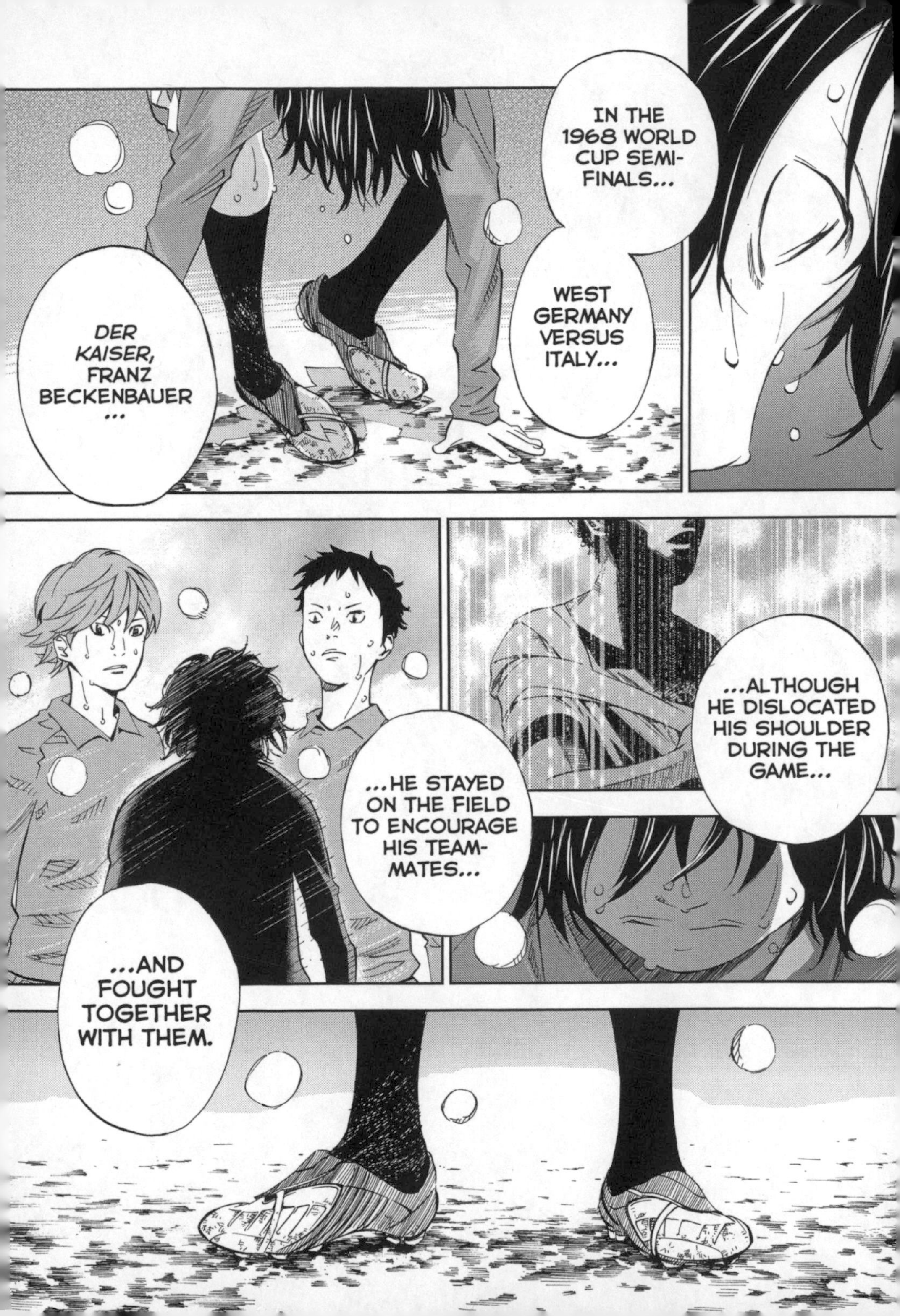
IN THE 1968 WORLD CUP SEMI-FINALS...
WEST GERMANY VERSUS ITALY...
DER KAISER, FRANZ BECKENBAUER ...
...ALTHOUGH HE DISLOCATED HIS SHOULDER DURING THE GAME...
...HE STAYED ON THE FIELD TO ENCOURAGE HIS TEAM-MATES...
...AND FOUGHT TOGETHER WITH THEM.

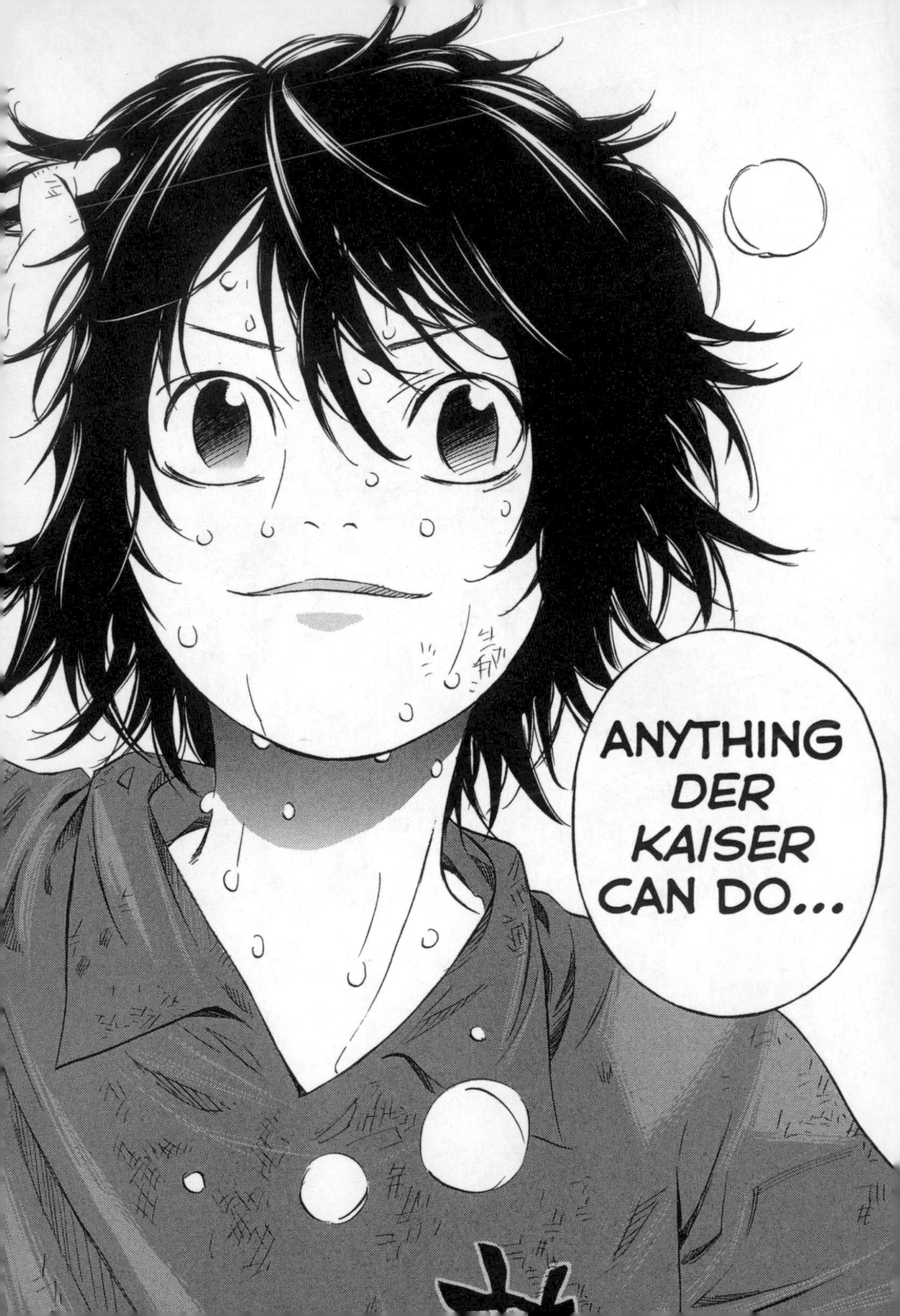
ANYTHING *DER KAISER* CAN DO...

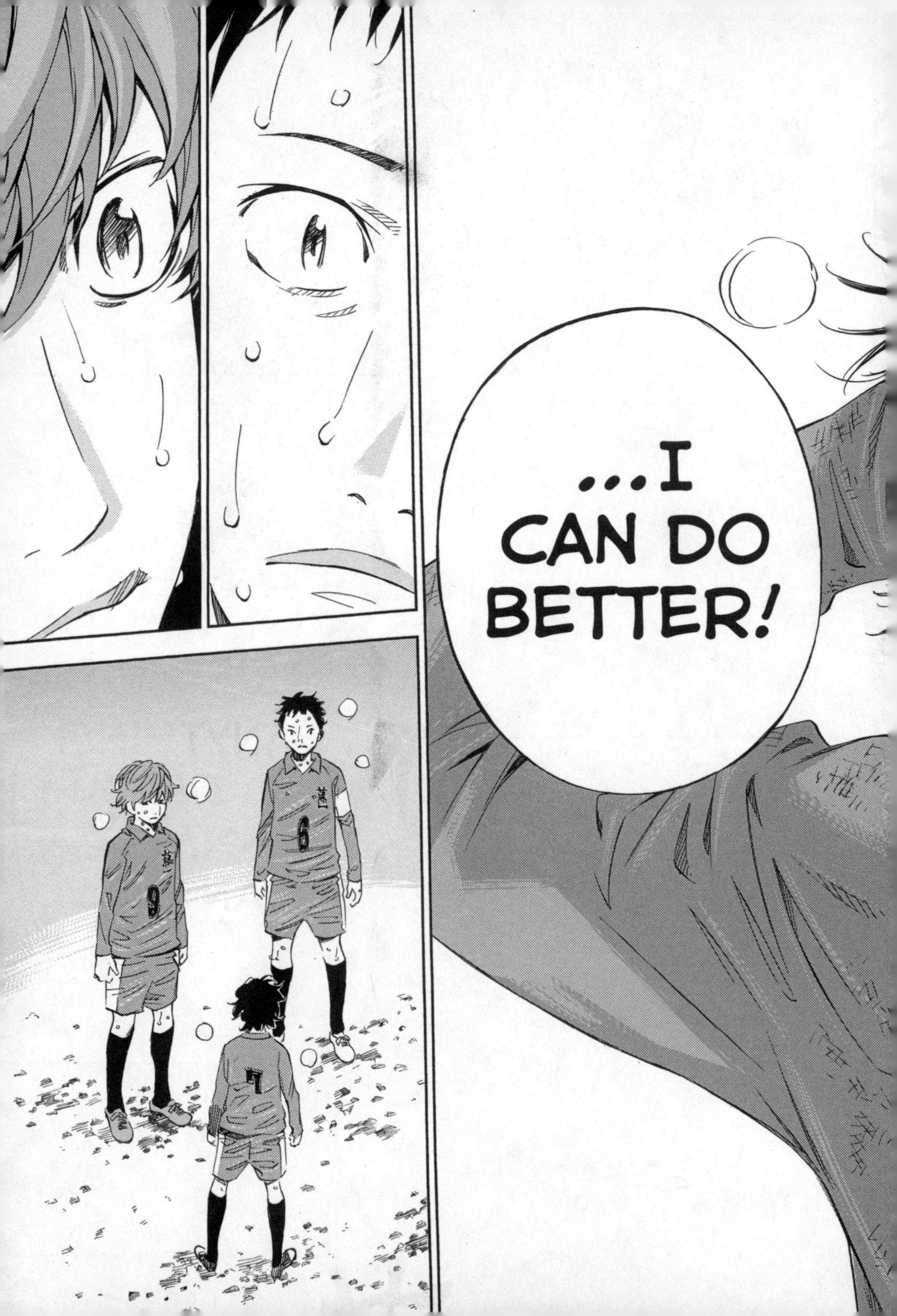
...I CAN DO BETTER!

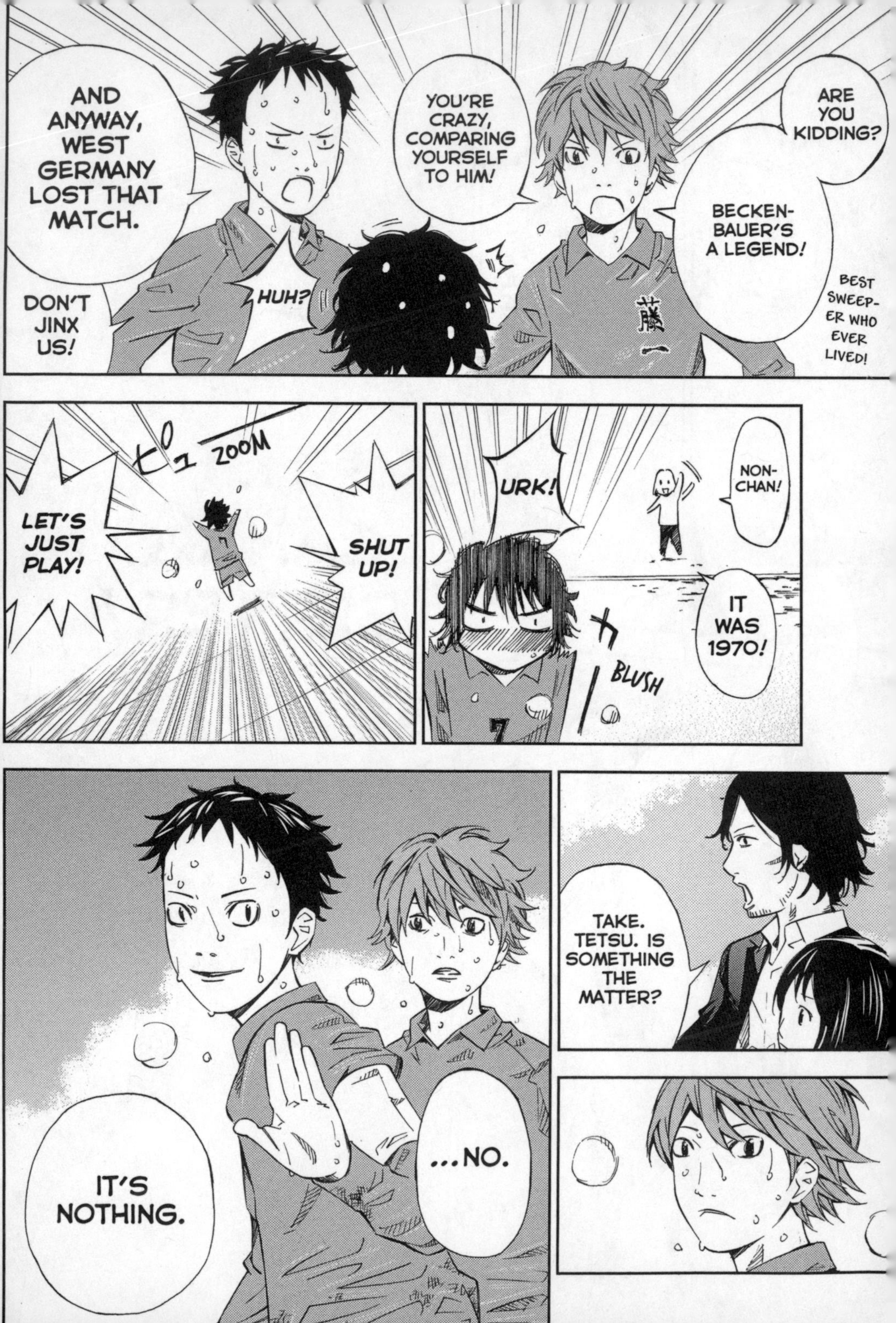
ARE YOU KIDDING?
BECKEN-BAUER'S A LEGEND!
BEST SWEEP-ER WHO EVER LIVED!
YOU'RE CRAZY, COMPARING YOURSELF TO HIM!
AND ANYWAY, WEST GERMANY LOST THAT MATCH.
HUH?
DON'T JINX US!
NON-CHAN!
URK!
IT WAS 1970!
BLUSH
SHUT UP!
ZOOM
LET'S JUST PLAY!
TAKE. TETSU. IS SOMETHING THE MATTER?
...NO.
IT'S NOTHING.

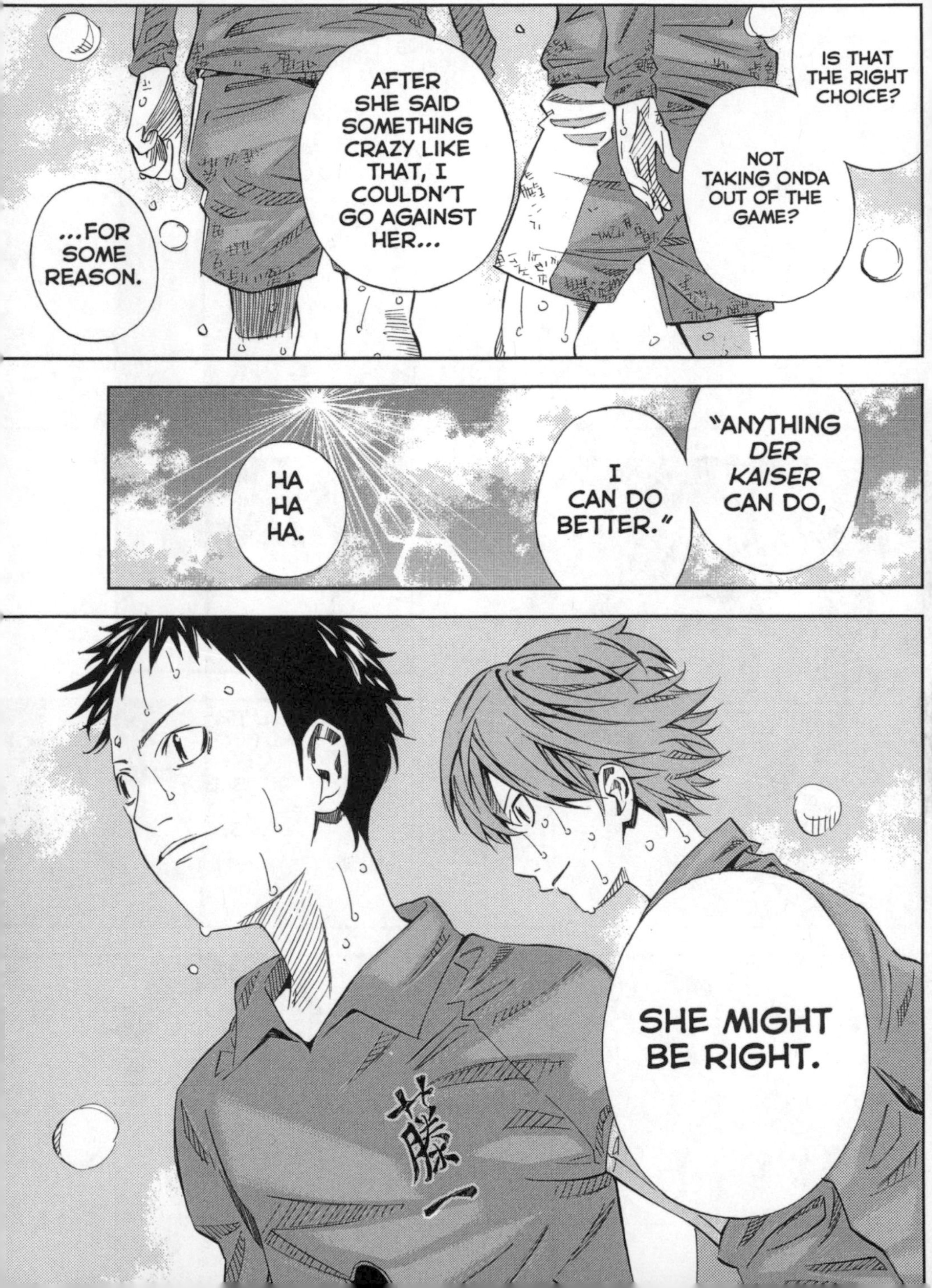
IS THAT THE RIGHT CHOICE?
NOT TAKING ONDA OUT OF THE GAME?
AFTER SHE SAID SOMETHING CRAZY LIKE THAT, I COULDN'T GO AGAINST HER...
...FOR SOME REASON.
"ANYTHING *DER KAISER* CAN DO,
I CAN DO BETTER."
HA HA HA.
SHE MIGHT BE RIGHT.

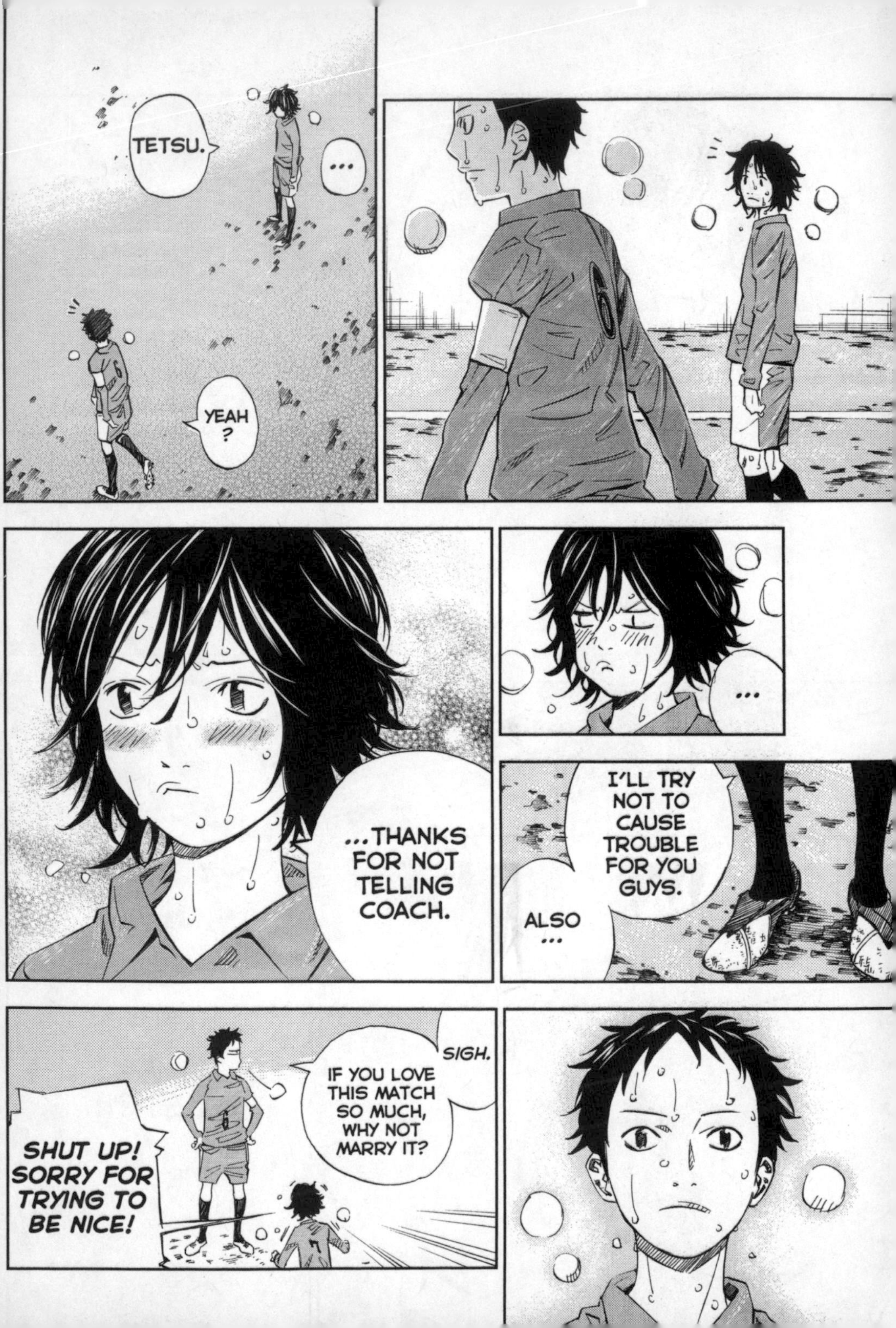
TETSU.
...
YEAH?
...
I'LL TRY NOT TO CAUSE TROUBLE FOR YOU GUYS.
ALSO ...
...THANKS FOR NOT TELLING COACH.
SIGH.
IF YOU LOVE THIS MATCH SO MUCH, WHY NOT MARRY IT?
SHUT UP! SORRY FOR TRYING TO BE NICE!

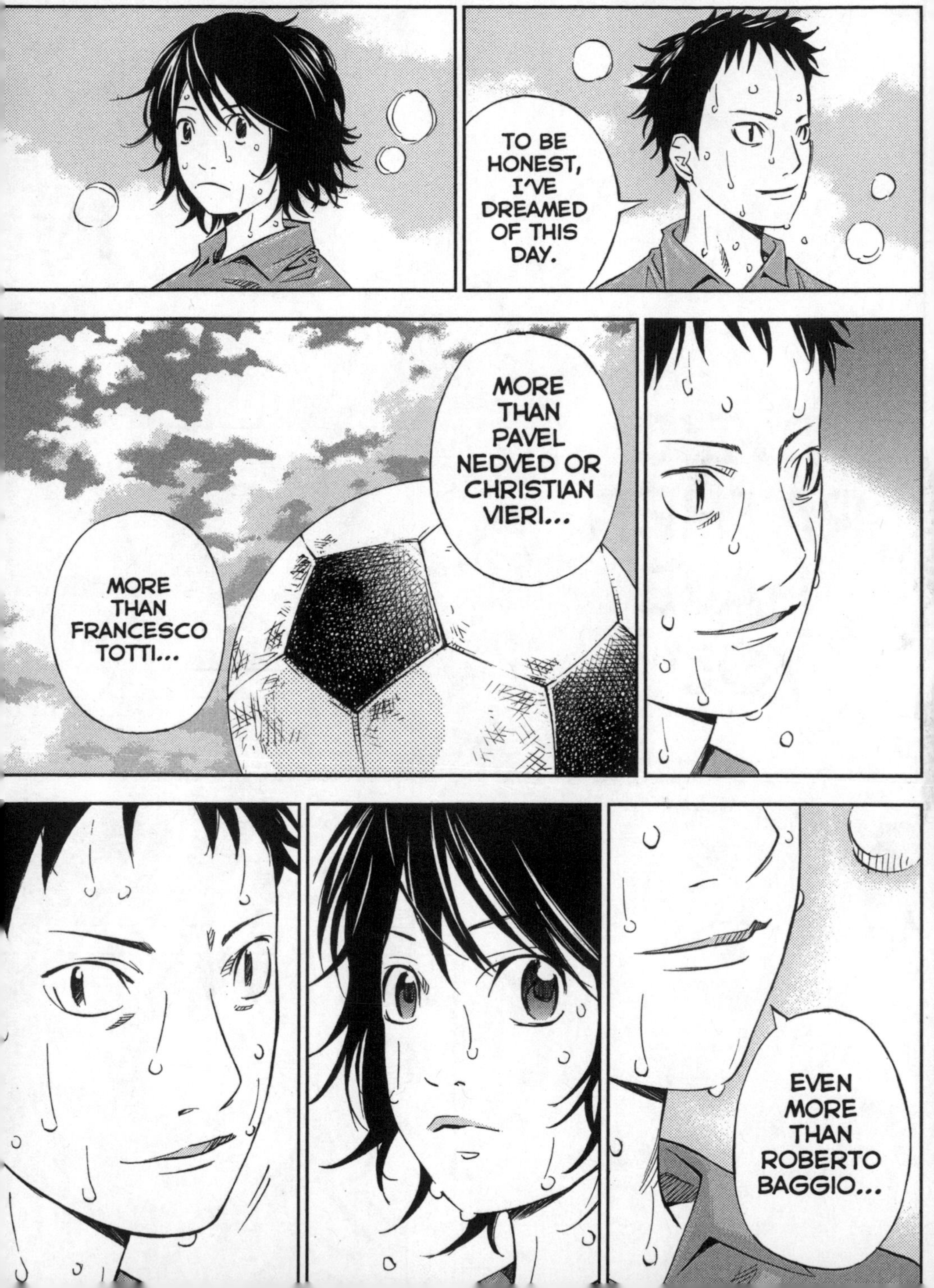
TO BE HONEST, I'VE DREAMED OF THIS DAY.
MORE THAN PAVEL NEDVED OR CHRISTIAN VIERI...
MORE THAN FRANCESCO TOTTI...
EVEN MORE THAN ROBERTO BAGGIO...

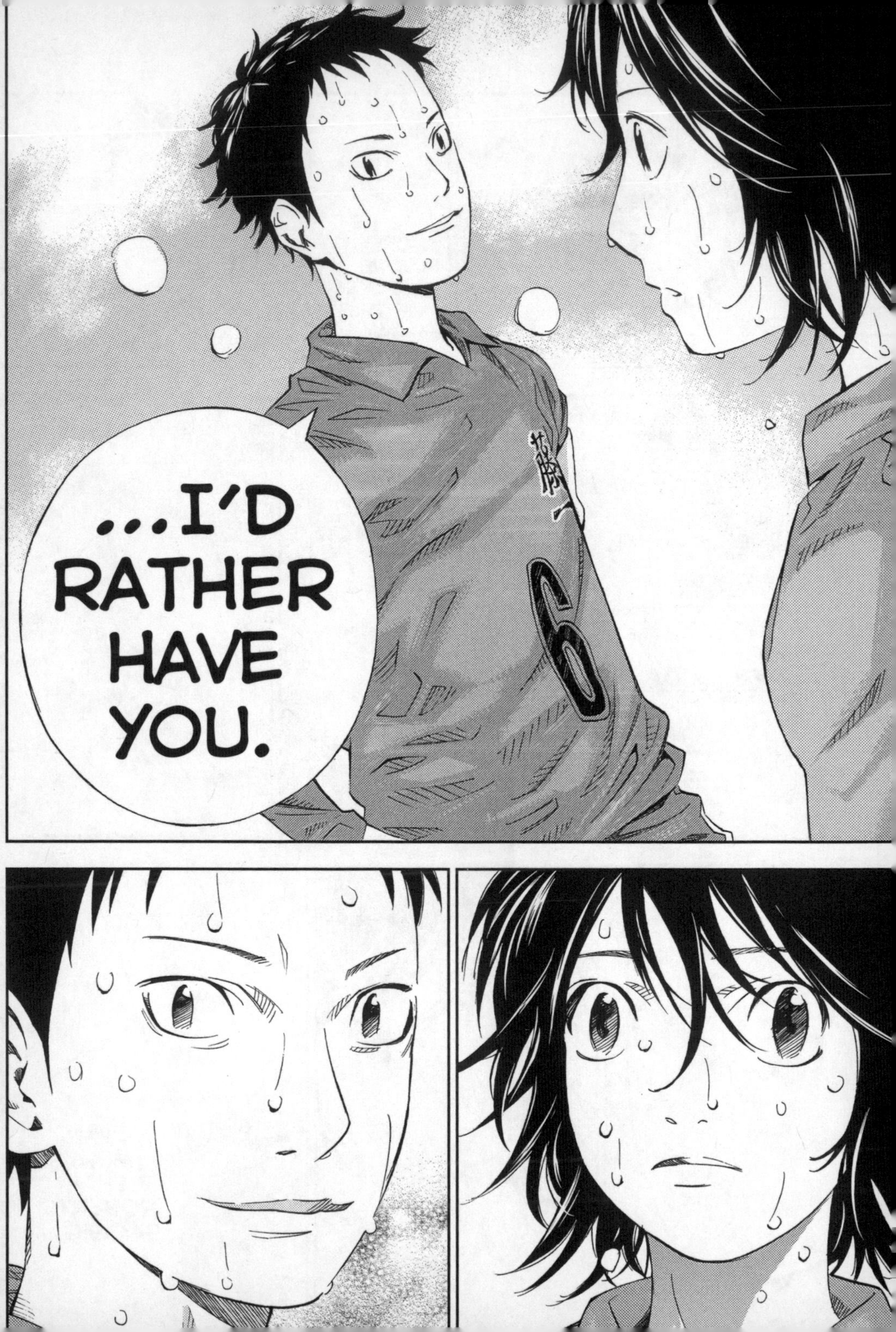
...I'D RATHER HAVE YOU.

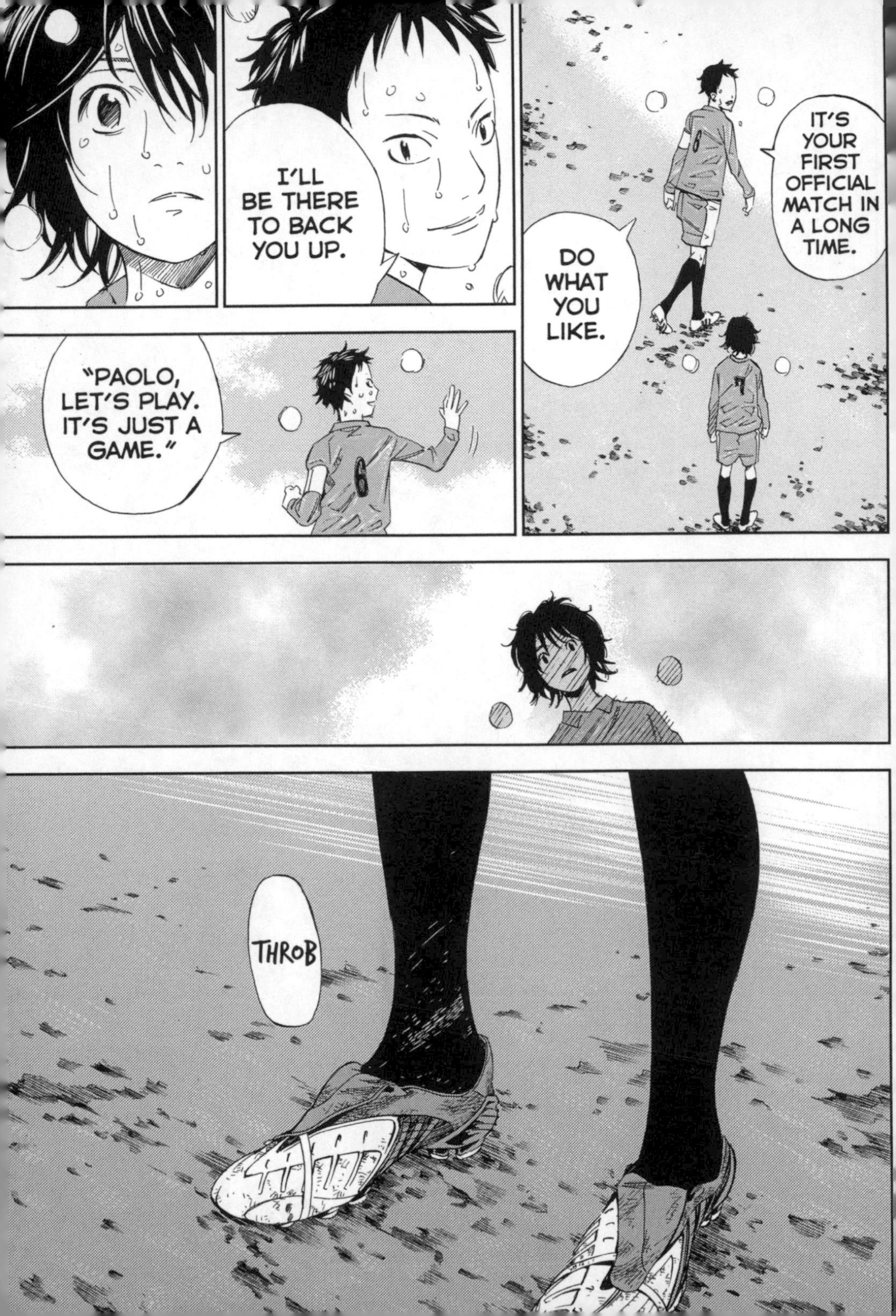
IT'S YOUR FIRST OFFICIAL MATCH IN A LONG TIME.
DO WHAT YOU LIKE.
I'LL BE THERE TO BACK YOU UP.
"PAOLO, LET'S PLAY. IT'S JUST A GAME."
THROB

SAYONARA FOOTBALL

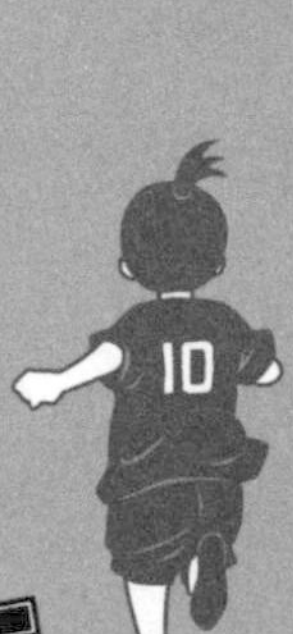
10

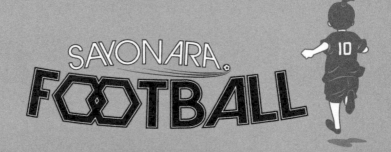

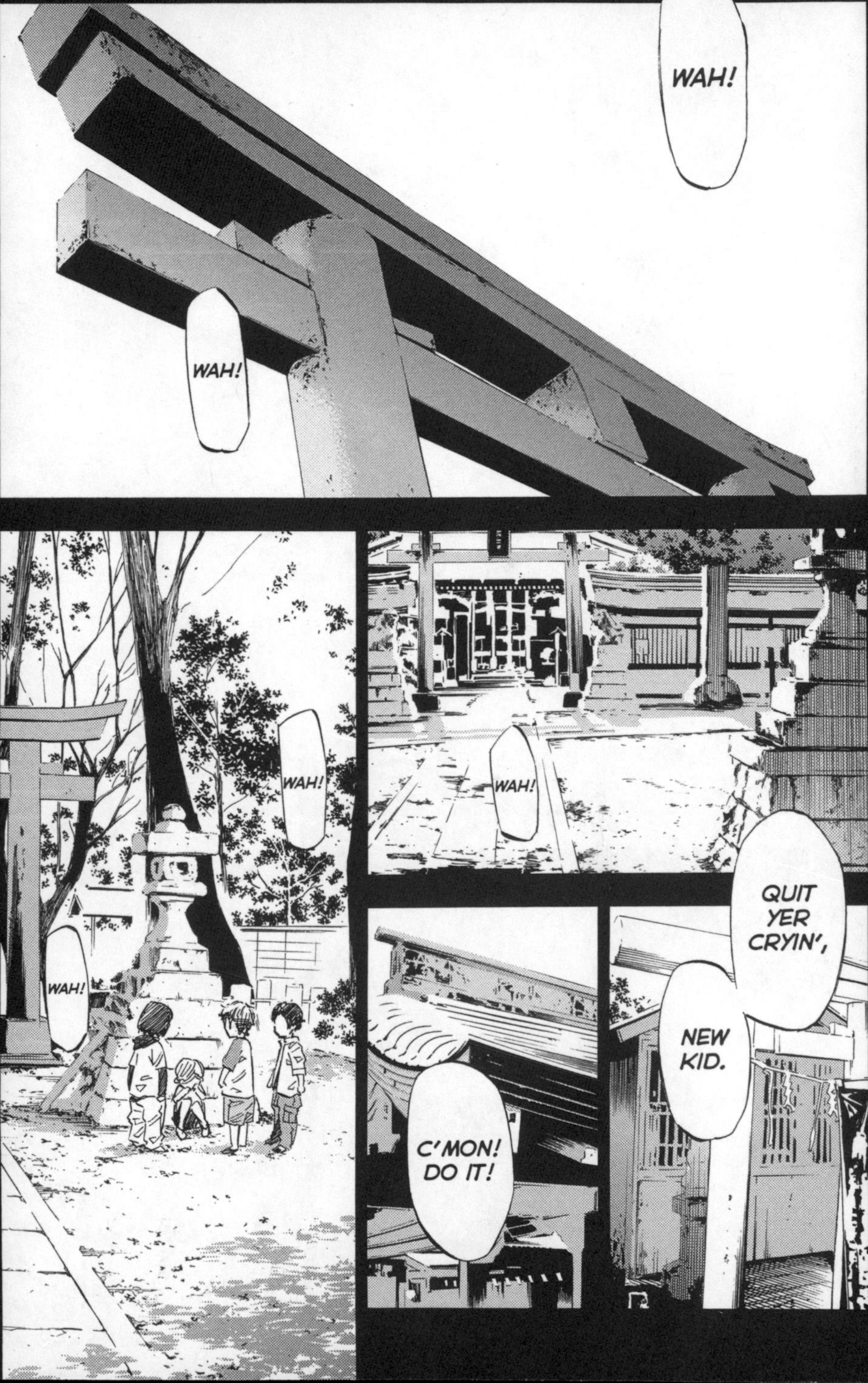
WAH!
WAH!
WAH!
QUIT YER CRYIN',
NEW KID.
C'MON! DO IT!
WAH!
WAH!

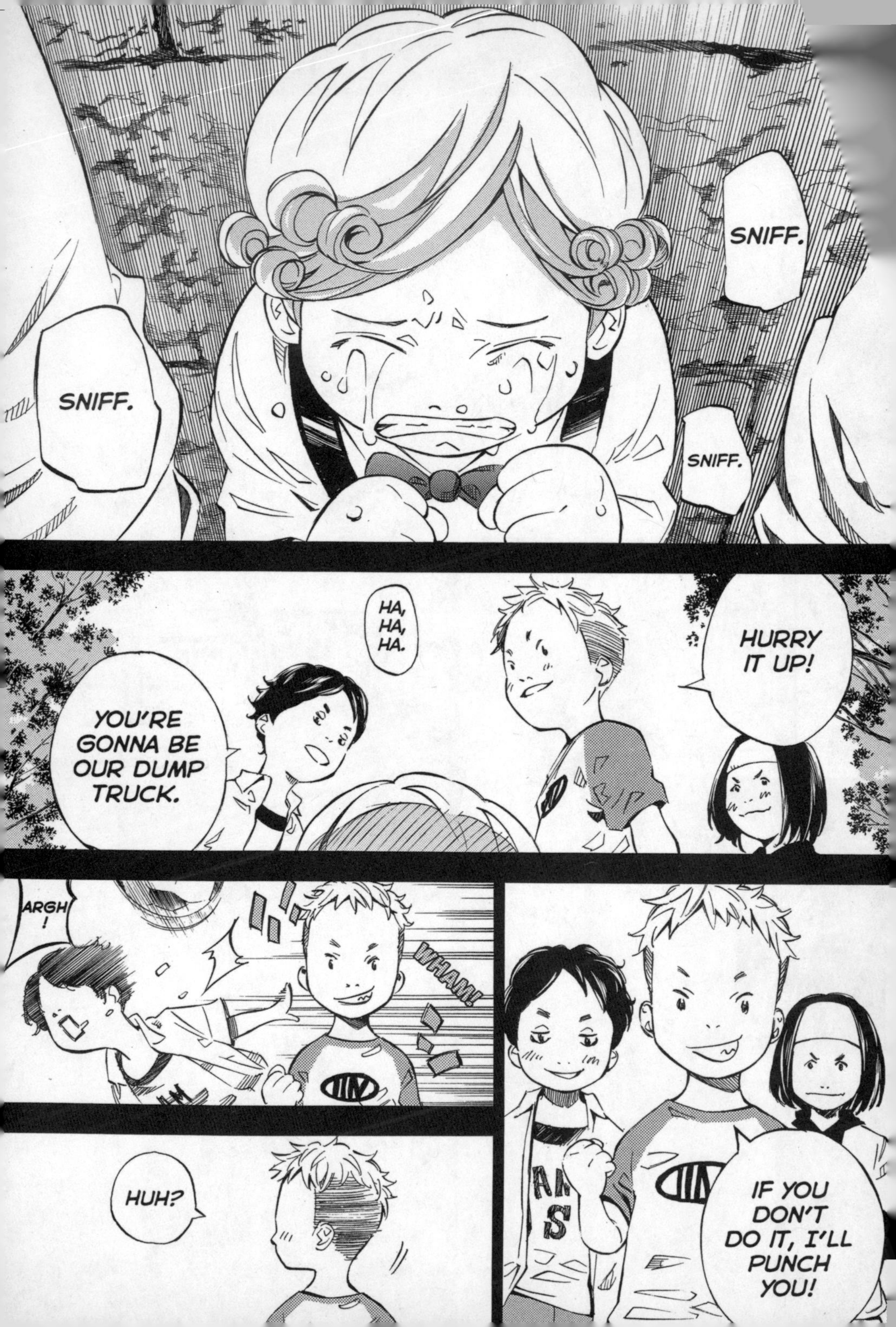
SNIFF.
SNIFF.
SNIFF.
HURRY IT UP!
HA, HA, HA.
YOU'RE GONNA BE OUR DUMP TRUCK.
IF YOU DON'T DO IT, I'LL PUNCH YOU!
WHAM!
ARGH!
HUH?

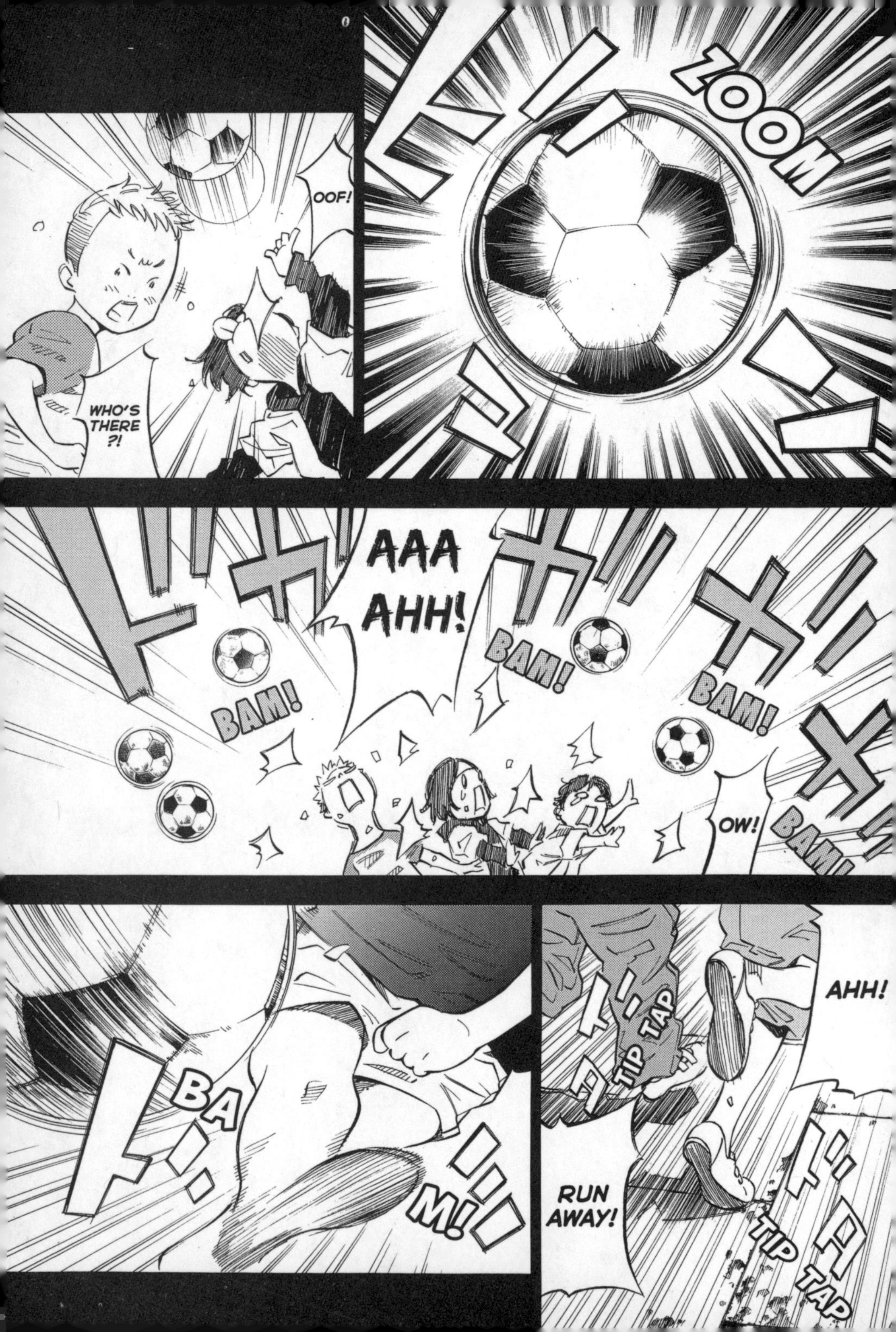
ZOOM
OOF!
WHO'S THERE ?!
BAM
OW!
BAM!
BAM!
AAA AHH!
BAM!
AHH!
TIP TAP
RUN AWAY!
TIP TAP
BA
M!

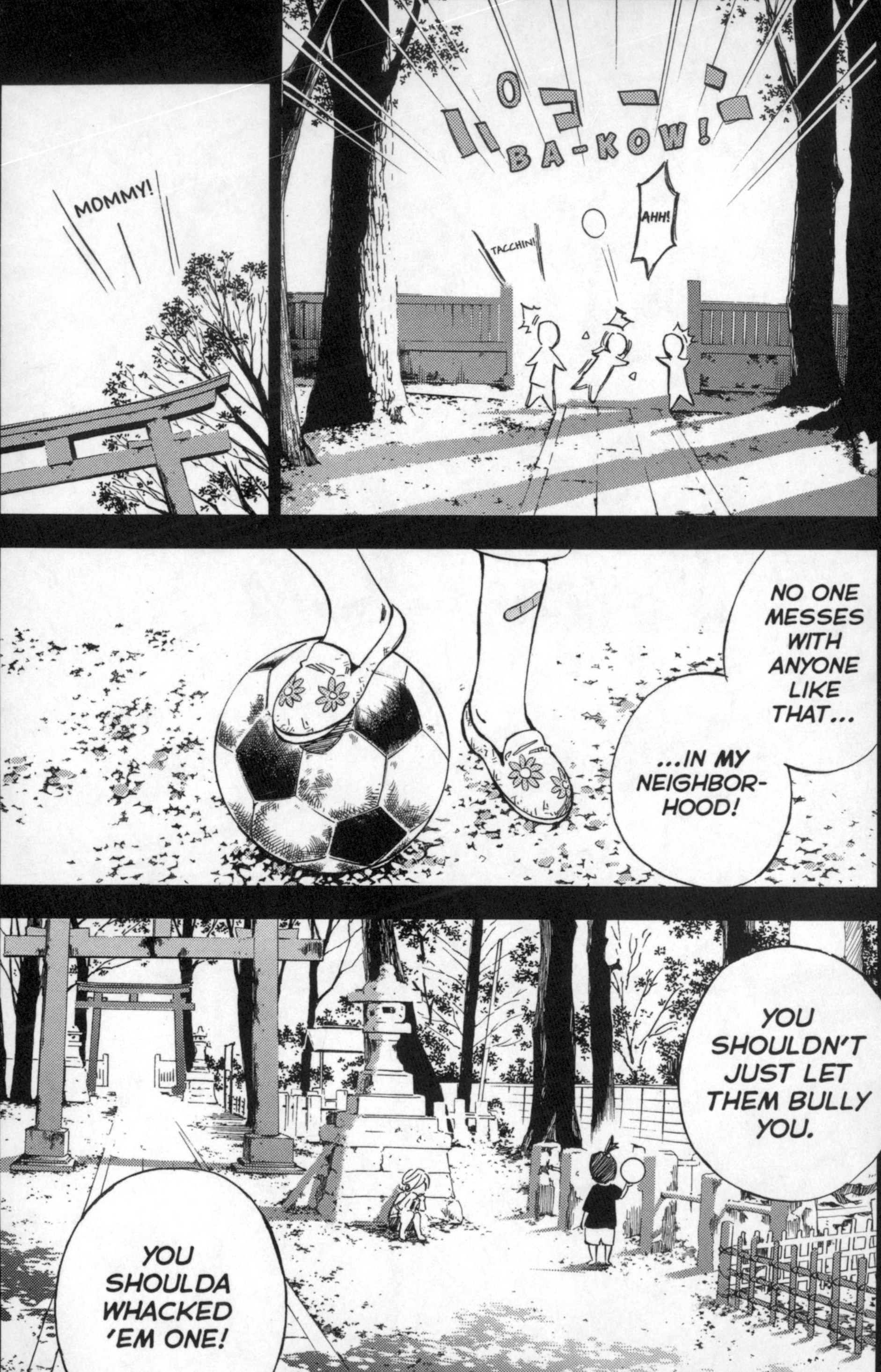
BA-KOW!
AHH!
TACCHIN!
MOMMY!
NO ONE MESSES WITH ANYONE LIKE THAT...
...IN MY NEIGHBOR-HOOD!
YOU SHOULDN'T JUST LET THEM BULLY YOU.
YOU SHOULDA WHACKED 'EM ONE!

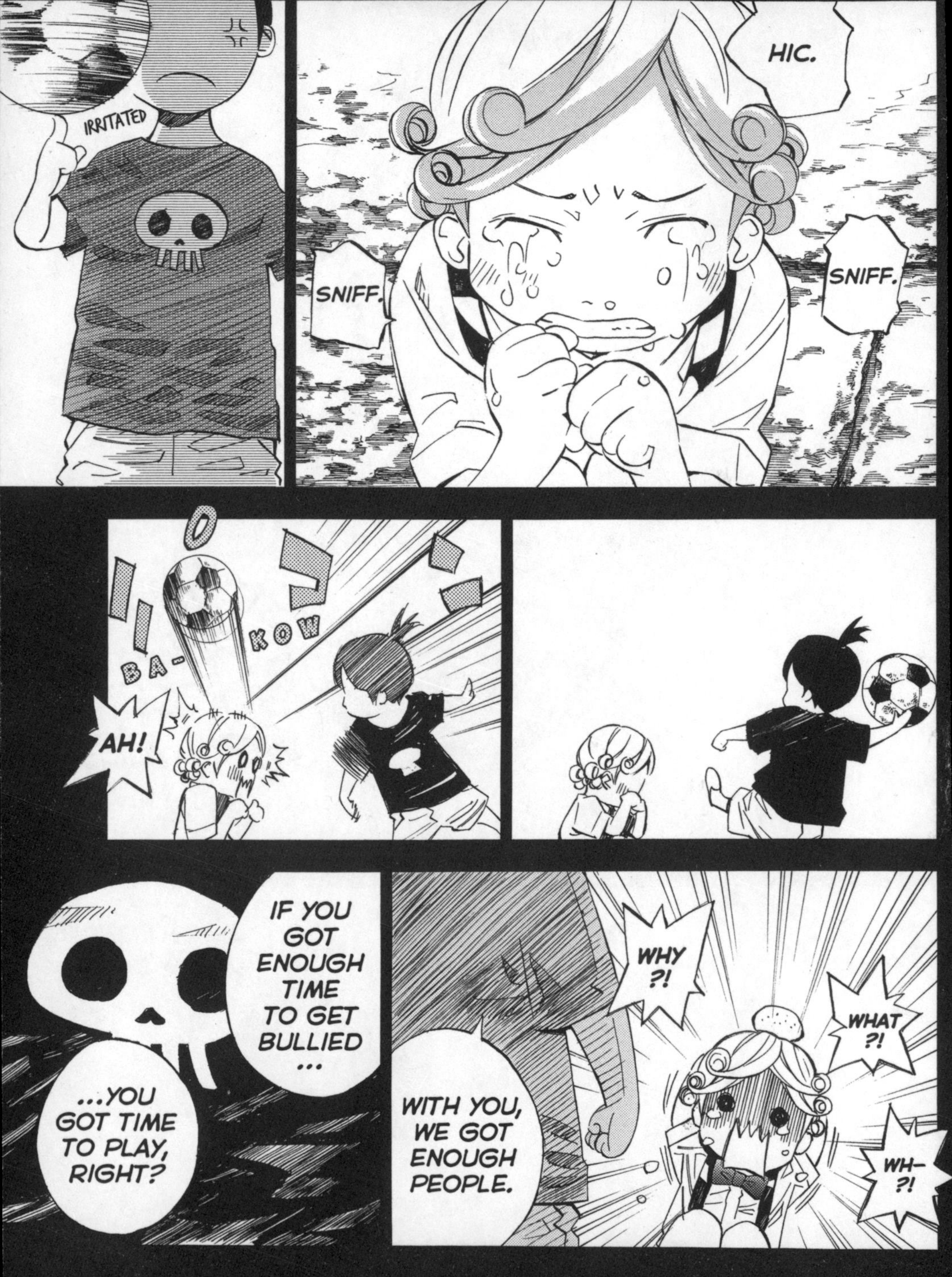
HIC.
SNIFF.
SNIFF.
IRRITATED
BA-KOW
AH!
WHY ?!
WHAT ?!
WITH YOU, WE GOT ENOUGH PEOPLE.
WH- ?!
IF YOU GOT ENOUGH TIME TO GET BULLIED ...
...YOU GOT TIME TO PLAY, RIGHT?

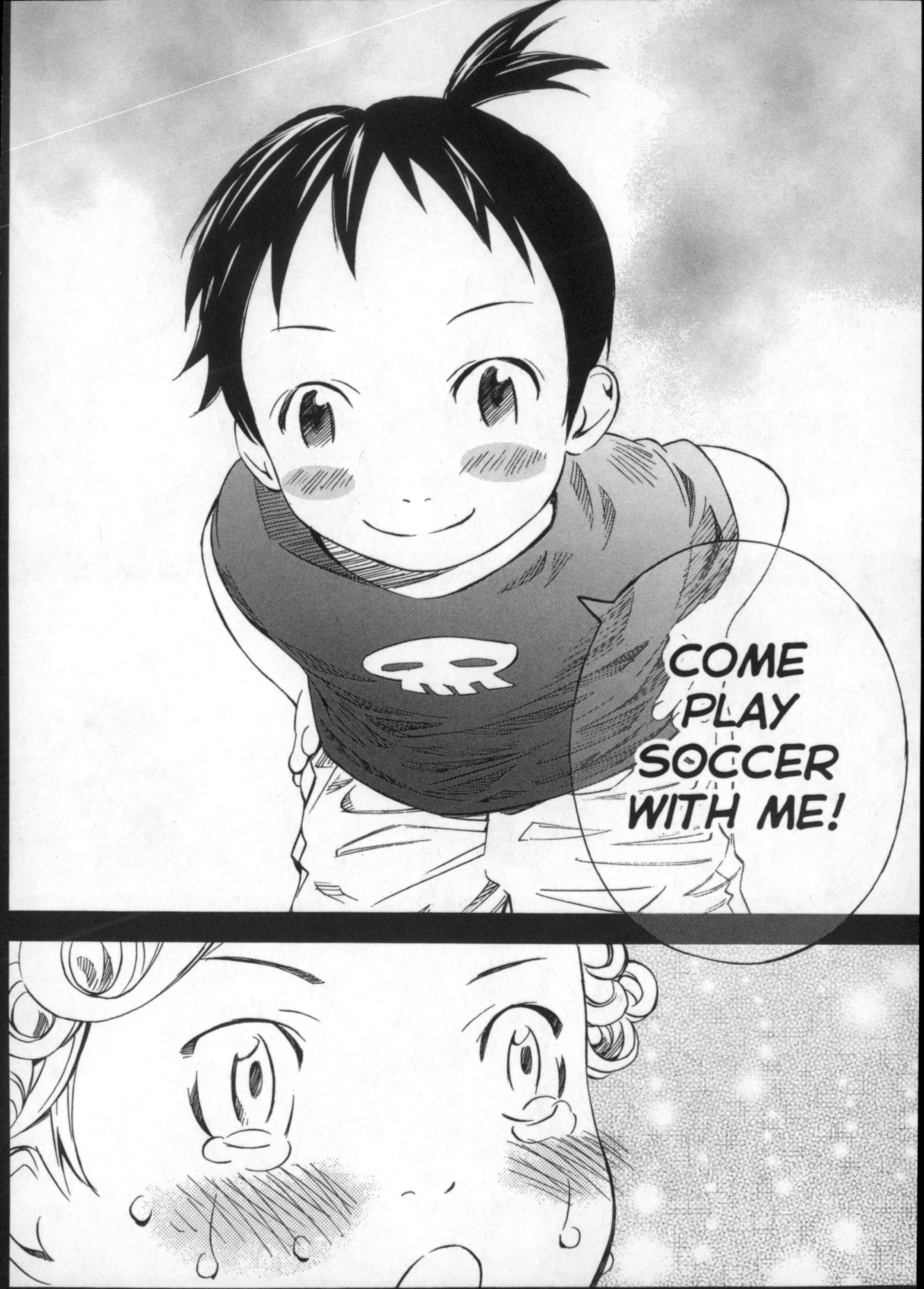
COME PLAY SOCCER WITH ME!

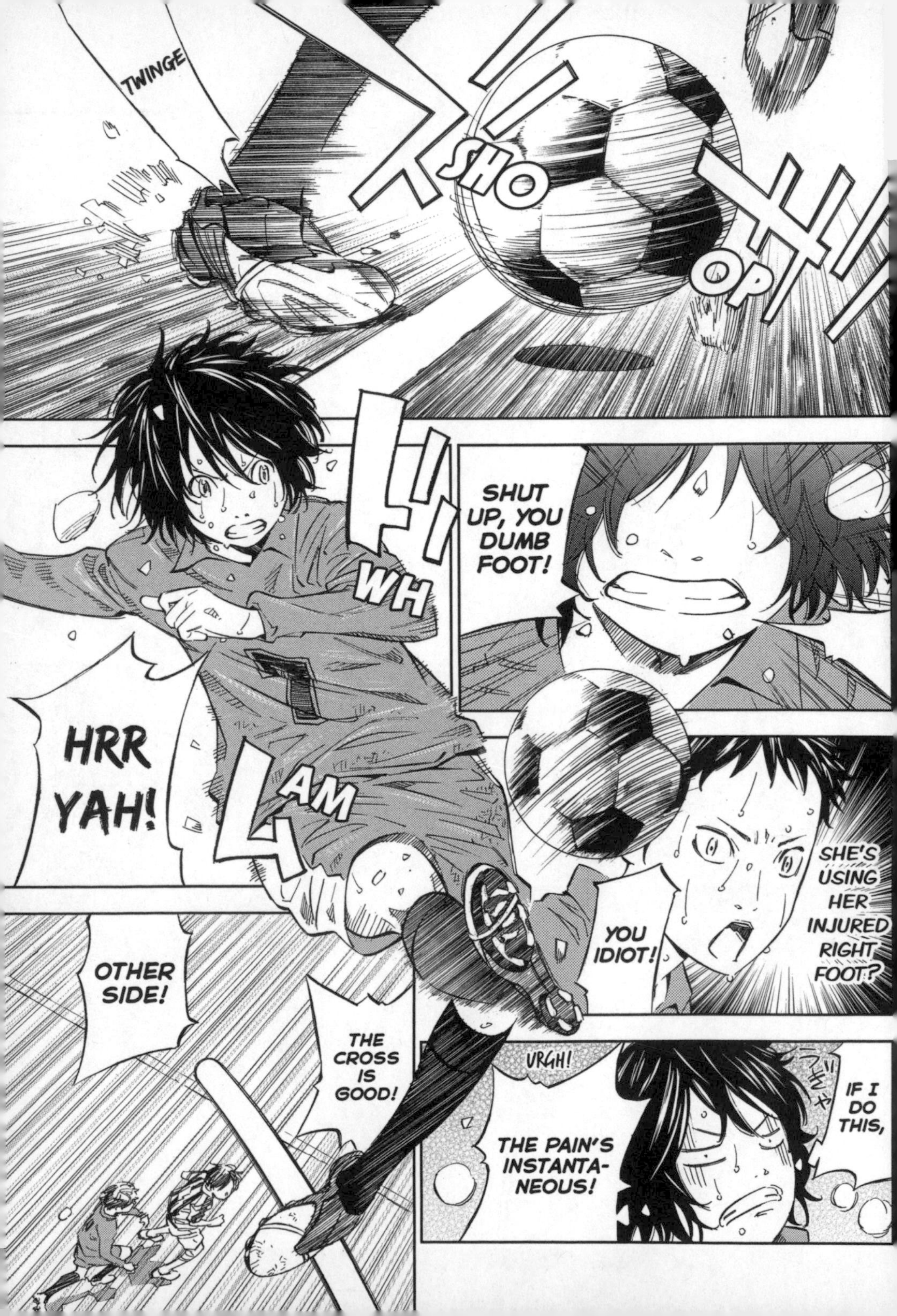
TWINGE
SHO
OP
SHUT UP, YOU DUMB FOOT!
SHE'S USING HER INJURED RIGHT FOOT?
YOU IDIOT!
IF I DO THIS,
URGH!
THE PAIN'S INSTANTA-NEOUS!
WH
AM
HRR YAH!
THE CROSS IS GOOD!
OTHER SIDE!

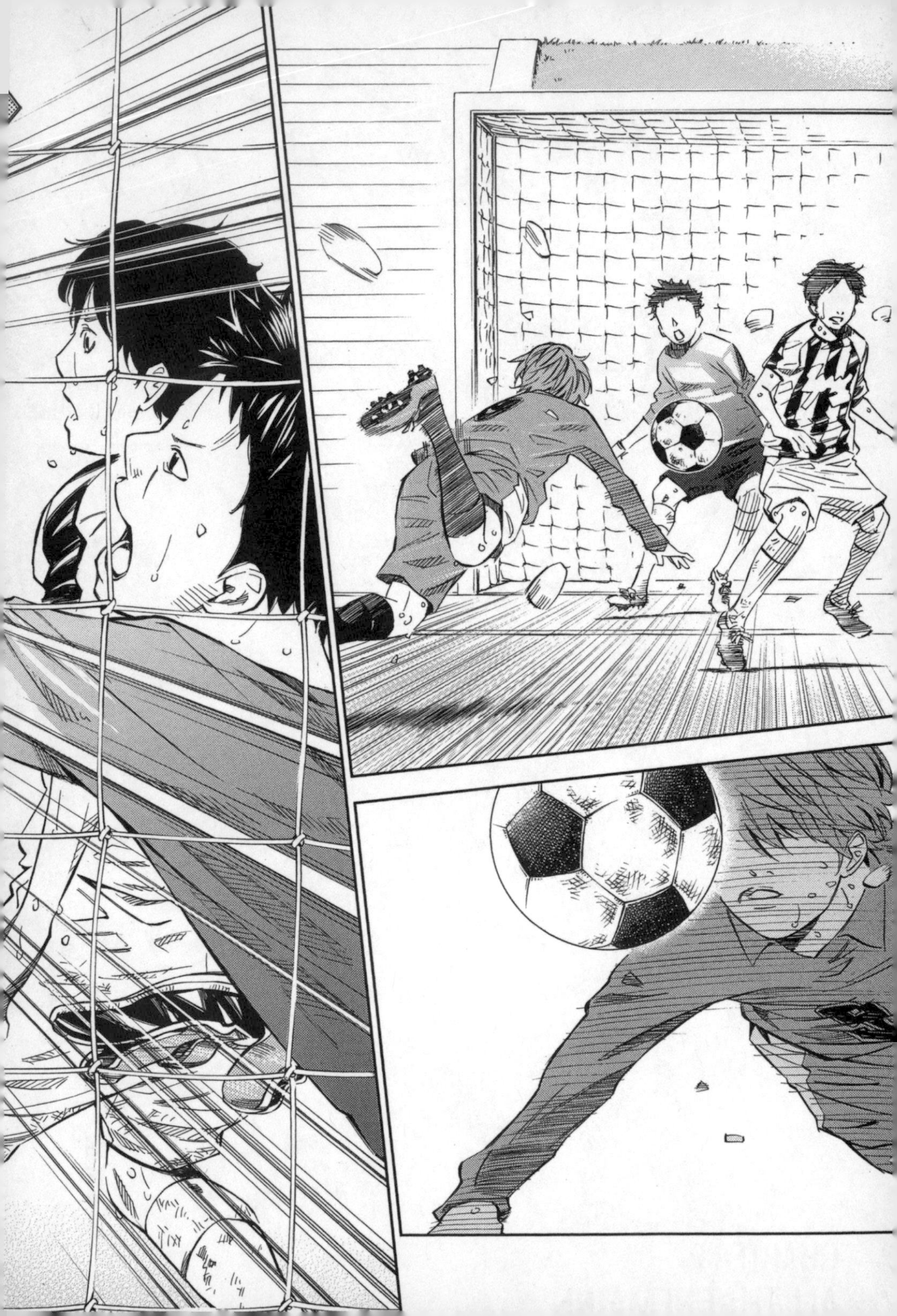

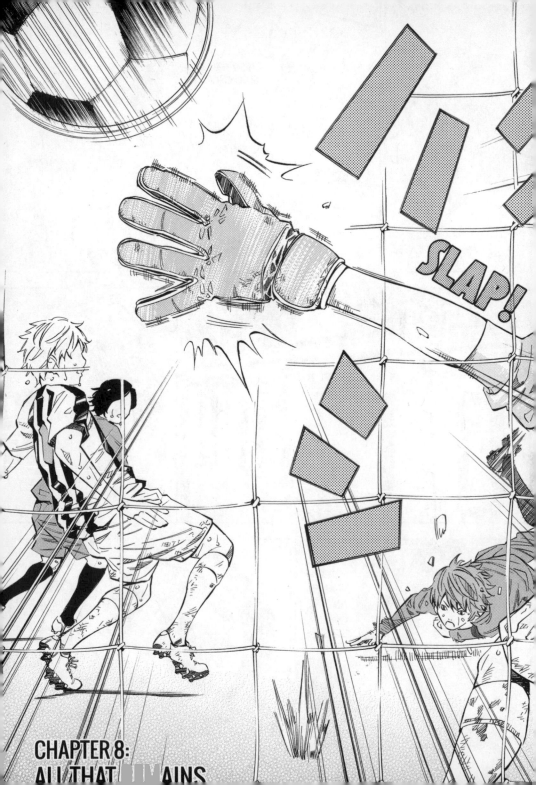

CHAPTER 8:
ALL THAT REMAINS

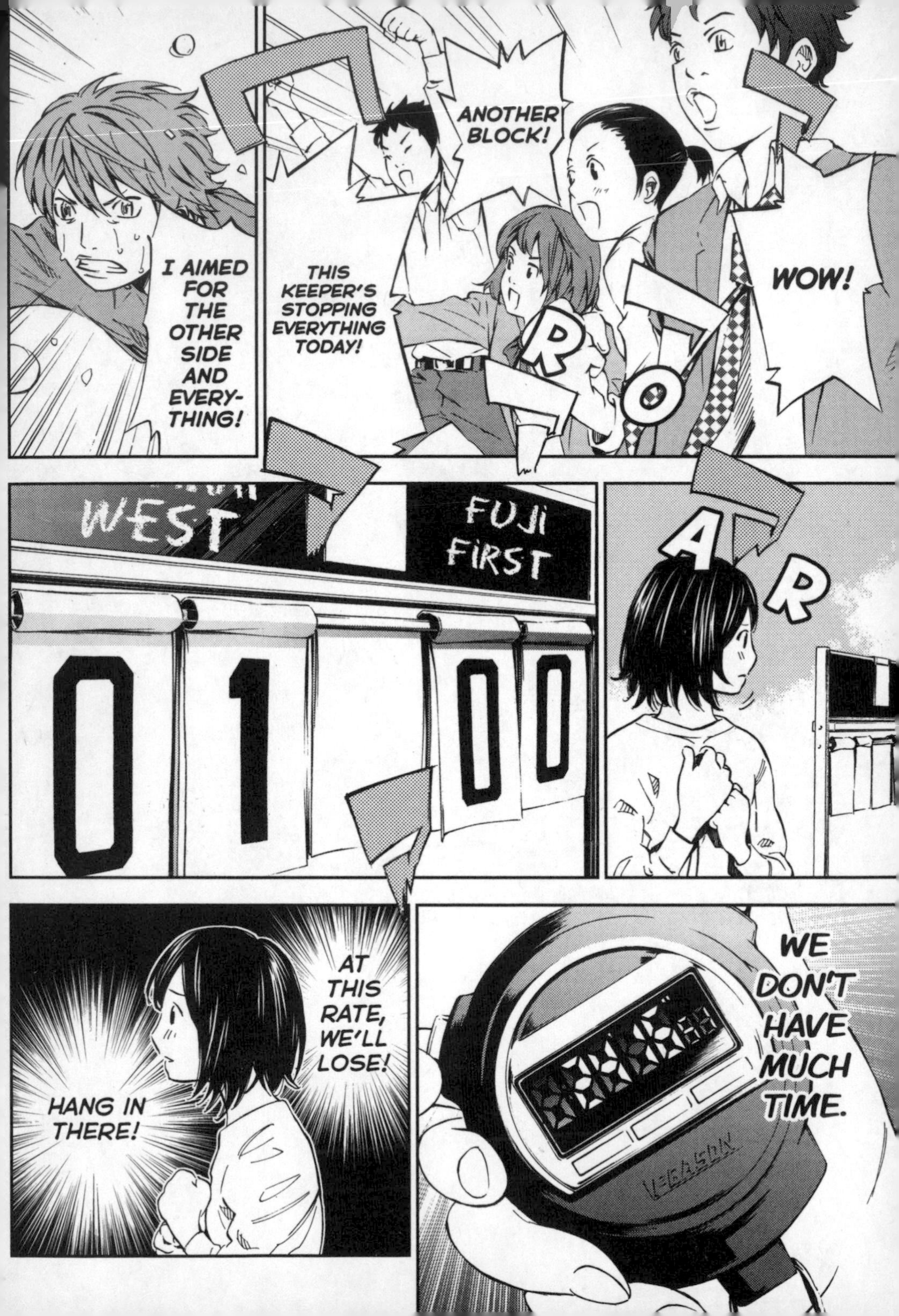
WOW!
ANOTHER BLOCK!
THIS KEEPER'S STOPPING EVERYTHING TODAY!
ROAR
I AIMED FOR THE OTHER SIDE AND EVERY-THING!
WEST
FUJI FIRST
0 1 0 0
WE DON'T HAVE MUCH TIME.
AT THIS RATE, WE'LL LOSE!
HANG IN THERE!

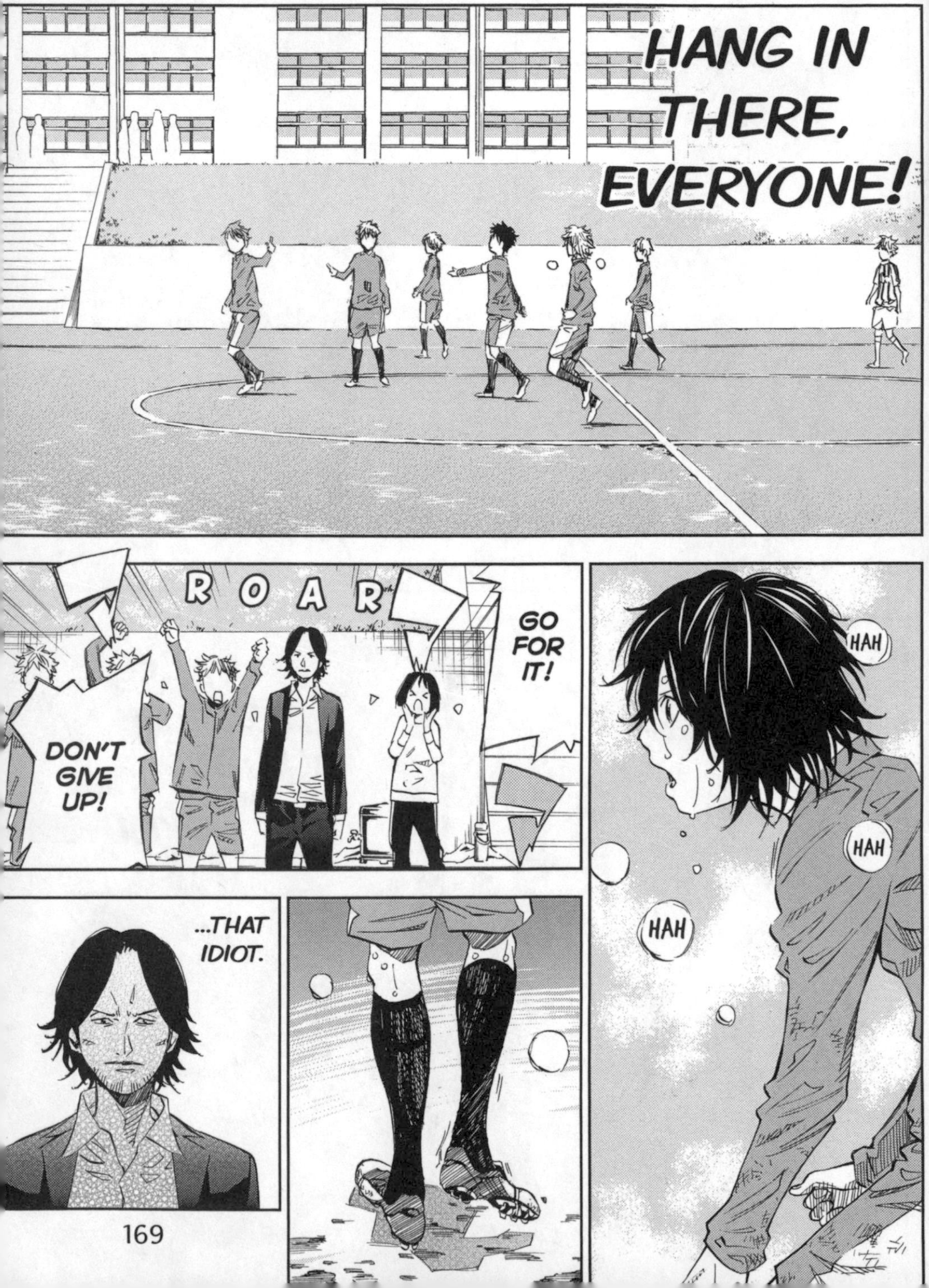
HANG IN THERE, EVERYONE!
HAH
HAH
HAH
GO FOR IT!
ROAR
DON'T GIVE UP!
...THAT IDIOT.

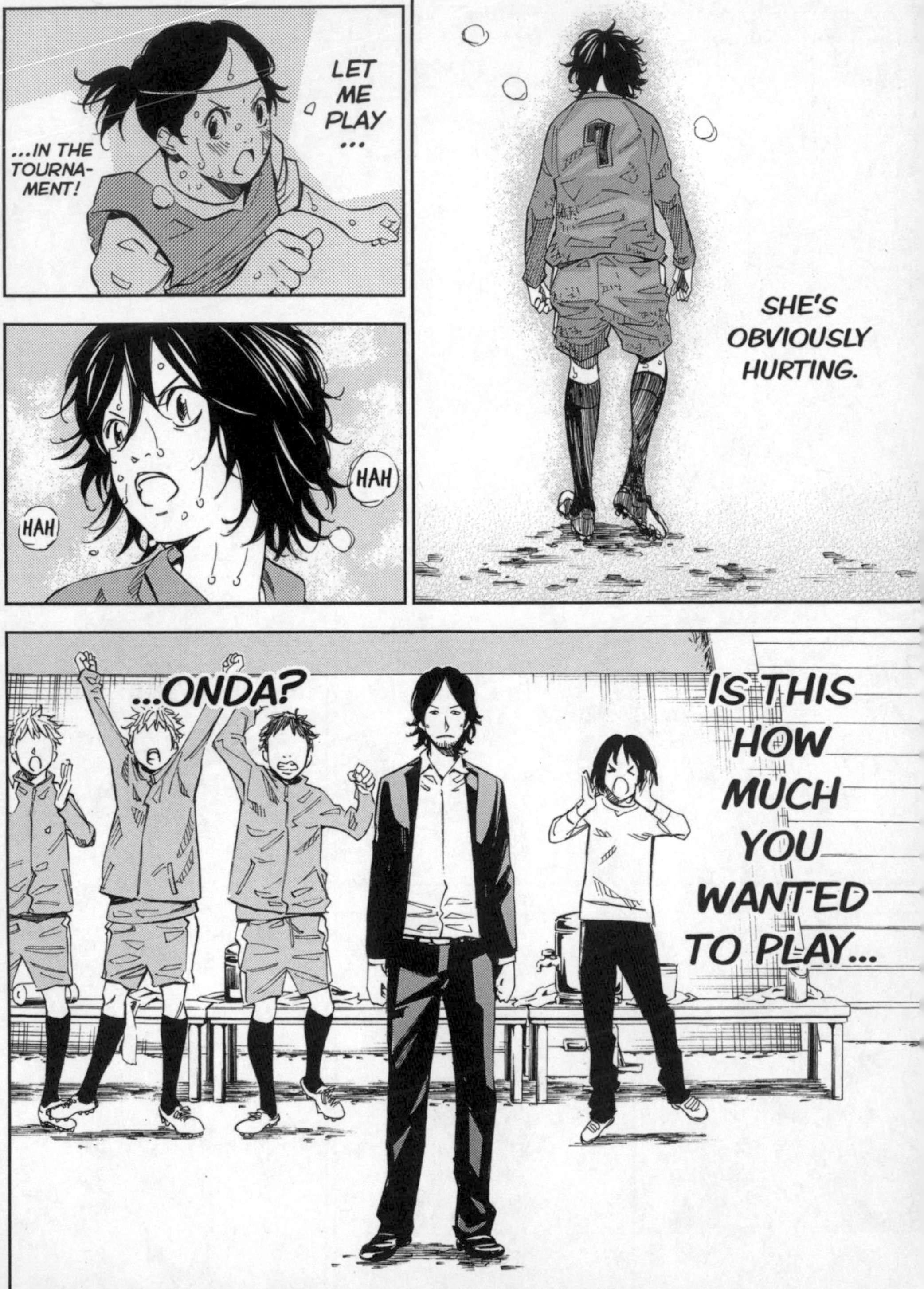
SHE'S OBVIOUSLY HURTING.
LET ME PLAY...
...IN THE TOURNAMENT!
HAH
HAH
IS THIS HOW MUCH YOU WANTED TO PLAY...
...ONDA?

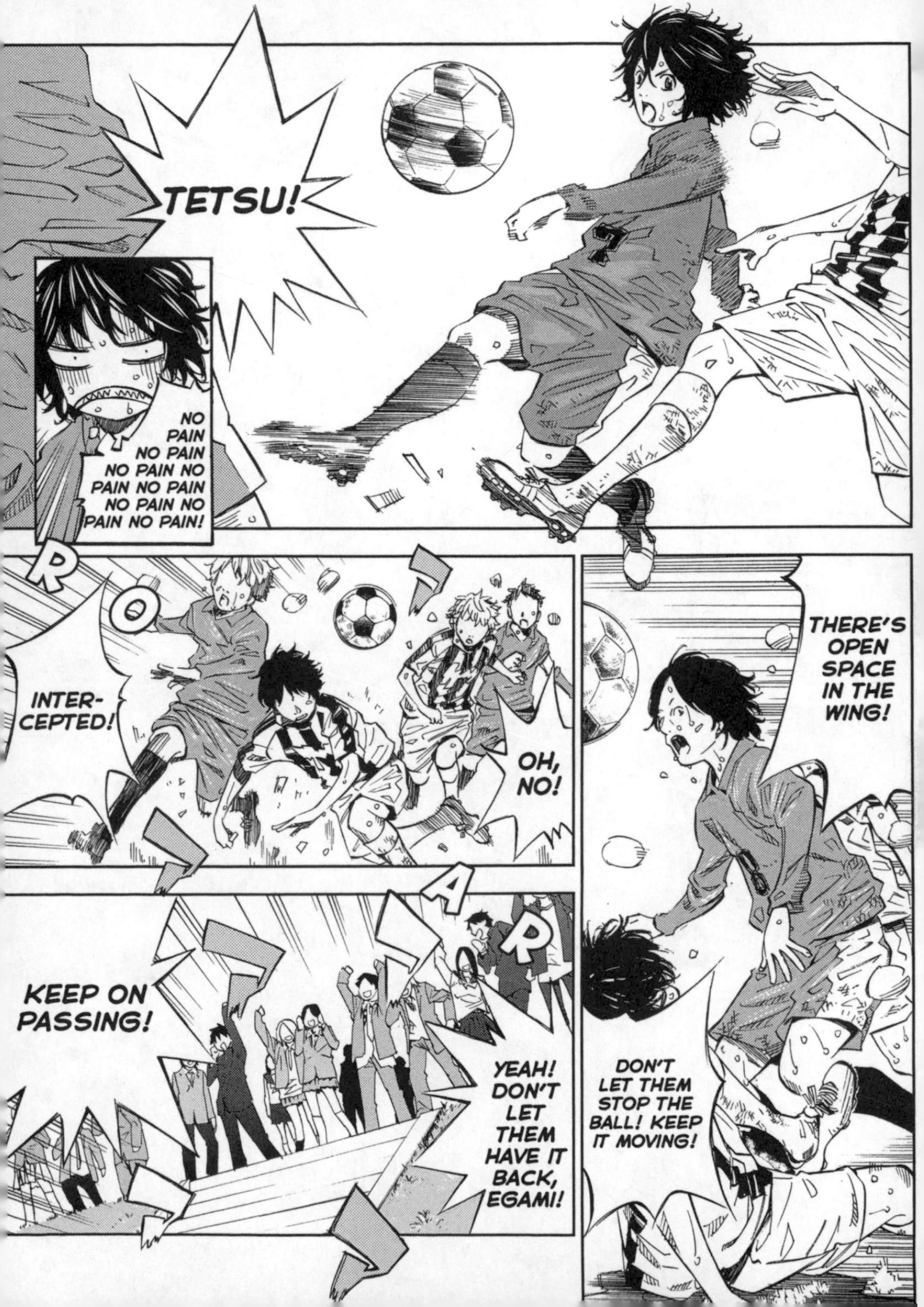
TETSU!
NO PAIN NO PAIN NO PAIN NO PAIN NO PAIN NO PAIN NO PAIN NO PAIN!
THERE'S OPEN SPACE IN THE WING!
DON'T LET THEM STOP THE BALL! KEEP IT MOVING!
OH, NO!
INTER-CEPTED!
ROAR
YEAH! DON'T LET THEM HAVE IT BACK, EGAMI!
KEEP ON PASSING!

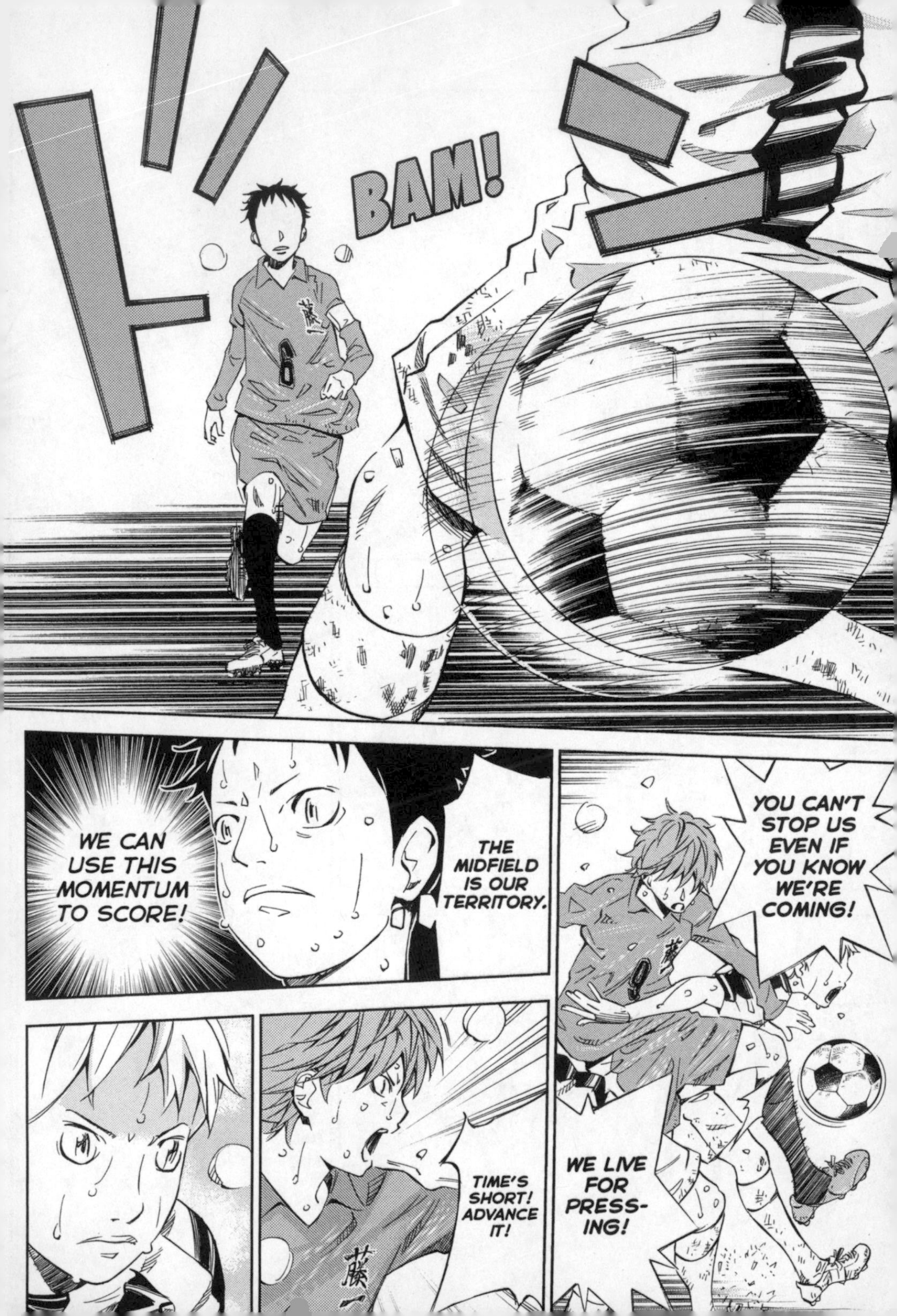
BAM!
YOU CAN'T STOP US EVEN IF YOU KNOW WE'RE COMING!
WE LIVE FOR PRESS-ING!
THE MIDFIELD IS OUR TERRITORY.
WE CAN USE THIS MOMENTUM TO SCORE!
TIME'S SHORT! ADVANCE IT!

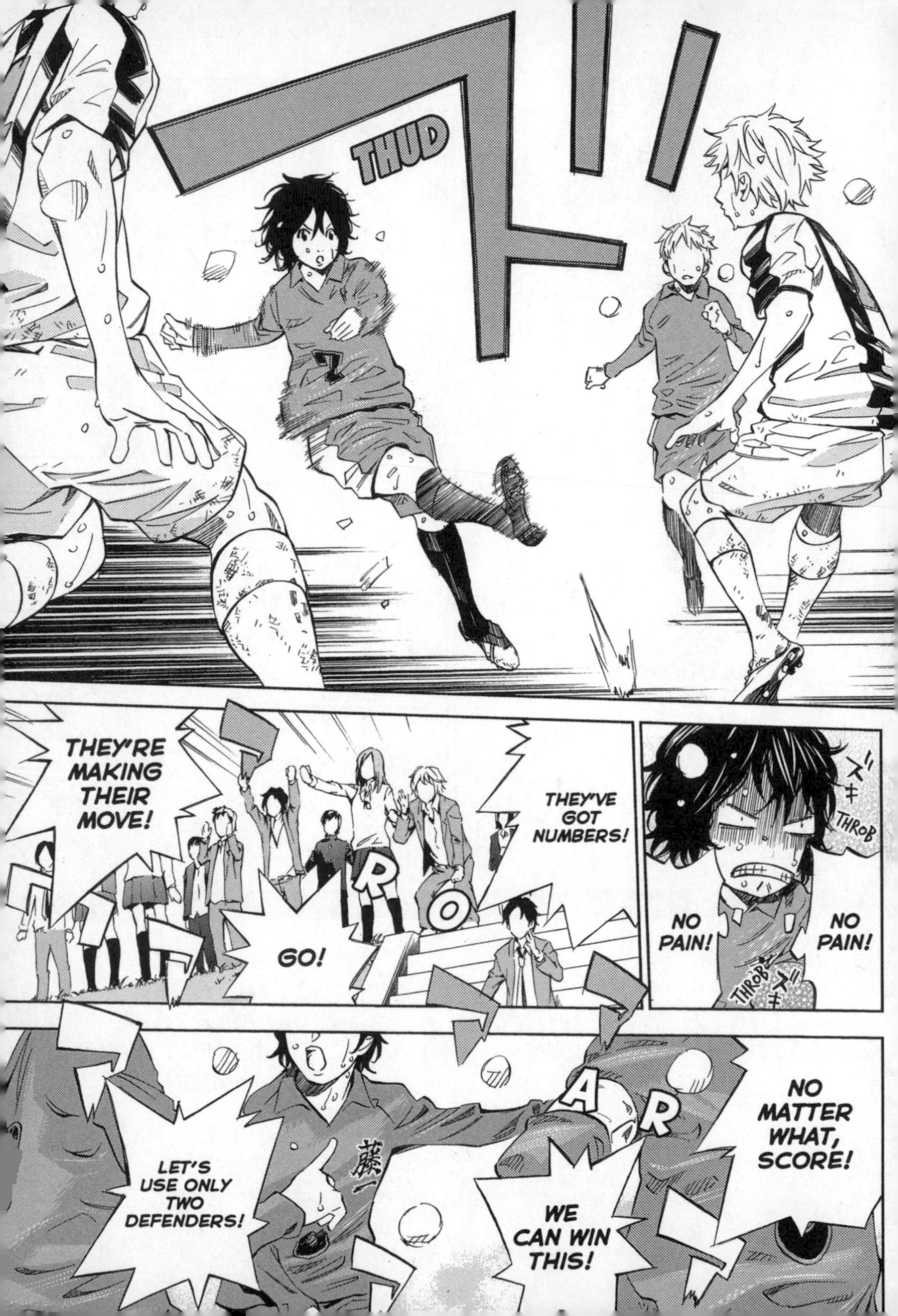
THUD
THROB
NO PAIN!
NO PAIN!
THROB
THEY'VE GOT NUMBERS!
THEY'RE MAKING THEIR MOVE!
R
O
GO!
NO MATTER WHAT, SCORE!
A
R
WE CAN WIN THIS!
LET'S USE ONLY TWO DEFENDERS!

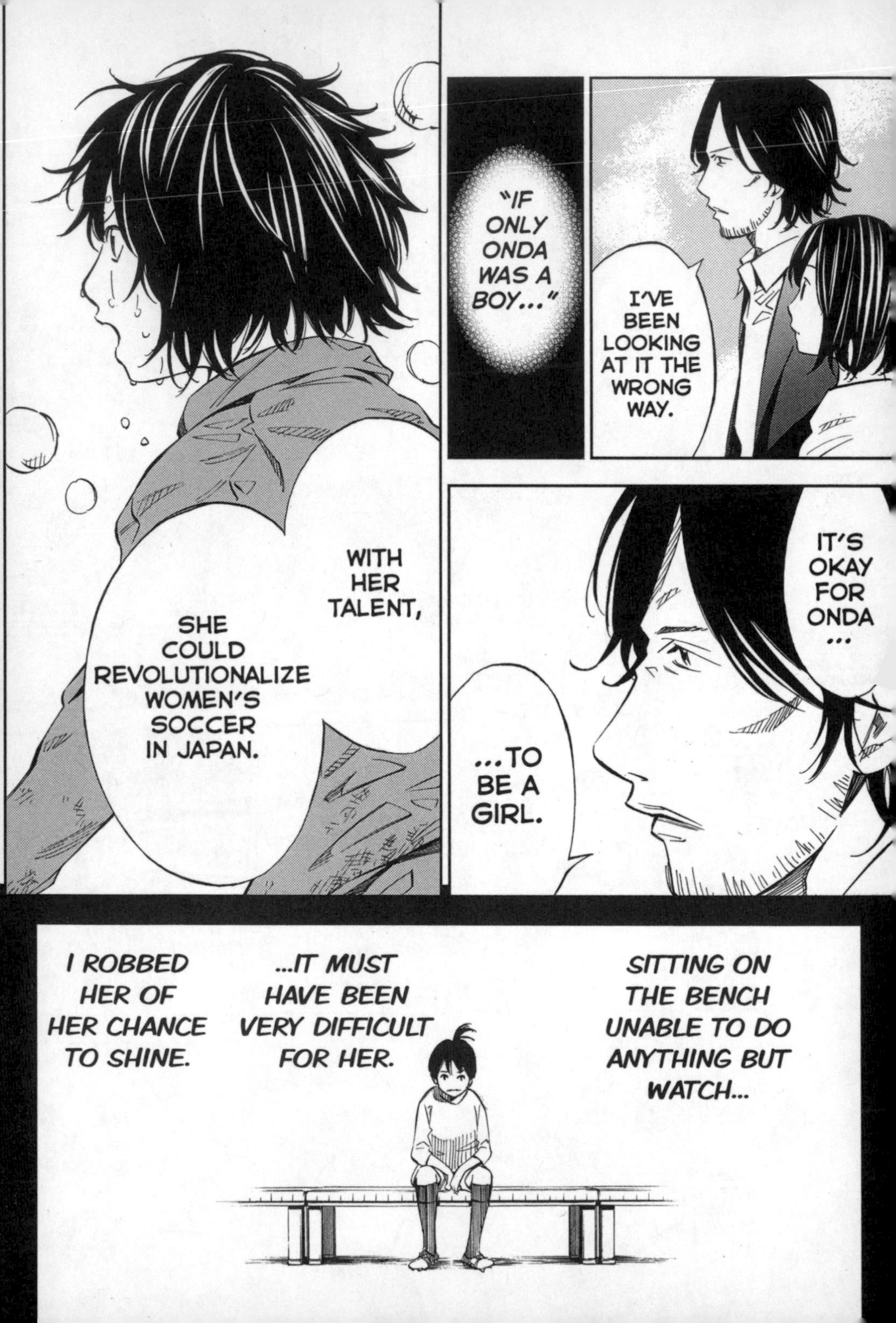
I'VE BEEN LOOKING AT IT THE WRONG WAY.
"IF ONLY ONDA WAS A BOY..."
IT'S OKAY FOR ONDA...
...TO BE A GIRL.
WITH HER TALENT,
SHE COULD REVOLUTIONALIZE WOMEN'S SOCCER IN JAPAN.
SITTING ON THE BENCH UNABLE TO DO ANYTHING BUT WATCH...
...IT MUST HAVE BEEN VERY DIFFICULT FOR HER.
I ROBBED HER OF HER CHANCE TO SHINE.

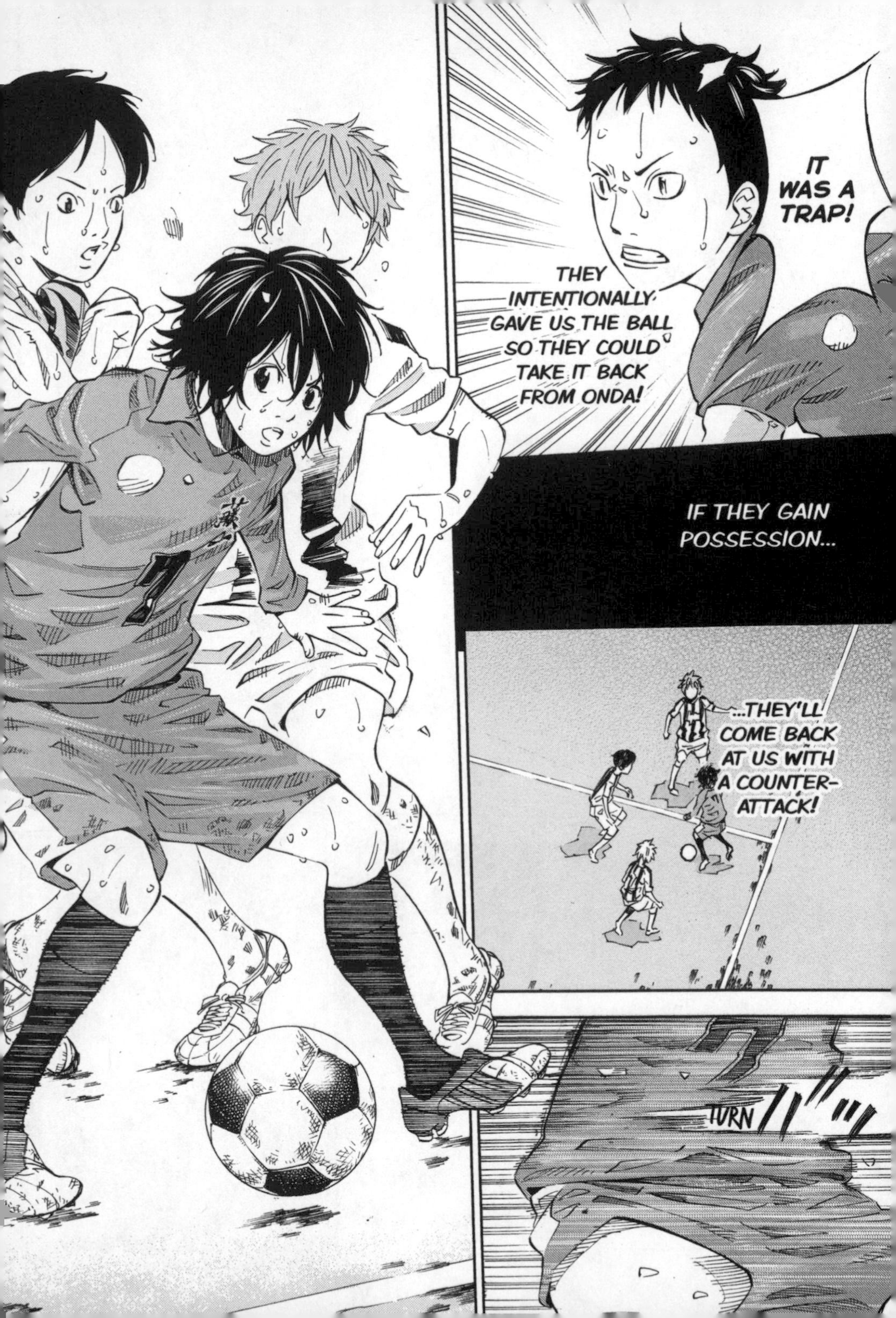
IT WAS A TRAP!
THEY INTENTIONALLY GAVE US THE BALL SO THEY COULD TAKE IT BACK FROM ONDA!
IF THEY GAIN POSSESSION...
...THEY'LL COME BACK AT US WITH A COUNTER-ATTACK!
TURN

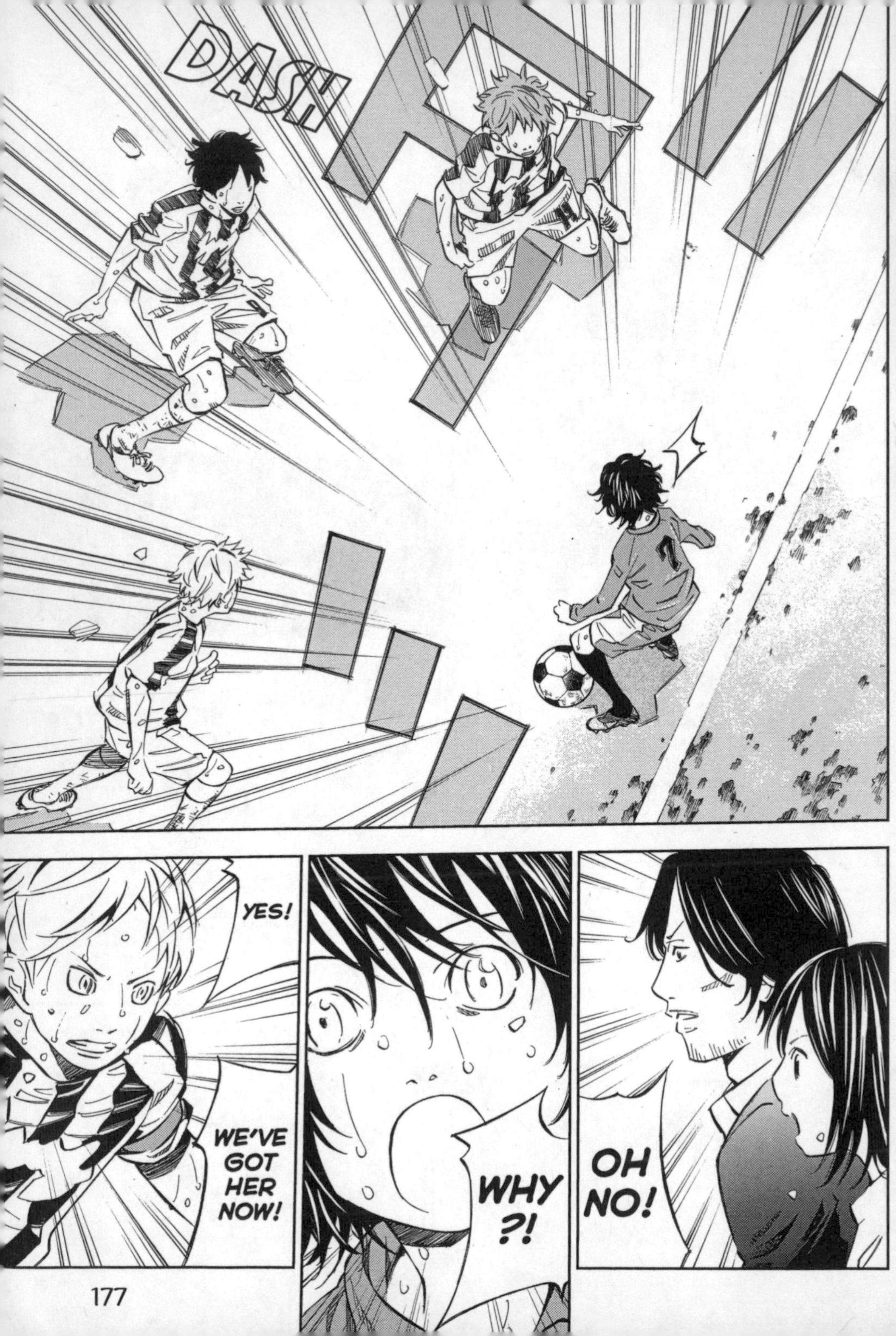
DASH
OH NO!
WHY ?!
YES!
WE'VE GOT HER NOW!

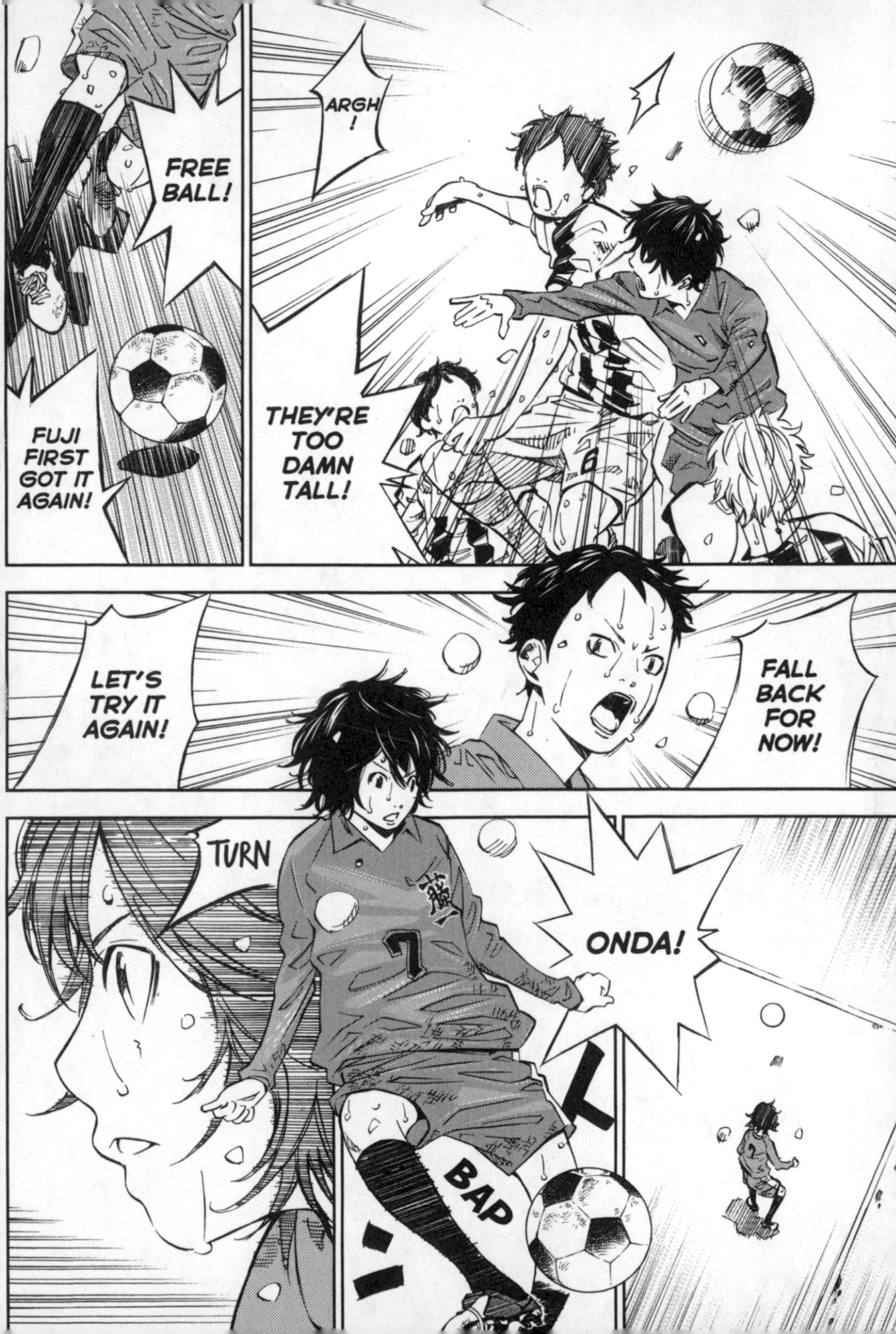
ARGH!
THEY'RE TOO DAMN TALL!
FREE BALL!
FUJI FIRST GOT IT AGAIN!
FALL BACK FOR NOW!
LET'S TRY IT AGAIN!
ONDA!
BAP
TURN

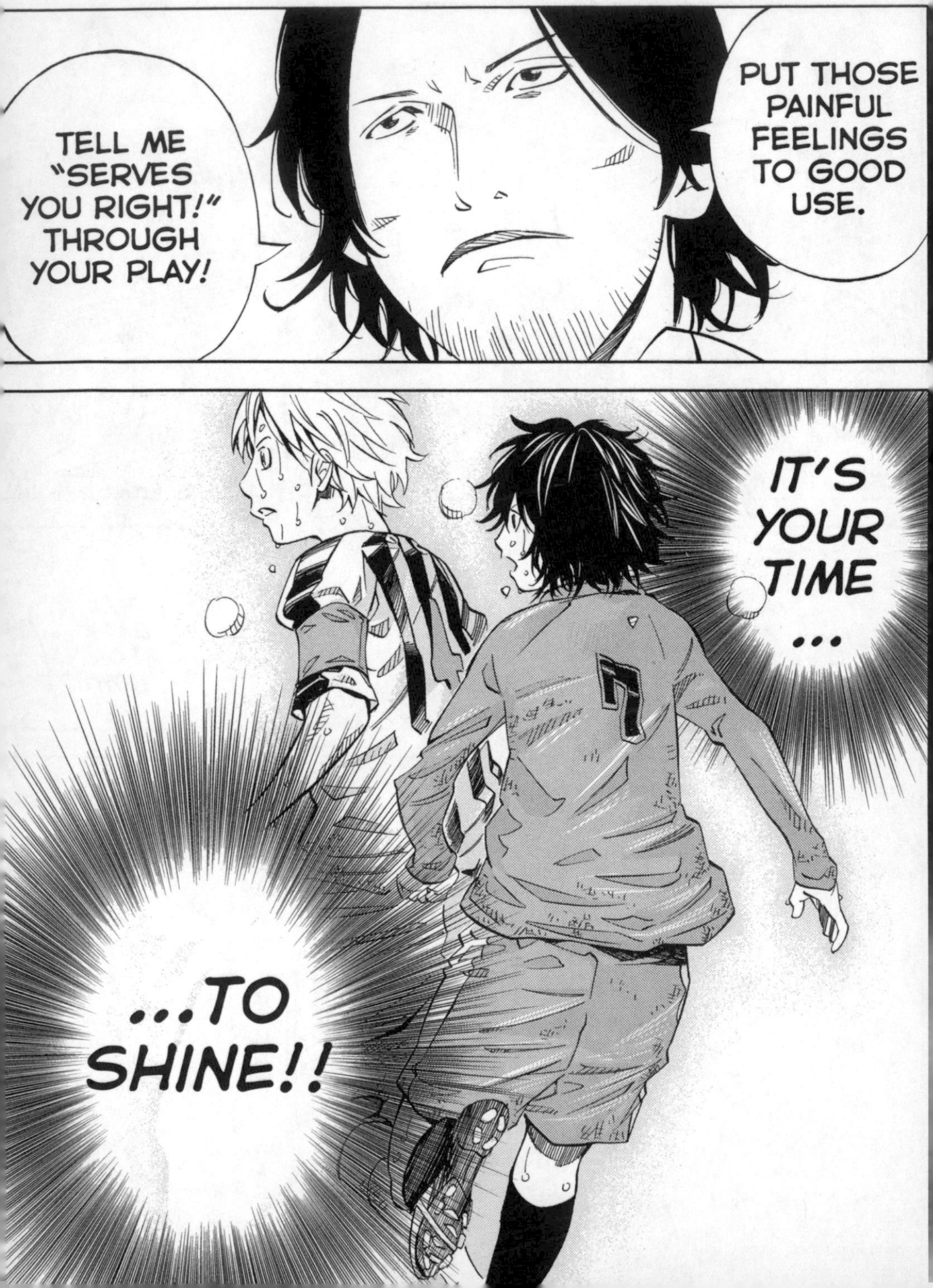
PUT THOSE PAINFUL FEELINGS TO GOOD USE.
TELL ME "SERVES YOU RIGHT!" THROUGH YOUR PLAY!
IT'S YOUR TIME...
...TO SHINE!!

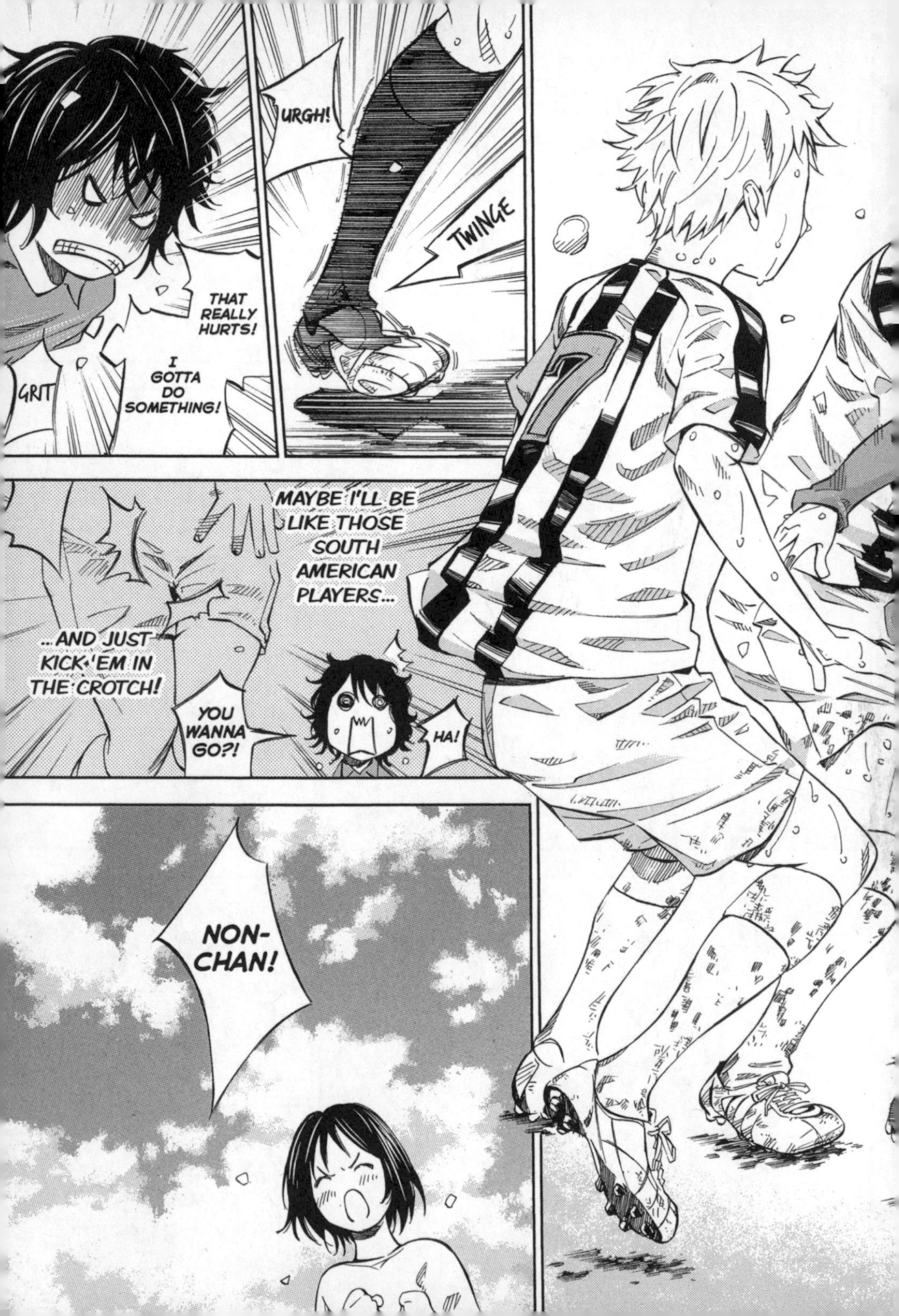
URGH!
TWINGE
THAT REALLY HURTS!
I GOTTA DO SOMETHING!
GRIT
MAYBE I'LL BE LIKE THOSE SOUTH AMERICAN PLAYERS...
...AND JUST KICK 'EM IN THE CROTCH!
HA!
YOU WANNA GO?!
NON-CHAN!

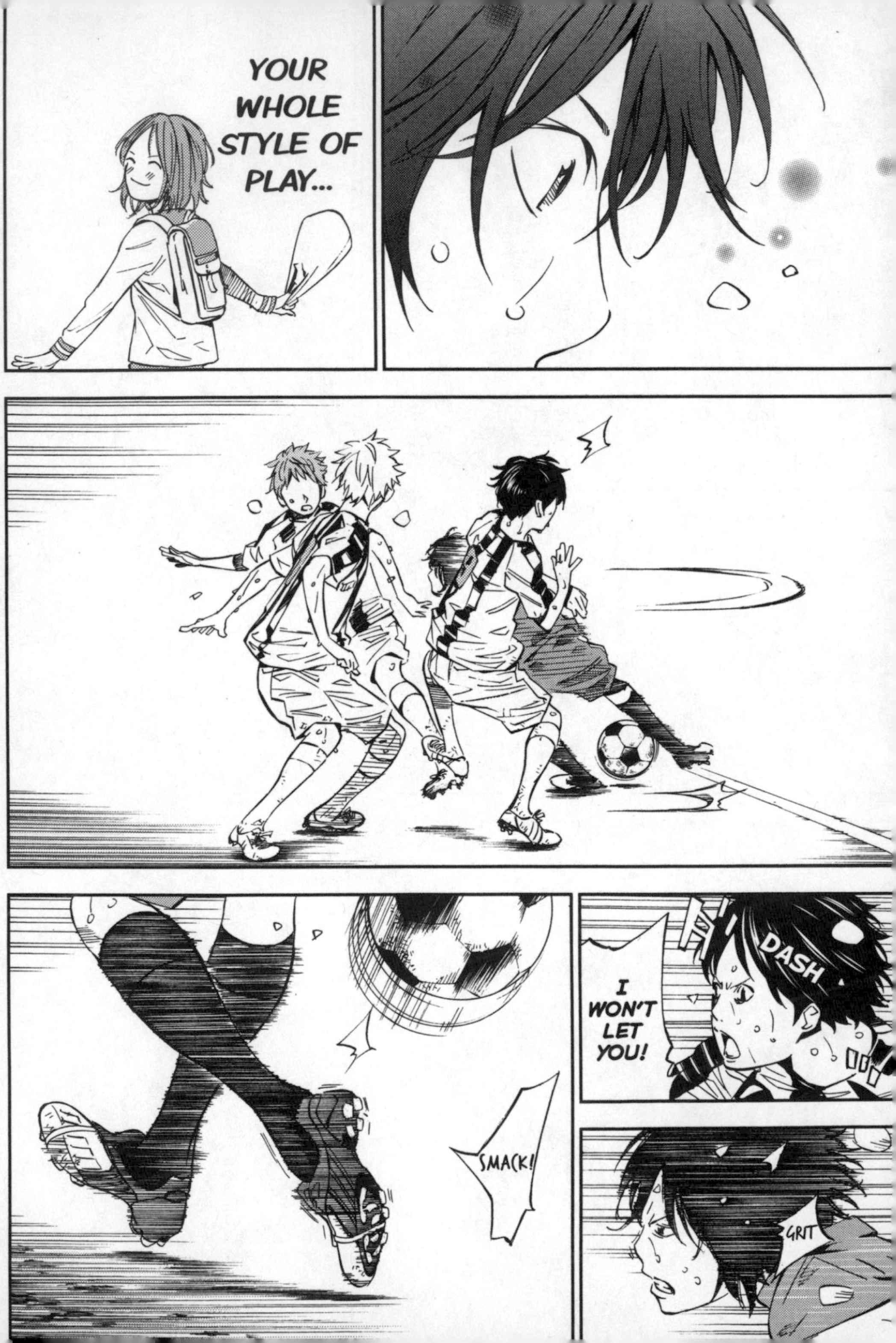
YOUR WHOLE STYLE OF PLAY...
DASH
I WON'T LET YOU!
GRIT
SMACK!

WE GOT HER!

OH... I SEE.

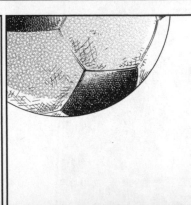

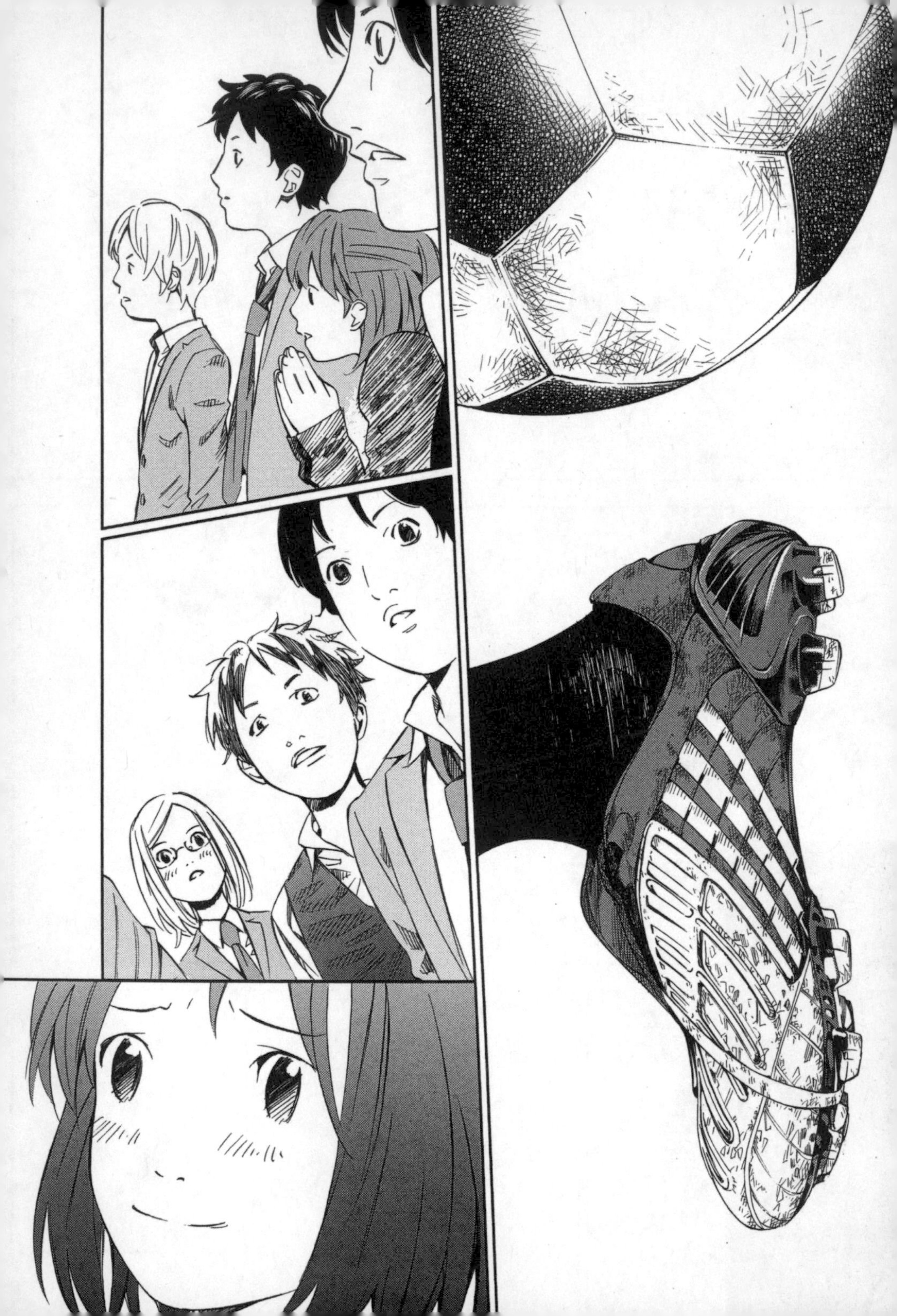

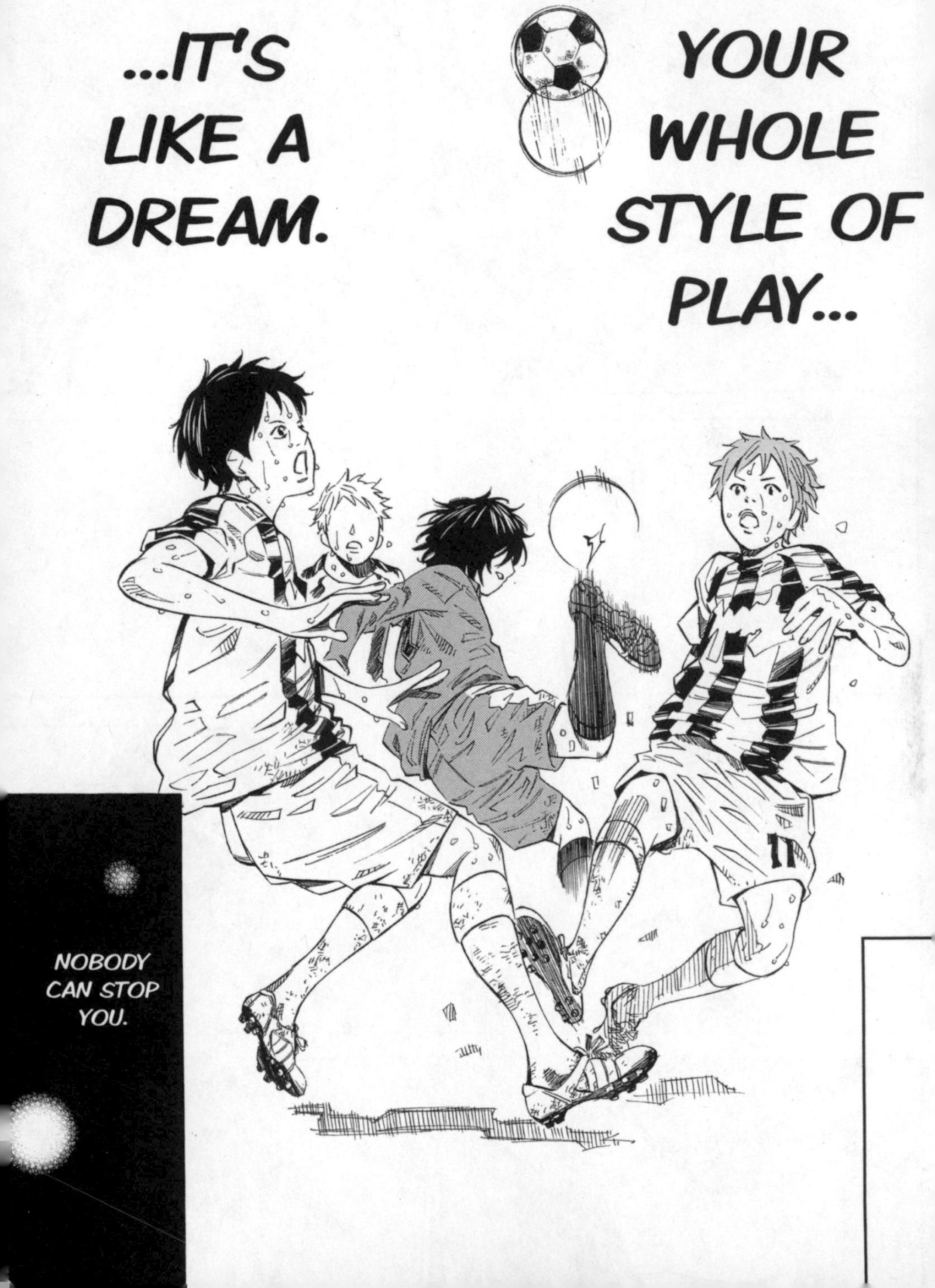
YOUR WHOLE STYLE OF PLAY...
...IT'S LIKE A DREAM.
NOBODY CAN STOP YOU.

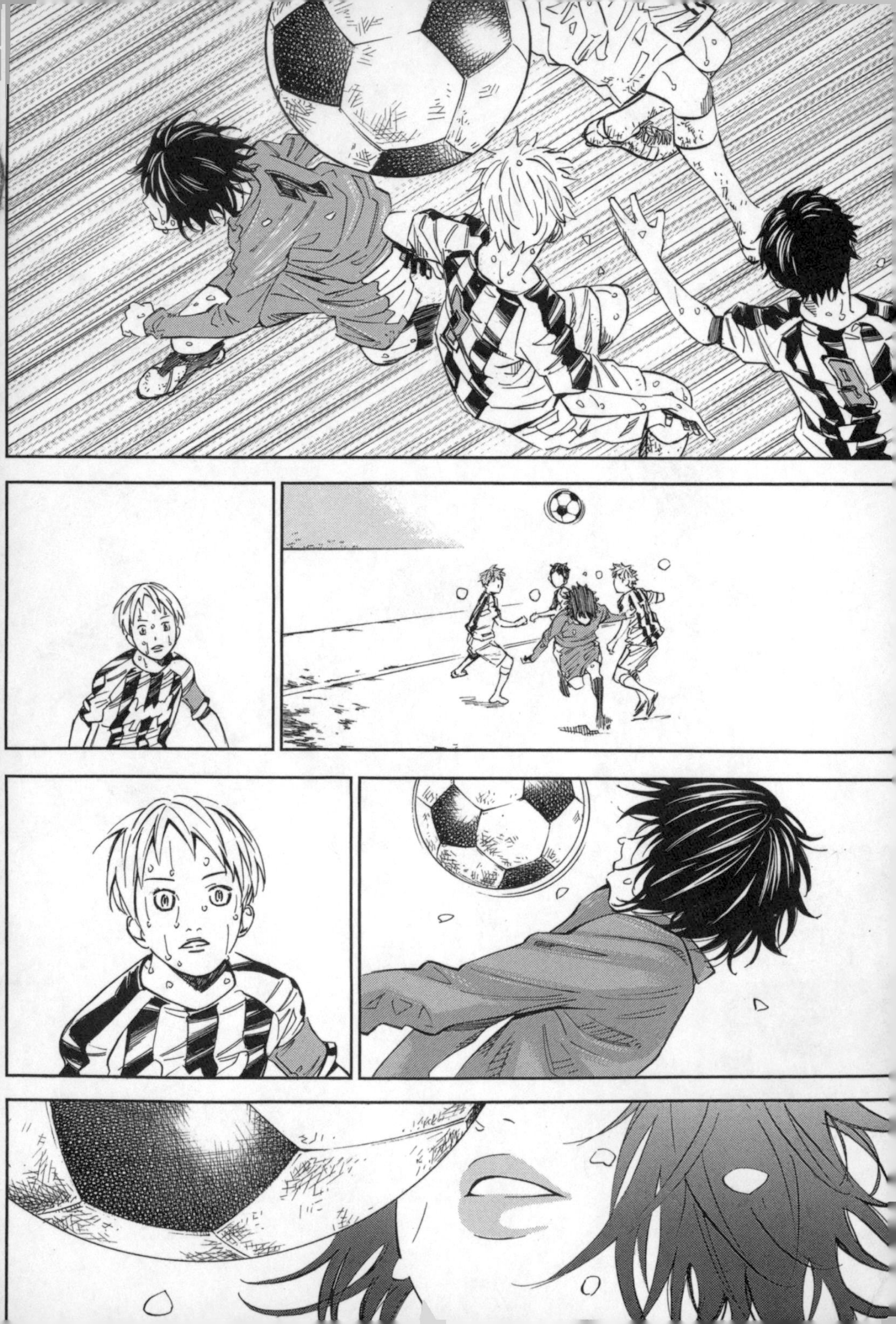

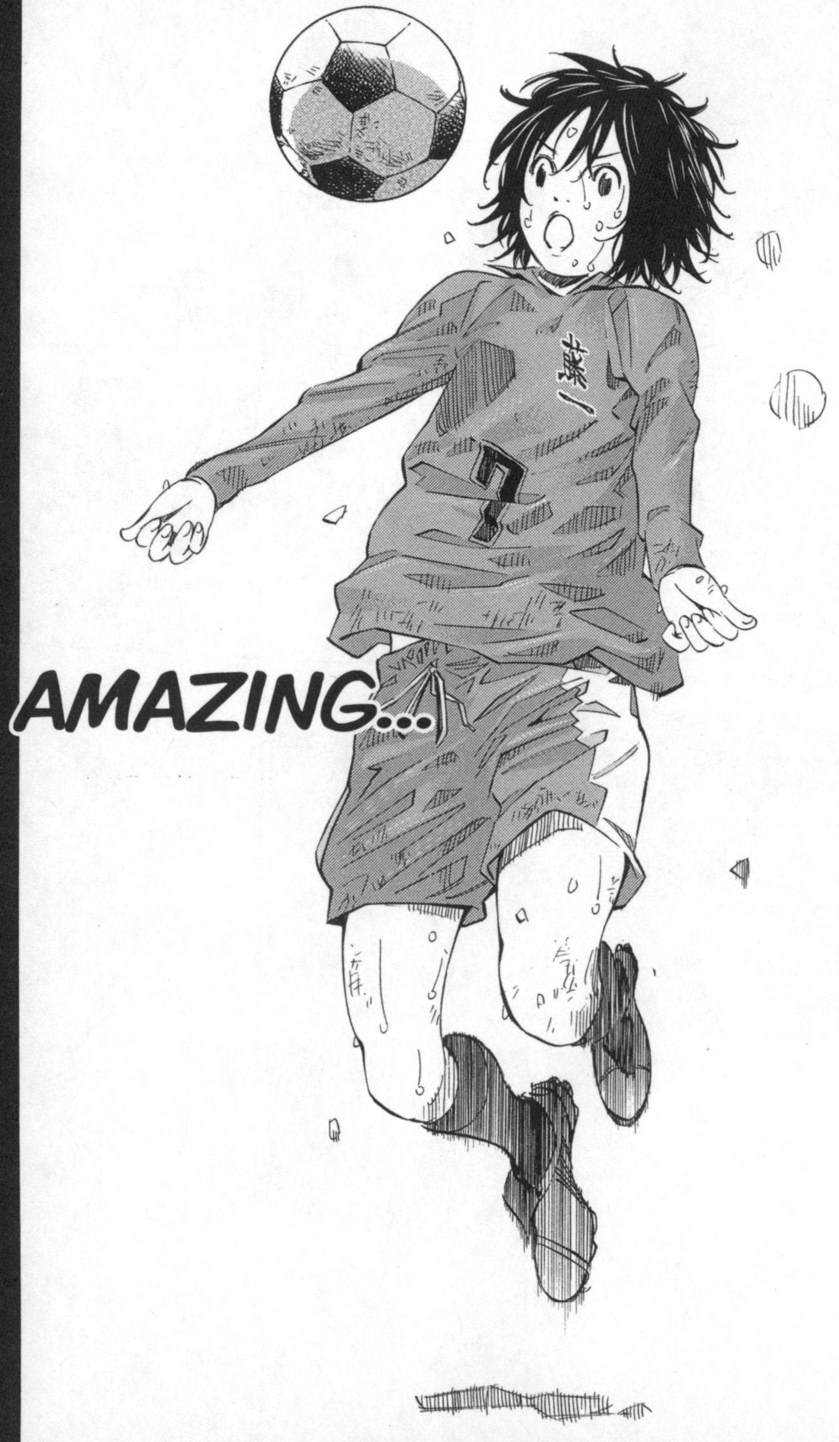
AMAZING...

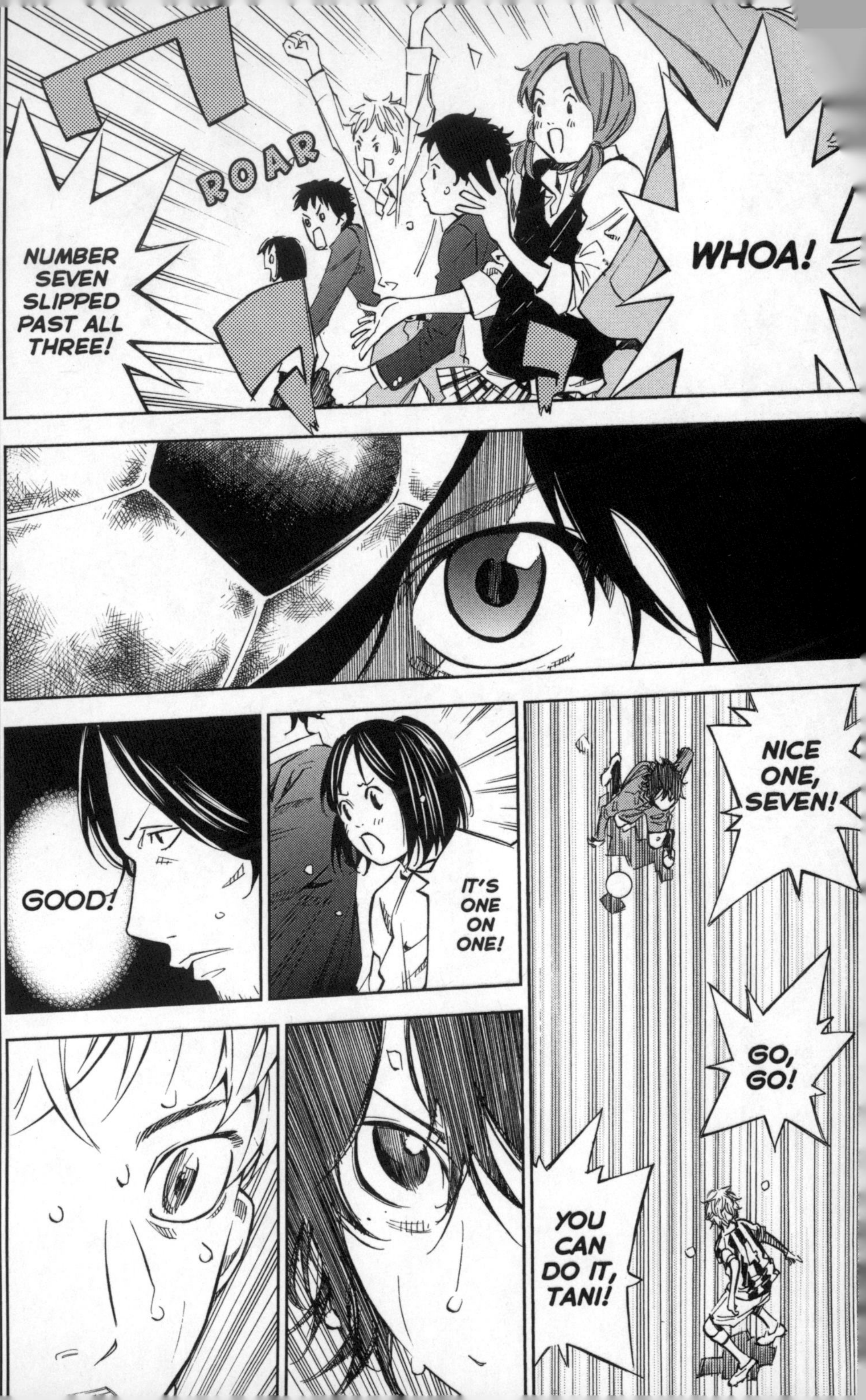
WHOA!
ROAR
NUMBER SEVEN SLIPPED PAST ALL THREE!
NICE ONE, SEVEN!
GO, GO!
YOU CAN DO IT, TANI!
IT'S ONE ON ONE!
GOOD!

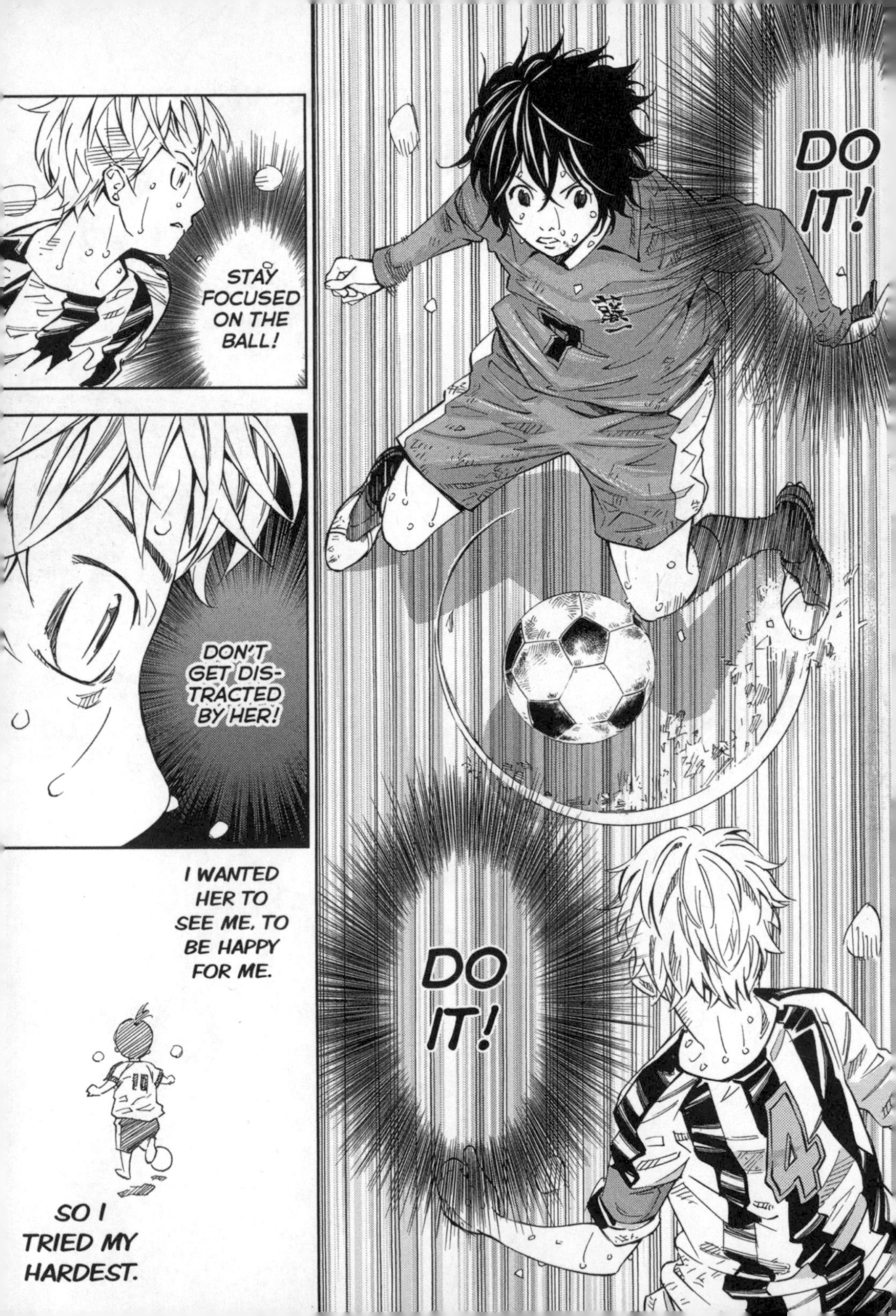
DO IT!
DO IT!
STAY FOCUSED ON THE BALL!
DON'T GET DISTRACTED BY HER!
I WANTED HER TO SEE ME, TO BE HAPPY FOR ME.
SO I TRIED MY HARDEST.

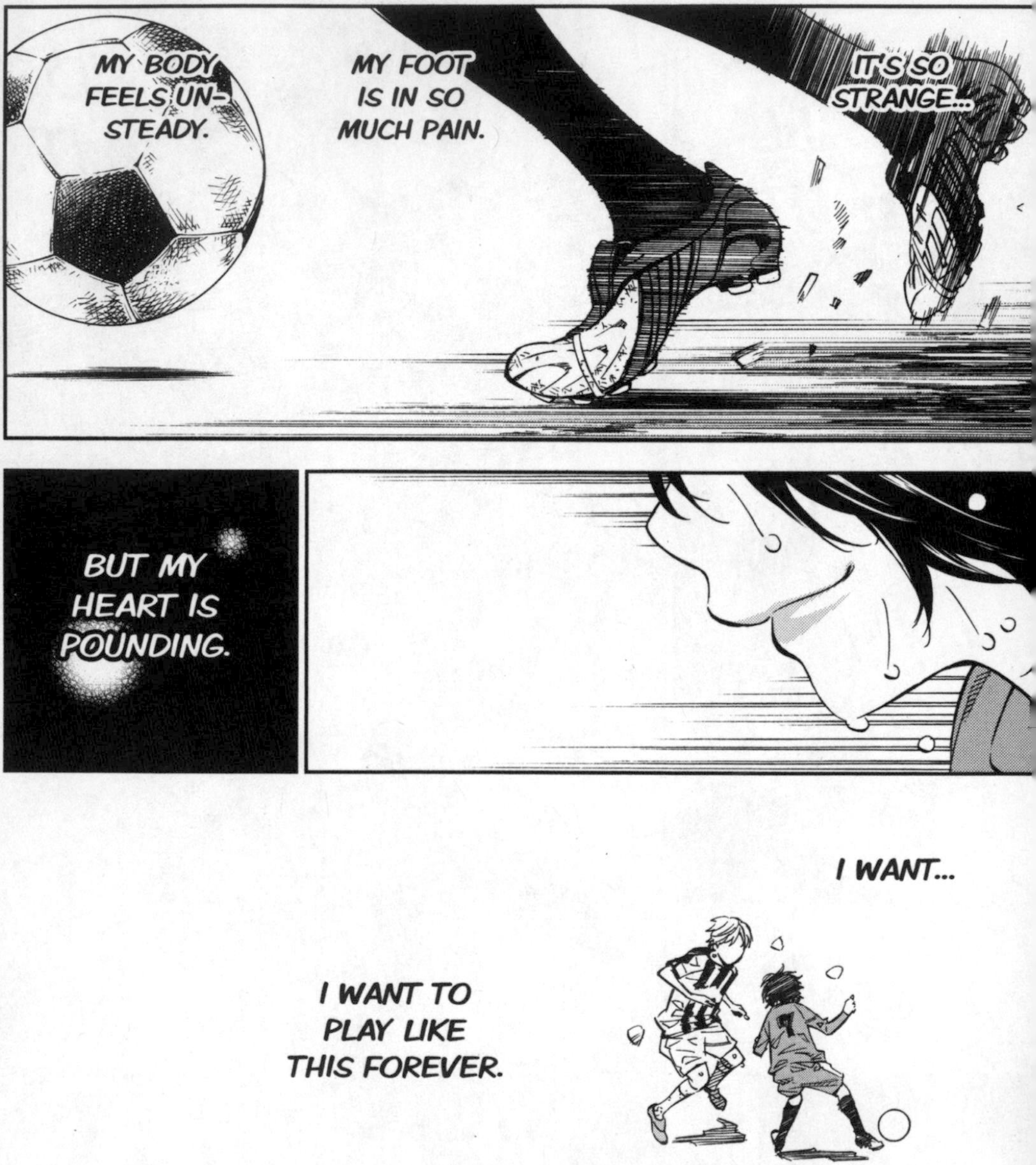
IT'S SO STRANGE...
MY FOOT IS IN SO MUCH PAIN.
MY BODY FEELS UN-STEADY.
BUT MY HEART IS POUNDING.
I WANT...
I WANT TO PLAY LIKE THIS FOREVER.

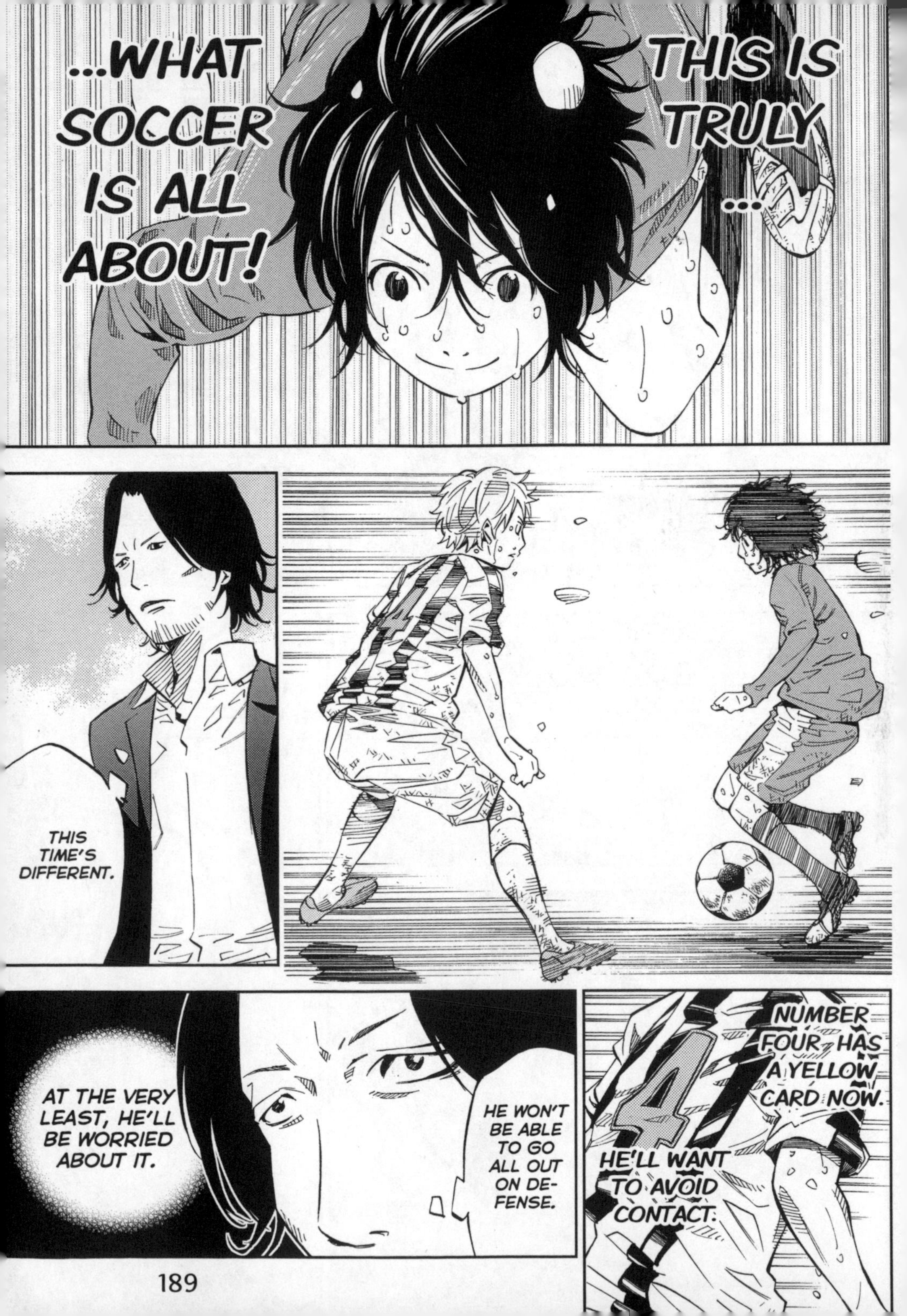
THIS IS TRULY ...
...WHAT SOCCER IS ALL ABOUT!
THIS TIME'S DIFFERENT.
NUMBER FOUR HAS A YELLOW CARD NOW.
HE'LL WANT TO AVOID CONTACT.
HE WON'T BE ABLE TO GO ALL OUT ON DE-FENSE.
AT THE VERY LEAST, HE'LL BE WORRIED ABOUT IT.

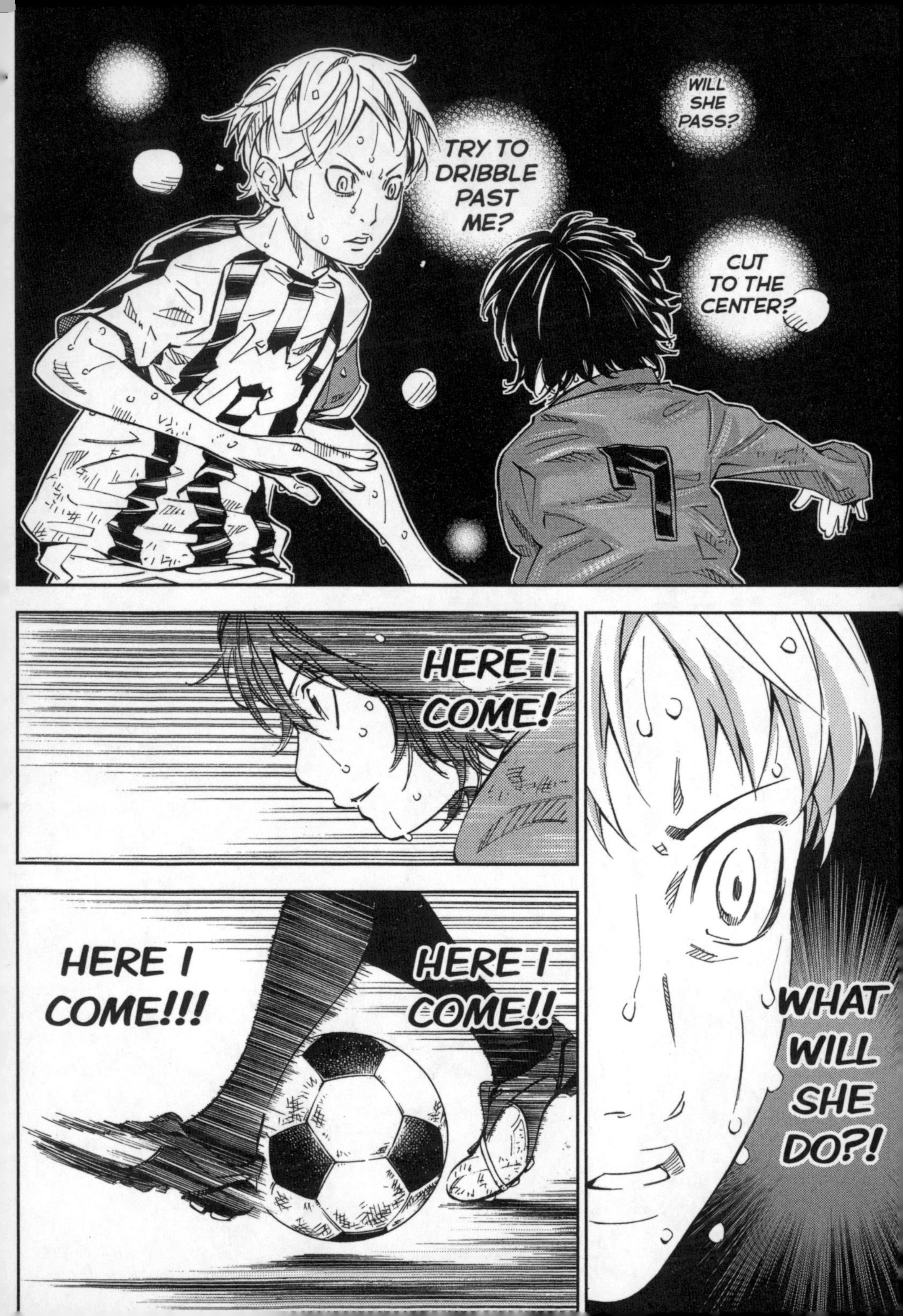
WILL SHE PASS?
TRY TO DRIBBLE PAST ME?
CUT TO THE CENTER?
WHAT WILL SHE DO?!
HERE I COME!
HERE I COME!!
HERE I COME!!!

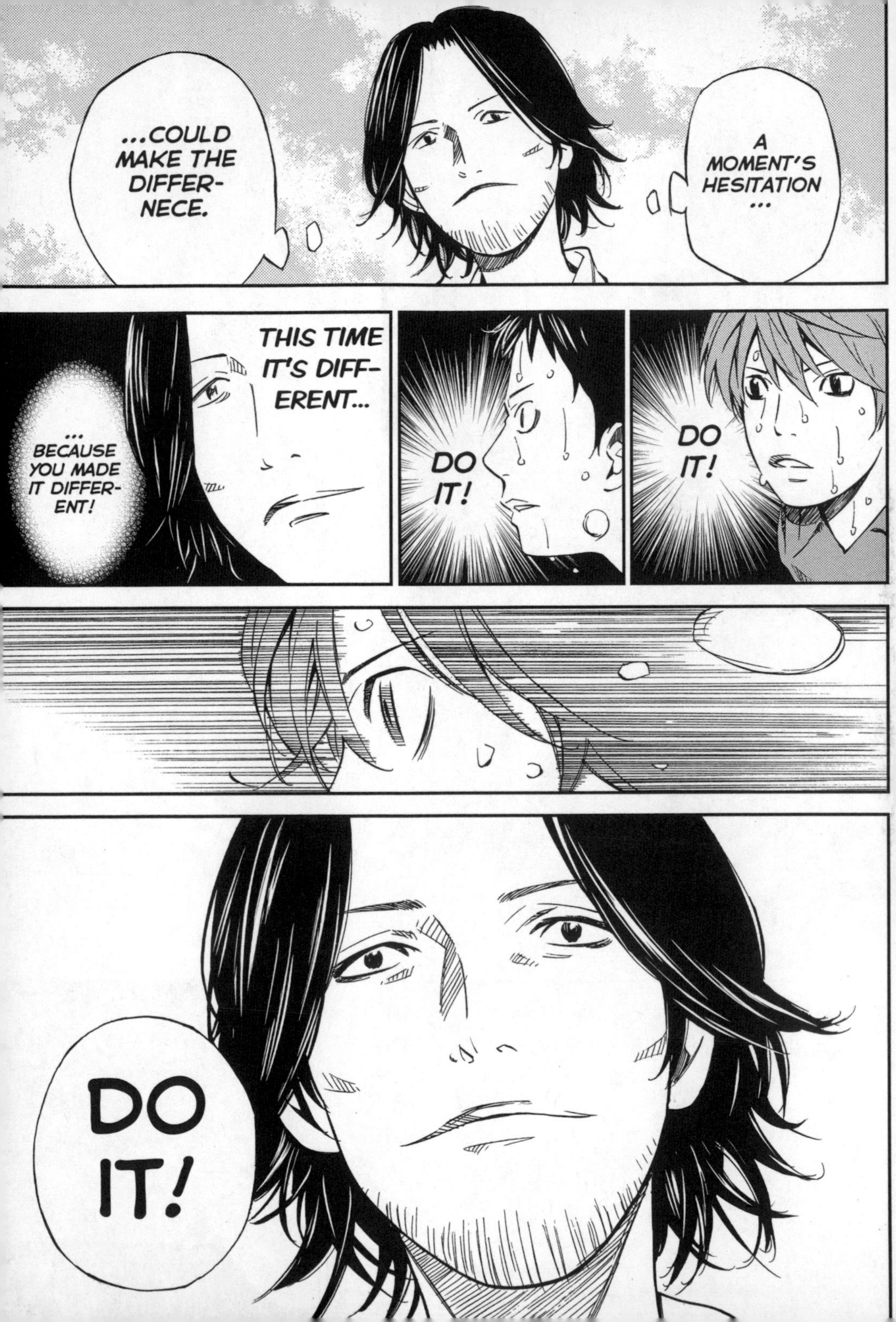
A MOMENT'S HESITATION ...
...COULD MAKE THE DIFFER-NECE.
DO IT!
DO IT!
THIS TIME IT'S DIFF-ERENT...
...BECAUSE YOU MADE IT DIFFER-ENT!
DO IT!

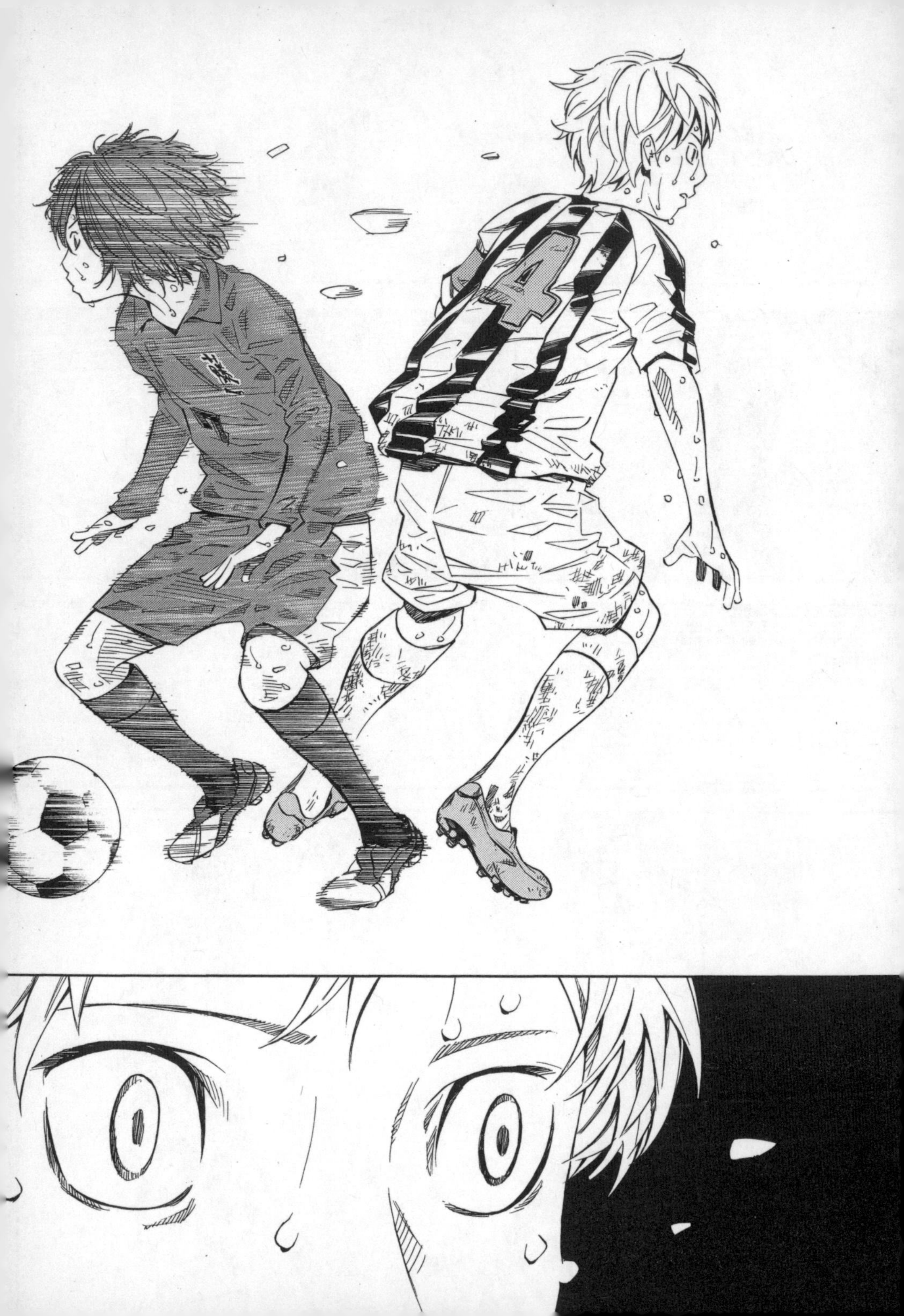

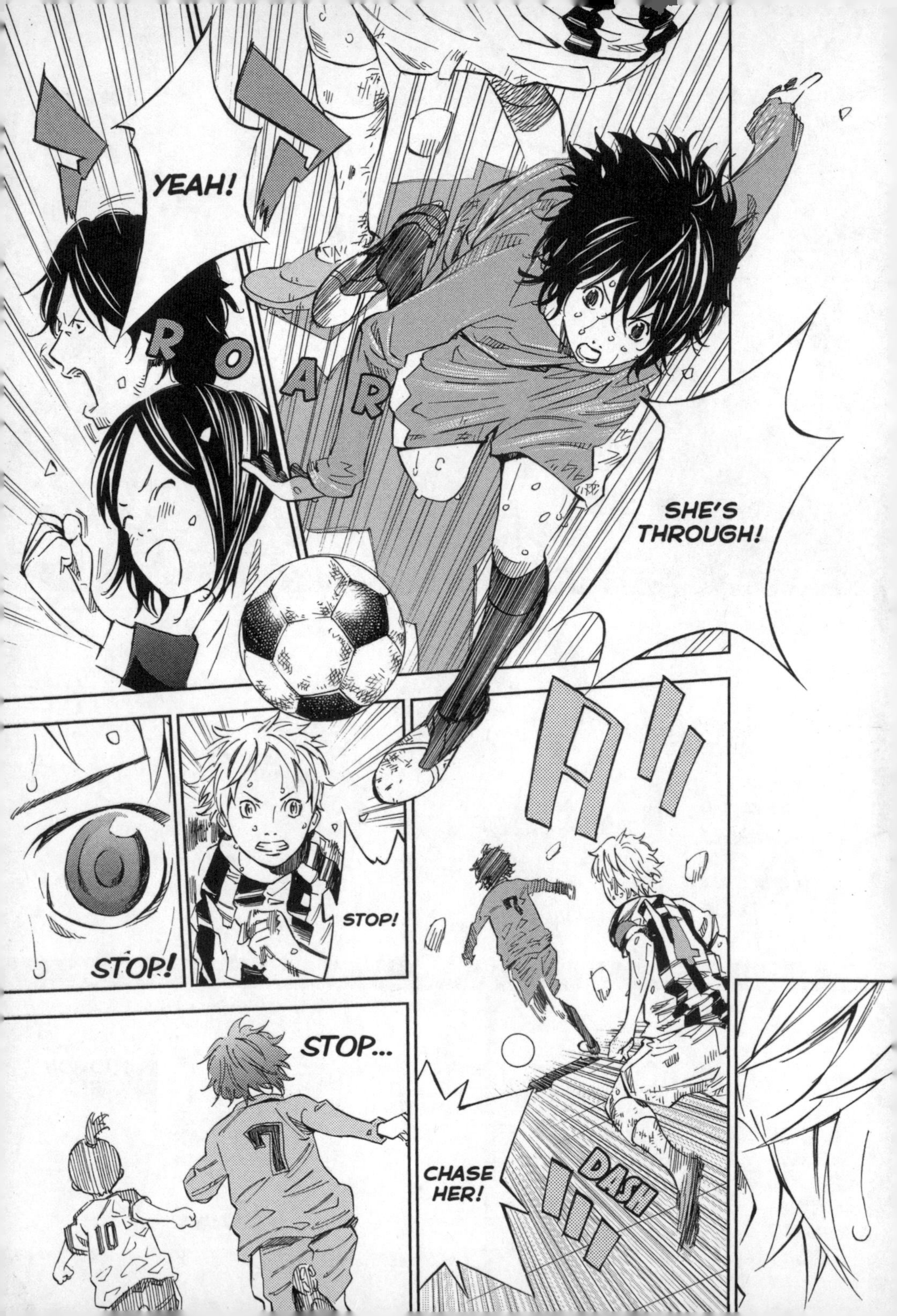
YEAH!
ROAR
SHE'S THROUGH!
A!!
CHASE HER!
DASH
STOP!
STOP!
STOP...

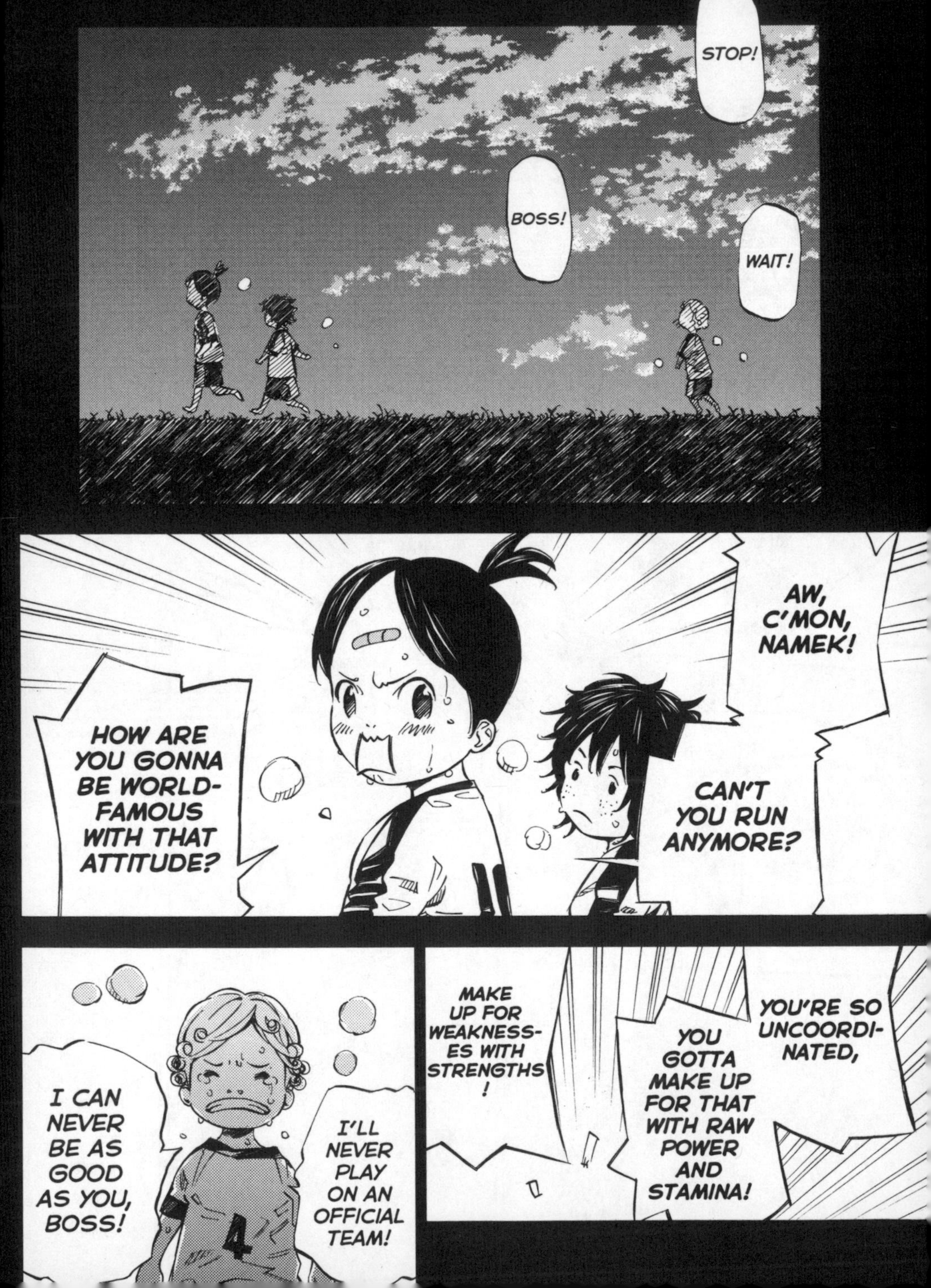
STOP!
BOSS!
WAIT!
AW, C'MON, NAMEK!
CAN'T YOU RUN ANYMORE?
HOW ARE YOU GONNA BE WORLD-FAMOUS WITH THAT ATTITUDE?
YOU'RE SO UNCOORDINATED,
YOU GOTTA MAKE UP FOR THAT WITH RAW POWER AND STAMINA!
MAKE UP FOR WEAKNESSES WITH STRENGTHS!
I'LL NEVER PLAY ON AN OFFICIAL TEAM!
I CAN NEVER BE AS GOOD AS YOU, BOSS!

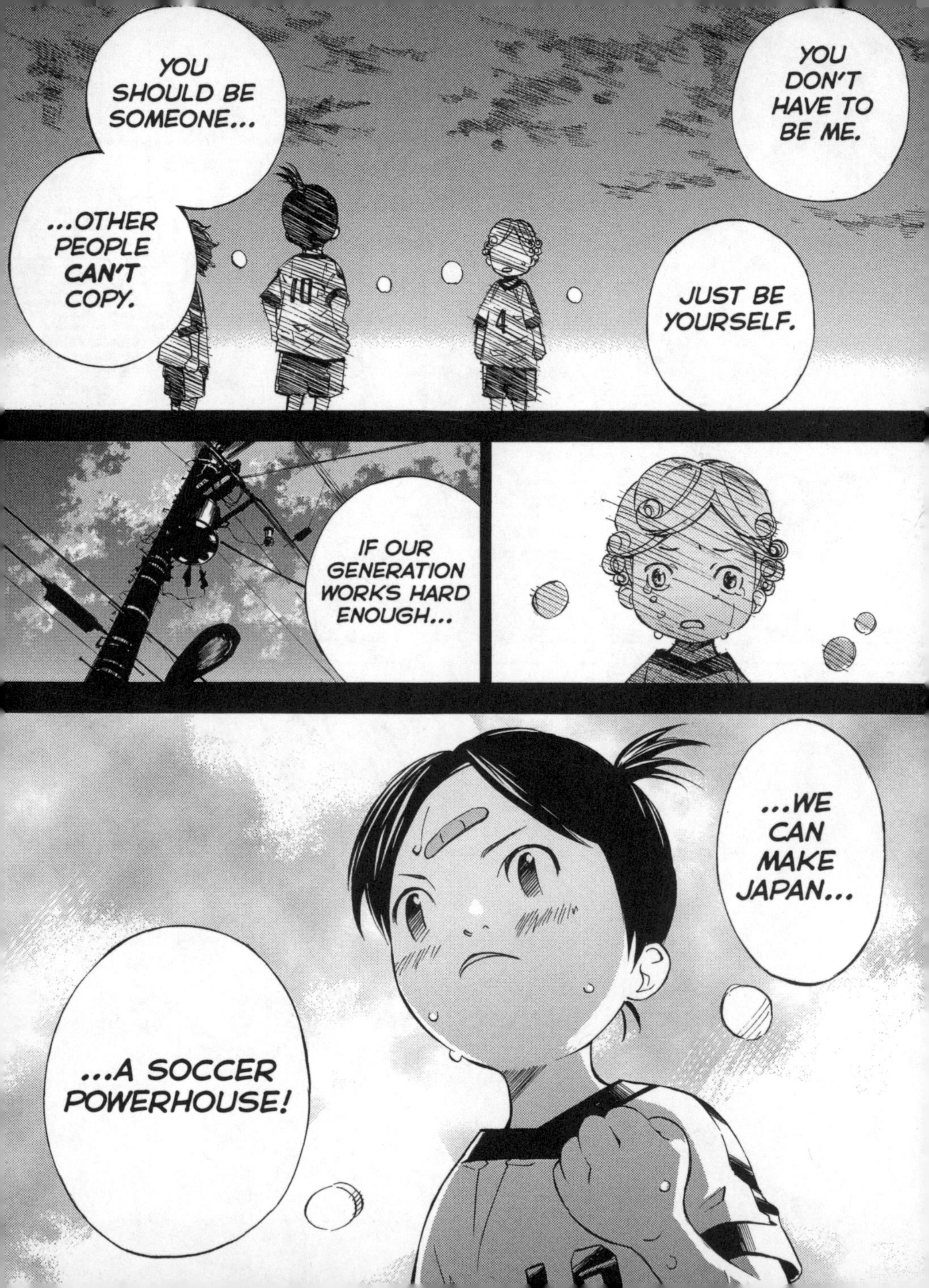
YOU DON'T HAVE TO BE ME.
JUST BE YOURSELF.
YOU SHOULD BE SOMEONE...
...OTHER PEOPLE CAN'T COPY.
IF OUR GENERATION WORKS HARD ENOUGH...
...WE CAN MAKE JAPAN...
...A SOCCER POWERHOUSE!

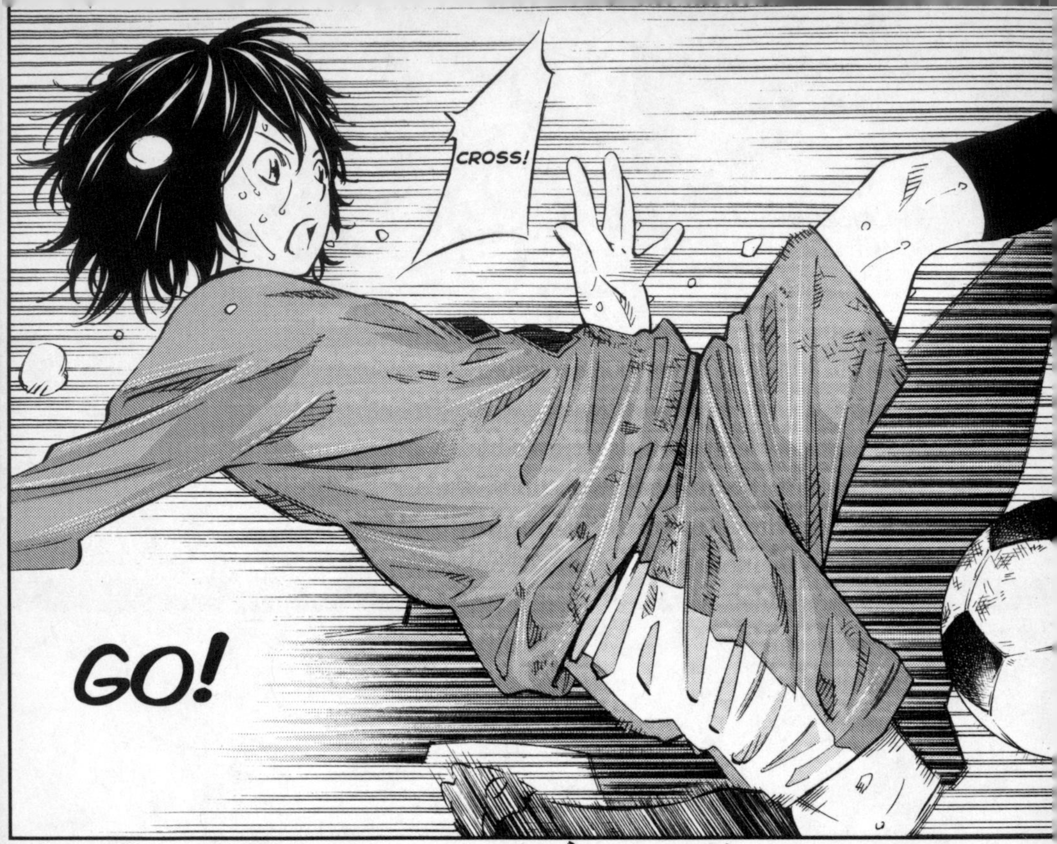
CROSS!
GO!
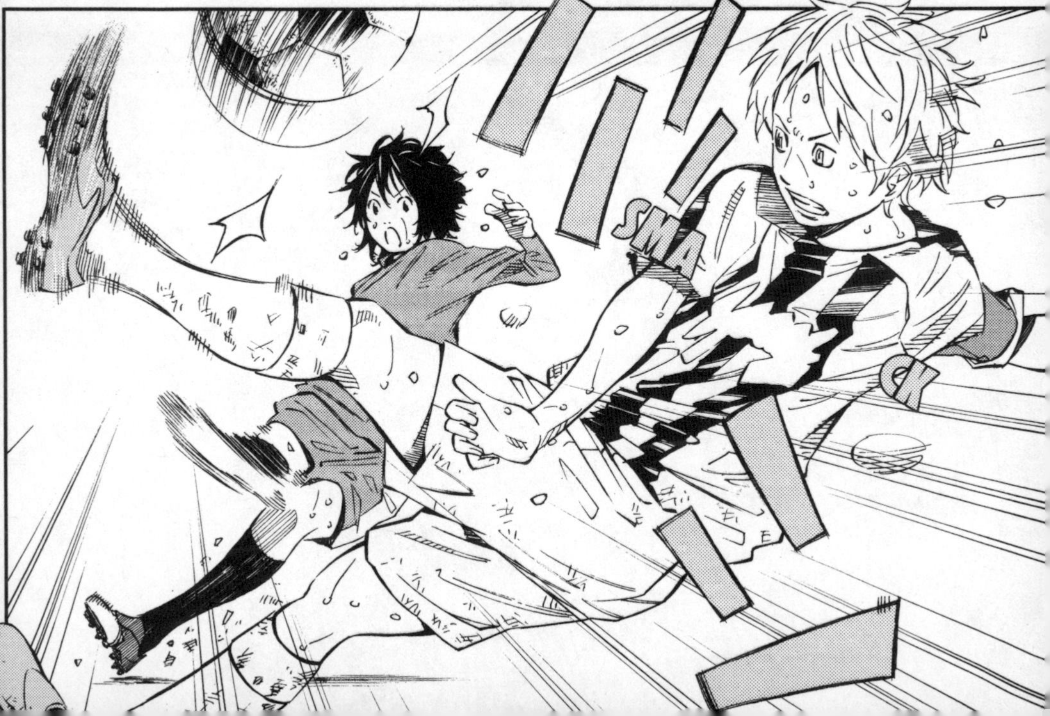
SMA
CK

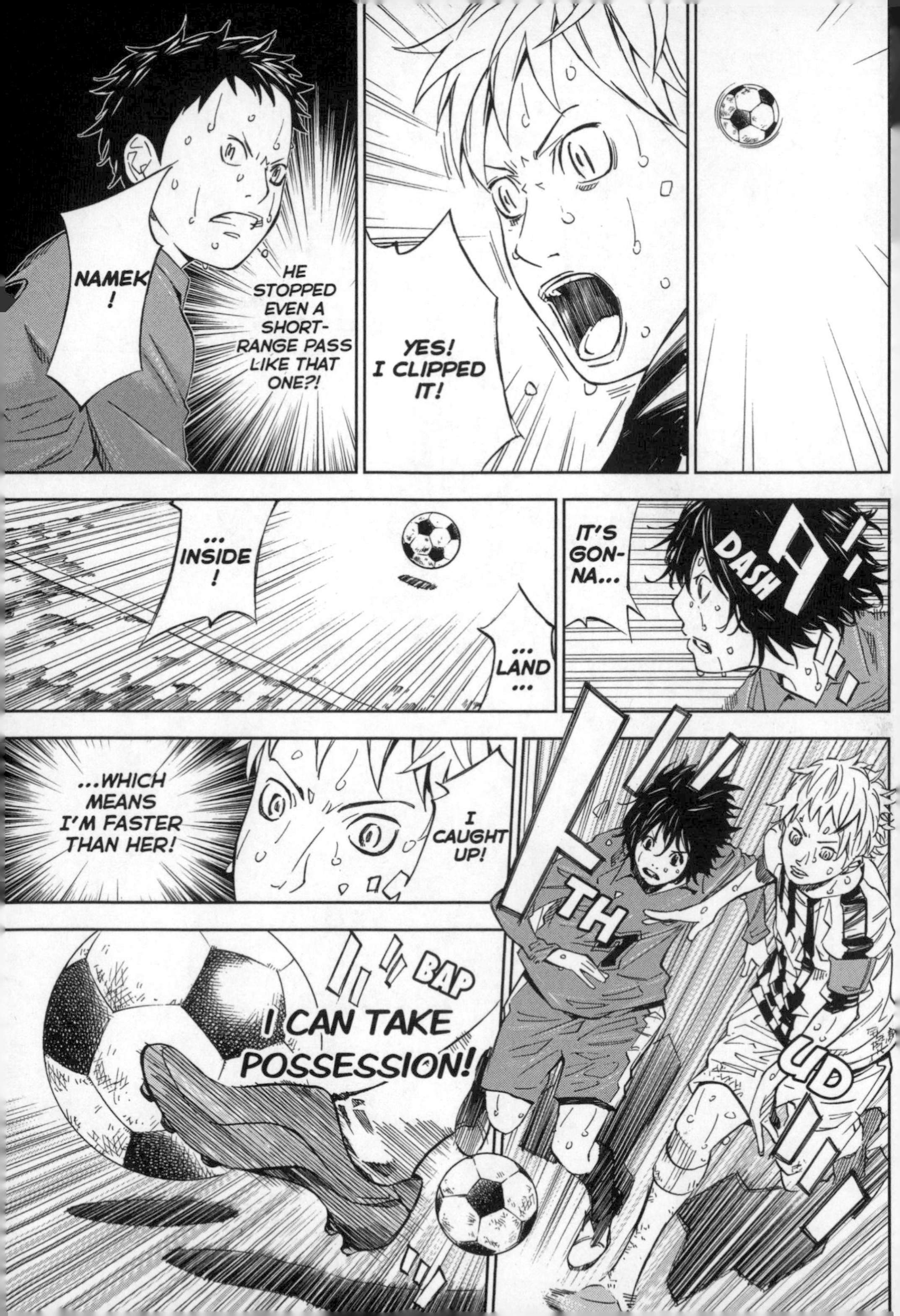
YES! I CLIPPED IT!
HE STOPPED EVEN A SHORT-RANGE PASS LIKE THAT ONE?!
NAMEK!
DASH
IT'S GON-NA...
...LAND...
...INSIDE!
TH
UD
I CAUGHT UP!
...WHICH MEANS I'M FASTER THAN HER!
BAP
I CAN TAKE POSSESSION!

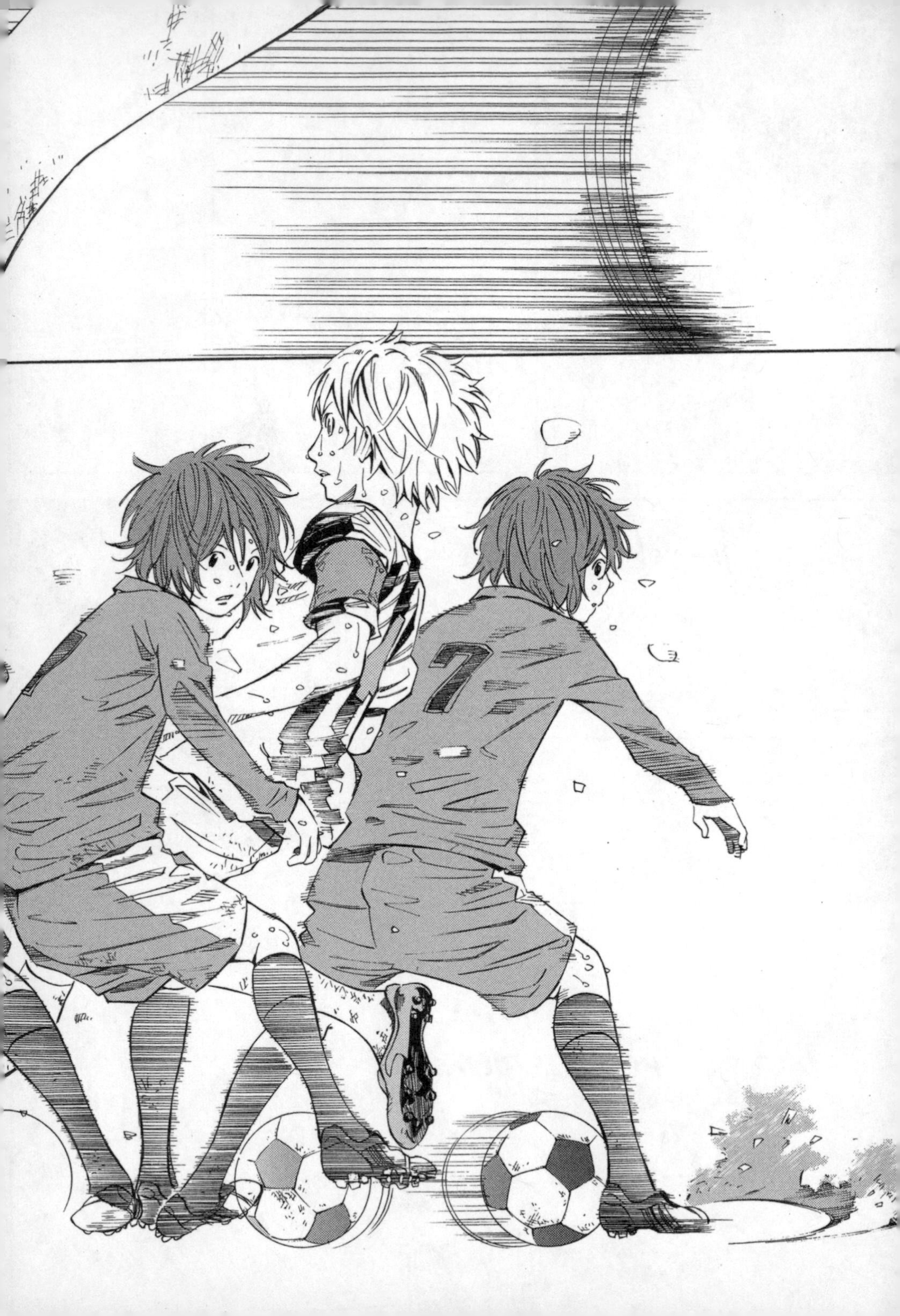

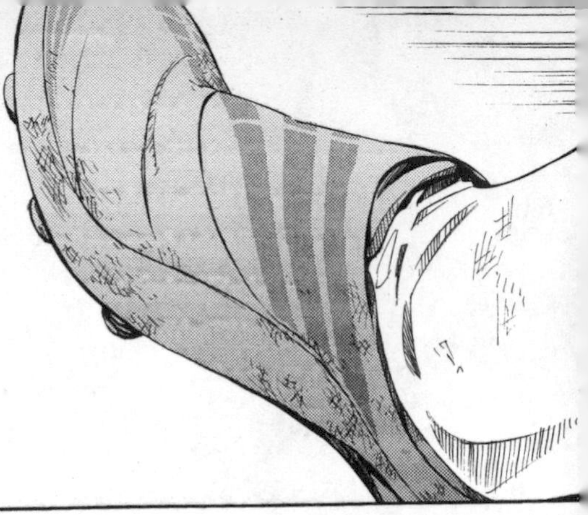
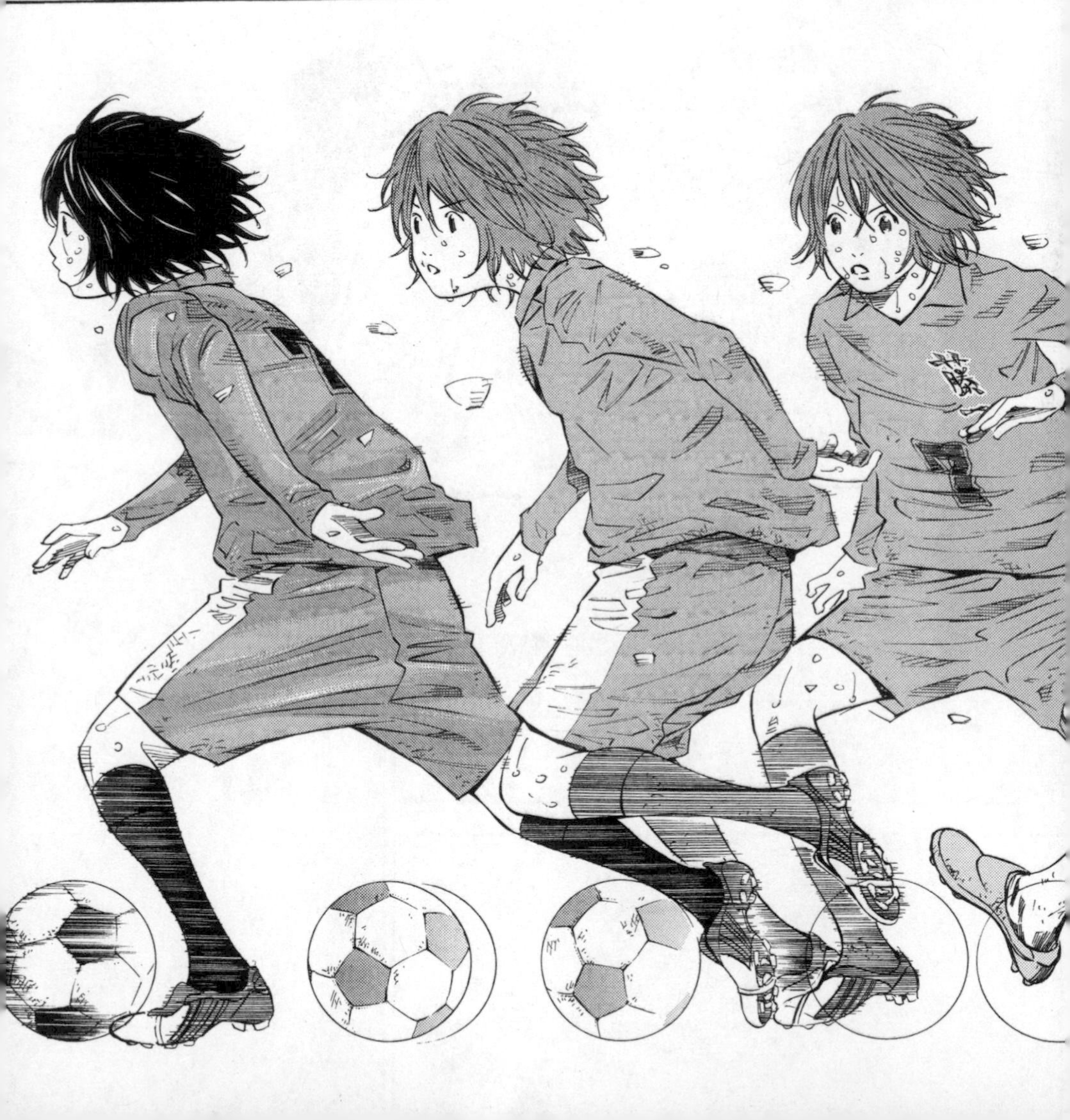

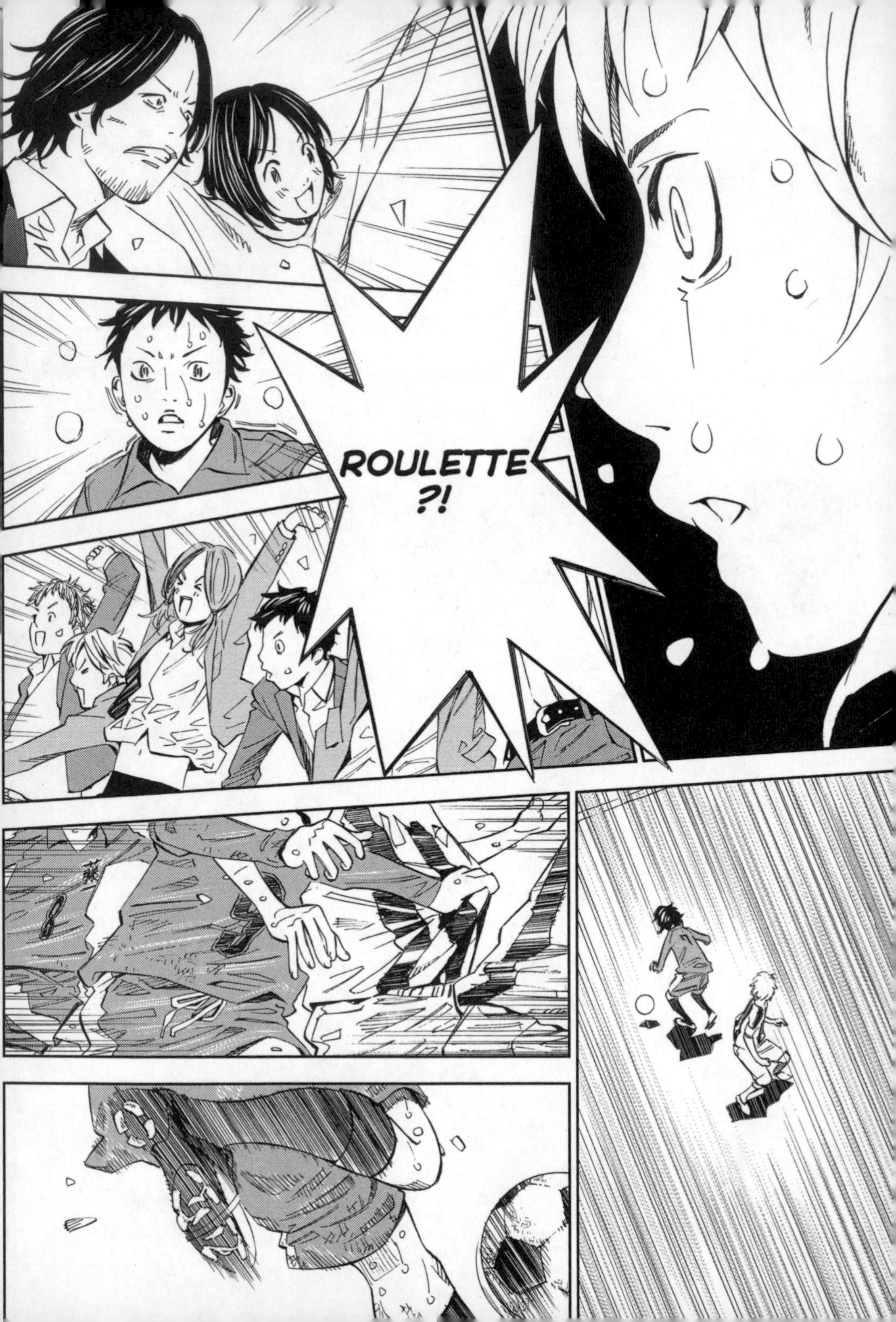
ROULETTE
?!

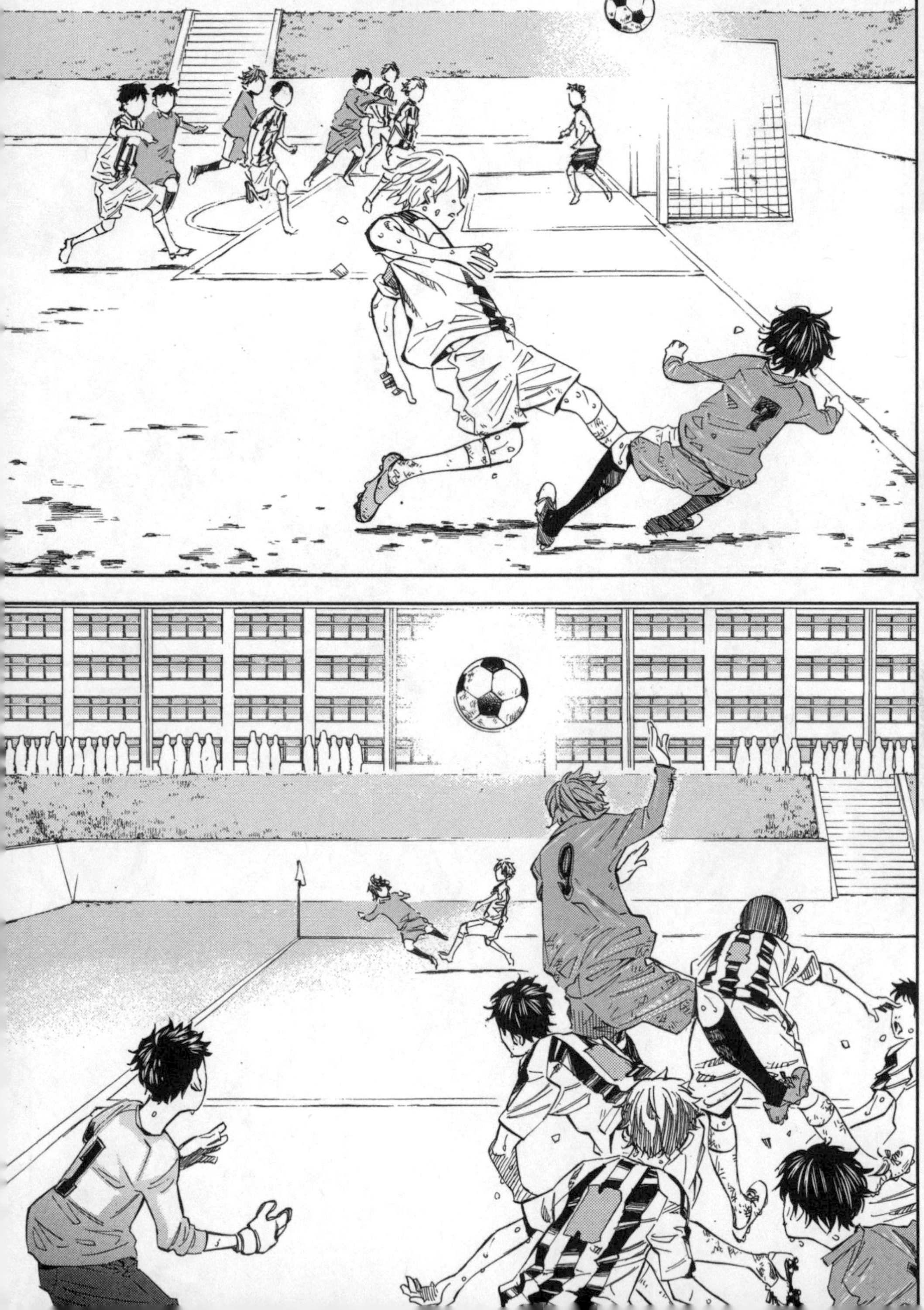

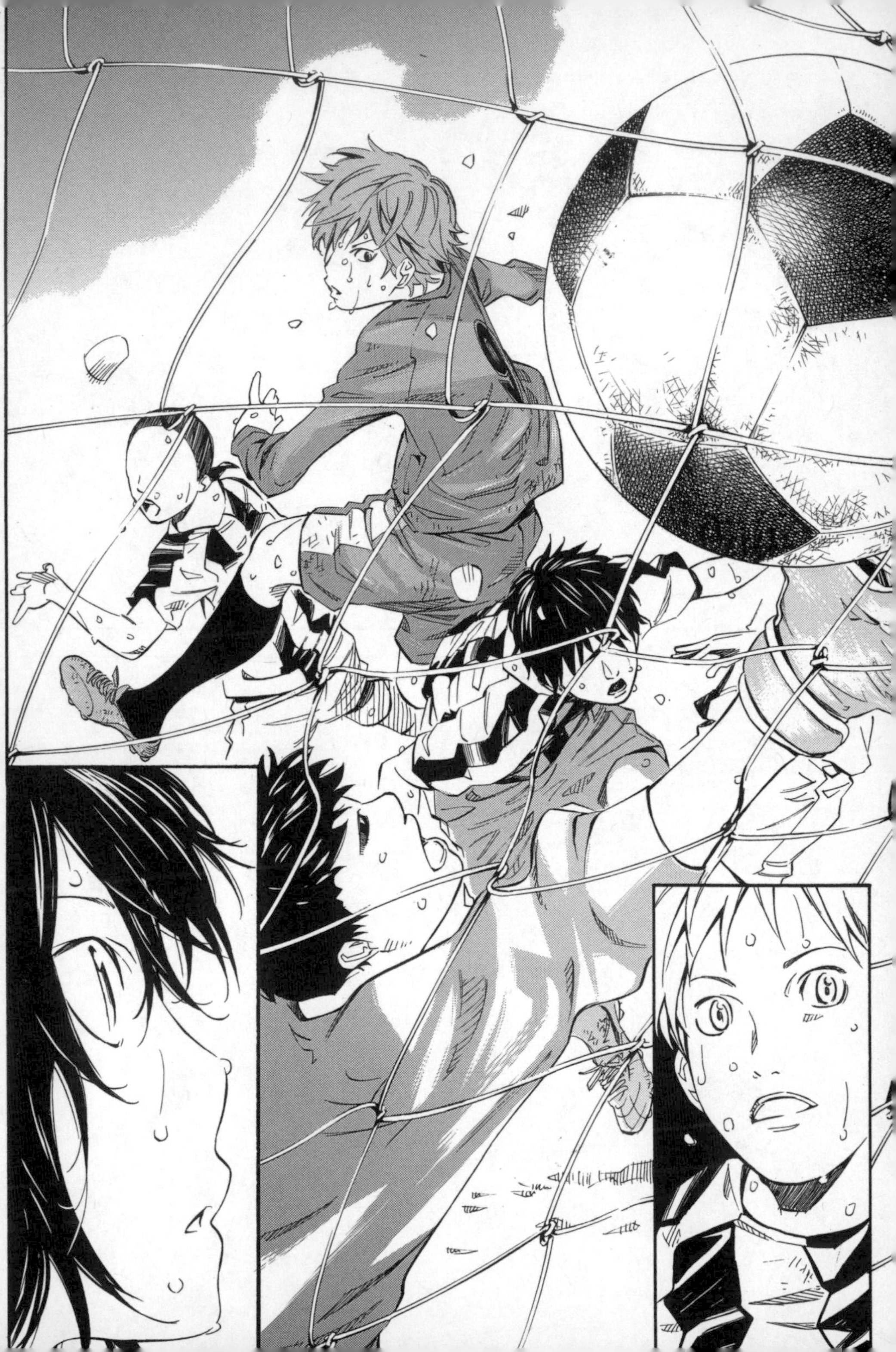

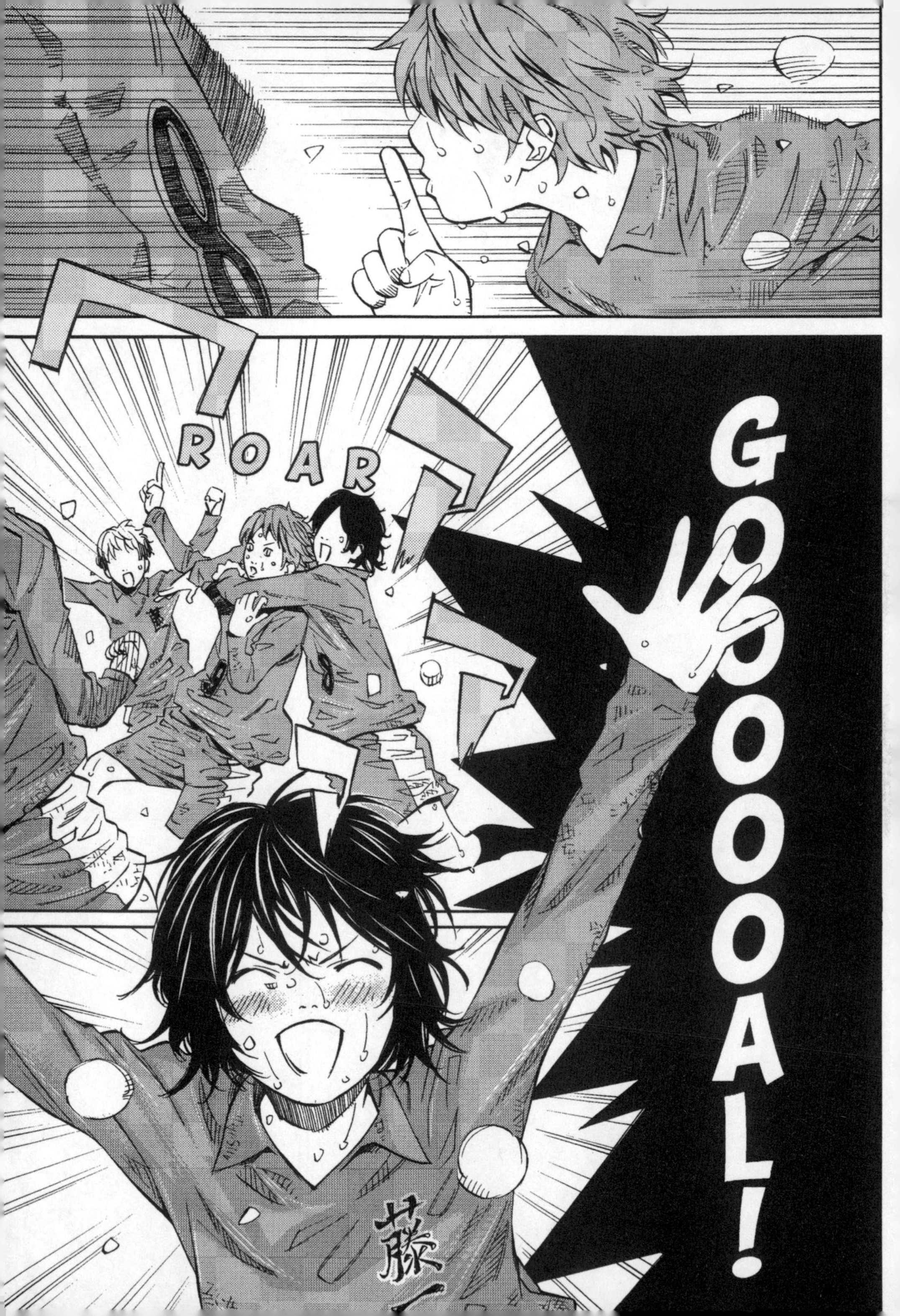
ROAR
GOOOOOAL!

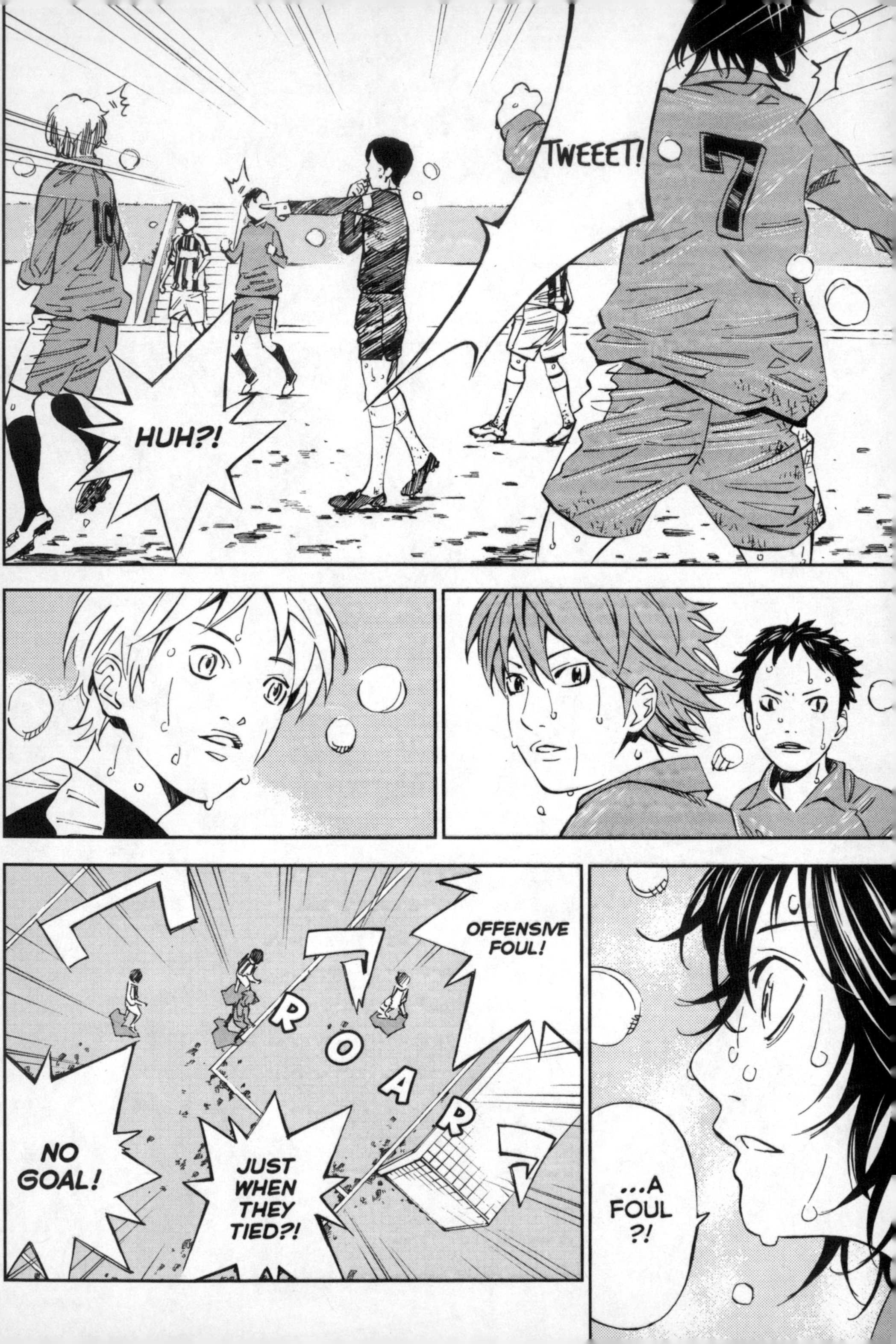
TWEEET!
HUH?!
...A FOUL ?!
OFFENSIVE FOUL!
ROAR
JUST WHEN THEY TIED?!
NO GOAL!

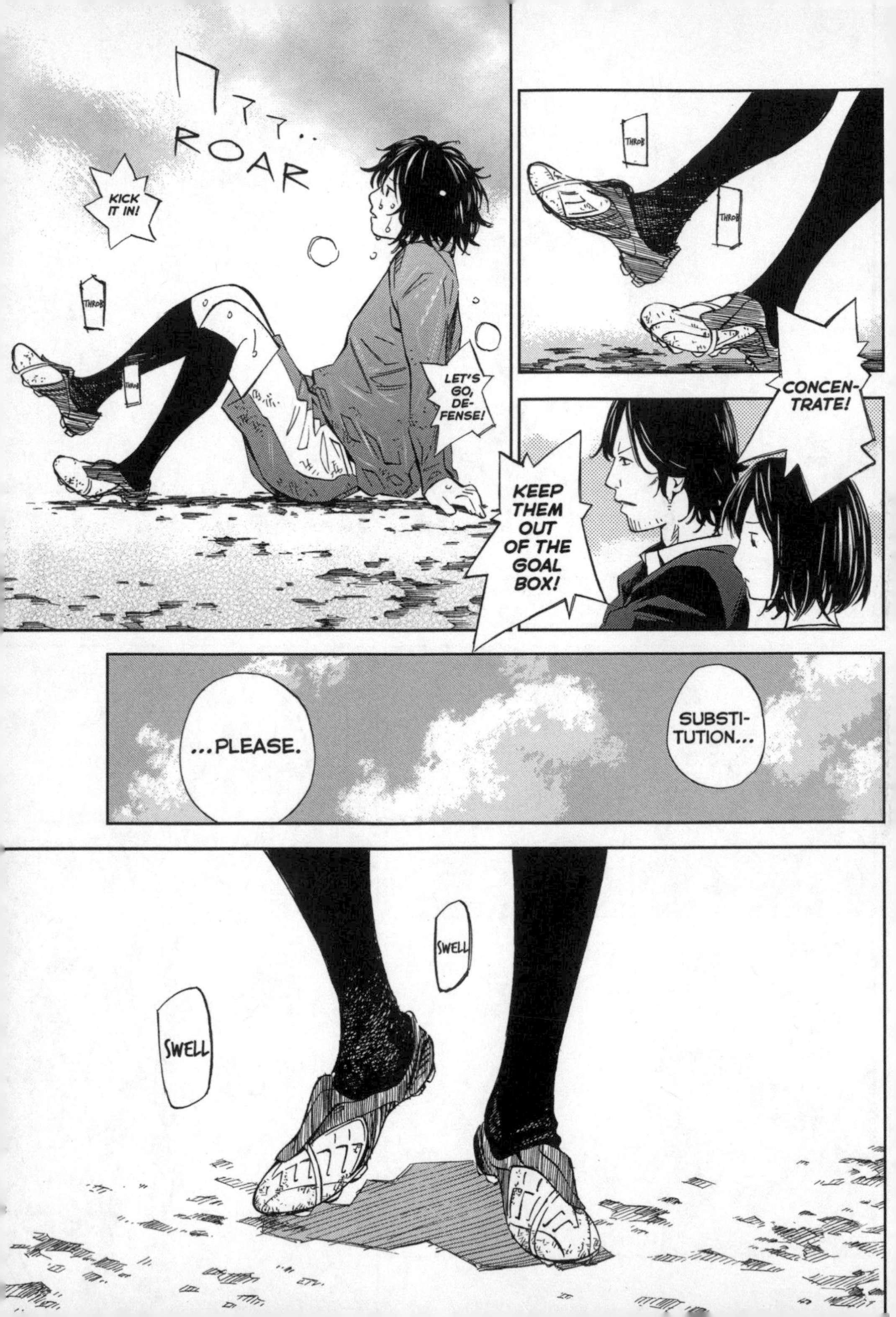
THROB
THROB
CONCENTRATE!
KEEP THEM OUT OF THE GOAL BOX!
ROAR
KICK IT IN!
LET'S GO, DEFENSE!
THROB
THROB
SUBSTITUTION...
...PLEASE.
SWELL
SWELL

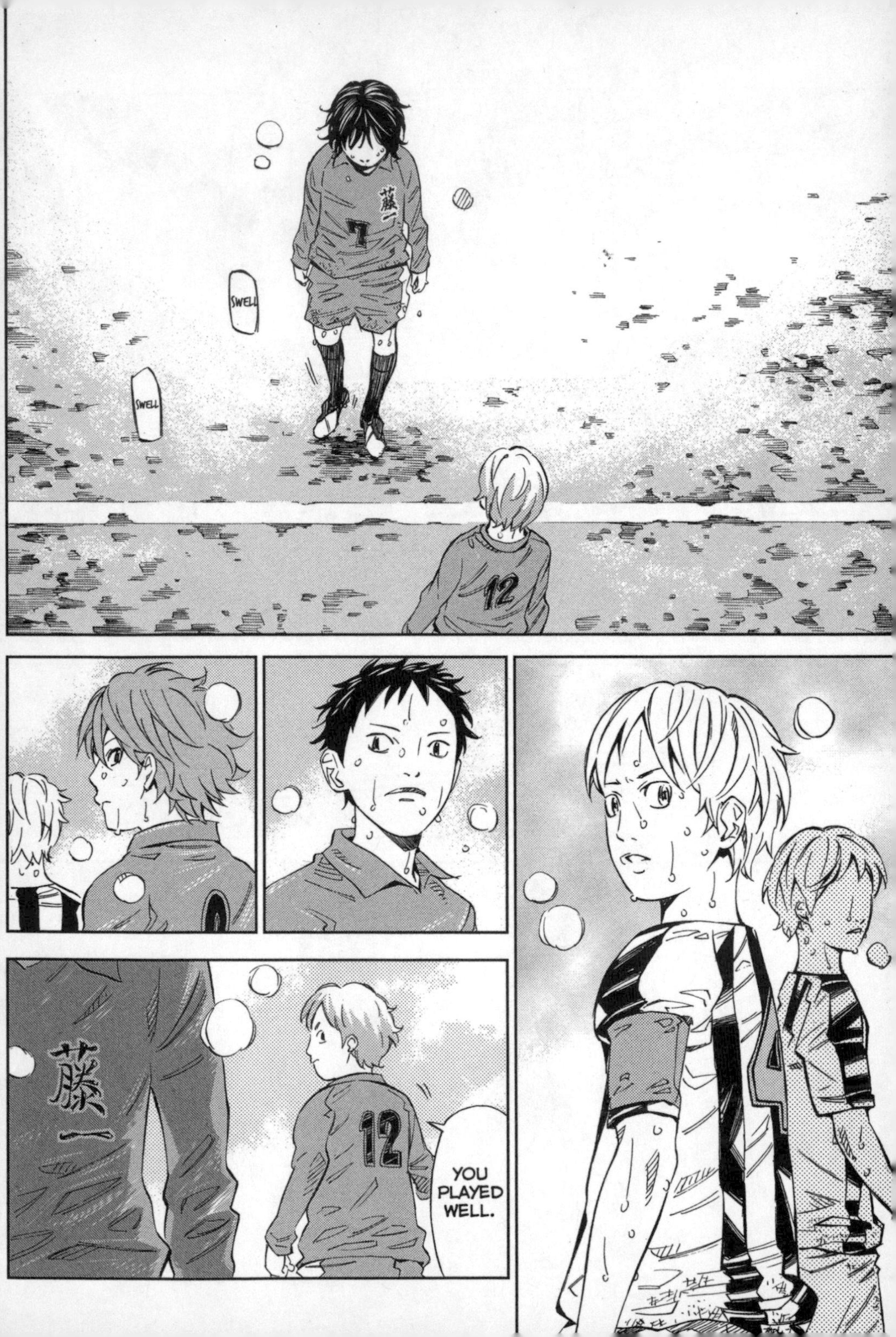
SWELL
SWELL
藤一
YOU PLAYED WELL.

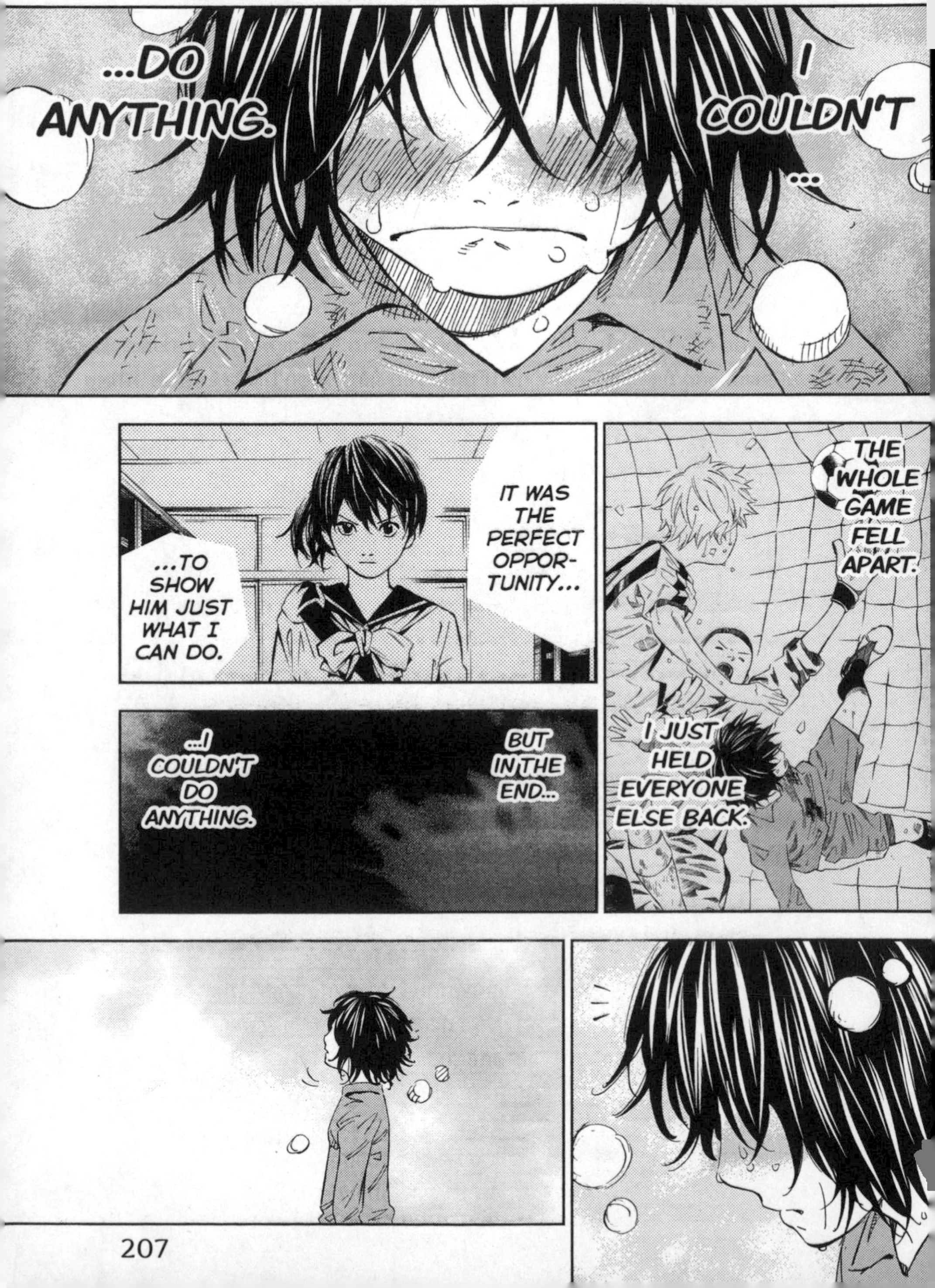
I COULDN'T ...
...DO ANYTHING.
THE WHOLE GAME FELL APART.
I JUST HELD EVERYONE ELSE BACK.
IT WAS THE PERFECT OPPOR-TUNITY...
...TO SHOW HIM JUST WHAT I CAN DO.
BUT IN THE END...
...I COULDN'T DO ANYTHING.

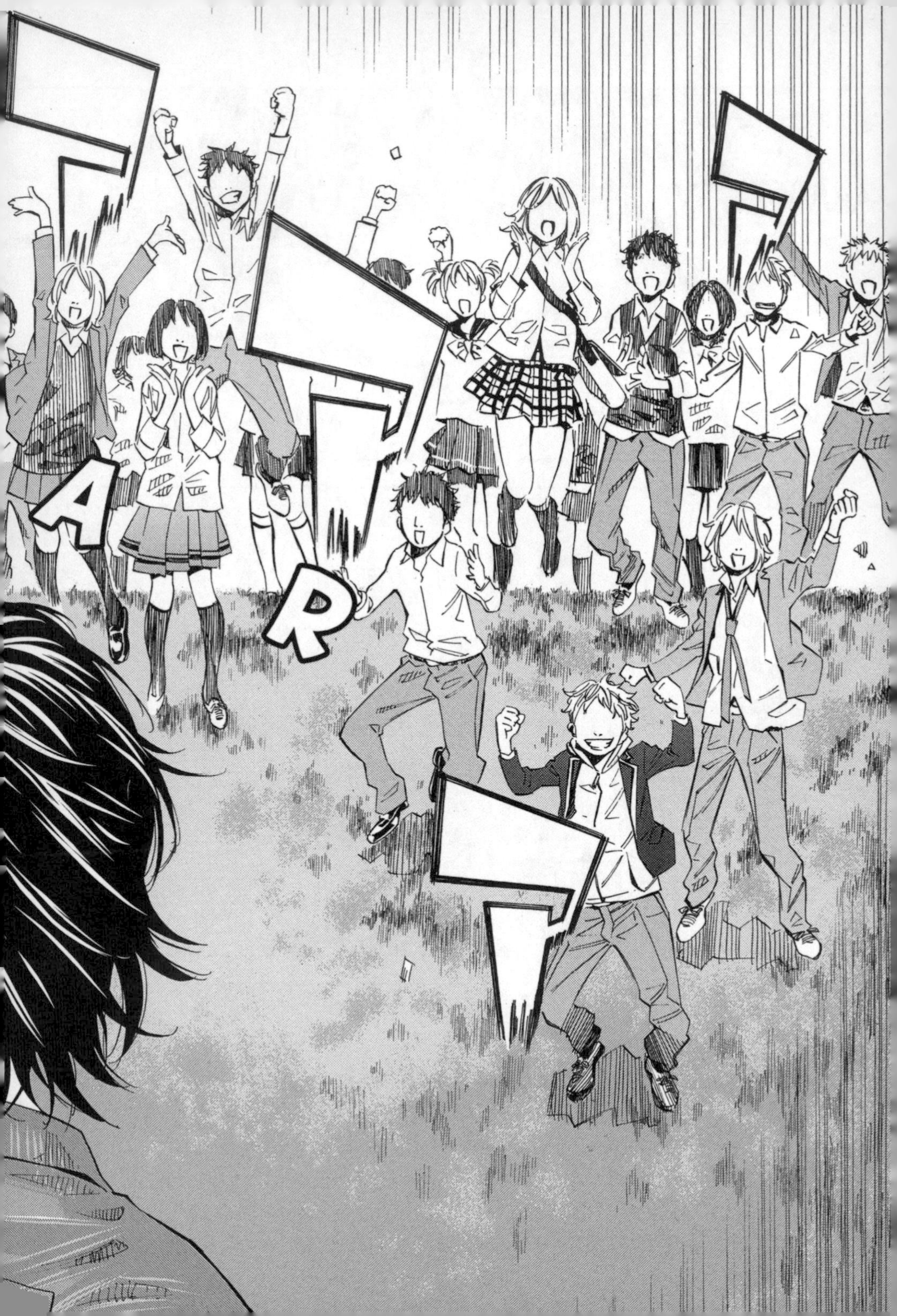
A
R

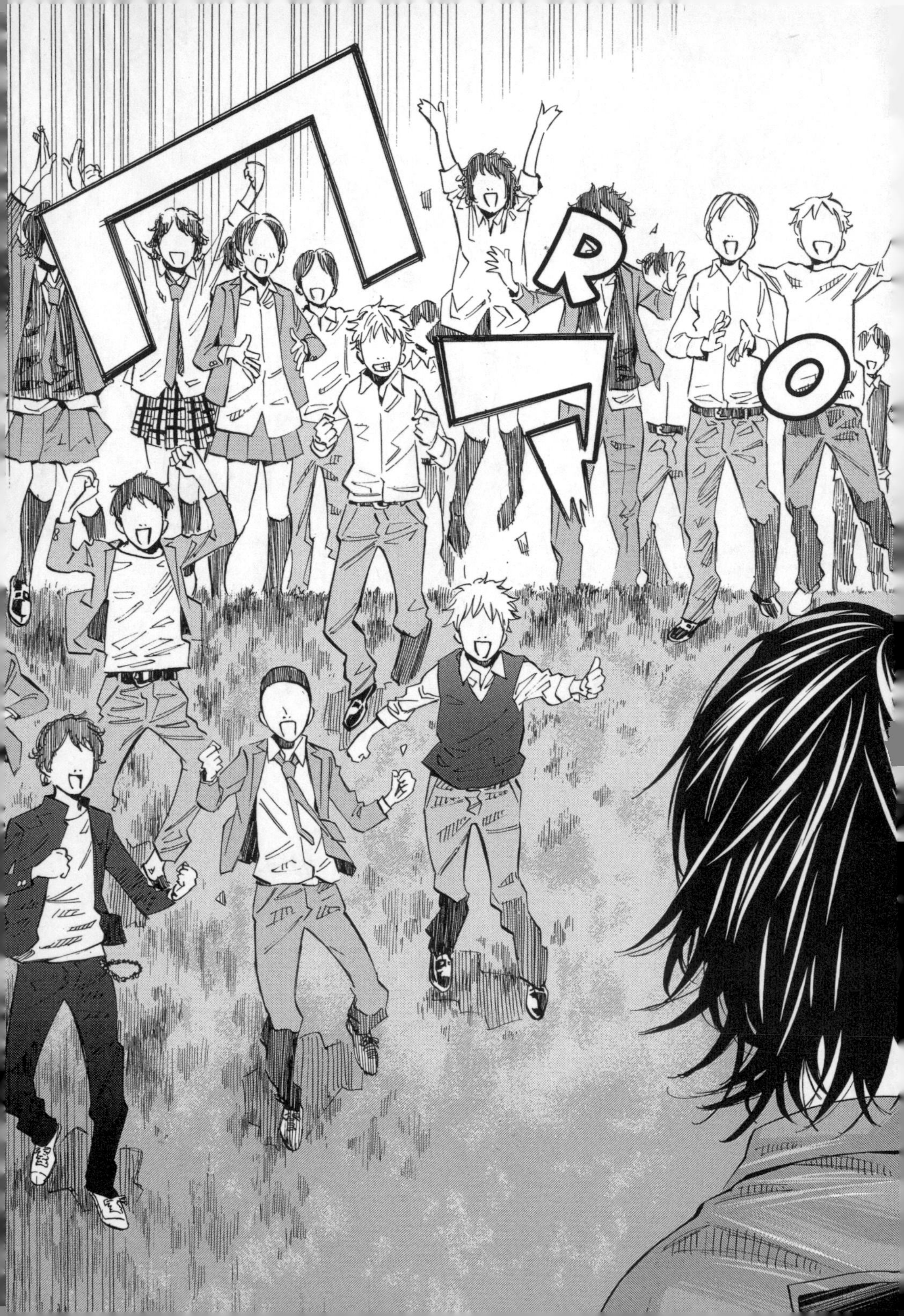

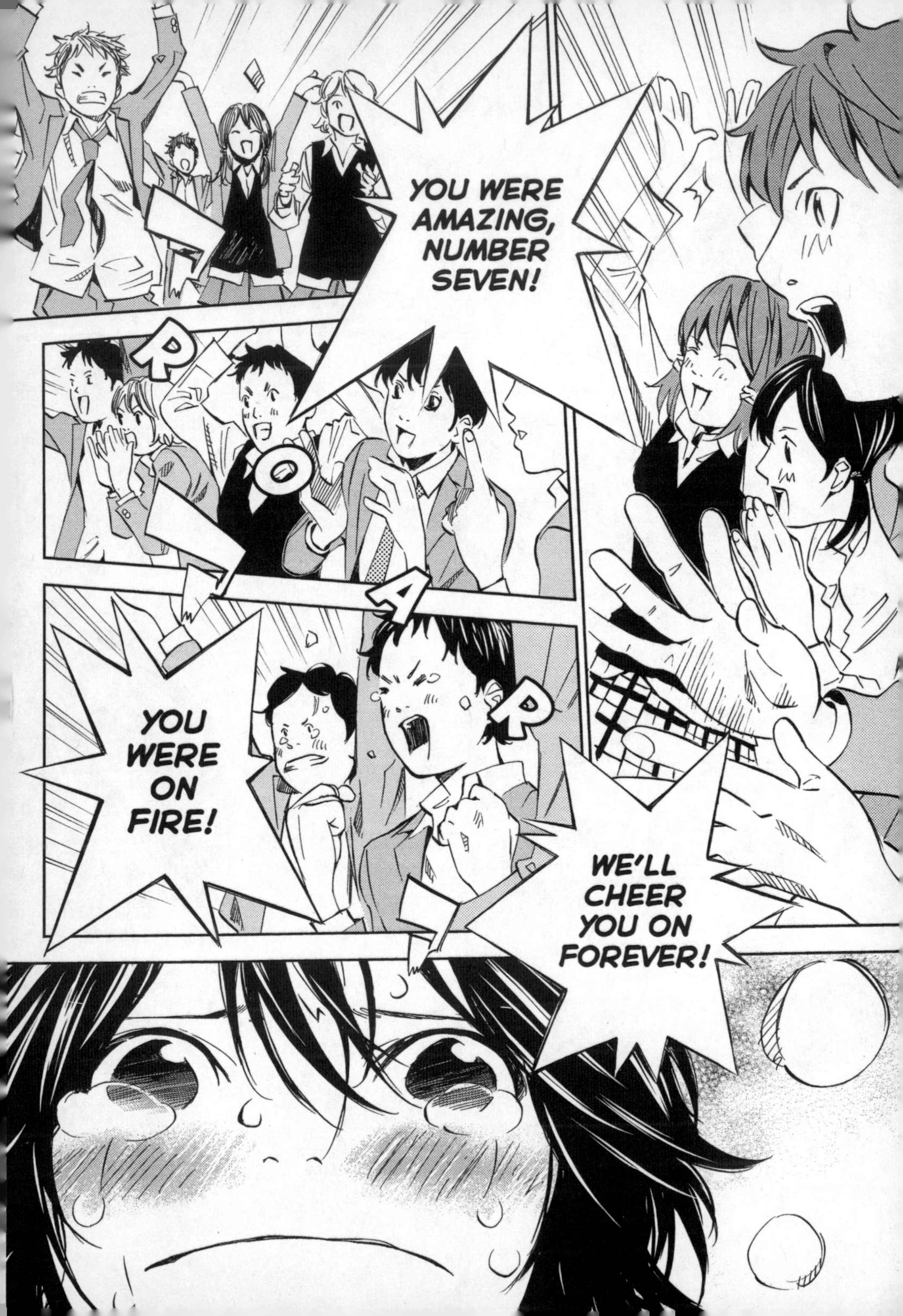
YOU WERE AMAZING, NUMBER SEVEN!
ROAR
YOU WERE ON FIRE!
WE'LL CHEER YOU ON FOREVER!

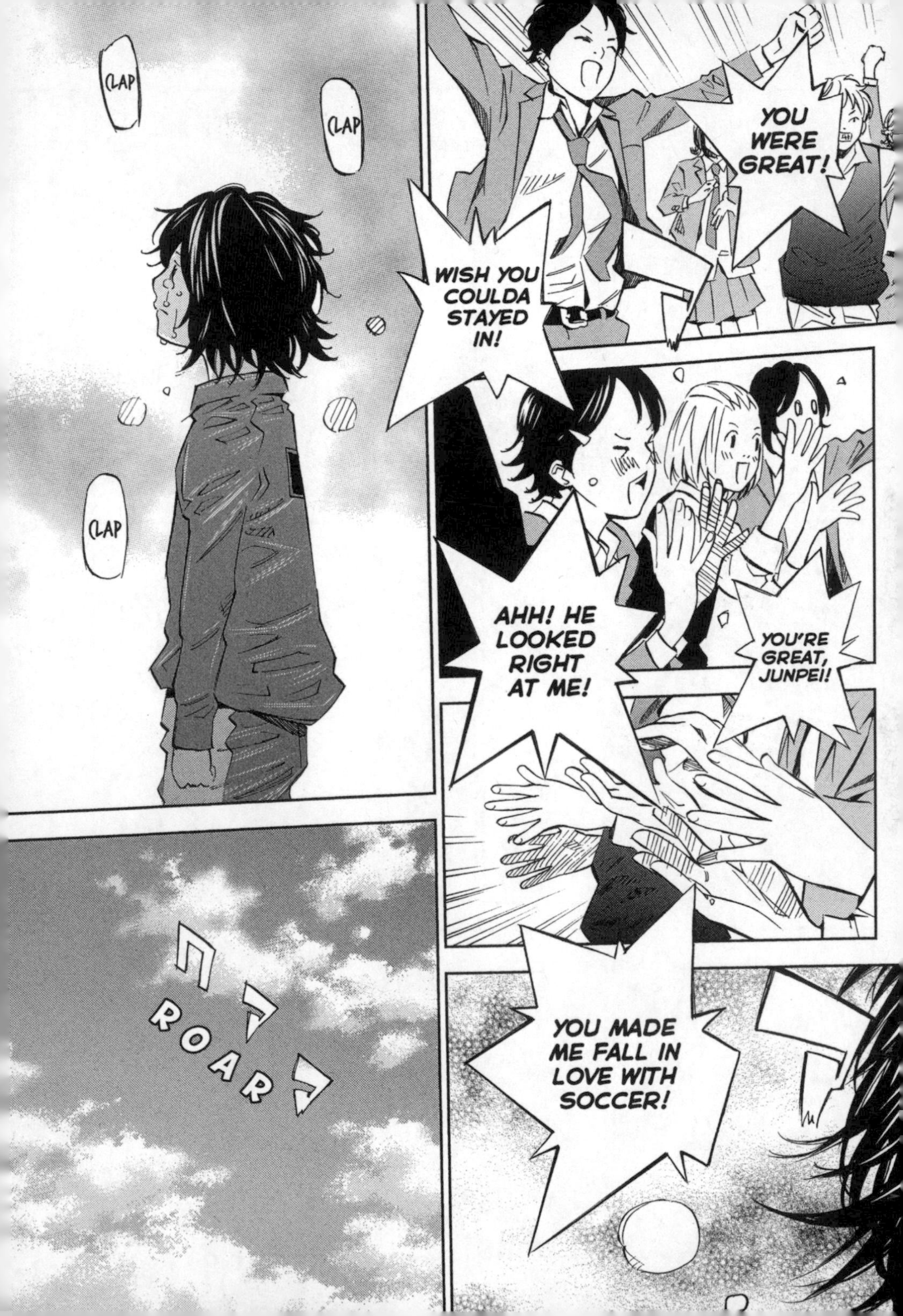
YOU WERE GREAT!
WISH YOU COULDA STAYED IN!
YOU'RE GREAT, JUNPEI!
AHH! HE LOOKED RIGHT AT ME!
CLAP
CLAP
CLAP
YOU MADE ME FALL IN LOVE WITH SOCCER!
ROAR

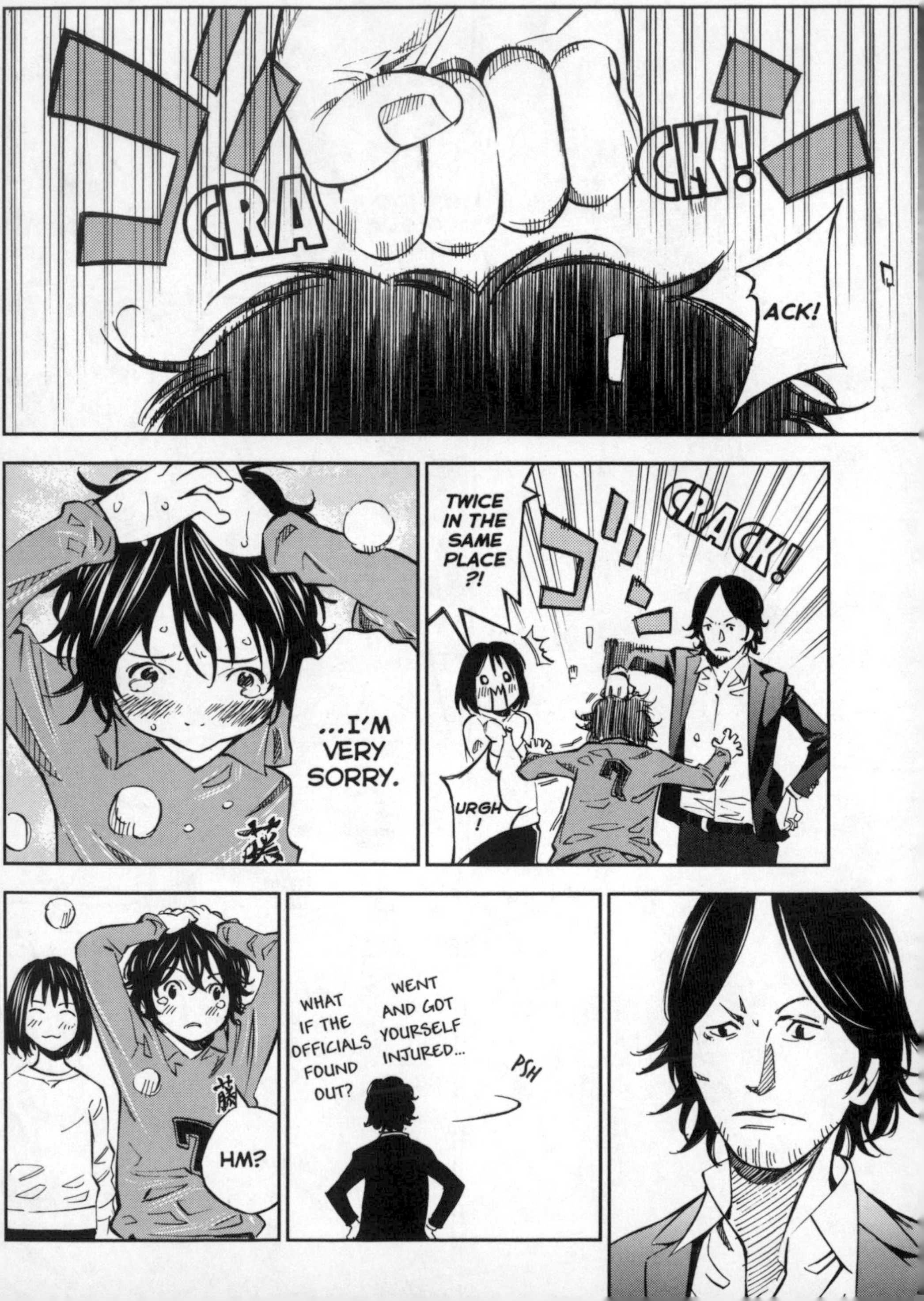
CRACK!
ACK!
TWICE IN THE SAME PLACE?!
CRACK!
URGH!
...I'M VERY SORRY.
WENT AND GOT YOURSELF INJURED...
WHAT IF THE OFFICIALS FOUND OUT?
PSH
HM?

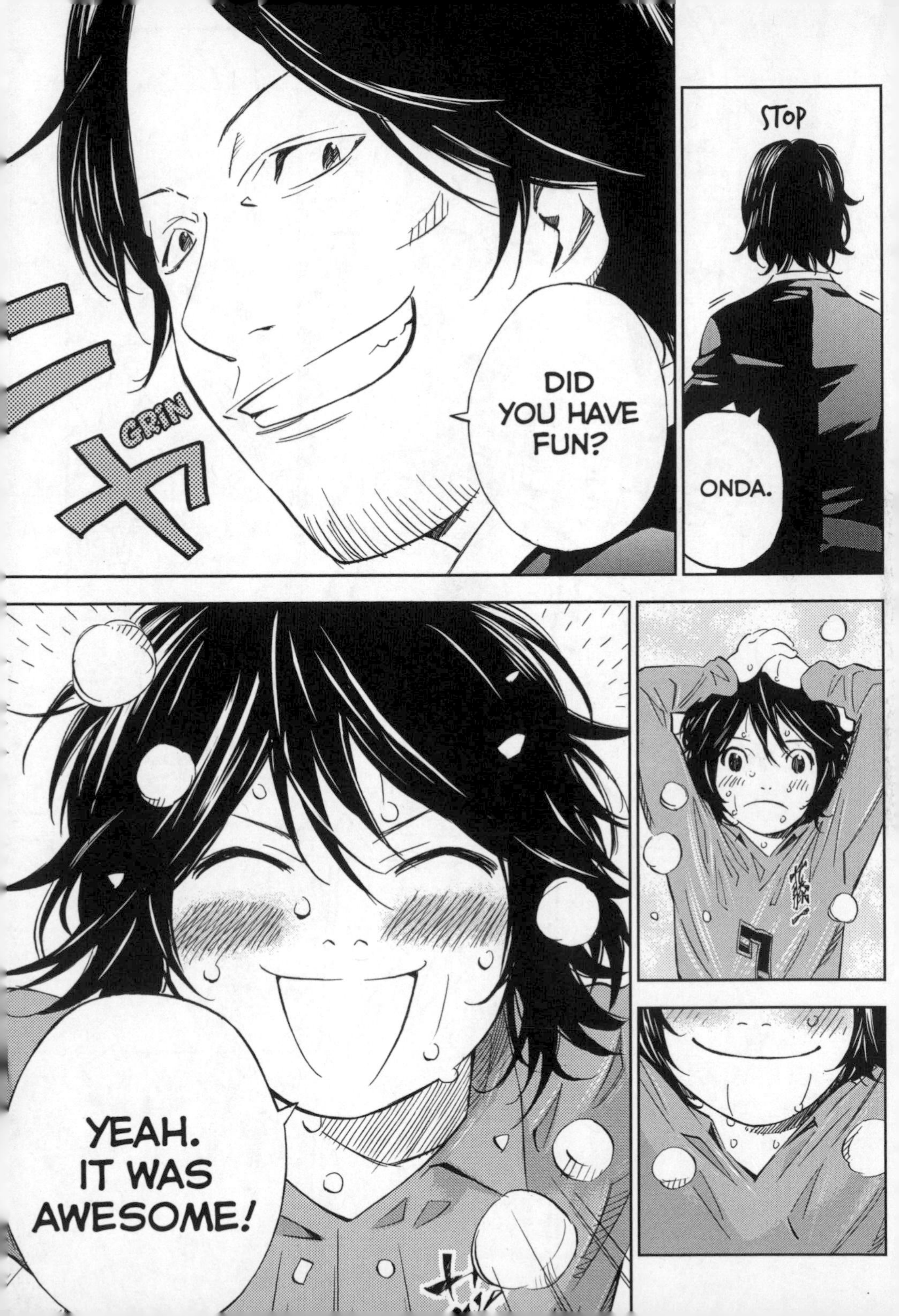
STOP
ONDA.
GRIN
DID YOU HAVE FUN?
YEAH. IT WAS AWESOME!

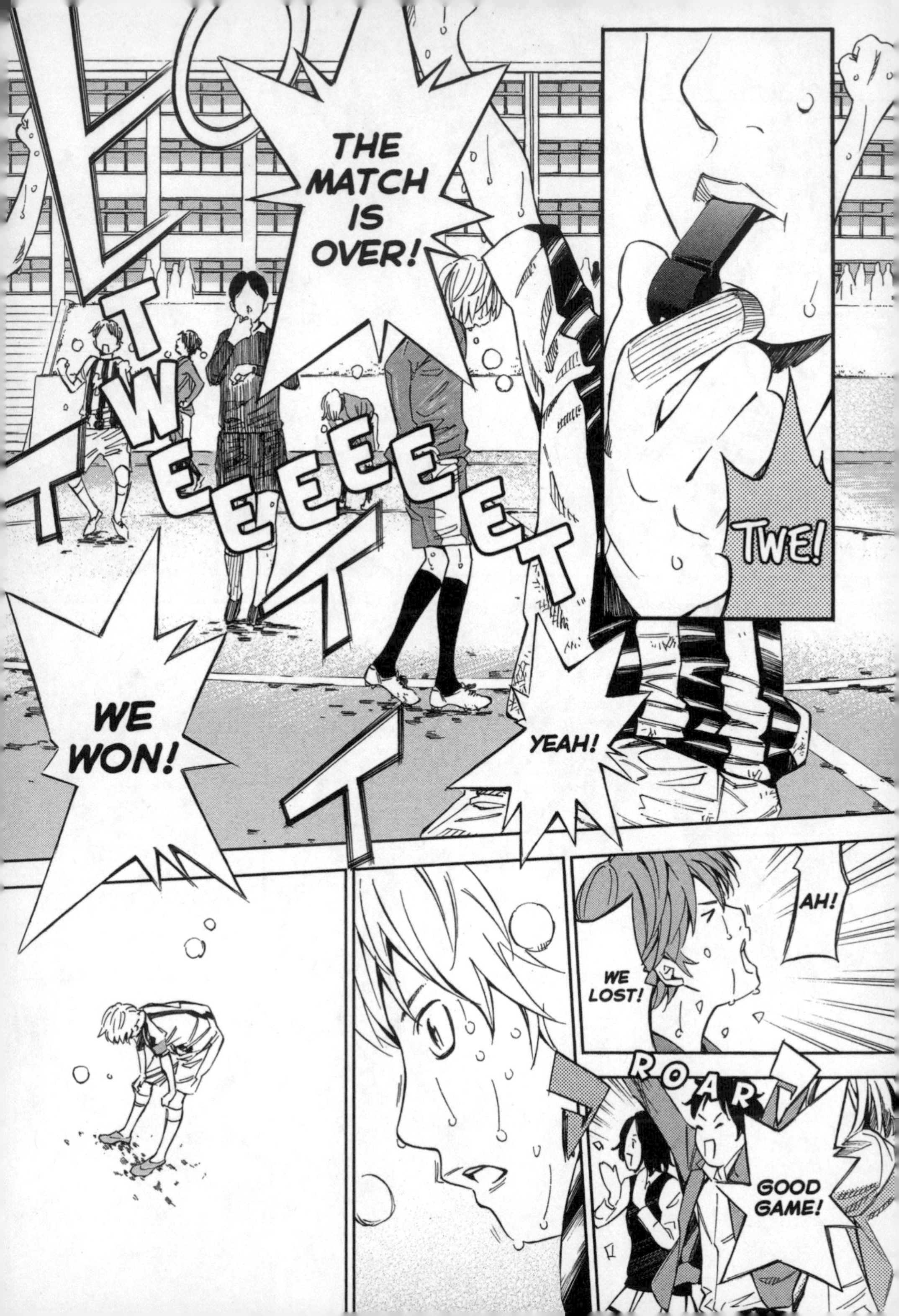
TWE!
THE MATCH IS OVER!
TWEEEEEET
YEAH!
WE WON!
AH!
WE LOST!
ROAR
GOOD GAME!

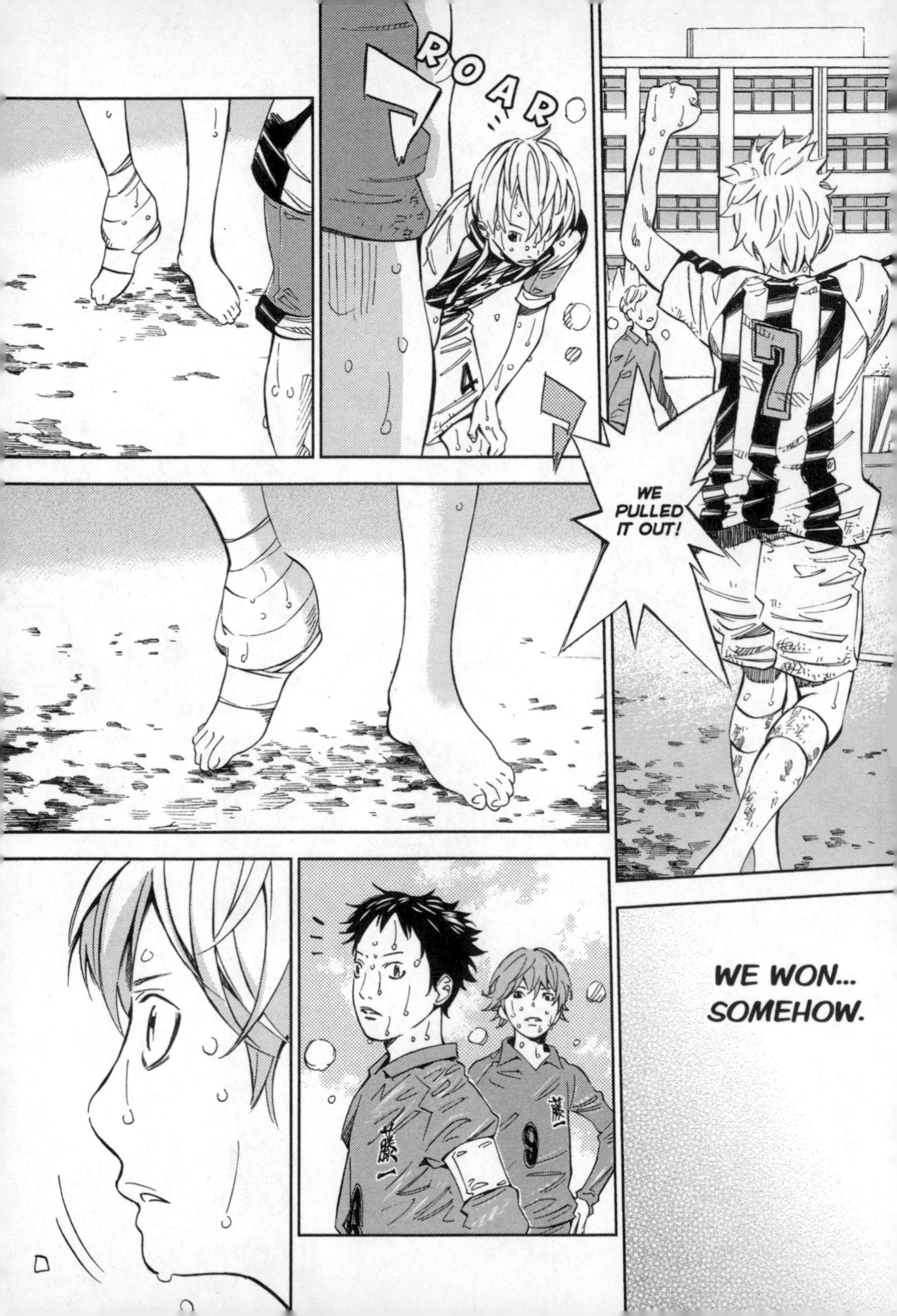
ROAR
WE PULLED IT OUT!
WE WON... SOMEHOW.

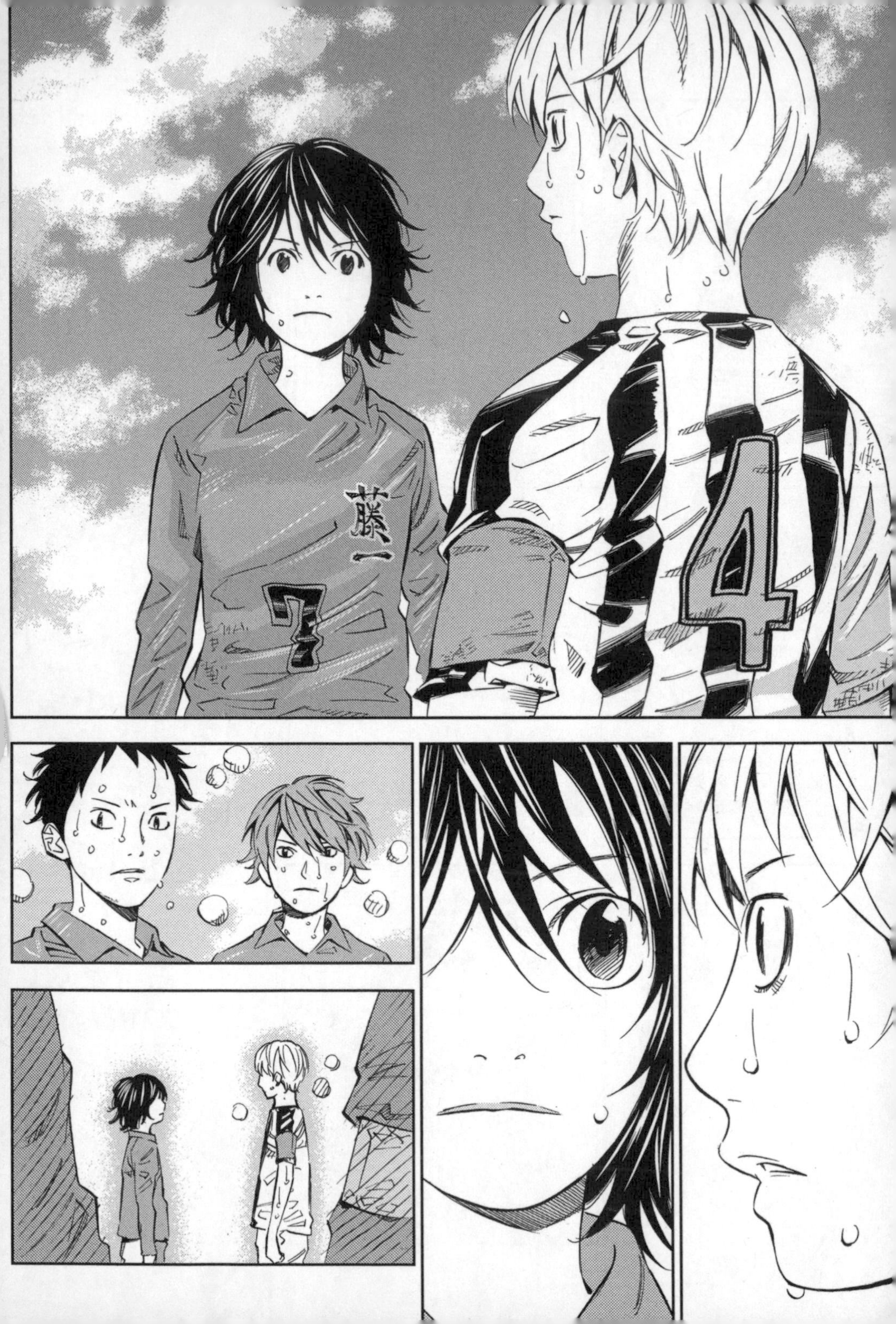
藤一
7
4

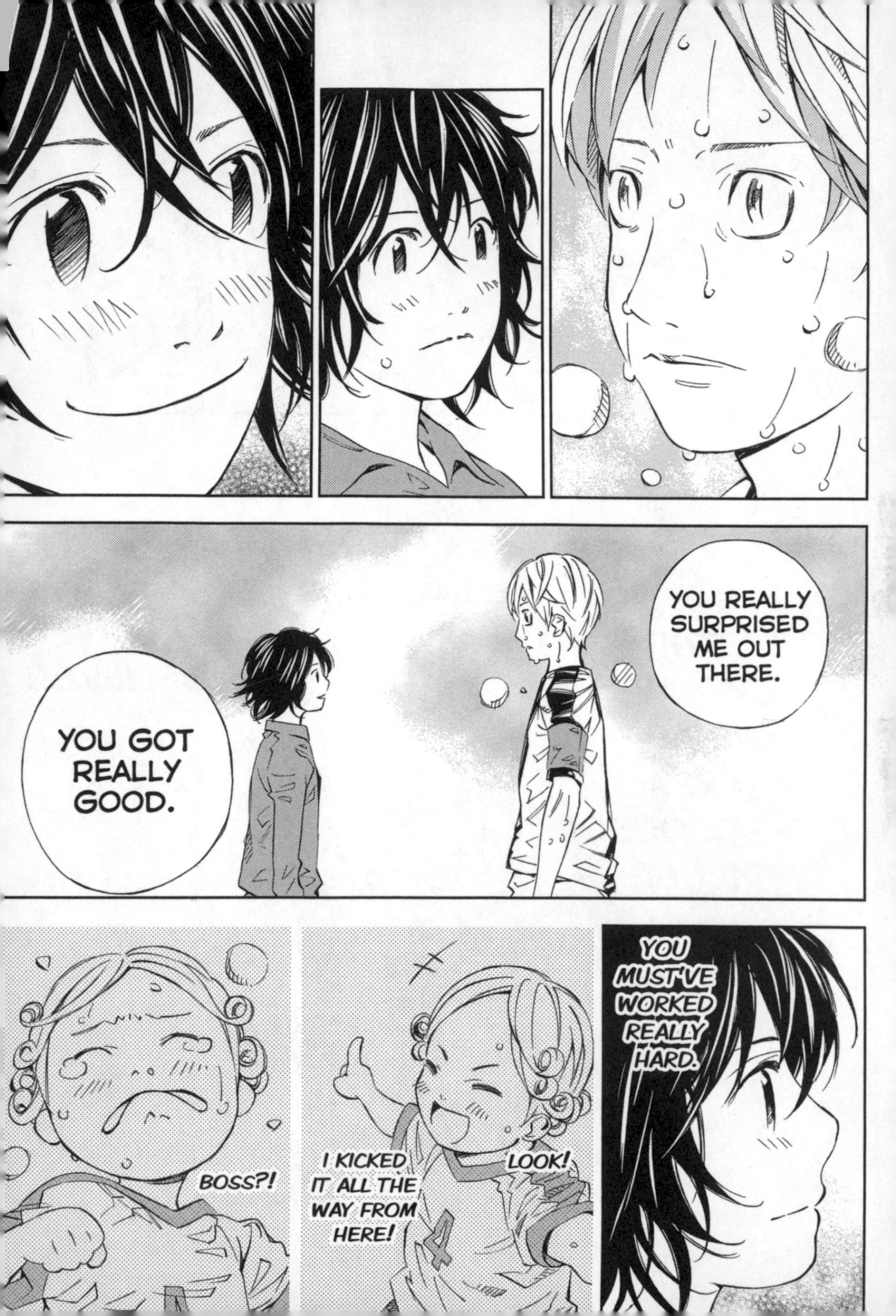
YOU REALLY SURPRISED ME OUT THERE.
YOU GOT REALLY GOOD.
YOU MUST'VE WORKED REALLY HARD.
LOOK!
I KICKED IT ALL THE WAY FROM HERE!
BOSS?!

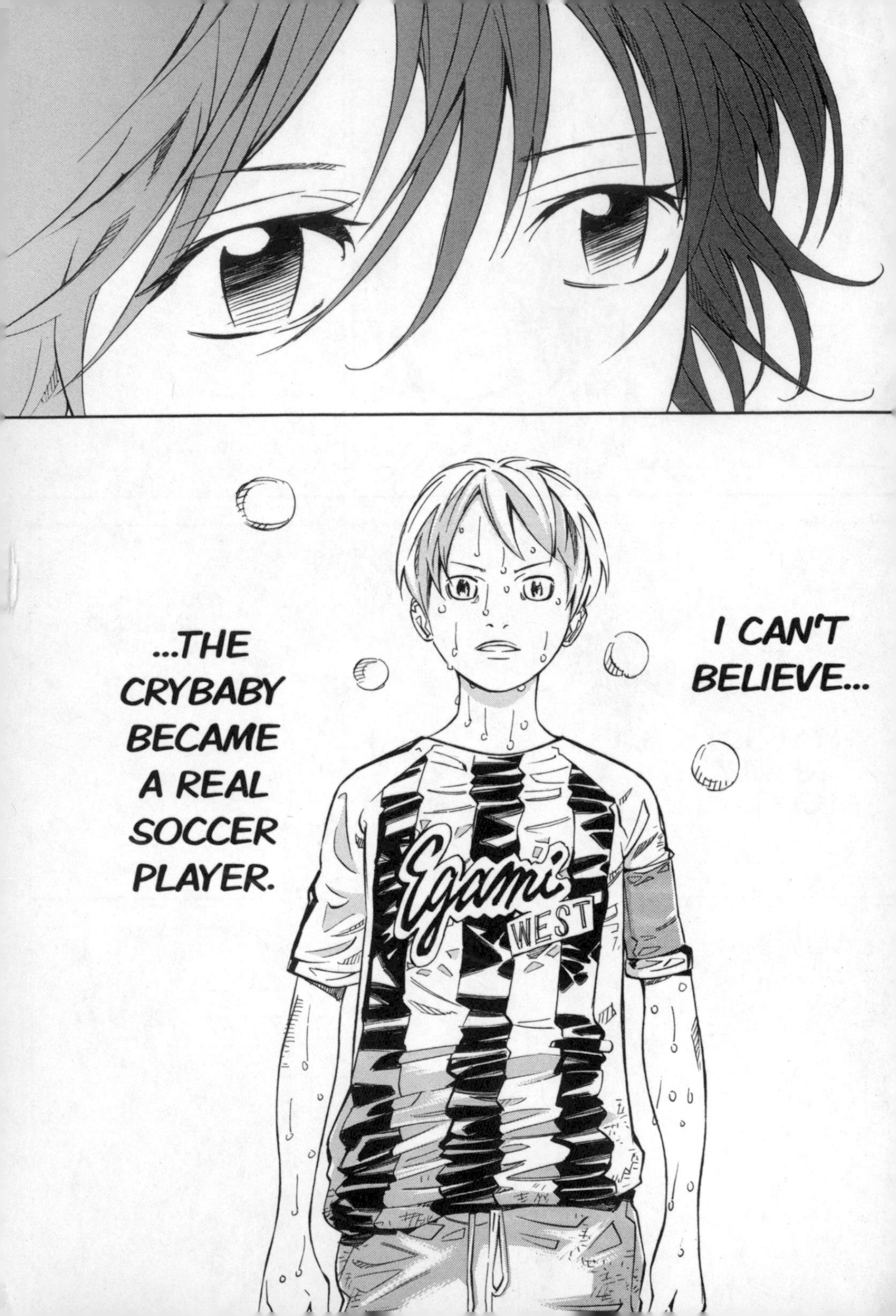
I CAN'T BELIEVE...
...THE CRYBABY BECAME A REAL SOCCER PLAYER.
Egami WEST

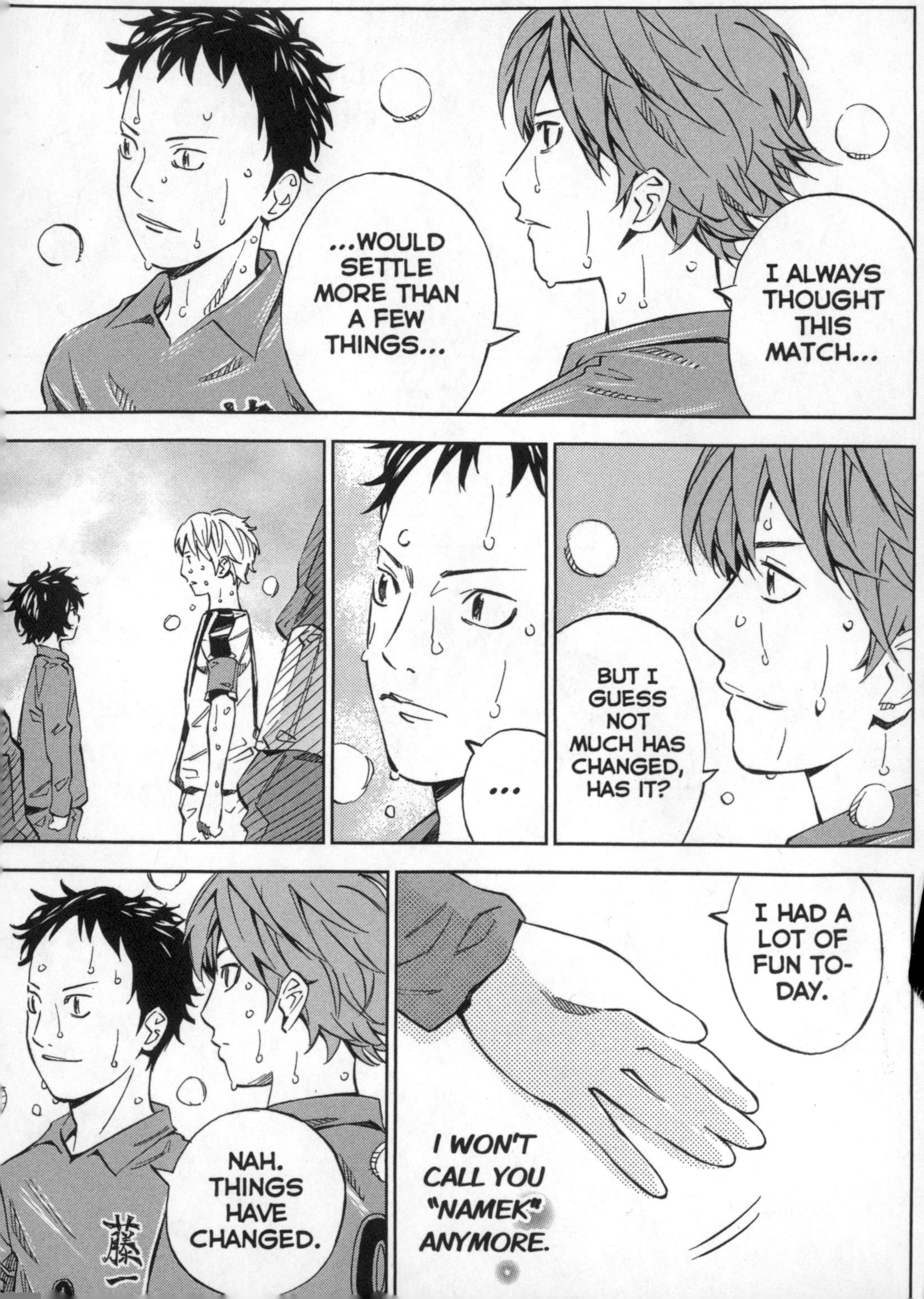
I ALWAYS THOUGHT THIS MATCH...
...WOULD SETTLE MORE THAN A FEW THINGS...
BUT I GUESS NOT MUCH HAS CHANGED, HAS IT?
...
I HAD A LOT OF FUN TO-DAY.
I WON'T CALL YOU "NAMEK" ANYMORE.
NAH. THINGS HAVE CHANGED.

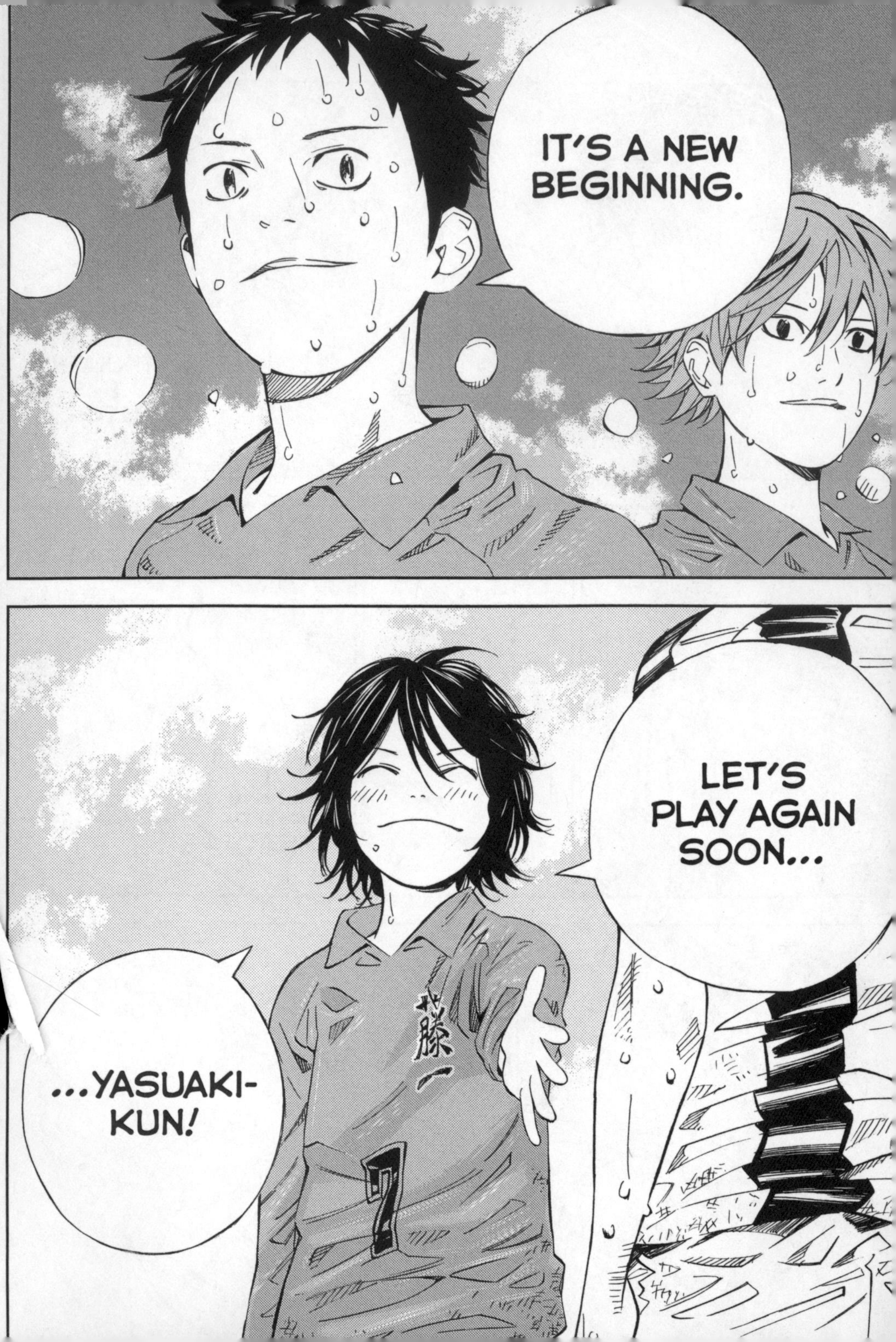
IT'S A NEW BEGINNING.
LET'S PLAY AGAIN SOON...
...YASUAKI-KUN!

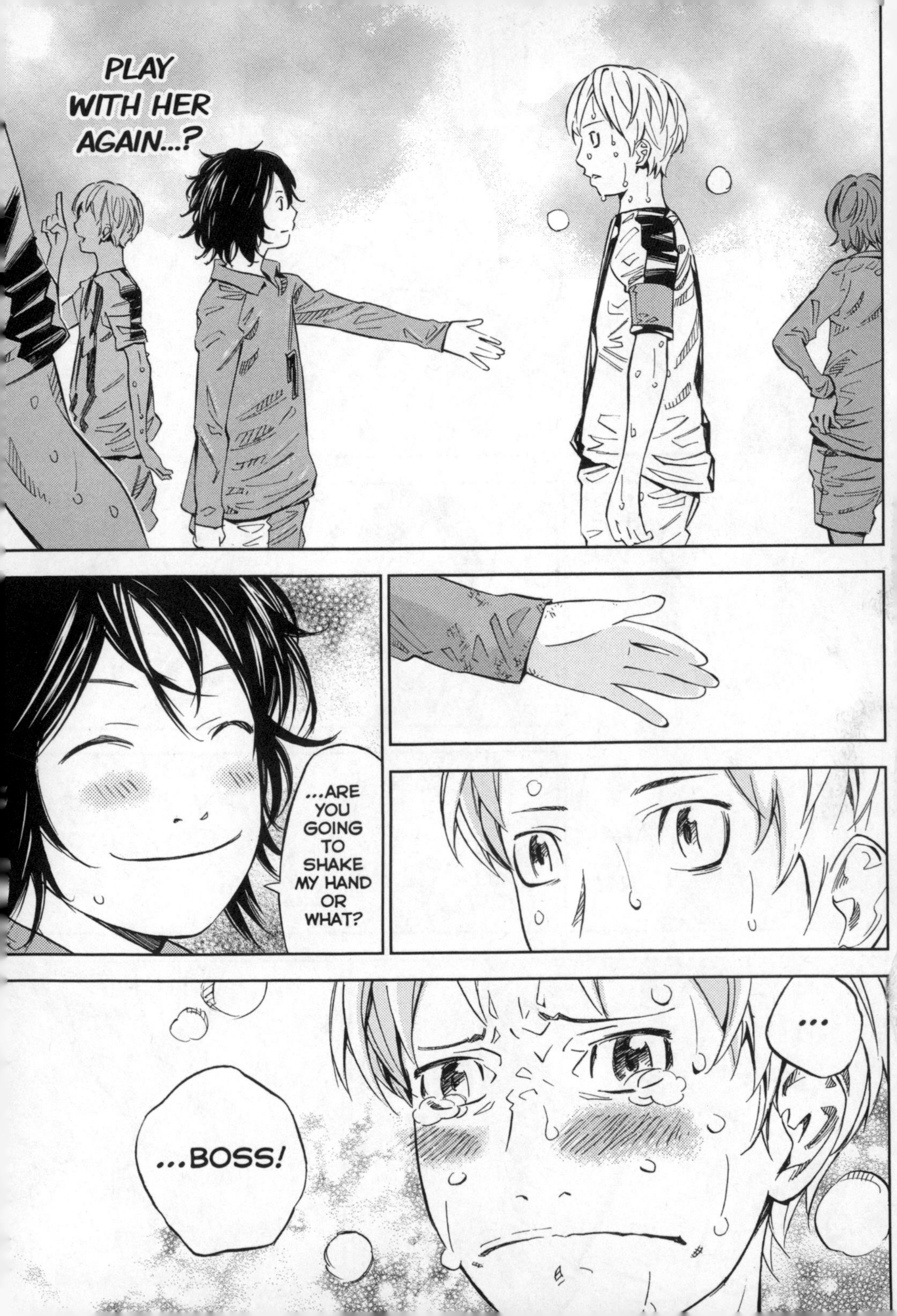
PLAY WITH HER AGAIN...?
...ARE YOU GOING TO SHAKE MY HAND OR WHAT?
...
...BOSS!

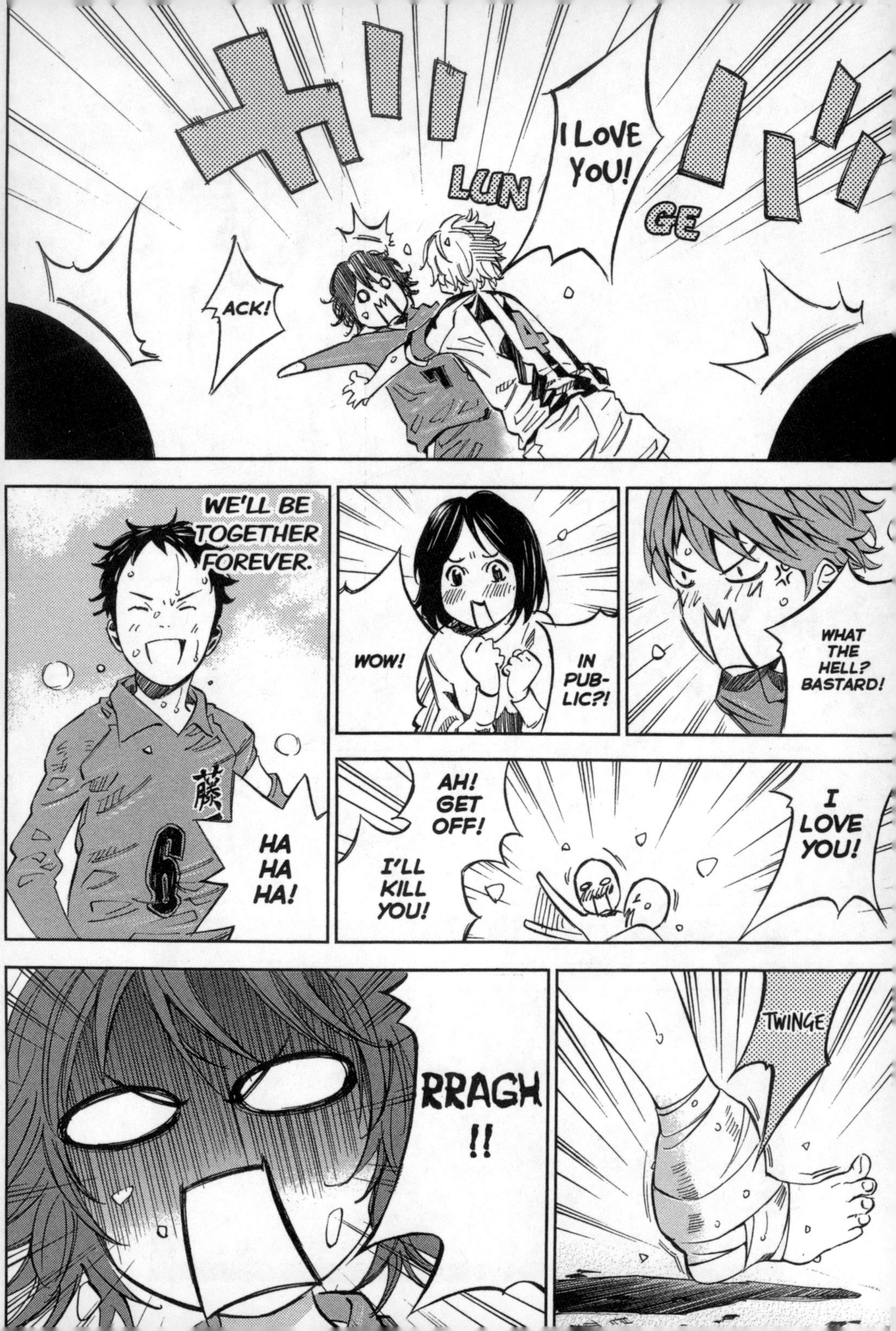
I LOVE YOU!
LUN
GE
ACK!
WHAT THE HELL? BASTARD!
IN PUB-LIC?!
WOW!
I LOVE YOU!
AH! GET OFF!
I'LL KILL YOU!
WE'LL BE TOGETHER FOREVER.
HA HA HA!
TWINGE
RRAGH !!

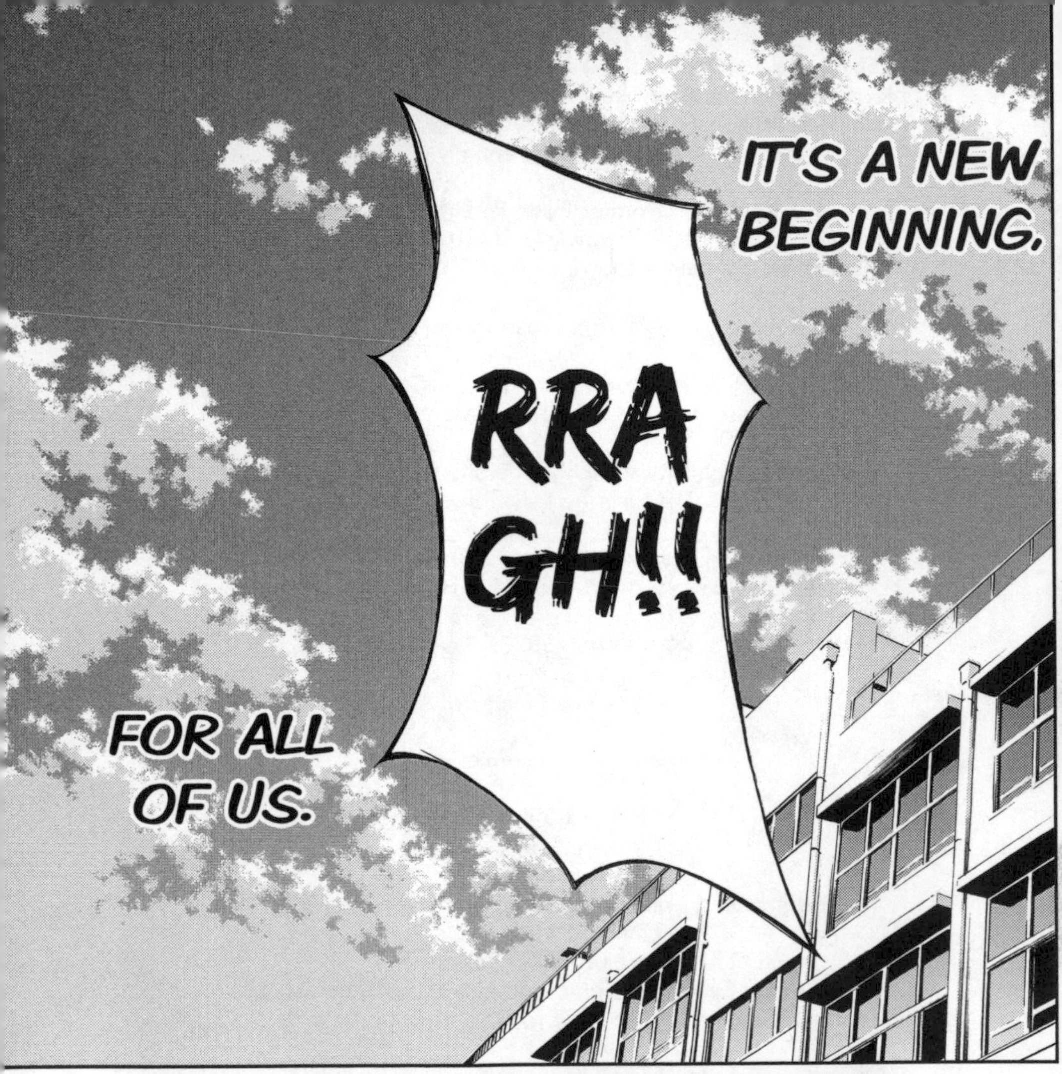
IT'S A NEW BEGINNING.
RRAGH!!
FOR ALL OF US.

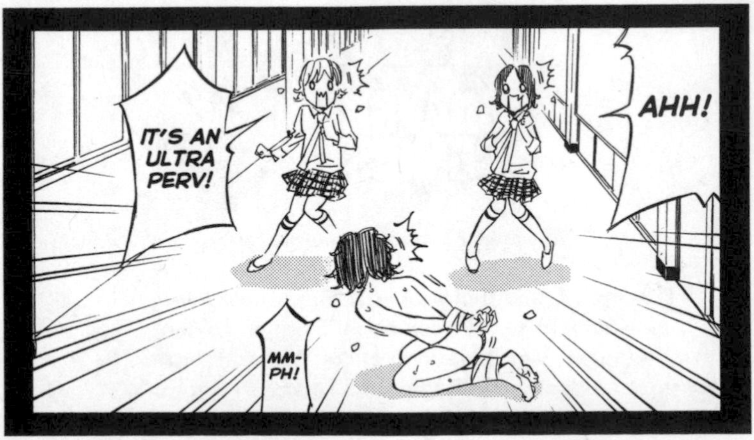
AHH!
IT'S AN ULTRA PERV!
MM-PH!

A Kodansha Comics Trade Paperback Original
Sayonara, Football 2 copyright © 2014 Naoshi Arakawa
English translation copyright © 2020 Naoshi Arakawa

All rights reserved.

Published in the United States by Kodansha Comics, an imprint of Kodansha USA Publishing, LLC, New York.

Publication rights for this English edition arranged through Kodansha Ltd., Tokyo.

First published in Japan in 2014 by Kodansha Ltd., Tokyo as *Sayonara futtobooru*, volume 2.

ISBN 978-1-63236-964-2

Printed in the United States of America.

www.kodanshacomics.com

9 8 7 6 5 4 3 2 1
Translation: Devon Corwin
Lettering: Allen Berry
Additional Layout and Lettering: Belynda Ungurath
Editing: PJ Hruschak
YKS Services LLC/SKY Japan, INC.
Kodansha Comics edition cover design by Adam Del Re

Publisher: Kiichiro Sugawara

Director of publishing services: Ben Applegate
Associate director of operations: Stephen Pakula
Publishing services managing editor: Noelle Webster
Assistant production manager: Emi Lotto, Angela Zurlo
Logo and character art ©Kodansha USA Publishing, LLC